S0-AZF-211

The WILSONIAN MOMENT

The WILSONIAN MOMENT

Self-Determination and the International Origins of Anticolonial Nationalism

EREZ MANELA

OXFORD
UNIVERSITY PRESS

2007

OXFORD
UNIVERSITY PRESS

Oxford University Press, Inc., publishes works that further
Oxford University's objective of excellence
in research, scholarship, and education.

Oxford New York
Auckland Cape Town Dar es Salaam Hong Kong Karachi
Kuala Lumpur Madrid Melbourne Mexico City Nairobi
New Delhi Shanghai Taipei Toronto

With offices in
Argentina Austria Brazil Chile Czech Republic France Greece
Guatemala Hungary Italy Japan Poland Portugal Singapore
South Korea Switzerland Thailand Turkey Ukraine Vietnam

Published by Oxford University Press, Inc.
198 Madison Avenue, New York, New York 10016

www.oup.com

Library of Congress Cataloging-in-Publication Data
Manela, Erez.
The Wilsonian moment: self-determination and the international
origins of anticolonial nationalism / Erez Manela.
p. cm.
Includes bibliographical references and index.
ISBN 978-0-19-517615-5
1. World War, 1914–1918—Peace. 2. World War, 1914–1918—Influence.
3. Nationalism. 4. Egypt—History—Insurrection, 1919. 5. India—History—British
occupation, 1765–1947. 6. China—History—May Fourth movement, 1919.
7. Korea—History—Independence movement, 1919. 8. Wilson, Woodrow, 1856–1924. I. Title.
D645.M38 2007
320.5409'041—dc22 2007005490

9 8 7 6 5 4 3 2 1

Printed in the United States of America
on acid-free paper

To

Bracha Manela

and the memory of

Yechiel Moshe Manela

and

Luba and Yitzhak Kornblit

It is not enough, I feel, to refer to these investigations as "Tales of the Old Wrangler."

Granted, the appellation could be stretched to fit; but one might, with as much justification, condense the whole of human history to "Anecdotes of the Famous and the Misguided."

—David Mamet, *Wilson: A Consideration of the Sources*

PREFACE

This book began with an unexpected discovery. I had set out to write a paper on U.S. contacts with Egypt before World War II, since I suspected (and still do) that the single-minded focus on the postwar period in most histories of U.S. relations with the Middle East had left some important stones unturned, even undiscovered. I began going through the State Department files on Egypt starting with World War I, and immediately came across a telegram from the Egyptian nationalist icon Sa'd Zaghlul to Woodrow Wilson, lavishing praise on the U.S. president and beseeching him to support Egypt's struggle for self-determination against Britain. I came upon one such message, and then another, and another. It soon became clear that the vast majority of the material on Egypt in the State Department files between the fall of 1918 and the spring of 1919 consisted of such documents: telegrams, letters, petitions, pamphlets, sent to Wilson not only by Zaghlul himself but by a long list of leading politicians, parties, professional organizations, women's groups, student groups, Egyptian organizations abroad, and even private Egyptian citizens, moved to write to the president of the United States as he arrived in Paris for the peace conference.

It was an intriguing discovery. I had seen no mention of this response to Wilson in the histories of Egyptian politics I had read, except perhaps in passing. I still wrote the paper on U.S.-Egyptian contacts in the interwar years,[1] but also mentioned the discovery to a colleague, who in turn told me the famous story about the man who would later become known as Ho Chi Minh, who was in Paris at the time of the conference and also petitioned Wilson for support in the Indochinese struggle against France. But Ho and Zaghlul were not the only anticolonial nationalists in 1919 searching for new allies, languages, and methods in their quests to challenge imperialism. As I read more about this moment in the histories of other colonial societies, what came into focus was a story of a broad anticolonial nationalist upheaval that was inherently international. After all, it could not be an accident that the 1919 Revolution in Egypt, which erupted as the British tried to suppress Zaghlul's activities, occurred simultaneously with the March First movement against Japanese rule in Korea, the launching of Gandhi's *satyagraha*, or nonviolent resistance movement in India, and the anti-imperialist May Fourth movement in China. There was, I found, much already written about each event within the respective national historiographies, but no substantial attempt to place them all together within a single field of vision, to frame them, as I have come to see them, as component parts of a single historical moment.

There is, of course, no shortage of writings on the international history of the Paris Peace Conference of 1919.[2] This literature, however, tends to focus on the perspectives of the great powers and the problems of the European settlement that occupied much of the conference. Since historians have generally followed the priorities and interests of the leading peace negotiators themselves, far less has been written about the perceptions and actions of the peoples in large swaths of the colonial or non-European world. The historical treatment of those extra-European issues that did receive a measure of attention at the peace table, such as the post-Ottoman settlement in the Middle East, has also emphasized great power perspectives and actions and minimized the agency of local actors.[3] Accounts of the international history of 1919 have said even less—in fact, often nothing—about the experiences of peoples in regions that the great power leaders did not discuss during the peace negotiations, such as India, Egypt, Korea, or French Indochina.[4] In the standard narrative of the peace conference, non-Western regions and peoples figure most often as inert masses of territory and humanity that the great powers carved up in an unprecedented expansion of imperialism.

Similar gaps exist, not surprisingly, in the literature on the U.S. role in the First World War and at the peace conference, with most of it focused on the interactions between the United States and its principal allies.[5] The impact of Wilsonian rhetoric in Europe has gotten some attention, but the perspectives of those beyond the continent remain largely absent.[6] Despite the central role that many authors assign to Wilson in the history of U.S. relations with the world—one described the past one hundred years as a "Wilsonian century," and another called Wilson "the hinge" of twentieth-century American foreign policy—Wilson's impact and image in much of the world remains unexplored.[7] Little wonder, then, that one recent survey of the literature, which emphasized the anti-imperial strain in Wilson's wartime thinking, concluded that "new studies of the expectations and disappointments generated by Wilsonian rhetoric are sorely needed,"[8] and another has noted that understanding how "the call for self-determination fired the imaginations of countless nationalists in the colonial world . . . is the most fertile ground for further writing about Wilsonianism."[9]

Such observations are part of the growing call among historians to "internationalize" the history of the United States.[10] Most of the recent work that has risen to this challenge has interpreted the task as showing how the impact of the world at large has been reflected in American history; that is, how aspects of the American historical experience, whether political, social, or cultural, unfolded within and have been shaped by a broader international context.[11] But there is another possible meaning, less often pursued, to the call to internationalize U.S. history, which is to examine how the United States has been reflected in the world, in the histories of other societies. This perspective is represented, for example, in recent work on the histories of anti-Americanism in regions such as Latin America or the Middle East.[12] But anti-Americanism is but one facet of the mirror that the world has placed before America. As the history of what I call the "Wilsonian moment" in the colonial world shows, a positive, even idealized image of America has been no less, and perhaps more influential in the history of the American impact on the world.[13] Moreover, in historical experience the attitudes of anti- and pro-Americanism are often closely related. As the history of the Wilsonian moment also shows, the roots of the former are firmly planted in the latter, feeding as they do on the fluctuating but ever-present gap between the promise of America's rhetoric and ideals and the realities of its policies and practices.

Thinking about the Wilsonian moment in the colonial world also provides an unusual perspective on the history of anticolonialism and decolonization, surely among the most important historical processes of the twentieth century. Much of the history of anticolonial movements has been written as if it occurred solely within the boundaries of the emerging nation, or of the imperial enclosure from which it emerged. Thus, the history of the Indian nationalist movement is written as part of Indian history, or of British imperial history; the history of Chinese nationalism as part of the history of China, and so on. The circular logic of this practice is easy to expose—Chinese nationalism in a sense "produced" China, and is therefore part of Chinese history—but it has not been easy to transcend. Nationalist histories have, of course, been challenged vigorously by historians of postcolonial societies, but such projects have tended to question the national and imperial frameworks by adopting subnational perspectives; that is, to historicize and denaturalize the national enclosure by breaking it down to its component parts, rather than by showing how it was forged in the first place within the broader context of international events.[14]

When we expand our field of vision and place anticolonial nationalist histories within an international context, it is easy to see, as Prasenjit Duara observed, that "after World War I, the circumstances for decolonization were generated as much from the international situation as any other."[15] This was not just due to the emergence of revisionist powers like the United States and the Soviet Union, but also, perhaps no less importantly, due to the establishment, for the first time, of international institutions and norms that allowed, indeed invited anticolonial nationalists to challenge colonial powers in an external arena, circumventing and thereby weakening the imperial relationship. This is why, as we will see, Edwin Montagu, the Secretary of State for India in 1919, was so worried over the admission of India into the League of Nations as a founding member, and why the Indian nationalist B. G. Tilak was so hopeful over the same event, despite the fact that Indian representation there remained under full British control. Though the League and its mandate system have traditionally been viewed as little more than fig leaves for empire, historians are now beginning to explore the importance of the notion that they introduced, that colonial powers were answerable to institutions and mechanisms higher than themselves, a notion that would evolve in the postwar decades into a powerful tool for undermining the legitimacy and therefore the viability of the arrangements of empire.[16]

Once we remove the Eurocentric lens through which the international history of 1919—and indeed, international history in general, especially prior to the Second World War—has most often been viewed, central events and experiences pertaining to non-European peoples come into focus, both enhancing our view of the international history of the period and illuminating those events and experiences themselves in a new light. Geoffrey Barraclough suggested some time ago that the shift away from the West as the focal point of modern history is one of the central features of the twentieth century, and close attention should therefore be paid to the rise of non-Western actors as active participants in world affairs. Examining contemporary history from non-Western perspectives, he wrote, "cuts into the past at a different angle," crossing traditional lines of inquiry, casting "doubts on the adequacy of the old patterns" and suggesting "the need for a new ground plan." Among other things, he said, it illuminates the transition from what he called the "old world" to the "new world" of international relations—from a world of empires to one of nation-states—a transition that acquired "a separate identity and an existence of its own" by 1918.[17] It is with the emergence of this new world into its own that this book is centrally concerned.

With a project of this scope I have inevitably accumulated even more than the usual share of debts in the course of the research and writing. The numerous research trips I made to far-flung archives on several continents would not have been possible without generous funding from many sources, including International Security Studies at Yale, the Dan David Prize scholarship, the George C. Marshall/Baruch Fellowship, the W. Stull Holt Fellowship of the Society for Historians of American Foreign Relations (SHAFR), the Council on East Asian Studies at Yale, the John Perry Miller Fund at Yale, and the Clark/Cooke Fund at Harvard. Much of the work of revising and preparing the manuscript for publication was done during a sabbatical year funded by grants from the Weatherhead Center for International Affairs and the National Endowment for the Humanities. Both International Security Studies at Yale and the John M. Olin Institute for Strategic Studies at Harvard provided welcoming intellectual communities at critical stages of the work, and for this I thank them.

Numerous archivists and librarians facilitated my research. The staff at the Academia Sinica in Taipei maintained their cheer in the face of my Mandarin and went beyond the call of duty in helping me to decipher some hastily scrawled characters in hand-written missives of the Chinese Foreign Ministry. At the National Archives of India they spared no effort in tracking down errant documents, and the Nehru Memorial Museum and Library in New Delhi, with peacocks roaming the grounds, was perhaps the most charming archive I have worked in; the only possible competitor was the French Army archive in Vincennes, housed in a grand chateau on the outskirts of Paris. The archivists at the U.K. National Archives in Kew and the British Library's India Office Records were unfailingly helpful and efficient, as were those at the U.S. National Archives in College Park, Maryland, and at the Library of Congress. My appreciation also goes to the staff at the French Foreign Ministry archive in the Quai d'Orsay, and at Harvard, Yale, Princeton, Columbia, the University of California–Berkeley, the University of Missouri–Columbia, the Hoover Institution at Stanford, the State Historical Society of Wisconsin in Madison, and the Presbyterian Historical Society in Philadelphia.

Opportunities to present my research to scrutiny have been invaluable to the development and refinement of my ideas throughout the course of the project. I thank the organizers, panelists, and audiences at numerous forums, including the SHAFR annual meetings in 2000 and 2003, the international history colloquia at Yale and Harvard, the Graduate Conference on International History at Harvard, the China workshop at Yale, and the Korea Institute workshop at Harvard. My work has benefited from the hospitality and critical acumen of Wm. Roger Louis and the British Studies seminar at the University of Texas at Austin; Peter Feaver and the Triangle Institute for Security Studies at Duke University; Mark Mazower and the Center for International History at Columbia University; Mike Reynolds and the Department of Near Eastern Studies at Princeton University; Eric Vettel and the Woodrow Wilson Presidential Library in Staunton, Virginia; Jun Furuya and the Symposium on Rethinking American Studies in Tokyo, Japan; and last but not least, of the Global History Network, run by Sebastian Conrad and Dominic Sachsenmaier in Germany and the United States.

The history departments at Yale, where I was a student, and at Harvard, where I now teach, have been exemplary homes for my intellectual pursuits. I am grateful to the many colleagues who have offered advice, support, and intellectual stimulation, including Sven Beckert, David Blackbourn, Sugata Bose, Vince Brown, Nancy Cott, Mark Elliott, Niall Ferguson, Andy Gordon, Akira Iriye, Mary Lewis, Charles Maier, Terry Martin, and Trygve Throntveit. John Milton Cooper and Thomas Knock welcomed me into the community of Wilson scholars and offered constant encouragement. Betsy Bartlett, Gregg Brazinsky, Mark Caprio, Israel Gershoni, Durba Ghosh, Leonard Gordon, Barbara Keys, Susan Pedersen, Mona Russell, and Jeremi Suri each read parts of the manuscript in its various incarnations and made countless helpful suggestions. I am especially grateful to those generous souls who took the time to read the entire text and offer detailed comments, including David Armitage, Elizabeth Borgwardt, William Keylor, James Kloppenberg, Frank

Ninkovich, Daniel Sargent, and Jay Winter. Lien-Hang Nguyen kept up morale over countless cups of coffee, Matthew Connelly lent inspiration over beer and tonic water, and Einat Wilf cast her famously discerning eye. It goes without saying that I bear sole responsibility for the errors that remain.

I am indebted to John Lewis Gaddis, without whom the project would have never been conceived, and to Paul Kennedy and Jonathan Spence, who supported it from the outset and offered steady encouragement and advice. Susan Ferber, my editor, showed great enthusiasm for the book when it was still scattered chapters and has shepherded it with her trademark professionalism and good cheer. I would also like to acknowledge the research assistants who helped with various pressing tasks at the last stages of the work: Noah Hertz-Bunzl, Ying Qian, Kevin Yang, and Nancy Zhang. Some passages in this book appeared previously in articles published in the journals *Diplomacy & Statecraft* 12:4 (2001) and the *American Historical Review* 111:5 (2006), and in an essay included in Wm. Roger Louis, ed., *Yet More Adventures with Britannia: Personalities, Politics and Culture in Britain* (London: I. B. Tauris, 2005). I thank the respective editors and publishers for their permission to use them here.

Finally, thanks are due to my family. My wife, Noga, and my daughters, Romi, Maya, and Daria, who joined us at various stages of this project, have been a constant source of comfort, humor, and wisdom. My parents, Jonah and Tova Manela, and my siblings, Lilach, Oren, and Alon, all lent encouragement and support over the course of many years. This book is dedicated to my grandparents, whose history deserves a book of its own.

CONTENTS

NOTE ON NAMES

In rendering the names of persons and places that originate in non-European languages, I have generally tried to use the transliteration systems that are most common in the recent English-language literature. For Chinese, I used the pinyin system (e.g., Mao Zedong rather than Mao Tse-tung, Shandong rather than Shantung, and Guangzhou, not Canton) and for Arabic, the *International Journal of Middle East Studies* (IJMES) system (though without diacritics, except in the bibliography). I made exceptions, however, in cases where this practice would have made familiar names unrecognizable to nonspecialists (e.g., Wellington Koo rather than Gu Weijun) and gave the alternate versions in parentheses at first mention. Names of East Asian persons are given in the Asian order (last name first), except when the "Western" variants are used (e.g., Syngman Rhee).

In the case of Indian names, I have simply given them as they appeared in the English-language sources I used. For names that had alternate spellings in the sources I chose the more prevalent form, but gave the alternate version in parentheses at first occurrence (e.g., Poona and Pune).

The WILSONIAN MOMENT

Introduction: A Spring of Upheaval

For a brief interval, Wilson stood alone for mankind. Or at least he seemed to stand for mankind. And in that brief interval there was a very extraordinary and significant wave of response to him throughout the earth. So eager was the situation that all humanity leapt to accept and glorify Wilson—for a phrase, for a gesture. It seized upon him as its symbol. He was transfigured in the eyes of men. He ceased to be a common statesman; he became a Messiah. Millions believed him as the bringer of untold blessings; thousands would gladly have died for him. That response was one of the most illuminating events in the early twentieth century. Manifestly the World-State had been conceived then, and now it stirred in the womb. It was alive.

And then for some anxious decades it ceased to stir.

—H. G. Wells, *The Shape of Things to Come*

In June 1919, Nguyen Tat Thanh, a twenty-eight-year-old kitchen assistant from French Indochina, set out to present a petition to the world leaders then assembled in Paris for the peace conference. The document, entitled "The Claims of the People of Annam," echoed the rhetoric of the president of the United States, Woodrow Wilson, who had recently emerged in the international arena as a champion of the right of all peoples to self-determination. In the tumultuous months following the end of the First World War, Wilson was hailed around the world as the prophet of a new era in world affairs, one in which justice, rather than power, would be the central principle of international relations. The young man from Indochina, who signed the petition as Nguyen Ai Quoc, or "Nguyen the Patriot," sought a personal audience with the American president to plead his people's case before Wilson. According to some accounts, he even rented a formal morning suit in preparation for the occasion. The meeting, however, did not materialize. Wilson probably never even saw Nguyen's petition, and he certainly did not respond to it. Within less than a year the man, who would later become known to the world as Ho Chi

Minh, adopted Bolshevism as his new creed, and Lenin replaced Wilson as his inspiration on the road to self-determination for his people.[1]

Ho's experience in the wake of the Great War was far from unique. The war, which had begun in August 1914, lasted more than four years and left many millions dead. When the armistice was finally declared on November 11, 1918, millions around the world celebrated the end of the carnage and hoped that the peace would bring a different world. The war saw the collapse of several major empires: the Russian empire of the Romanovs, the Austro-Hungarian empire of the Habsburgs, the Ottoman Empire, and the German empire under the Hohenzollerns. It delivered serious blows, too, to some who were among the victors: Britain and France both suffered great losses, human and economic, that left them far weaker than they had been before the war. The United States, on the other hand, was the one major power to emerge from the war more powerful, economically, militarily, and politically. Its material and financial resources had underpinned the Allied war effort, its entry into the war in April 1917 appeared to have tipped the scales in favor of the Allies, and, finally, the armistice agreement had been based on the principles outlined in Wilson's famed Fourteen Points. When the U.S. leader shortly thereafter announced his decision to travel to Europe to participate personally in the peace negotiations—an unprecedented move for a sitting American president—he seemed to be poised to lead the world into a new era in international affairs.

The major leaders who convened for the peace conference in Paris in January 1919 were concerned mainly with fashioning a settlement in Europe. But Europeans were not the only ones who had high hopes for the conference. For colonized, marginalized, and stateless peoples from all over the world—Chinese and Koreans, Arabs and Jews, Armenians and Kurds, and many others—the conference appeared to present unprecedented opportunities to pursue the goal of self-determination. They could now take the struggle against imperialism to the international arena, and their representatives set out for Paris, invited or otherwise, to stake their claims in the new world order. A largely unintended but eager audience for Wilson's wartime rhetoric, they often imagined the president as both an icon of their aspirations and a potential champion of their cause, a dominant figure in the world arena committed, he had himself declared, to the principle of self-determination for all peoples.

Based on these perceptions, groups aspiring to self-determination formed delegations, selected representatives, formulated demands, launched campaigns, and mobilized publics behind them. They composed and circulated a flood of declarations, petitions, and memoranda directed at the world leaders assembled in Paris and directed at public opinion across the world. Many of the petitioners adopted Wilson's rhetoric of self-determination and the equality of nations to formulate their demands and justify their aspirations, both because they found his language appealing and, more importantly, because they believed it would be effective in advancing their cause. They quoted at length from the president's Fourteen Points address and his other wartime speeches, praised his plan for a League of Nations, and aimed to attract his support for their struggles to attain self-determination.

Hundreds of such documents, many addressed to President Wilson himself, made their way to the Paris headquarters of the American Commission to Negotiate Peace at the Hôtel Crillon, but most got no further than the president's private secretary, Gilbert Close. The president read only a small fraction of them, and he acted on fewer still. The complex and contentious issues of the European settlement were foremost on his mind during his months in Paris, and relations with the major imperial powers—Britain, France, Japan—loomed larger in the scheme of U.S. interests as Wilson saw them than did the aspirations of colonized groups or weak states. Though the dispensation of territories that belonged to the defunct empires—German colonies in Africa and the Pacific, Ottoman possessions in the Arab Middle East—was an important topic in the peace negotiations, the leading peacemakers had no intention of entertaining the claims for self-determination of dependent peoples elsewhere, least of all those that ran against their own interests. To himself and to others, Wilson explained this lapse by asserting that the peace conference already had enough on its plate and that the League of Nations would take up such claims in due time.

Many in the colonial world who had followed Wilson's increasingly dramatic proclamations in the final months of the war, however, came to expect a more immediate and radical transformation of their status in international society. As the outlines of the peace treaty began to emerge in the spring of 1919, it became clear that such expectations would be disappointed and that outside Europe the old imperial logic of international relations, which abridged or entirely obliterated the sovereignty of most non-European peoples, would remain largely in place. The disillusionment that followed the collapse of this "Wilsonian moment" fueled a series of popular protest movements across the Middle East and Asia, heralding the emergence of anticolonial nationalism as a major force in world affairs. Although the principle of self-determination was honored in Paris more in the breach, the events of 1919 established it at the center of the discourse of legitimacy in international relations. Thus, the Wilsonian moment began the process that Hedley Bull called "the expansion of international society" in the twentieth century. It launched the transformation of the norms and standards of international relations that established the self-determining nation-state as the only legitimate political form throughout the globe, as colonized and marginalized peoples demanded and eventually attained recognition as sovereign, independent actors in international society.[2]

This book is an effort to reconstruct the story of the colonial world at the Wilsonian moment. Most historians have told the story of the Paris Peace Conference from the inside out, focusing on the views and actions of the leaders of the great powers of Europe and North America. This book aims to tell it from the outside in, from the perspectives of peoples who were on the margins of the peace conference and of international society more generally. The period on which the narrative centers opened with the U.S. entry into the war in April 1917, when it began to appear that Wilson would play a major role at the peace table, and ended with the conclusion of the Versailles Treaty in June 1919. During this time, Woodrow Wilson's vision for the postwar world was disseminated to a growing global audience, and, when peace came, colonial peoples moved to claim their place in that world on the basis of Wilson's proclamations. The crucial period—the Wilsonian moment itself—lasted from the autumn of 1918, when Allied victory appeared imminent and Wilson's principles seemed destined to shape the coming new world order, until the spring of 1919, as the terms of the peace settlement began to emerge and the promise of a Wilsonian millennium was fast collapsing.

The use of the phrase the "Wilsonian moment" to describe this eventful time does not suggest that Wilson alone conceived or articulated the vision that became so intimately associated with him. Others, including the British prime minister David Lloyd George and, much more forcefully, the Russian Bolshevik leaders V. I. Lenin and Leon Trotsky, had preceded Wilson in advocating a peace settlement based on the principle of self-determination. Nor does the term imply that rhetoric alone was responsible for creating the far-reaching expectations that so many entertained in the wake of the war. The experiences of the war itself, with its unprecedented decimation of human lives and the myriad political, social, and economic dislocations it caused, served as the crucial context for the articulation and dissemination of the Wilsonian message and shaped the perceptions and responses to it. Nevertheless, the term the "Wilsonian moment" captures the fact that, during this period, the American president became for millions worldwide the icon and most prominent exponent of the vision, which many others shared, of a just international society based on the principle of self-determination. His name, and in many cases also his image, came to symbolize and encapsulate those ideas, and Wilson appeared, for a brief but crucial moment, to be the herald of a new era in international affairs.

In retrospect, of course, we know that the Wilsonian moment ended in ignominious collapse, its promise fading into bitter disillusion. But if we are to see the events of the time in their proper context, we must suspend for a while this retrospective knowledge. It may be tempting, for example, to construe the ideological essence of 1919 as a clash between Wilsonian and communist internationalism; "Wilson vs. Lenin" is the influential phrase that Arno

Mayer coined some decades ago.[3] But while the Wilson versus Lenin framework is helpful, as Mayer used it, for understanding the struggle over the European Left at the time, it cannot be extended to the colonial world in 1919. Socialist ideas were influential among some colonial intellectuals at the time, and the Russian Bolsheviks also used the language of self-determination, but until late 1919 Wilson's words carried far greater weight in the colonial world than Lenin's. The United States, after all, was a leading world power whose intervention in the war had appeared to tip the scales in favor of the Allies; Wilson had set the terms of the armistice and seemed poised to do the same for the peace settlement. The Bolsheviks, on the other hand, were struggling for control of a land that was devastated by the war and were engaged in a brutal civil war whose outcome was far from certain. It was only after the collapse of the Wilsonian moment and the stabilization of the Soviet state that Lenin's influence in the colonial world began to eclipse Wilson's.

Wilson's promise of a new world order captured imaginations across the world. In the wake of a war whose consequences were widely felt, his words captured the attention not only of political elites but also of much broader publics, even if their meanings and implications varied considerably among different groups. Some, of course, remained skeptical, and they were soon joined by many others who grew disillusioned with their erstwhile hero as the developments in Paris and elsewhere failed to fulfill their expectations. But for a while, from mid-1918 to the early spring of 1919, the future of international society seemed to belong to Wilson's vision and to depend on his influence as the leading figure in world affairs. The Wilsonian moment, therefore, should be examined and understood as an international phenomenon not because every individual on the face of the planet was aware of Wilson's rhetoric, but because the scope of its dissemination and import transcended the usual geographic enclosures of historical narratives.

Quite apart from Wilson's own intentions when he uttered the words of the Fourteen Points address or his other well-known speeches, different groups and individuals adopted the language of self-determination to varying extents and adapted it to varying circumstances. Perhaps most famously, it was used by many of the national groups that emerged from the wreckage of the Habsburg and Romanov empires in East-Central Europe, and helped shape the postwar settlements that created Czechoslovakia, Poland, and the Kingdom of the Serbs, Croats, and Slovenes as independent states.[4] But the language of self-determination was also adopted by groups that made claims directed at the victorious powers, either to demand political independence, as in Ireland, or to ask for recognition of rights within an existing polity, as with leading African-American activists like W. E. B. Du Bois and William Monroe Trotter.[5] The adoption of the language of self-determination, moreover, was not limited to groups that saw themselves as oppressed or marginalized. In fact, as the H. G. Wells quote that opens this chapter testifies, a wide array of progressives and radicals in Europe and North America entertained for a time near-millennial expectations for a more peaceful world order based on Wilsonian principles.[6]

The focus of this book is on the specific significance of the Wilsonian moment in the colonial world, defined broadly as the dependent or semi-dependent territories that encompassed at the time almost all of Asia and Africa.[7] Even within these narrower geographical and conceptual bounds, however, an effort to cover the colonial world in its entirety would have yielded either a broad, general synthesis or else required a multivolume work of encyclopedic proportions. On the other hand, telling the story of the Wilsonian moment in only one region or within a single group would have failed to capture fully the international context of the experiences of colonial peoples at the time, and would have forgone the insights that a broad, integrated perspective can provide. In order to combine fine-grained detail with a broad perspective, therefore, the book focuses on the experiences of four groups: Egyptians, Indians, Chinese, and Koreans. It recounts the responses of these four emergent nations to the Wilsonian moment, probing their evolving perceptions of its challenges and opportunities and tracing its impact on their rhetoric, actions, and goals. It also reconstructs the sprawling international campaigns they launched, in which diasporic communities and unprecedented popular mobilizations both played important roles, and relates them to the broad, transformative protest movements that erupted in all four places in the spring of 1919. Nationalism, as an ideology and as a form of political practice, evolved conceptually and historically within an international context, and it cannot be fully understood outside that context.

There were, of course, many differences among these societies in their histories, structures, and relationships to imperialism. Still, Egyptians, Indians, Chinese, and Koreans shared important elements of historical condition and experience. All four societies had long histories as integrated socioeconomic and political entities and well-established elites imbued with consciousness of distinct cultural and historical identities. Moreover, in each of these four societies there had developed by 1914 influential groups of literate, socially mobile individuals, whose members were conversant in Western languages and ideas and had begun to develop and circulate notions of national identity articulated in modern idioms.[8] The Wilsonian moment presented these elites with unprecedented opportunities to advance claims in the name of these emerging national identities and thus bolster and expand their legitimacy both at home and abroad. The language of self-determination and the international forum afforded by the peace conference prompted nationalist leaders to rethink their strategies, redefine their goals, and galvanize larger domestic constituencies than ever before behind campaigns for self-determination. In the spring of 1919, sweeping protest movements against imperialism erupted almost simultaneously in all four societies: the May Fourth movement in China, the launching of Gandhi's nonviolent resistance movement in India, the 1919 Revolution in Egypt, and the March First movement in Korea.

In all four societies, and not only there, the period between 1917 and 1920 saw a sharp escalation of resistance to imperial penetration and control and the emergence or realignment of institutions and individuals that would play central roles in subsequent anticolonial struggles. In Egypt, Sa'd Zaghlul, a veteran political figure who before the war had long worked within the British-controlled political system, now established a delegation that demanded the opportunity to put before the peace conference a claim for Egyptian independence. To lead this campaign, Zaghlul, who is remembered in Egypt as the "Father of the Nation," established a new political party that came to dominate Egyptian politics in the interwar years.[9] A similar shift from accommodation to confrontation occurred in India's relationship with the empire during the same period, as the Indian National Congress, which before the war adhered to moderate positions toward the empire, became a vehicle for mobilizing resistance to it. By 1920, the Congress came under the control of Mahatma Gandhi, who had himself shifted in 1919 from a position of firm if critical support for Indian membership in the British empire to one of determined opposition to it. The newfound radicalism of the Gandhian Congress augured an era of nationalist struggle that culminated in the dissolution of British rule in 1947.[10]

In China, the May Fourth protests that erupted in response to Chinese disillusion with the Wilsonian promise unleashed broad currents of change in the realms of thought, culture, literature, and politics. In the wake of May Fourth, protests against foreign influence in China broadened and intensified. Among the intellectual and political classes, the erstwhile admiration for the liberal ideals advanced by Wilson was widely replaced with a growing interest in other ideologies as models for building a strong Chinese nation and establishing its status and dignity internationally. And in Korea, too, the March First movement, which began as an effort to draw the attention of Wilson and the peace conference to Korean claims for independence, escalated and broadened the resistance to Japanese colonial rule. In the Korean case, even more than in the others, diasporic organizations played a crucial role in the movement, establishing a provisional government in exile headed by Syngman Rhee, a long-time independence activist and former acquaintance of Wilson at Princeton University. The provisional government survived, though barely, through the interwar years, and in 1948 the United States helped the tenacious Rhee actually attain the position he had claimed since 1919, the presidency of an independent Korean republic.[11]

As this convergence of transformative events around the spring of 1919 suggests, one of the central features of the Wilsonian moment was its simultaneity across the boundaries of nations, regions, and empires within which the histories of the anticolonial movements of the period are usually enclosed. It was a brief but intense period in which people across the world directed attention and actions toward the drama unfolding in Paris, with the U.S. president as its leading protagonist. In part, the story of the Wilsonian moment is one of the articulation and circulation of ideas, most prominently the idea that all peoples had a right to self-determination and the related notion of a liberal international order structured around a league of nations in which all members would be equal in status if not in power. The emergence of Wilson's ideas about the postwar international order, their gradual articulation and refinement in his wartime rhetoric, and their dissemination—both intentionally through the efforts of U.S. wartime propaganda, and circumstantially through the contemporary infrastructure of global communications, which was dominated by pro-Allied news agencies such as Reuters—are all important components of the story told here.

But this is not only, nor even primarily, an intellectual history, a history of the emergence, articulation, and circulation of ideas. To a greater degree, the story of the Wilsonian moment in the colonial world is one about the role of power, both real and perceived, in the dissemination, adoption, and operationalization—the conversion into purposeful political action—of the new norms of international legitimacy and practice that Wilson championed. For anticolonial nationalists, Wilson's utterances were surely attractive as well as, to some extent, also innovative. The most crucial feature of his utterances, however, was that they came from a man widely viewed at the time as the most powerful leader in the world arena, whose influence on the shape of the postwar international order, it was assumed, would be decisive. Thus, the perception of the stature of the United States as a major world power and of Wilson's commitment to his peace plan were just as important as the content of the president's wartime proclamations in creating the impact of the Wilsonian moment in the colonial world. For a time in 1918 and early 1919, Wilson, who appeared to wield extraordinary leverage over the Allies and enjoy unprecedented popularity among their peoples, seemed to possess both the will and the power to implement his vision.[12]

Wilson himself, it is true, had at best only a vague idea of how the principle of self-determination would be practically implemented even in Europe, and he devoted little attention to its implications elsewhere. Nevertheless, the president's talk about the right to self-determination and his advocacy of the League of Nations implied a new and more equitable model of international relations, and they took on a life of their own, independent of Wilson and his intentions. For colonial nationalists, the acceptance of these principles as a basis for the armistice and their establishment as central tenets of the coming peace settlement were sufficient reasons to expect great changes in their own positions in international affairs. Wilson, in his wartime addresses, especially those that he delivered in the final months of the war, had couched his principles explicitly in sweeping, universal terms. Egyptians, Indians, Chinese, Koreans, and other colonial nationalists saw little reason that they should not apply outside Europe as well as within it.

The Versailles peace is often seen as heralding the apex of imperial expansion, and indeed the empires of the victorious powers, especially the British, French, and Japanese, made significant territorial gains in the wake of the war. Empire, however, cannot survive on territorial control alone. It requires accommodation and legitimacy, at least among a portion of the populations in both the metropole and the periphery.[13] The adoption of the language of self-determination by colonial nationalists, as well as by anti-imperialists in the metropole, weakened these underlying supports of the imperial edifice. It rendered the relationship between imperial powers and subject peoples, as Henri Grimal noted, "markedly different from the idea of timeless domination which had characterized the previous period" and presented a major challenge to the legitimacy and permanence of the imperial order in the international arena.[14] As James Mayall has observed, at Versailles Lloyd George and the French premier, Georges Clemenceau, may have succeeded in the short run in outwitting Wilson in their efforts to protect the interests of their empires. But in an age of advancing popular democracy they could offer no substitute, either domestically or internationally, to the principle of self-determination "as an ordering principle for international society."[15] Rather than bolster or expand the imperial order, the events of 1919 in fact laid the groundwork for its demise.

The First World War itself had no doubt set the stage for the expectations for radical change that spread in its wake. It dealt a severe blow to the power and prestige of the leading imperial powers, and so made it easier for colonial nationalists to challenge them. The war strained the resources of the European powers, exposed as hollow their claims to superior civilization, and decimated the image of Western military invincibility already tarnished by the Japanese defeat of Russia in 1905.[16] Moreover, peoples from the periphery who had made significant contributions to the Allied war effort felt it entitled them to a greater voice in their own government and in the international arena. If they could die alongside Europeans, why could they not govern alongside them? Almost a million Indians saw combat in the war and hundreds of thousands of Chinese went to Europe as laborers, and many returned home with new experiences and ideas about rights and freedom.[17] The economic crises and dislocations of the war also contributed to postwar discontent in places like Egypt and India, though this factor did not operate everywhere; in Korea, for example, the war was a time of relative prosperity.

The impact of the war alone, however, cannot explain the events that occurred in its wake in the colonial world. Despite the war's drain on European power and prestige, there was surprisingly little agitation against empire during the war itself, when the imperial powers were militarily most vulnerable, neither did uprisings break out immediately after the war ended. It is true, as a number of historians have noted, that the wartime spectacles of material destruction and moral depravity helped to launch a broad critique of Western civilization among Afro-Asian intellectuals. This insight, however, neglects the widespread if short-lived adulation of that quintessential representative of the West, Woodrow Wilson, as a quasi-millennial figure whose vision could redeem the suffering of the war and usher in a new era of peace.[18] At the time of the armistice in November 1918, nationalists across the colonial world believed that the road to self-determination passed through Paris, and they launched broad campaigns to receive a hearing there. It was only in the spring of 1919, as it became clear that their efforts to claim these rights had failed, that upheaval erupted. Thus, the campaigns to advance demands for self-determination and international equality and the subsequent failure and disillusionment helped launch major anticolonial protest movements and mobilize widespread popular support behind them.

Other factors, political and economic, figured prominently in these postwar anticolonial mobilizations. The burdens of wartime inflation and conscription among Egyptian and Indians, anger about the suspicious death of a former emperor among Koreans, and mounting industrial grievances among the rising Chinese working class were all significant in the respective uprisings of 1919. Those factors can help to account for the prevalence of popular disturbances and for the hostility toward foreign powers or colonial rulers. Alone, however, they do not explain the specific timing, character, and goals of the uprisings. The campaigns for self-determination and equality in the international arena each had roots in internal developments within each society. But they were also intricately enmeshed in the international context of the Wilsonian moment, as the demands that nationalist leaders made on the international forum assembling in Paris channeled a mix of grievances and frustrations into anticolonial uprisings in the cause of self-determination. The campaigns to lodge these demands, and the failure of the great powers to meet or even address them, helped convert the expectations for a new era in international affairs into demonstrations in the streets of Cairo, Delhi, Beijing, Seoul, and elsewhere, and endow those demonstrations with coherent meanings and purposes. The anticolonial revolts of 1919 owed at least as much to the peace as they did to the war.

The international scope of the story of the Wilsonian moment in the colonial world is not merely an artifact of a particular historiographical approach, and this book should not be read as an exercise that juxtaposes several distinct events for comparative purposes. Rather, its scope reflects the ways that the historical actors themselves perceived their conditions, planned their actions, and proceeded to carry out their plans. Indeed, the Wilsonian moment as it was perceived, experienced, and enacted by colonial peoples was both international and transnational in its scope, if we take "international" to refer primarily to interactions between established nation-states and "transnational" to mean actions and interactions that cross the borders of states but are not necessarily performed by them.[19] It is abundantly clear that Wilson saw himself as acting on a global stage. But an equally important insight, one to which we will return in more detail in the conclusion of the book, is that the anticolonial movements of 1919—commonly viewed in only the context of their respective national histories—profoundly transcended national enclosures in their genesis, conduct, and aims. They were shaped by transnational networks of nationalist activists who imagined themselves as part of a global wave, operated explicitly on an international stage, and aspired to goals that were specifically international; namely, the recognition of the peoples and territories they claimed to represent as self-determining, sovereign nation-states within a new international society whose structure and dynamics would reflect Wilsonian precepts.

In retrospect, it is easy to see that the expectations for a more inclusive international order that Wilson's rhetoric and global stature raised among colonial nationalists went far beyond the president's intentions and even further beyond what he would achieve. But at the time, most Egyptian, Indian, Chinese, and Korean nationalists, along with the millions who lined the streets in the capitals of Europe to cheer Wilson as he drove by in his carriage, believed that the peace conference would transform international order in ways that would help them gain the right to self-determination. They were neither naive victims of Wilson's hypocrisy nor, outside a few exceptions, radicals intent on revolutionary transformation, but rather savvy political actors who, keenly aware of their weakness vis-à-vis the British and Japanese imperial projects, sought to harness Wilson's power and rhetoric to the struggle to achieve international recognition and equality for their nations. They moved with dispatch and energy to seize the opportunities that the Wilsonian moment seemed to offer to reformulate, escalate, and broaden their campaigns against empire, and worked to mobilize publics both at home and abroad behind their movements. When it became clear that the postwar settlement would fall far short of these expectations and the visions of international equality that Wilson had evoked collapsed, these mobilized nationalists launched the simultaneous revolts that convulsed the colonial world in the spring of 1919. Despite the title of this book, it is they, and not Wilson, who are the main protagonists of the story that follows.

PART

I

The Emergence of the Wilsonian Moment

On December 4th, 1918, Woodrow Wilson, the first president to leave the territory of the United States during his presidency, sailed for France aboard the George Washington, the most powerful man in the world.

—John Dos Passos, *1919*

Woodrow Wilson, true to biblical form, was a reluctant prophet, and his rise to the status of the herald of a new order did not begin until several years into the Great War. When the conflict began with a cascade of declarations of war between the European powers between July 28 and August 4, 1914, Wilson, though caught by surprise, nevertheless immediately announced that the United States would follow its long-standing tradition and observe strict neutrality in the conflict. Drawing on his long-standing notions of civilized behavior, Wilson declared on August 3 that America, unlike the other powers, would maintain its "self possession" and "calmness of thought." He called on the American people to remain neutral "in fact as well as in name" and to preserve "the dignity of self-control" so that they could serve the cause of peace.[1] For much of the first year of the war, Wilson ignored the critics, led by former president Theodore Roosevelt and Massachusetts senator Henry Cabot Lodge, who called for building up the armed forces of the United States in the name of "preparedness." Even as Japan entered the war on the Allied side in late August, the Ottoman Empire joined the Central Powers in November, and Italy, initially neutral, joined the Allies in May 1915 after receiving secret promises for extensive territorial gains, the United States remained staunchly neutral.

The German submarine campaign against merchant shipping in the Atlantic, which culminated in the sinking of the British steamship *Lusitania* in May 1915 that killed 128 Americans, forced a change in the administration's position. Wilson now moved to implement preparedness, but he still resisted the calls to throw U.S. support fully behind the Allies. As the fighting increasingly jeopardized U.S. commercial interests he intensified his diplomatic efforts with the belligerents, and by May 1916, he obtained a German promise to restrict its submarine campaign. By then, moreover, Wilson began to inch away from the detached posture and back-channel contacts that had characterized his diplomacy, and started to articulate publicly an ambitious vision for the postwar world. A lasting peace, he said, required a reordering of international society on the basis of the principles of government by consent, the equality of nations, and international cooperation, but his "Peace without Victory" speech of January 1917, the first comprehensive presentation of his plan, met with a cold reception from European governments committed to victory. The following month, Germany resumed unrestricted submarine warfare, and news of a German plan to encourage Mexico to wage war on the United States—the famous Zimmermann Telegram—raised a public outcry. After several weeks of pained hesitation, Wilson came before Congress on April 2 to ask for a declaration of war on Germany. He still insisted, however, on standing apart from the European allies, styling the United States an "associated power." In taking the United States to war, Wilson hoped to ensure that he would have a dominant position in the eventual peace conference, a position that would allow him to implement his vision for the postwar restructuring of international relations.

Wilson continued to develop his plans for the peace, most famously in the address he gave before Congress on January 8, 1918, which became known around the world as the "Fourteen Points." On November 11, 1918, when the armistice was concluded on the basis of his Fourteen Points, the president appeared to have achieved his goal: he was the dominant figure in the international arena, cheered by millions worldwide, and poised, so it seemed, to transform international relations. A week after the armistice, he announced that he would travel to Europe himself—an unprecedented move for a sitting president—to lead the U.S. delegation to the peace conference. He had no choice but to do it, he thought, since only he could face down the entrenched interests of the European powers in the old order and defend the cause of justice. French and British leaders, he said, opposed his presence in Paris because they feared that he "might lead the weaker nations against them,"[2] and this made him even more determined to go. Wilson no doubt imagined himself primarily as the defender of the "weaker nations" of Europe—Belgians, Poles, Czechs—rather than those of the colonial world. Nevertheless, his impact on largely unintended audiences in the colonial world proved no less significant.

The two chapters that follow in Part I explore two central aspects of the relationship between the U.S. president's efforts to use the peace conference to construct a new international order and the efforts of peoples outside Europe to use that same forum to overcome their subjugated status and win recognition as independent actors in international society. Chapter 1 probes the origins of Wilson's plan for the postwar world and seeks to outline the place that non-European peoples were to have within it. Wilson's position on this issue was both more complex and more dynamic than most historians have recognized. In order to recover its nuances and evolution, we need to look beyond the president's wartime rhetoric and examine both his domestic record on race relations and the development of his position toward the U.S. imperial project overseas in the wake of the Spanish-American War of 1898, when he began to think seriously about international questions. Chapter 2 then tracks Wilson's wartime rhetoric down to the armistice as it evolved in response to both domestic and international developments. Among other things, it seeks to explain how Wilson came to be seen by the end of the war as the champion of the principle of self-determination, a term he never used publicly before February 1918. To do so, the chapter outlines the channels and mechanisms of the worldwide dissemination of Wilson's rhetoric and image, including the massive American wartime propaganda campaigns abroad. By the time Wilson arrived on the shores of Europe in December 1918, he carried great hopes and expectations upon his shoulders.

1

Self-Determination for Whom?

The USS *George Washington*, which carried President Woodrow Wilson across the Atlantic, steamed into the harbor of Brest on the coast of Brittany, France, at noon on Friday, December 13, 1918. It was the first time that a sitting American president had come to Europe and Wilson's decision to go had been controversial at home. But the president, who believed thirteen was his lucky number, saw the date of arrival as a good omen for his mission. And he seemed to have every reason to think so as the cheering throngs that gathered at the docks to meet him came into view. Everyone—high officials in formal suits, local peasants in Breton caps, groups of schoolchildren in their holiday best—had come to see the great man land, hoisting banners that welcomed the "Champion of the Rights of Man" and praised the "Founder of the Society of Nations." The mayor of Brest, greeting the president as he disembarked, delivered a resounding speech hailing him as an apostle of liberty come to release the peoples of Europe from their suffering. The next morning, as the president drove down the Champs Élysées in an open-top automobile, girls in Alsatian costumes threw flowers on him and the cheering crowds called, "*Vive Wilson! Vive l'Amérique! Vive la liberté!*" The French press across the political spectrum sang his praises, and labor leaders hailed him as "the incarnation of the hope of the future."[1] Over the next five weeks, Wilson met with similar receptions in England and Italy as he toured the continent before the peace conference opened in Paris on January 18.[2]

The prevailing sentiments across much of Europe were echoed by the French pacifist author and Nobel Laureate Romain Rolland, who in grand language depicted the president as a prophet, heir to a great line of American liberators destined to transform humanity, and called on him to fulfill his promise of a better, more just world:

> You alone Mr. President are endowed with an [*sic*] universal moral authority. All have confidence in you. Respond to the appeal of these pathetic hopes! Take these outstretched hands, help them to clasp each other. Help these groping peoples to find their way, to establish the new Charter of enfranchisement and of union whose principles they are all passionately if confusingly seeking.

The hero's welcome that Woodrow Wilson received upon his arrival in Europe in December 1918 was widely reported across the colonial world and helped foster the impression that the U.S. president possessed the power to affect a lasting change in international affairs. *Princeton University Library, Woodrow Wilson Coll., Box 42, Folder 5.*

> Descendant of Washington, of Abraham Lincoln! Take in hand the cause, not of a party, of a people, but of all! Summon to the Congress of Humanity the representatives of the peoples! Preside over it with all the authority which your lofty moral conscience and the powerful future of immense America assures to you! Speak! Speak to all![3]

Great wars are transformative events; they destroy not only lives and property but also established orders—norms, institutions, ideas, perceptions—in short, the old ways of thought and practice. The Great War of 1914–1918 was an event unprecedented in the sheer scale of its destruction. It extinguished millions of lives and caused untold devastation; it also threatened the collapse of order and stability in international relations. In the wake of the war, many around the world hoped, and expected, the postwar world to be entirely different from what had come before it. In the aftermath of the First World War, moreover, such sentiments and expectations were unusually strong, even compared to the aftermaths of other cataclysmic conflicts such as the Napoleonic wars some hundred years earlier or the Second World War a quarter century later. There were no messiahs on the horizon in the wakes of those wars, only hardheaded men of affairs working to refashion a semblance of order out of the chaos of war.[4] In 1919, as H. G. Wells suggested, there did appear to be such a figure, a prophet of a new world order who, however briefly, came to symbolize to millions worldwide their own hopes and aspirations.

Such perceptions of Wilson as possessor of a "universal moral authority" backed by the "powerful future of immense America" emerged gradually as the shape of Wilson's vision for the postwar world developed and disseminated from mid-1916 on, when he began to make more concerted and visible efforts to play a role in ending the war.[5] His pronouncements came most often in the form of addresses before the U.S. Congress; from the beginning of his term in office Wilson had cast aside more than a century of precedent, opting to come speak before Congress in person rather than send messages to be read by an emissary, as previous presidents had done. From this pulpit, he issued his most important foreign policy declarations, uttering memorable, soaring phrases that echoed around the world. He called on the warring parties to make "peace without victory" when the United States was still neutral, and he vowed to make the world "safe for democracy" after he took his country into the war on the Allied side in April 1917. Though ostensibly addressed to Congress and the American public, Wilson often used these speeches as moves on the chessboard of open diplomacy, intended to mobilize support for his ideas among peoples abroad, sometimes against the positions of their own governments.

As the next chapter will show in detail, the American wartime propaganda machine, of unprecedented scope and efficiency, facilitated the dissemination of his words, amplifying and often exaggerating their import. The salesmen of the American creed who managed U.S. propaganda saw Wilson's idealistic language and image as a defender of right against might as a major asset in convincing the world of the righteousness of America's war effort and its vision for the peace. By the time of the armistice, Wilson's name and image were recognizable, and his principles for the peace settlement known to a broad array of people across the world, often to individuals and groups who had not before paid close attention to the words of a foreign leader nor been attuned to international issues. As one study of the U.S. wartime propaganda effort concluded, by the time of the armistice, "the name Woodrow Wilson, and a general idea that he was a friend of peace, liberty, and democracy, were . . . familiar in some of the remote places of the earth."[6] An American president had never before spoken, as Wilson did during the war, on such a grand stage, to such a broad audience, and with such a widespread effect. Arguably, none has done so since.[7]

First, however, we must explore in more detail how the central principles of Wilson's rhetoric, those that oppressed peoples found most appealing, developed in the course of the war. Wilson's plans for the peace changed and evolved considerably during the war and its aftermath, but a number of consistent elements appeared especially important to colonized or marginalized peoples.[8] Those elements included Wilson's oft-repeated emphasis on the "equality of nations": the idea that small, weak nations were entitled to the same treatment and rights in international society as the major powers. A related principle, summarized by its proponents at the time as "right over might," was that international disputes should be resolved through peaceful means, relying on international law, voluntary mechanisms such as arbitration, and institutional arrangements eventually embodied in the League of Nations, rather than through resort to armed conflict. And third, perhaps the best known and most celebrated of the Wilsonian mantras, was the rejection of any international arrangements that would not receive the consent of the populations concerned. This was the principle of the "consent of the governed," a term for which, for reasons explained below, Wilson began after February 1918 to substitute what would become his most famous and memorable phrase: the right of peoples to "self-determination."[9]

The Wilson administration adhered to a policy of neutrality for almost three years after the war in Europe began—"He Kept Us Out of War" was the slogan of Wilson's successful reelection campaign in 1916.[10] From early on, however, the president sought a way to play a central role in the postwar negotiations and in the new international order that would emerge from them. Wilson delivered the first major public address in which he detailed a plan for the postwar settlement on May 27, 1916, almost a year before U.S. entry into the war, and in it there were already present the main elements of the vision for the postwar world that would become identified with him. He called for the establishment of a mechanism for international cooperation among sovereign states based on two related principles: one was that political arrangements, whether national or international, should be based on popular legitimacy or, in the phrase Wilson favored, "the consent of the governed." The second was that all political units constituted through such arrangements of consent should relate to each other as equals. "We believe," he declared then before a gathering of William Howard Taft's League to Enforce Peace, "that every people has a right to choose the sovereignty under which they shall live" and that "the small states of the world shall enjoy the same respect for their sovereignty and for their territorial integrity."[11]

Several weeks later, Wilson also inserted these same phrases into a plank of the Democratic party platform for the 1916 elections to highlight his determination to stand for a just peace in Europe.[12] Then, on January 22, 1917, shortly after his reelection, Wilson came before the Senate to elaborate further on his plan for peace. Calling for a "peace without victory," he urged European leaders to work toward a negotiated settlement. At the same time, he emphasized that the United States, though it was not then a belligerent, would have to play a central role in shaping and guaranteeing the peace settlement and that the peace must therefore conform to American values and principles. Law and morality, he said, must replace brute force in governing international relations, and the "balance of power" must make way for a "community of power." The United States would be a pivotal member of that community and would uphold and guarantee the peace, but the arrangement could only work if postwar international relations adhered to and defended the twin principles of equality among nations and popular government.[13] The new international society must be constituted on the basis of "an equality of rights" that would "neither recognize nor imply a difference between big nations and small, between those who are powerful and those that are weak." Equality of rights, however, would not mean equality of circumstances, since "equality of territory or of resources there of course cannot be," nor would there be enforced equality "not gained in the ordinary peaceful and legitimate development of the peoples themselves." International equality, then, could not be absolute nor imposed by violent or revolutionary means. But that, he said, would be fine. No one who adhered to American principles as he saw them expected or asked for "anything more than an equality of rights."[14]

The source of these concepts in traditional republican notions about the status and rights of individuals in society is clear, and the president projected both the extent and the limits on individual equality within society that were inherent in his progressive political creed onto states in the international order he envisioned.[15] The ideals on which American society was founded, he had no doubt, would appeal to all peoples. Their implementation would respond to the popular will of the world's people and was therefore necessary for the achievement of lasting peace. Any arrangement that contravened them was bound to fail since it would not muster popular consent and would spark resistance among "whole populations" that "will fight subtly and constantly against it, and all the world will sympathize." These principles were quintessentially American—the United States, he said, "could stand for no others"—but at the same time could and should be applied universally, since they held "the affections and convictions of mankind" and were shared by "forward looking men and women everywhere, of every modern nation, of every enlightened community."[16] But what of those nations that were not deemed sufficiently "modern," those communities not sufficiently enlightened? And who would be the judge? Wilson did not say. For now, he and most of his audiences simply ignored the question.

This second central principle, the consent of the governed, was also drawn directly from the core ideas of the Anglo-American liberal tradition and Progressive Era conventional wisdom and was therefore no less fundamental in Wilson's scheme. Ruling by popular consent rather than fiat, he insisted, must serve as a basis for the international legitimacy of governments and for the legitimacy of the international system as a whole. "No peace can last, or ought to last," he intoned in January 1917, in a phrase that representatives of colonized peoples later repeated often, "which does not recognize and accept the principle that governments derive all their just powers from the consent of the governed, and that no right anywhere exists to hand peoples about from sovereignty to sovereignty as if they were property." International peace required that no one nation seek to dominate another, but that every people should be left to determine their own form of government, their own path of development, "unhindered, unthreatened, unafraid, the little along with the great and powerful."[17] This principle, Wilson believed, had been at the heart of the foreign policy of the United States since the promulgation in 1823 of the Monroe Doctrine, which he, like most U.S. leaders at the time, saw as the guarantor of self-government in the Americas. His own project was, he said, to extend the reach of that doctrine over the entire globe.

The "Peace without Victory" address, the most complete and detailed plan for the postwar world articulated by any major statesman up until that time, was widely disseminated and discussed around the world and established Wilson's stature in the popular mind as a leading figure in the international arena.[18] The logic of Wilson's argument, that a durable peace required government rule by popular consent, appeared to pose a direct challenge to the imperial arrangements that spanned much of the world at the time. The historian Thomas J. Knock has concluded that the address constituted "the first time that any statesman of stature" had launched what amounted to a "penetrating critique of European imperialism."[19] But Wilson, though he articulated his vision in terms of universal maxims—no right *anywhere* exists—was primarily referring to the situation in Europe, with little thought of dependent territories elsewhere. In the address, he gave the restoration of an independent Poland as an example of the principle of consent. Imperialists could still take comfort in Wilson's words if they parsed them carefully enough. If certain groups were not sufficiently "modern," certain communities not fully "enlightened," they could be excluded, at least for the time being, from the brave new world that the president envisioned.

Wilson's own secretary of state, Robert Lansing, wrote later that the principle of self-determination clearly did not apply to "races, peoples, or communities whose state of barbarism or ignorance deprive them of the capacity to choose intelligently their political affiliations." Lansing was convinced of the "danger of putting such ideas into the minds of certain races," which was bound to "create trouble in many lands" and to "breed discontent, disorder and rebellion."[20] Wilson himself in his wartime utterances did not explicitly exclude non-European peoples from the right to be governed by consent. At the same time, he did not elaborate at any length his views on colonial questions nor explain how and to what extent that principle applied in colonial situations. Some historians, following the principle that actions speak louder than words, have taken the failure of the great powers, including the United States, to apply the principle of self-determination meaningfully outside Europe in the peace settlement as evidence that Wilson "believed that national self-determination applied almost exclusively to Europeans."[21] In this view, colonial peoples who expected any support from the American president were simply naive.

Wilson's view, however, was somewhat more complicated than this approach suggests. Though there is little evidence that Wilson considered the impact that his rhetoric on self-determination would have on colonial peoples or expected the peace conference to deal with colonial questions beyond those arising directly from the war, he also did not exclude non-European peoples from the right to self-determination as a matter of principle. Rather, he envisioned them achieving it through an evolutionary process under the benevolent tutelage of a "civilized" power that would prepare them for self-government. Wilson, historian N. Gordon Levin has written, envisioned an international order that would transcend traditional imperialism and in which "the human, political, and territorial rights of underdeveloped peoples would be respected," and in which their self-determination would obtain through a "careful and orderly" process of liberal reform. "Unlike Lenin, Wilson was not prepared in the immediate postwar period to challenge the entire imperialist system with a call for the instantaneous and universal establishment of self-determination for all colonial peoples."[22] Non-European populations would eventually practice self-determination, but they would get there through gradual reforms and international institutional and legal processes, not violent revolutions. This was the logic behind Wilson's struggle in Paris to establish League of Nations "mandates" over colonial territories, in which "advanced" powers, supervised by the League, would serve as "trustees" of populations deemed not yet ready to govern themselves.[23]

Beyond the establishment of the mandate principle, however, Wilson did not give much thought during his time in Europe to colonial questions. Britain and France, the main colonial powers among the Allies, were naturally unwilling to entertain discussion of their own colonial possessions and policies at the peace table. The conference dealt only with colonial issues that arose directly from the war, largely those related to former German and Ottoman possessions outside Europe, and in any case, Wilson spent most of his energy and attention in Paris on the complex issues of the European settlement.[24] A broader perspective on the development of his thinking on colonial issues, one that goes beyond his wartime rhetoric, would therefore help reconstruct the conceptual world behind Wilson's advocacy of self-determination and reveal how and to what extent he might have seen his principles of self-determination and equality as applicable to non-Europeans. Two aspects of Wilson's prewar thinking and policies are especially relevant in this regard. First, his attitude toward the United States' own imperial possessions, initially as a prominent academic and then as a rising political leader, and second, Wilson's views on race relations and his attitude toward African Americans in the domestic American context.

Perhaps the most glaring contradiction to the universalist message of Wilson's wartime pronouncements on self-determination was his record on race relations in the domestic American context. Woodrow Wilson was a son of the American South. He was born in 1856 in antebellum Virginia and raised in Augusta, Georgia, where he lived through the Civil War as a boy, and later in Columbia, South Carolina. He was raised with racial assumptions typical of that time and place, and he appears never to have seriously challenged them, viewing blacks as his inferiors and generally disapproving of social mixing between the races. Throughout his academic career, he never made any efforts to advance minority rights. As president of Princeton University, he did nothing to open the college to black enrollment, writing in 1903 that though "there is nothing in the law of the University to prevent a negro's entering, the whole temper and tradition of the place are such that no negro has ever applied for admission." The same year, Wilson voiced his opposition to a suggestion that students at the University of Virginia, where he had once studied law, take part-time work as waiters in campus dining rooms. Such work, he explained, was "ordinarily rendered by negroes" and would therefore cause white students "an inevitable loss of self-respect."[25] In his public orations, Wilson was wont to display his prejudices, entertaining white audiences with jokes and anecdotes that featured uneducated, simple-minded "darkies."[26] Even a biographer as sympathetic to Wilson as Arthur Link concluded that although Wilson "never shared the extreme anti-Negro sentiments of many of his contemporaries," he "remained throughout his life largely a southerner on the race question."[27]

As president of the United States, too, Wilson's record on race issues was bleak. Early in his first administration, he allowed several members of his cabinet, most notably Postmaster General Albert S. Burleson and Treasury Secretary William Gibbs McAdoo, Wilson's close adviser and son-in-law, to introduce racial segregation among employees in their departments.[28] Wilson still nominated a black man, Adam Edward Patterson, for register of the treasury, a position traditionally reserved for an African American. The move, however, outraged many southerners in Congress and elsewhere, who saw Wilson's election victory, the first by a southern Democrat since the Civil War, as an opportunity to promote segregation in the federal government. White-supremacist author Thomas Dixon, who had known Wilson at Johns

Hopkins University in the 1880s, wrote him an angry letter to protest the appointment of a "Negro to boss white girls." The South, he warned darkly, would never forgive this "serious offense against the cleanness of our social life." Wilson's reply was carefully hedged and ambivalent. On the one hand, he emphasized his commitment to segregation in the federal bureaucracy and explained that his administration was implementing "a plan of concentration" which would put black employees "all together and will not in any one bureau mix the two races." At the same time, he distanced himself from Dixon's virulent rhetoric, noting that he was trying to handle the issue "in the spirit of the whole country."[29] In any event, Patterson soon withdrew his own candidacy in the face of congressional opposition.

The tensions between Wilson's progressive principles and his racist attitudes were on stark display during his White House confrontation, in November 1914, with prominent black journalist William Monroe Trotter, chair of the National Equal Rights League and editor of the *Boston Guardian*. Trotter led a group of black activists who had supported Wilson in the 1912 election as a progressive reformer and had now come to the White House to express their disappointment with his policies toward African Americans. Confronted with Trotter's pointed criticisms of the administration's segregation plans, Wilson replied with a patronizing lecture about his desire "to help colored people" and defended segregation as a form of preferential treatment that would allow blacks to develop their skills without the pressures of direct competition with whites. Straining to reconcile his principles with his policies, he admitted that both whites and blacks had "human souls" and were "absolutely equal in that respect" but added that the question was one of "economic equality—whether the Negro can do the same things with equal efficiency." Things, he assured his visitors, would "solve themselves" once blacks proved that they could do so, though it would "take generations to work this thing out."[30] By reiterating the principle of equality but relegating its attainment to some distant, indeterminate future, Wilson tried to resolve the dissonance between his ideals and his prejudices. When Trotter suggested that this policy would cost him the support of black voters, the president took violent offense and abruptly showed him the door.[31]

Wilson's racism was a matter of intellectual and social habit. He never seems to have questioned this legacy nor rebelled against it, and his conduct with Trotter leaves little doubt that he felt instinctively superior to blacks and most likely to nonwhites more generally. Wilson biographer Kendrick Clements reckoned that although Wilson "undoubtedly wished blacks well" and his record in the White House was "marked more by indifference to racial discrimination than by its active promotion," his "conservative paternalism was an inadequate response to the need" of the era and he showed "no commitment . . . to solving racial problems." John Milton Cooper, a leading and sympathetic biographer, notes Wilson's belief that blacks were "inferior" to whites but adds that he thought that they would eventually achieve parity, and evaluates Wilson's racial views as "surprisingly mild" for someone of his background.[32] Like most educated whites of his era, Wilson saw nonwhite peoples generally as "backward," but he also believed that, with "proper instruction," they could eventually learn the habits of "civilization," including self-government.

This was Wilson's general framework for thinking about questions related to nonwhite peoples, and he employed it during the debate over the U.S. conquest and rule over the Philippine Islands. Prior to the Spanish-American War of 1898, Wilson, though an avid student of American history and politics and of comparative politics, had written very little about international affairs or the question of imperialism. It was only when the issue of overseas expansion moved to the forefront of the American political debate with the acquisition of the Philippines, Cuba, Puerto Rico, and Guam that Wilson, then a prominent faculty member at Princeton University and a popular essayist and public speaker, set his mind to that question. Though not initially an ardent expansionist, once the annexation of the Spanish possessions by the United States was settled in the 1898 Treaty of Paris, Wilson spoke in its favor. America's new role as a colonial power, he asserted, would profit both the United States and the native populations of its new possessions. In the United States, an imperial mission would help to overcome domestic divisions and to "restore the unity of national purpose to the American people and government." The duties of empire would also offer an outlet for the energies of American youth, affording the "impetuous, hot-blooded young men of the country" an opportunity to make their mark on the world. To the native populations, U.S. rule would bring progress, both material and political. Indeed, it could be justified only if it pursued this purpose.[33]

Despite his subsequent reputation in the popular mind as a zealous advocate of spreading democracy, Wilson's position was actually quite circumspect. In his earliest pronouncements on U.S. rule in the Philippines, at the turn of the twentieth century, Wilson emphasized that its ultimate goal must be to prepare the islanders for self-government, but that attaining that goal would require time and training and hence a significant period of direct rule. It would not be enough, he warned, for the United States merely to institute the forms and documents of constitutional government in the Philippines and then leave. Free institutions could not be "spread by manuscripts," and the United States would have to install and then nurture them for a considerable period.[34] The Filipinos, Wilson found, were not yet ready to exercise responsibly the rights that come with a full-fledged democracy and should not therefore have those rights: "Freedom is not giving the same government to all people, but wisely discriminating and dispensing laws according to the advancement of a people." The United States should not attempt to implement the American system of government in the Philippines prematurely, and would "have to learn colonial administration, perhaps painfully." At the same time, Wilson spoke against the colonial authorities' early efforts to suppress Filipino criticisms of America's imperial policies. The United States should "do everything openly and encourage those in our new possessions to express freely their opinions," in order to prove to Filipinos that it had "only their welfare at heart."[35] Americans should teach by example and work to earn the goodwill of the native population.

On the other hand, Wilson also criticized American anti-imperialists, who opposed the annexation of the islands, as irresponsible. Their argument that the United States was constitutionally ill suited for colonial rule and should leave the Philippines to another power reminded him, he told one audience, of a vain woman who had recently found religion. Asked about her newly plain appearance, she replied: "When I found that my jewelry was dragging me down to hell, I gave it to my sister."[36] It was America's duty to govern the Philippines for the advancement of the native population, and it could not shirk it. He ridiculed the anti-imperialists who compared Emilio Aguinaldo, the leader of the Filipino resistance to the American occupation, to George Washington as ignorant of the true nature of liberty. Liberty, Wilson said, quoting his intellectual hero, Edmund Burke, in his assessment of the French Revolution, must be "combined with government; with the discipline and obedience of armies; with the collection of an effective and well-distributed revenue; with morality and religion; with the solidity of property; with peace and order; with social and civil manners." Aguinaldo offered the Philippines liberty without order, which was not true liberty at all.[37] Filipinos could have liberty eventually—they were not inherently incapable of it—but it would come in a process of gradual, measured progress, supervised by the United States.

Wilson summarized the task of the United States in the Philippines, as well as in Puerto Rico, as the establishment of self-government "if they be fit to receive it,—so soon as they can be made fit." A long-time admirer of the British political system and especially of the reformist tradition epitomized by one of his early heroes, the liberal Victorian statesman William Ewart Gladstone, Wilson held British colonial administration in high regard. The United States, he thought, should follow in that tradition in order to instruct "less civilized" peoples in "order and self-control in the midst of change" and in the "habit of law and obedience." The ultimate goal was to lift the colonized to the level of the colonizers and make them "at least equal members of the family of nations."[38] But it would be a gradual process, which might take as long as three or four generations and would require conceptual flexibility and sensitivity to cultural difference. The Anglo-American form of self-government, Wilson often reminded audiences, emerged out of historically specific social and political circumstances, and so self-government in the Philippines, even when attained, could well look quite different from that in the United States.[39]

But how could colonial rule be reconciled with the principle of government by consent, which Wilson always saw as the bedrock of legitimate government? At the time, Wilson was unsure. In a revealing reply in 1900 to a former student who had inquired how that principle might apply to the new American possessions in the Philippines, Wilson wrote somewhat evasively that he had not studied the question in depth and so he could not give a firm opinion. Nevertheless, he ventured to suggest that the principle could not possibly mean the same thing, nor apply in the same manner, to Americans and to Filipinos:

> "The Consent of the Governed" is a part of constitutional theory which has, so far, been developed only or chiefly with regard to the adjustment or amendment of established systems of government. Its treatment with regard to the affairs of politically undeveloped races, which have not yet learned the rudiments of order and self-control, has, I believe, received next to no attention. The "consent" of the Filipinos and the "consent" of the American colonists to government, for example, are two radically different things,—not in theory, perhaps, but in practice.

That difference, however, had "never been fully or adequately explained." You should work on this question on your own, the professor suggested, and "I shall be very much interested to know where your thinking lands you. I shall have to tackle the problem myself more formally than I have yet tackled it."[40]

Soon after this exchange, Wilson became president of Princeton University, and he apparently never found the time to tackle the problem "more formally." But the view that many if not all of the nonwhite "races" were unfit for self-government was a common one in American public discourse, as it was in Europe, in the early decades of the twentieth century. Both supporters and opponents of imperialism invoked it, with the former using it to justify colonial rule while the latter argued that backward, racially different populations could not be "developed" and should therefore be left alone.[41] For Wilson, the lack of fitness of many nonwhite populations for self-government reflected their lower levels of development and could therefore be remedied by time and training. But the process, he usually stressed, would take many years. U.S. colonial rule would eventually allow such underdeveloped populations to exercise self-government. In the meantime, however, they were students to be taught, or children to be raised, by their American masters. Independence would come only after a lengthy period of tutelage and cultural and institutional development.

In the decade from 1902 to 1912, Wilson said little, and apparently thought little, about colonial issues as he rose quickly in the world, first becoming president of Princeton University, then governor of New Jersey, and finally the Democratic candidate for president in 1912. Despite the earlier paeans for empire of Wilson the public intellectual, Wilson the politician showed his flexibility during the campaign when he adopted the traditional anti-imperialist position of the Democratic party, and upon taking office his administration moved quickly to implement it. He appointed Francis Burton Harrison, a liberal-minded Democrat, as governor of the islands with instructions to give native Filipinos majorities in both houses of the Philippine legislature and to respect the decisions of that legislature.[42] Wilson explained this move as part of the developmental progression toward self-government, since it would allow the Filipinos to prove their "sense of responsibility in the exercise of political power" and, if successful, would allow them to proceed toward full independence. The United States, he said, would gradually extend and perfect the system of self-government on the islands, testing and modifying it as experience required, giving more control to the indigenous population, and increasingly relying on their counsel and experience in order to learn how best to help them establish their independence.[43]

The United States' success in this task, Wilson added, was more than just an issue of domestic interest. It was also a practical test of American ideals and principles, conducted before a global audience. The eyes of the world, Wilson told Congress, were on the American experiment in the Philippines, and the United States had the opportunity, indeed the obligation, to instruct the whole world on how to manage the benevolent transformation of a backward people.[44] Reflecting the view that he would later attempt to implement in the League of Nations' mandate system, Wilson declared that America was a "trustee" of its overseas possessions. It was not there to do as it pleased nor to further its own narrow interests, but rather to carry out a duty. A new era had dawned in relations between the advanced powers and developing regions: "Such territories, once regarded as mere possessions, are no longer to be selfishly exploited; they are part of the domain of public conscience and of serviceable and enlightened statesmanship." The aim of U.S. policy in the Philippines must be the country's ultimate independence, and the transition to independence must move forward "as steadily as the way can be cleared and the foundations thoughtfully and permanently laid."[45] This view no doubt appeared perfectly logical to Wilson, as it did to many of his contemporaries, but it had inherent tensions. The "civilizing" power had to stay in order to allow it, eventually, to leave; colonial populations had a right to self-government, but the implementation of that right could be deferred, perhaps indefinitely, until the colonial power judged them ready to exercise it.

Other aspects of Wilson's prewar foreign policy also illustrated both his ambivalence toward independence as practiced by peoples outside "Anglo-Saxon civilization" and the difficulty he had, oft noted by later scholars, of reconciling goals with means, ideals with policy instruments. When Wilson came into office, the Mexican Revolution, launched in 1910, was already under way, and he declared his wish to assist the people of Mexico in determining their own future. But the means he tried to use to advance that aim often undermined it instead. In response to a minor incident in April 1914 between Mexican soldiers and a group of U.S. sailors that had come ashore in the Mexican port of Tampico, Wilson authorized the occupation of the major port city of Veracruz, hoping to destabilize the autocratic regime of General Victoriano Huerta and help his more liberal opponents. Wilson, however, underestimated the force of Mexican nationalist sentiment. His ham-handed intervention antagonized Mexicans of all stripes and did little to endear the United States, and Wilson himself, to Mexican liberals. Less than two years later, Wilson authorized a military invasion of Haiti in the name of restoring order, precipitating an American occupation of the country that lasted until 1934. In both cases, Wilson imagined and tried to present himself as a friend of the common people of these nations, defending them, as well as U.S. interests, against unscrupulous leaders and chaotic conditions; but his policies aroused local anger and resistance and left a legacy of suspicion and mistrust.[46]

The lessons of these failed interventions were not entirely lost on Wilson. Moreover, as the world war itself gradually prompted him to adopt and articulate an expanded conception of America's world role, it also influenced his stand on U.S. colonial policy. By 1916, as the administration launched its preparedness program and the president began to contemplate the possibility of joining the conflict, colonial policy became even more directly linked in his mind to the larger context and goals of the United States' growing world role. In its actions and policies in the Philippines, Wilson declared in February 1916, the United States had to prove its disinterested and benevolent attitude toward peoples of all races and in all regions of the globe. What America had to give the world was of universal value, transcending differences of geography, ancestry, or race. The American flag, he said, "stands for the rights of mankind, no matter where they be, no matter what their antecedents, no matter what the race involved; it stands for the absolute right to political liberty and free self-government, and wherever it stands for the contrary American traditions have begun to be forgotten."[47] Self-government, then, was a universal right, not a privilege limited to specific geographical regions or racial groups.

The war increasingly led Wilson to imagine American society as a model for the world, one whose internal conflicts and contradictions were being performed before a global audience. This new context prompted Wilson to begin to voice more forceful opposition than he had previously to domestic practices that were in clear breach of the exalted principles for which, he was trying to convince the world, the United States stood. If the United States was to be a light unto the world, the antithesis of the militarism and barbarity that Wilson attributed to the Central Powers, then the stakes involved in American race relations were higher than ever before. No longer were they crucial only for the future of American society, but for the future of the world. Thus, in July 1918, the president delivered a sharp if shamefully belated public denunciation of acts of lynching directed both at African Americans and, as happened repeatedly during the war, at those deemed "German sympathizers." The perpetrators of such acts, he charged, were emulating the "disgraceful example" of Germany and harming the war effort by sullying the image of the United States abroad:

> We proudly claim to be the champions of democracy [but] every American who takes part in the actions of a mob [is] its betrayer, and does more to discredit her by that single disloyalty to her standards of law and of right than the words of her statesmen or the sacrifices of her heroic boys in the trenches can do to make suffering people believe her to be their savior. How shall we commend democracy to the acceptance of other peoples, if we disgrace our own by proving that it is, after all, no protection to the weak?[48]

On the long-standing issue of female suffrage, too, Wilson's wartime conception of America's global responsibilities seemed to have helped to change his attitude. Initially reluctant to support a constitutional amendment guaranteeing women the vote, he changed his position by 1918, telling the Senate in September that passing the amendment would help the United States to retain the faith and trust of the common people of the world. "The plain, struggling, workaday folk . . . are looking to the great, powerful, famous Democracy of the West to lead them to the new day for which they have so long waited; and they think, in their logical simplicity, that democracy means that women shall play their part in affairs alongside men."[49] The next day, the amendment came up for a vote in the Senate and fell only two votes short of achieving the requisite two-thirds majority. It finally passed the following summer and was ratified in August 1920.

By mid-1918, then, Wilson had come to view the major social and political issues within American society as intimately connected to the global role he envisioned for it in the postwar world, as a model for the new international society he wanted to build. In the end, however, the reception of Wilson's rhetoric among nationalists in the colonial world was not defined by the intentions of its author but by the perceptions, goals, and contexts of its often-unintended audiences. The interpretations and import that colonial nationalists gave to Wilson's words often went far beyond his views or intentions. The message stood independently of the man, and it could be used without regard, sometimes in conscious disregard, of his intent. Perhaps no one knew better the limits of Wilson's faith in equality than William Monroe Trotter, the black leader whom Wilson had thrown out of his White House office several years earlier for urging him to fulfill his election promises to African Americans. But despite that experience, in 1919 Trotter was quick to adopt the language of self-determination to make the case for black liberation, within the United States and elsewhere. The peace conference, he wrote, "with its talk of democracy and self-determination," could "provide a stage from which to tell the world about the plight of blacks in the United States." Circumventing State Department objections, Trotter arrived in Paris in April 1919 to launch a campaign for black self-determination, inundating the assembled press and conference delegates—including Wilson—with letters and memoranda aimed at "letting the world know that the Negro race wants full liberty and equality of rights." Black Americans, Trotter argued, were "an ethnical minority denied equal rights," and they demanded the same rights as everyone else.[50] Like Egyptians, Indians, Chinese, and Koreans, as well as many others, Trotter enlisted Wilsonian language on self-determination for purposes far different and more radical than Wilson himself had intended.

2

Fighting for the Mind of Mankind

On March 5, 1917, in the inaugural address of his second term in office, Woodrow Wilson once more articulated a vision for the postwar world order. The plan he outlined then included all of the practical elements that have since come to be associated with the Wilsonian, or liberal internationalist, prescription for the conduct of international relations: institutions of collective security, the reduction of armaments, free trade. International order and cooperation, he declared once again, could not last long unless it stood on the principles of the equality of nations and of government by consent, and the United States would insist both on "the actual equality of nations in all matters of right and privilege" and on the principle that "governments derive all their just powers from the consent of the governed." Autocratic rulers like the German Hohenzollerns could no longer lay claim to legitimacy in the international arena, since they would not be "supported by the common thought, purpose, or power of the family of nations."[1] Coming from a leader of one of the great powers, this idea was a radical departure from the accepted norms and practices of international relations. It suggested that the international legitimacy of a government—its claim to membership in the community of nations—rested not only in its ability to exercise effective sovereignty over its territory, as international law traditionally stipulated, but also on the nature of its internal regime, which had to be based on popular consent.[2]

A week after Wilson's inaugural address, the most obviously autocratic regime fighting on the Allied side of the war—the Russian empire under Czar Nikolai II—succumbed to the revolution of March 1917, making it easier for the president both to imagine and to portray the war in Europe as one of democracy against autocracy. Soon after, on April 6, the United States officially declared war on Germany, joining the conflict on the Allied side, and Wilson's peace plan now became part of the war aims of the United States. Though its details evolved over the course of the war, the essential vision did not change much: the establishment of postwar international relations based on equality among legitimate polities governed by popular consent.[3]

In the address he gave on April 2 asking Congress for a declaration of war against Germany, Wilson said that the kaiser's government, lacking the demonstrated consent of its own people, was illegitimate, and that the people of Germany were little more than "pawns and tools" in Berlin's hands. The American people harbored no ill will toward them, only feelings of "sympathy and friendship," and had Germany been a self-governing nation there would have been no war. Now, the United States had to enter the fray to fight for its long-time fundamental values: "for democracy, for the right of those who submit to authority to have a voice in their own governments, for the rights and liberties of small nations."[4] Again, Wilson explicitly cast himself and America as defenders of the weak against the powerful, of common folk against autocratic regimes, of small nations against great powers.

The president devoted special praise in his message to the recent democratic revolution in Russia, speaking in glowing terms of the Russian people's toppling of the Romanov autocracy and the establishment of a democratic government. It seemed a perfect illustration of the worldwide trend away from rule by fiat and toward government by consent that would, he said, define the postwar world and would henceforth undergird the preservation of international peace. The Russian people, "in all their naïve majesty and might," had joined the forces that were "fighting for freedom in the world, for justice, and for peace" and could now assume their rightful place in the international partnership of self-governing peoples.[5] In a note he sent in late May to the provisional government of Russia, Wilson reiterated that message, assuring the new government that the United States was "fighting for the liberty, the self-government, and the undictated development of all peoples." Moreover, he was not merely interested in making "pleasing and sonorous" statements but was rather committed to taking effective measures that would guarantee the incorporation of these principles into the postwar settlement. One such measure would be a yet-unnamed mechanism for international cooperation based on a "common covenant," which would defend the principle of government by consent and provide an institutional framework that would reflect the "brotherhood of mankind."[6]

The text of Wilson's declaration of war address of April 1917 was widely reported, printed, and translated around the world. Now that the United States had entered the war, Wilson could be expected to have more influence at the peace table, and his pronouncements were therefore given much greater prominence in the world press. British and French opinion, especially liberals and socialists, generally greeted Wilson's war message and his subsequent proclamations with enthusiastic acclaim. In Britain, groups such as the Union of Democratic Control, whose membership included such luminaries as philosopher Bertrand Russell, author Norman Angell, and Labour party leader Ramsay MacDonald, had long called for a peace settlement in which any territorial adjustment would require the consent of the peoples involved. Their ideas, marginal and isolated in British public discourse at the outset of the war, increased in popularity as the war progressed, and Wilson's ringing rhetoric and rising prominence on the international stage greatly encouraged them.[7] Organizations such as the League of Nations Society, founded in mid-1916 by a group of liberal British intellectuals, called for peace based on Wilsonian principles, and the British Labour party had already announced its support for the president's proposals after his "Peace without Victory" address of January 1917. By mid-1917, Wilson had clearly emerged on the world stage as the champion of the new diplomacy of liberal internationalism.[8]

In the meantime, the revolutionary events in Russia seemed to confirm Wilson's contention that the age of autocracy was at an end. In March, a coalition of left-wing revolutionary groups had toppled the Romanov dynasty and several weeks later, on April 9, 1917—only three days after the American declaration of war on Germany—the new provisional government released a statement of its war aims. Unlike the old imperial regime, the new, democratic Russia would no longer seek to dominate foreign peoples or occupy their territories, but rather would promote and support "the establishment of permanent peace on the basis of the self-determination of peoples."[9] That statement, composed under the influence of the Bolshevik-controlled Petrograd Soviet, represented the first instance that a belligerent government invoked the term "self-determination" as a basis for its war aims and called explicitly for a peace settlement based on that principle.

For the Russian Bolsheviks, who were influential in the provisional government even before they overthrew it in November, the use of the term both made perfect sense and carried a specific meaning. For V. I. Lenin, the Bolshevik leader, the term implied the dismantling of colonial empires that was a crucial stage in the progress he envisioned toward world revolution. Lenin held this process to be particularly important, and the Bolsheviks issued scathing denunciations of the suppression of self-determination under imperialism. The question of national self-determination and its proper relationship to proletarian revolution had long been a topic of debate in European socialist circles, and Lenin's ideas on the subject crystallized in 1915–1916, while he was composing his major work, *Imperialism: The Highest Stage of Capitalism*, and were summarized in an article on "The Socialist Revolution and the Right of Nations to Self-Determination," which he completed in March 1916.[10] For Lenin, the principle of national self-determination, which he defined as the right of peoples to secede from oppressive regimes, was an important tool for undermining the capitalist-imperialist world order and, more specifically, for destabilizing the old regime in Russia and gaining the support of non-Russian minorities for the revolution.[11] As early as March 1917, Lenin declared publicly that when the Bolsheviks took power in Russia, their peace plan would include "the liberation of all colonies; the liberation of all dependent, oppressed, and non-sovereign peoples."[12]

When the Bolsheviks seized control of the revolution in November, they published from the captured czarist archives copies of the secret treaties that the European Allies had concluded among themselves to divide the spoils of war, exposing and denouncing the imperialist designs of the "old diplomacy." In the Bolshevik peace plan, announced on December 29, Leon Trotsky, the newly appointed commissar of foreign affairs, denounced as hypocritical Allied claims that they were fighting to guarantee the freedom of small nations, such as Belgium and Serbia. The imperial powers, he said, could not claim to be fighting for the rights of small nations in Europe while at the same time oppressing other national groups within their own empires:

> Are they willing on their part to give the right of self-determination to the peoples of Ireland, Egypt, India, Madagascar, Indochina, et cetera . . . ? For it is clear that to demand self-determination for the peoples that are comprised within the borders of enemy states and to refuse self-determination to the peoples of their own state or of their own colonies would mean the defence of the most naked, the most cynical imperialism.

Such behavior on the part of the capitalist governments of the Allies, Trotsky declared, was hardly surprising. They had shown no inclination to work for a truly democratic peace nor, given their "class character," could they ever do so: "Their attitude towards the principle of 'national self-determination'" was inevitably "not less suspicious and hostile than that of the Governments of Germany and Austria-Hungary."[13]

The dual challenge of Lenin and Wilson to the old ways of European politics and the growing appeal of their proclamations for large segments of the British and French publics increased the pressure on leaders in London and Paris to announce their support for more progressive, enlightened war aims. While the Allied leaders could dismiss Lenin's critique as that of a dangerous radical, they could not so easily ignore the president of the United States, an indispensable ally on whose supplies, credit, and arms the European Allies depended. Though the British and the French leaders, the president told his long-time close aide and confidant, "Colonel" Edward Mandell House, did not share his views on the peace, their dependence on American capital and supplies would compel them in the end to accept "our way of thinking."[14]

By late 1917, the pressure on the British government, a coalition of Liberals and Conservatives headed after December 1916 by the leader of the Liberal party, David Lloyd George, was mounting to accommodate "the development of American thinking and the public pronouncements of President Wilson" and to adopt more Wilsonian war aims.[15] On December 28, the British Labour party issued a public statement that echoed Wilson's pronouncements, declaring that the war could no longer be justified unless it would make the world "safe for democracy," and that Labour would withdraw its support for the war effort unless the government redefined its aims clearly in those terms.[16] At the same time, the Bolsheviks appeared ready to conclude a separate peace with Germany at the Brest-Litovsk negotiations and take Russia out of the war, releasing the German forces on the eastern front for transfer to the west. With the Allied position thus in danger of fraying both at home and abroad, Lloyd George decided to make a declaration of war aims that would regain the diplomatic initiative for the Allies. Such a statement was necessary, his adviser Philip Kerr told him, to rally labor and liberals, both at home and abroad, to the Allied cause. Victory was still necessary, but "the old war arguments" would no longer do. The prime minister entrusted the drafting of the statement to two of Wilson's most prominent ideological allies in British officialdom: Lord Robert Cecil, a cabinet minister and a leading liberal internationalist, and the South African general Jan Smuts, a member of the Imperial War Cabinet. Both would later work with Wilson to establish the League of Nations and the mandate system for international supervision over colonial possessions.[17]

On January 5, 1918, speaking before the British Trades Union League at Caxton Hall, the prime minister delivered a major address outlining Great Britain's updated war aims.[18] He designed the speech to appeal to the British Left, to shore up Allied morale, and to sway neutral opinion by meeting the challenge of the Bolsheviks' rhetoric of liberation and presenting the Allied aims as moderate and liberal. The postwar territorial settlement, Lloyd George declared on that occasion, must respect "the right of self-determination or the consent of the governed."[19] Thus, in a promiscuous rhetorical flourish, the prime minister bundled the Bolshevik term "self-determination" together with Wilson's favorite phrase, "consent of the governed," casually obfuscating the wide gap between the radical anti-imperialist agenda suggested by the former and the liberal reformism implied in the latter. The Caxton Hall speech was a pivotal moment in the emergence of self-determination as one of the most celebrated and contested principles of the postwar settlement. Wilson himself would complete this conflation in the following months, adopting "self-determination" as his own with growing gusto. The prime minister would later claim in his memoirs that his (and Wilson's) statements supporting the right to self-determination had pertained only to Europe and the non-Turkish portions of the Ottoman Empire, but neither of them mentioned any such qualification at the time. In fact, in his speech Lloyd George clearly suggested that the principle of self-determination would, for example, apply to the disposition of the German colonial possessions in Africa and the South Pacific.[20]

Lloyd George's bold proclamation spurred Wilson to regain the diplomatic initiative and reassert his own standing as the leading world statesman. Three days later, on January 8, he came before Congress to give the most detailed exposition to date of the United States' war aims and his vision for the postwar world. The address, which quickly became famous worldwide as the Fourteen Points, enumerated fourteen planks on which peace must be based. These included the general principles of open diplomacy rather than secret treaties, freedom of the seas and of trade, the reduction of armaments, and the establishment of an "association of nations" that would guarantee the "political independence and territorial integrity" of "great and small states alike." Most of the points, however, were geographically specific: They called for the evacuation and restoration of all Russian, Belgian, and French territories and supported the "autonomous development" of the peoples of the Austrian and Ottoman empires. Contrary to popular perceptions both at the time and later, the term "self-determination" itself was nowhere to be found in the text of the address, though several of the points—the call for a "readjustment of the frontiers of Italy" along "clearly recognizable lines of nationality" and for reconstituting a Polish state along similar lines—seemed to imply Wilson's support for that principle, at least in some instances.

The general outline of the peace plan proposed in the Fourteen Points address was similar to that of Wilson's previous addresses. For the first time, however, the president made an explicit reference to colonial questions, calling for any settlement of colonial issues to take into account the interests of colonial populations. Colonial claims, said point five of the fourteen, would have to be resolved in a "free, open minded, and absolutely impartial" manner, and their resolution would be "based upon a strict observance of the principle that in determining all such questions of sovereignty the interests of the populations concerned must have equal weight with the equitable claims of the government whose title is to be determined."[21] Point five was hardly an unambiguous endorsement of colonial self-determination. First, it called for the "interests" of colonial peoples to be taken into account rather than their express wishes or preferences, and so left open the question of just who would decide what those interests were: the people themselves or the colonial powers? In addition, Wilson also balanced those interests, however determined, against the "equitable claims" of the colonial governments, which would receive equal consideration.

Nevertheless, the inclusion of an explicit reference to the rights of colonial peoples, however tentative and equivocal, signaled the president's dissatisfaction with the reigning imperial order in international society. Most of the fourteen points were based on the recommendations included in the memorandum that was submitted a few days earlier by members of the Inquiry, a group of experts gathered by Colonel House to advise the government on issues related to the peace settlement. But the Inquiry memorandum made no reference to colonial issues, and it was Wilson himself who added point five to the text of the address.[22] House himself testified that "at first it was thought we might have to evade this [colonial question] entirely," but "the President began to try his hand on it and presently the paragraph which was adopted was acceptable to us both, and we hoped would be to Great Britain." Wilson did not consult the Allies on this question, so germane to their interests, and House was clearly concerned about their reaction.[23] The decision to refer in the Fourteen Points address to the colonial question and to the interests of colonial peoples was Wilson's alone.

Why did he make that choice? One influential interpretation of the origin of the Fourteen Points has seen the address as essentially a response—a "countermanifesto"—to the challenge that Lenin and Trotsky had presented with the announcement of their own radical peace plan.[24] In this context, point five might be seen as a rejoinder, albeit a hedged, tentative one, to the Russian Bolsheviks' sweeping call for the destruction of imperialism and the self-determination of colonial peoples. At the same time, however, the call made in point five was consistent with Wilson's previous wartime pronouncements, as well as with his long-standing position on the nature and purpose of colonialism. While the specific timing of the Fourteen Points address reflected the recent Bolshevik challenge, its content drew on principles that had long been part of the worldview Wilson had articulated in successive speeches prior to the appearance of Lenin. The essential elements of the Wilsonian scheme for international order, both in the colonial realm and elsewhere, had been expressed in Wilson's repeated assertions of the right to "self-government" and the requirement that legitimate governments receive the "consent of the governed."[25]

Wilson's position on the colonial question in the Fourteen Points was still hedged and equivocal, but his rhetoric soon grew bolder. Within weeks of that address, on February 11, 1918, the president came before Congress again and delivered another speech, known as the Four Points address, outlining once more his plan for the peace. It was in this speech that he first publicly uttered the phrase "self-determination." In the coming settlement, he intoned, "national aspirations must be respected," and people may be "dominated and governed only by their own consent." Self-determination was not "a mere phrase" but rather "an imperative principle of action, which statesmen will henceforth ignore at their peril," and "every territorial settlement involved in this war must be made in the interest and for the benefit of the populations concerned." Again, as he did in point five of the Fourteen Points, he spoke of the population's "benefit," not necessarily its wishes, and there were other qualifications on the unfettered exercise of the right to self-determination. Only "well-defined national aspirations" would receive consideration and only to the extent that they would not create or perpetuate "elements of discord."[26]

In invoking the principle of self-determination, Wilson incorporated the novel term into his wartime ideological lexicon, adopting this phrase as his own and assimilating it into his program for the postwar international order. Calls for a peace based on self-determination would henceforth largely replace in Wilson's rhetoric the previously ubiquitous references to the consent of the governed. This substitution aimed to neutralize Bolshevik critiques of the Allied war aims by co-opting their language, but it did not change the essence of Wilson's vision in his own mind. To him, the advocacy of "self-determination" was simply synonymous with calling for "self-government" and lecturing on the importance of "government by consent."

Some of Wilson's contemporary critics, including his secretary of state, Robert Lansing, observed early on that Wilson used the novel term self-determination to convey old ideas. Lansing, an international lawyer with a conservative bent of mind, noted that the term self-determination was essentially equivalent, in Wilson's usage, to the time-honored liberal principle of consent of the governed. It was, Lansing said, a theoretically appealing idea that was nevertheless "unsusceptible of universal application," since any such attempt would lead to excessive "change and uncertainty" in world affairs. Lansing, in common with other critics of Wilson's performance in Paris, observed in the aftermath of the peace conference that the principle of self-determination, loudly proclaimed in wartime pronouncements, had been violated repeatedly in the terms of the peace treaties. At the same time, it served as an "excuse for turbulent political elements in various lands to resist established governmental authority."[27]

Partly, the disappointment in the principle and its leading champion was a result of the ambiguous and multiple meanings that attached to the term at the time and since. Although Wilson did borrow the term self-determination itself from the language of the Bolsheviks—socialist and Marxist theorists had been using the term for some time—he gave it a different meaning and used it for a different purpose. For the Bolsheviks, who always talked specifically about "national" self-determination, it was a call for the revolutionary overthrow of colonial and imperial rule through an appeal to the national identity and aspirations of subject peoples. Wilson, on the other hand, rarely if ever qualified self-determination as specifically national. Rather, he used it in a more general, vaguer sense and usually equated the term with popular sovereignty, conjuring an international order based on democratic forms of government. He did at times, as in the cases of Poland or Italy, advocate redrawing borders according to ethnic lines, but he still saw the principle involved as one of consent rather than of ethnic homogeneity as such. Indeed, acutely aware as he was of the multiethnic character of American society, his model of a self-determining people, he could hardly have thought that ethnic homogeneity was a prerequisite for the exercise of the right to self-determination.[28]

In addition, while Lenin saw self-determination as a revolutionary principle and sought to use it as a wrecking ball against the reactionary multiethnic empires of Europe, Wilson hoped that self-determination would serve precisely in the opposite role, as a bulwark against radical, revolutionary challenges to existing orders, such as those he saw in the Russian and Mexican revolutions. If revolution, as he and other progressives believed, was a reaction to oppression by autocratic, unaccountable regimes, then the application of self-determination, defined as government by consent, would help remove the revolutionary impulse and promote change through rational, gradual reforms. In the case of colonialism, as already noted, he envisioned that self-determination would emerge through gradual processes of reform carried out with the cooperation of the colonial powers, rather than through the abrupt overthrow of colonial rule.[29]

However, these distinctions between the Wilsonian and Leninist versions of self-determination, compelling as they may appear in retrospect, were hardly so clear-cut at the time. To many around the world, and especially in the colonial world, Wilson and Lenin appeared to be more similar than different. Both advocated a new, open diplomacy, both were sharply critical of imperialism, both called for a radical transformation of international relations, and both advocated a peace based on the principle of self-determination. There was one important difference, however. In 1918, Wilson appeared by far the more prominent and powerful of the two in the international arena, and the one far likelier to wield direct and decisive influence on the upcoming peace negotiations. Wilson's adoption of Bolshevik language, though leaving his vision largely unchanged in his own mind, lent a more radical hue to his rhetoric in the eyes of those groups, in Europe and elsewhere, that were already anxious for a radical change in the way international society operated. Thus, just as Wilson appropriated the notion of self-determination from the Bolsheviks and assimilated it into his own program for international transformation, so too would colonial nationalists move to adopt and appropriate that language from Wilson and adapt it to their circumstances and purposes.

By the summer of 1918, as the tide of the war began to turn decisively in favor of the Allies, Wilson's rhetoric grew bolder still. On the Fourth of July, in a brief Independence Day address he delivered at George Washington's former estate at Mount Vernon, the president described his vision for the postwar world order in sweeping terms. Anchoring his ideas in the most sacred images of American iconography, he invoked the legacy of the founding fathers in support of his own mission. They, he said, had "entertained no private purpose" and "desired no particular privilege" in their historic endeavors, but were "consciously planning that men of every class should be free" and were striving to make America a haven for "the rights and privileges of free men."

The United States went to war for that same goal, to secure not only the liberty of the United States "but the liberties of every other people as well." The war was an epic struggle between autocratic regimes whose time had passed and the progressive ideals of the present. The aftermath of this conflict would see American ideals extended over the entire globe, embraced by many races and in many regions:

> On the one hand stand the peoples of the world,—not only the peoples actually engaged, but many others who suffer under mastery, but cannot act; peoples of many races and in every part of the world. . . . Opposed to them, masters of many armies, stand an isolated, friendless group of governments who speak no common purpose but only selfish ambitions of their own which can profit but themselves . . . governments clothed with the strange trappings and the primitive authority of an age that is altogether alien and hostile to our own.[30]

No compromise, therefore, was conceivable, not only with the Central Powers but also with the prewar principles of international relations. The postwar order, Wilson said, would have to be based on popular legitimacy rather than on great power interests. It would be predicated on "the settlement of every question, whether of territory, of sovereignty, of economic arrangement, or of political relationship, upon the basis of the free acceptance of that settlement by the people immediately concerned." The peace settlement would have to replace an international system based on power with an international society in which interaction among nations would comport with the "principles of honour and of respect for the common law of civilized society that govern the individual citizens of all modern states in their relations with one another." An international organization to deter aggression and arbitrate conflicts would embody and manage this arrangement: "What we seek is the reign of law, based upon the consent of the governed and sustained by the organized opinion of mankind."[31] The address at Mount Vernon was Wilson's boldest formulation yet of his postwar plans, and as we will see, it resonated widely around the world.

In the following months, Wilson continued in his public rhetoric to present the war, and the United States' role within it, in idealistic terms. The purpose of the war, he declared repeatedly, was to secure the right of peoples to determine their own futures, to establish the principle of equality among nations, and to defend the rights of weak nations against the might of strong ones. The peace settlement, he said, would have to reflect "full and unequivocal acceptance of the principle that the interest of the weakest is as sacred as the interest of the strongest."[32] It was during these months that he made the statements denouncing lynching and in support of female suffrage, explaining that American society must present itself to the world as a model of the principles of righteousness and justice for which it was fighting abroad. Once he arrived in Europe, moreover, Wilson continued to insist from every podium that the peace settlement would have to follow these principles: at the Sorbonne in Paris, at Buckingham Palace, in London and Manchester, in Rome and Genoa, in Milan and Turin.[33] The British economist John Maynard Keynes, who would become one of the most scathing and influential critics of the Versailles Treaty and of Wilson himself, wrote that in the immediate wake of the war, the president "enjoyed a prestige and a moral influence throughout the world unequalled in history."[34]

Throughout the final years of the war, the machinery of global communications carried Wilson's increasingly heady rhetoric to audiences around the world. International news agencies and wartime propaganda organs alike reported and reproduced the messages, and disseminated them through the cable and wireless networks that by then spanned the globe. The use of telegraphic communications began in Europe and North America in the 1840s and then spread elsewhere, often following the logic of imperial expansion and administration. The first dependable telegraph cables to the British domains in Egypt and India were laid in the 1870s, and they soon became among the busiest in the world. In China, telegraph lines began to spread in the 1860s, following the path of European penetration into the domains of the crumbling Qing dynasty. After the turn of the century, the use of wireless communication as an alternative or supplement to the cables grew more common, and by 1914 the wireless reached deeply into Asia and the Middle East. The rise of telegraphic communications dramatically reduced the time that it took information to move across continents and oceans, and news that previously would have taken weeks or even months to travel from America or Europe to the Middle East, India, or China could now arrive in a matter of hours.[35]

The spread of the telegraph and its revolutionary impact on the speed of information travel led to the growth and expansion of international news agencies that supplied wire copy to thousands of newspapers around the world. Charles Havas, a news service pioneer, founded his eponymous agency in Paris in 1835. Initially, Havas used pigeons for the speedy reporting of news across the English Channel, but he soon began to employ telegraphy as it spread in Western Europe in the 1840s and 1850s. In 1850, Julius Reuter, who had immigrated to England from Germany, established his own news service in London. Reuter's agency also relied on pigeons at first but quickly moved to telegraphy, and by 1865 it became a public company, the Reuters Telegram Company. The first major journalistic scoops that made its reputation were the reports on the start of the war for Italian unification in 1859 and the assassination of President Abraham Lincoln in 1865. News from Reuters' service became so ubiquitous in British papers that one commentator noted in 1861: "All our earliest information from America, India, and China, the Cape, and even Australia, is derived from this gentleman's telegrams."[36] By the 1860s, news agencies like Reuters had become indispensable in the rapid dissemination of information around the world and began to expand beyond Europe. The first Reuters branch outside Europe opened in Alexandria in late 1865, and its first Asian branch was set up in Bombay the following year.

As they spread around the globe, the three largest international news agencies—Havas, Reuters, and the German news service Wolff—initially fought over territory, but eventually they concluded agreements that divided the world's news markets among them. Havas naturally got the French empire and Southern Europe; Wolff provided international reporting in the Habsburg empire, Scandinavia, and Russia; and Reuters largely monopolized news services throughout the territories controlled by the British empire, in East Asia, and in the United States, though in the latter regions it saw growing competition from Japanese and American news agencies. A few areas, such as Turkey, Egypt, and Greece, were shared between Reuters and Havas. But British control over the global network of undersea telegraph cables meant that Reuters, which had developed intimate ties with British officialdom, controlled practically all news coming into Europe from other continents, supplying the other news services with information that they in turn passed on to their subscribers. By 1914, Reuters had become a "semi-official institution of the British Empire," so ubiquitous that it became in many places a "household word."[37]

During the world war, Reuters provided most of the international news across the British empire, and its bureaus in Bombay, Cairo, and Shanghai were the main suppliers of war news to newspapers in India, Egypt, and China, respectively. The Associated Press, founded in 1848, was the leading news agency supplying international news to U.S. papers, while the countries of Latin America received their foreign news primarily through Havas.[38] The spread of telegraphy and the global penetration of international news services meant that the war was reported across the world simultaneously and almost instantaneously. Readers across much of the globe could learn of events on the battlefronts and read the proclamations of leading statesmen within a day or two of their occurrence. Many news outlets, especially in the regions outside Europe, did not have the resources to hire numerous foreign correspondents who could provide them with independent perspectives on events abroad, and they therefore depended heavily on international services for foreign news. And since the agencies that supplied international news to much of the globe—Reuters, Havas, the Associated Press—were associated with the Allied powers, the tenor of the reporting was often favorable to the Allies and hostile to the Central Powers even beyond the considerable reach of Allied censors.

Allied propaganda, then, had relatively easy access to newspapers around the globe, and no one was better positioned to make use of this access than the United States.[39] The American propaganda campaign during the First World War was of unprecedented scope and scale in U.S. history. The decades leading up to the war saw the rise of telegraphy and fast-moving international news, and governments were growing increasingly aware of the importance of public opinion in wartime, not only in their own societies but also among those of allies, enemies, and neutral powers. The Great War, which introduced mass warfare that engaged entire societies and demanded the raising of huge conscripted armies, saw the scale and significance of wartime propaganda increase dramatically both at home and abroad. All of the major belligerent powers in the war engaged in propaganda activities that went beyond anything they had done before, but their approaches, techniques, and styles differed. The Germans treated war propaganda as a military activity and managed it as a branch of military intelligence. The French government tended to view propaganda as a diplomatic affair best left to the experts at the Quai d'Orsay. The British conducted their propaganda campaign largely as a literary enterprise, enlisting some of the leading authors of the period in the patriotic cause. In the United States, however, the task of wartime propaganda was planned and managed as "a huge advertising campaign," with American ideals the product to be marketed and President Wilson their leading spokesman.[40]

Wilson, like many of his contemporaries, saw the war as much as a conflict of ideals and worldviews as it was a clash of arms or interests, and therefore viewed propaganda as a central component of the American war effort. The British novelist H. G. Wells wrote shortly after the outbreak of the fighting that the conflict would be about the demise of old ideas and the rise of new ones: "The ultimate purpose of this war is propaganda, the destruction of certain beliefs, and the creation of others."[41] For Wilson, spreading the American gospel and winning "world opinion" to the side of U.S. ideals was a crucial war aim. The American mission to transform international affairs, he thought, could succeed only if others were convinced that a transformation was necessary and desirable: "Everything that affects the opinion of the world regarding us," the president told his secretary of state, "affects our influence for good."[42] The propaganda campaign that accompanied the U.S. war effort, therefore, sought to disseminate Wilson's vision of transformation around the globe and convince the world that only the United States, under his leadership, could bring it about. The image of the United States abroad, the perception of its benevolence, disinterestedness, and fairness, and the assumption of its good will were all to Wilson concrete and precious assets that had to be safeguarded and promoted.

On April 13, 1917, a mere week after the United States declared war on Germany, Wilson issued an executive order establishing the Committee on Public Information (CPI) as the organ responsible for the U.S. war propaganda effort at home and abroad. The members of the committee included the secretaries of war, state, and the navy, but the real force behind it was its chair, George Creel. Creel, a forty-one-year-old veteran muckraking journalist, was a long-time progressive and a keen partisan of Wilson's reform programs. He had supported Wilson's reelection campaign, and his 1916 book *Wilson and the Issues*, which defended the president's record, was said to have "mightily pleased" the president.[43] Fiercely loyal to the president and his ideals, Creel saw the CPI as an opportunity to spread the Wilsonian gospel of progressivism and democracy both domestically and abroad, "to drive home the absolute justice of America's cause, the absolute selflessness of America's aims."[44] It was his inventiveness and his zeal for the liberal internationalist ideals he worked to propagate that transformed the committee from an ad hoc improvisation into a highly effective propaganda machine of global reach.[45]

In their campaign to advertise America's war aims and peace plans at home and abroad, Creel and his deputies at the CPI made widespread use of recent advances in communications, such as wireless technology, and in media, such as motion pictures, in addition to deploying more traditional propaganda methods. There was "no medium of appeal that we did not employ," Creel boasted. "The printed word, the spoken word, the motion picture, the poster, the signboard—all these were used in our campaign."[46] The CPI produced and distributed movies about the successes of the American war effort, which aimed to impress audiences, both domestic and foreign, with the inevitability of U.S. victory. It also worked to depict American society as prosperous and its citizens as upright and diligent, and tried to carry these images "to every community in the United States and to every corner of the world." In addition, the committee controlled the export of commercially produced films to overseas markets and sought to block films that it judged to be "giving false or misleading impressions of American life" by dealing with such unsavory themes as crime, corruption, or dissolute behavior.[47]

The CPI issued daily news bulletins to the U.S. and foreign press in numerous languages and supplied magazines with ready-made feature articles extolling the United States, its society, economy, and contributions to the Allied war effort. On the domestic front, the CPI established special divisions that concentrated on getting out the message to specific sectors of the media, such as the rural press, the religious press, and the labor press. The committee also recruited speakers to praise the U.S. war effort and administration policy to domestic audiences, most famously the "Four Minute Men," so called because they would give four-minute patriotic speeches about the war effort at theater intermissions. Millions of pamphlets extolling American ideals and

Wilson delivering his Independence Day Address on July 4, 1918, at Mt. Vernon, Virginia. Wilson's second wife, Edith, is at right. Also visible behind Wilson's left shoulder is George Creel, the progressive journalist who headed the U.S. wartime propaganda organ known as the Committee on Public Information. The texts of Wilson's public addresses were a crucial component of Creel's campaign. *Library of Congress, LC-USZ62-63878.*

life, in dozens of languages, were printed and circulated at home and abroad. The CPI also drafted the commercial advertising industry into the propaganda effort. It recruited artists to produce a variety of posters, cartoons, and window cards for public display, supplied state fairs with exhibits about the war effort, and prepared and distributed still photographs about it. Special emphasis was put on reaching the foreign-born populations within the United States, who were seen as requiring special persuasion, and the foreign-language press in the U.S.—in Swedish, Polish, Ukrainian, Lithuanian, Czech, German, Hungarian, Italian, Russian, Serbian—was provided with translated articles designed to combat the "ignorance and disaffection" assumed to prevail among its readers.[48]

Although the CPI did not launch its foreign operations until late 1917, foreign news services filed quotes from its news summaries and pamphlets from the outset and supplied them to the press in Europe and elsewhere. By early 1918, the CPI had opened its first offices abroad; some of the most active offices were located in Bern, Rome, Madrid, and Lisbon. The goal of the foreign operations, Creel declared, was to "fight for the mind of mankind" and to "convince the world that hope for the future lay in Wilson alone."[49] The United States, CPI propaganda aimed to convince the people of the world, was a disinterested power, which joined the war in order to establish peace and to spread justice and liberty, not for selfish gain. It would play a crucial role in winning the war and would have a powerful voice in the peace settlement, and the weaker nations could be sure that it, unlike its imperialist allies, would safeguard their rights there. The U.S. influence at the peace table would guarantee that the victory would usher in a new era in which all nations would be equal, peoples would determine their own futures, and government by consent would replace autocratic rule.[50]

The CPI's Foreign Press Bureau, which was headed by the journalist and Pulitzer prize–winning novelist Ernest Poole, provided foreign news outlets with short articles extolling the virtues of American society: its "social and industrial progress," its schools, its laws, and its "treatment of workers, women and children."[51] The vast majority of the CPI's efforts abroad were in Europe, and to a lesser extent in Latin America, but Creel's aggressive promotion of the progressive Wilsonian message did not ignore other regions. Special materials were prepared for use in East Asia, including window displays with texts in Asian languages for China, Korea, Japan, and parts of India.[52] Though State Department diplomats often resented the activities of Creel's agents abroad since they could not control them, for the duration of the war Wilson's confidence in Creel and his determination to keep control of wartime propaganda in his own hands protected the committee from its domestic critics.[53]

The use of wireless radio technology facilitated the CPI's reach overseas since it reduced American reliance on the undersea cable network largely controlled by the British. The CPI often sent copy intended for foreign venues by wireless from the navy station in Tuckerton, New Jersey, which was relayed through receiving stations in London and Paris to various locales in Europe and into Russia. Wire service in Spanish went by cables and radio to Mexico and South America for distribution by CPI agents there. In regions where the

CPI lacked official branches, networks of resident American diplomats, businessmen, or missionaries who volunteered to serve the wartime propaganda effort often helped to distribute the information. By "balloons, mortars, and aeroplanes," Creel claimed, CPI propaganda had even reached across enemy lines into the territories controlled by the Central Powers.[54]

President Wilson's major public addresses and declarations—the Fourteen Points, the Four Points address of February 1918, and the Fourth of July address at Mount Vernon, among others—quickly became the central instruments of CPI propaganda, especially in its foreign operations. Wilson's messages were disseminated worldwide in order to "tell all the people on earth what President Wilson was saying about the war and what the aroused American people were doing to win it."[55] The CPI, Creel later reported, decided early on that it would emphasize the "distribution throughout the world" of Wilson's speeches, since the president "was looked upon as the spokesman for the Allies" and "it was he who sounded the keynote of America's policy in the war."[56]

According to its own records, the CPI circulated Wilson's speeches to England, France, Italy, Spain, Switzerland, Holland, Scandinavia, Russia, Australasia, Japan, China, Siberia, South America, Central America, Mexico, India, South Africa, Greece, Egypt, and Canada. In order to reach Asia, the CPI often sent the texts by wireless from New York to San Diego, and from there, through the navy station at Cavite in the Philippines, to Shanghai, and thence to Beijing, Tokyo, and Vladivostok for distribution in Siberia. They were also broadcast—a new technology at the time—from the navy's wireless stations for interception by ships at sea and by "whatever stations desired to listen in." In addition, the CPI distributed the speeches by mail to Persia and Liberia. International news agencies also played a role in disseminating Wilson's messages. In India, Egypt, and China, the addresses were distributed by the local branches of Reuters, in the latter case with the assistance of the local CPI branch in Shanghai after it opened in the summer of 1918. Creel boasted to Wilson that "for the first in history the speeches of a national executive were given universal circulation, and I am proud to tell you, sir, that your declarations had the force of armies."[57]

Upon their arrival, local CPI agents had the texts of Wilson's speeches translated and then printed and circulated them through numerous channels and methods: They were "printed on post cards and embodied in moving-picture films and interpreted by the committee's speakers." The message, Creel reported, was disseminated in Asia as well as in Europe, with Teheran and Tokyo receiving it "as completely as Paris or Rome or London or Madrid."[58] The text of the Fourteen Points, as the most detailed articulation of the president's peace plan, played a central part in this effort, and it was propagated by the CPI as an authoritative statement of the Wilsonian vision for the new world order. Within days of the address in January 1918, the CPI produced hundreds of thousands of poster copies of the text, both in the original and translated into numerous languages, and these were distributed everywhere the committee could reach.[59] Wilson's subsequent major addresses received similar treatment. By the end of the war, the president's calls for a peace based on the principles of self-determination and the equality of all nations were widely familiar to reading publics around the world and helped to shape their expectations regarding the nature and possibilities of the postwar international order.

The CPI efforts to project Wilson as the preeminent leader in the international arena gained in force and credibility as the tide of war turned in favor of the Allies in the summer of 1918, and Wilson's principles were accepted by the belligerents as the basis for the armistice.[60] By then, the phrase Fourteen Points had accumulated meanings that far transcended the literal content of the text itself, becoming for many shorthand for the transformation of international society along the principles of equality, self-determination, and justice. Although the Bolsheviks had been the first to call for a peace based on self-determination, and though the term itself did not appear in the text of the Fourteen Points address, Wilson had made the term his own by the time of the armistice, and he had become identified with it in the eyes of millions around world. He had declared repeatedly after February 1918 that the principle of self-determination was central to his vision of postwar international society, and though his specific references were always located in Europe, Egyptians, Indians, Chinese, Koreans, and others in the colonial world had little doubt that the principle should, and would, apply to them.

Wilson's success in overshadowing Lenin as the chief icon of self-determination may appear puzzling in retrospect. It is less mysterious, however, if we consider the relative stature and renown of the two men at the time and their perceived influence in international affairs. In the colonial world, where newspapers had few foreign correspondents, the Bolsheviks were often viewed through the Reuters lens (or that of the French Havas Agency) and so usually appeared in a singularly unattractive light, especially after they left the war in March 1918 with the Treaty of Brest-Litovsk. Reports of events in Russia thus warned of the "Bolshevist peril" spreading "destruction" and facing imminent defeat by the anti-Bolshevik White forces. In contrast to Wilson's ubiquitous presence and great acclaim in reports on world affairs, Lenin, if named at all, was often described as a mysterious, even sinister figure.[61]

Moreover, for colonial nationalists who sought to seize the opportunity they perceived at the peace conference, the crucial distinction between Wilson and Lenin lay in their perceived power to shape a postwar settlement that would be favorable to demands for self-determination. The Bolsheviks, excluded from Paris and mired in civil war, were hardly in a position during this period to lend much succor to movements for colonial self-determination.[62] The United States, on the other hand, emerged from the war more powerful than ever, and Wilson appeared to wield unparalleled influence in world affairs. With the other major powers—Britain, France, Japan—clamoring for the reinforcement and even expansion of the imperial order, Wilson remained, until the spring of 1919, the only world figure who seemed to have both the will and the power to produce a settlement that would implement self-determination as a principle of the international order.

For the time being, therefore, all eyes were fixed on Wilson. The president's rhetoric, propelled by the recent expansion of communications technologies and mass print media in many regions of the colonial world, echoed among nationalists in Asia and the Middle East, fostering among them anticipation for the establishment of an international society in which all peoples, strong and weak, would be equally entitled to exercise the right to self-determination. Wilson's rhetoric, moreover, offered colonial nationalists a new language of rights that they could use to demand an independent role in this emerging international order. It seemed to open a window of opportunity that made it appear feasible, even compelling, for marginalized groups to invoke the principle of self-determination in order to articulate demands for the recognition of their rights in the international arena. Colonial nationalists, who closely followed the emergence of the Wilsonian moment in the international arena, were determined that they would not be excluded from the opportunities it presented. A new world order was about to be forged in Paris. They, too, would have to stake their claims.

Part II

The Internationalization of Nationalism

Imagination fails to picture the wild delirium of joy with which he [Wilson] would have been welcomed in Asiatic capitals. It would have been as though one of the great teachers of humanity, Christ or Buddha, had come back to his home, crowned with the glory that the centuries had brought him since he last walked the earth.

—V. S. Srinivasa Sastri, *Woodrow Wilson's Message for Eastern Nations*

A new era unfolds before our eyes. The old age of force is gone and an age of justice is here. A humane spirit, nurtured through all the centuries of human experience, has begun to cast the brilliant light of a new civilized morality upon human history.

—Korean Declaration of Independence, March 1919

In the five weeks that passed between Woodrow Wilson's acclaimed arrival in France on December 13 and the opening of the peace proceedings on January 18, the president traveled around the continent and was everywhere received as a conquering hero. Ecstatic crowds surrounded him on his arrival in Paris as he drove past the city's great monuments through the Arc de Triomphe and down the Champs Élysées. He was received with much pomp at the Élysée Palace, made an honorary citizen of the city of Paris, and awarded a doctorate *honoris causa* in a splendid ceremony at the Sorbonne. The president then spent the Christmas holiday with American troops at Chaumont, on the upper Marne, where the American Expeditionary Force was headquartered, and left for England the next day. In London, he met with King George V at Buckingham Palace. He traveled to Manchester, where he spoke at the Free Trade Hall, and to his mother's birthplace in Carlisle in the north of England. There, he visited the Presbyterian church where his grandfather, the Reverend Thomas Woodrow, had preached. After a brief respite for the New Year's holiday, Wilson continued on a whirlwind tour of Italy. He visited Rome, Genoa, and Milan, and met with Pope Benedict XV, a first for a U.S. president. Everywhere, he was greeted by large, cheering crowds. The people of Europe, Wilson thought, were firmly behind him.[1]

The enthusiastic receptions notwithstanding, most of the president's travels during these five weeks had to be improvised at the last minute. Wilson had landed in France thinking that the inter-Allied consultations would begin within a week, but quickly discovered that the French had not even named their delegates and that the British representatives had yet to set sail for France. Lloyd George sent word that they were occupied with the general election in that country and that they could not arrive until after the new year. The election took place on December 14 and brought an overwhelming victory to the coalition of Conservatives and Liberals led by Lloyd George. Unlike Wilson, whose party had lost control of both houses of Congress in the midterm elections of the previous month and who had alienated many Republicans when he denied them any significant role in the peace negotiations, Lloyd George secured solid support on his domestic flank before he arrived at the table.

Before Wilson set out for Paris, many, including supporters, advised him to take along leading Republicans, such as former president William Howard Taft or Massachusetts senator Henry Cabot Lodge, in order to secure their party's support for the treaty that would emerge. But Wilson, determined to keep control of the negotiations in his own hands, refused and appointed to the American peace commission only men who had no independent political standing and could not contradict him. They included Secretary of State Lansing, whom he largely ignored; General Tasker Bliss, a former army chief of staff; and Henry White, a former ambassador to Italy and France, who served as the delegation's token Republican. All three passed their days in Paris in luxurious ineffectuality amid the chandeliers and red carpets of the Hôtel Crillon, the former palace on the northern edge of the Place de la Concorde that served as the headquarters for the U.S. delegation. The fifth delegate, Wilson's confidant Colonel House, was the only member to whom the president paid any heed, but as the negotiations went on even House eventually lost the confidence of his increasingly harried, ailing chief. Unlike Lloyd George and the French premier, Georges Clemenceau, who generally made effective use of their advisers and experts in Paris, Wilson, convinced that none of his subordinates could understand his vision as clearly or advance it as forcefully as he could, largely did battle alone.[2]

The proceedings that began in Paris on January 18 were not actually intended to be part of the peace conference at all. Rather, they were planned as a preliminary consultation among the victorious Allies, in which they would discuss and prepare their peace proposals and then bring them before the representatives of the Central Powers at the official peace conference. The conference plenary, officially the central organ of the proceedings, included the countries that had declared war on Germany or severed relations with it, each represented by delegates whose number reflected the country's relative power and contribution to the war. The major Western Allies—Britain, France, Italy, and the United States—each had five seats in the plenary. So did Japan, despite its relatively minor contribution to the war effort; as Britain's main ally in East Asia, and with Lloyd George's support it, too, was recognized as a major power. The British also demanded and received separate representation for each of their self-governing dominions—Canada, South Africa, Australia, and New Zealand—as well as for India, though the Indian representatives were selected by the British. Serbia and Belgium, which among the small nations had suffered the most in the war, were recognized for their sacrifices with three delegates each. The rest mostly got one or two. They included small European nations that fought alongside the Allies, like Portugal, Greece, and Rumania; new nations emerging from the wreckage of fallen empires, like Poland and Czechoslovakia; a number of Latin American countries; and representatives from Liberia, Siam, and China. The Chinese, as we will see, strongly protested their relegation to the ranks of the small nations, especially given Japan's recognition as a major power. Their protests, however, were ignored.

The real decisions at Paris, in any case, were made not at the plenary, which convened only infrequently and ceremoniously. They were made by the leaders of the great powers, who met in an increasingly smaller group as the conference stretched on, crises mounted, and decisions became more urgent. Initially, there was the Council of Ten, where each of the five major powers had two representatives. By March, it had shrunk to become the Council of Four, which included only the leaders of Britain, France, and the United States and

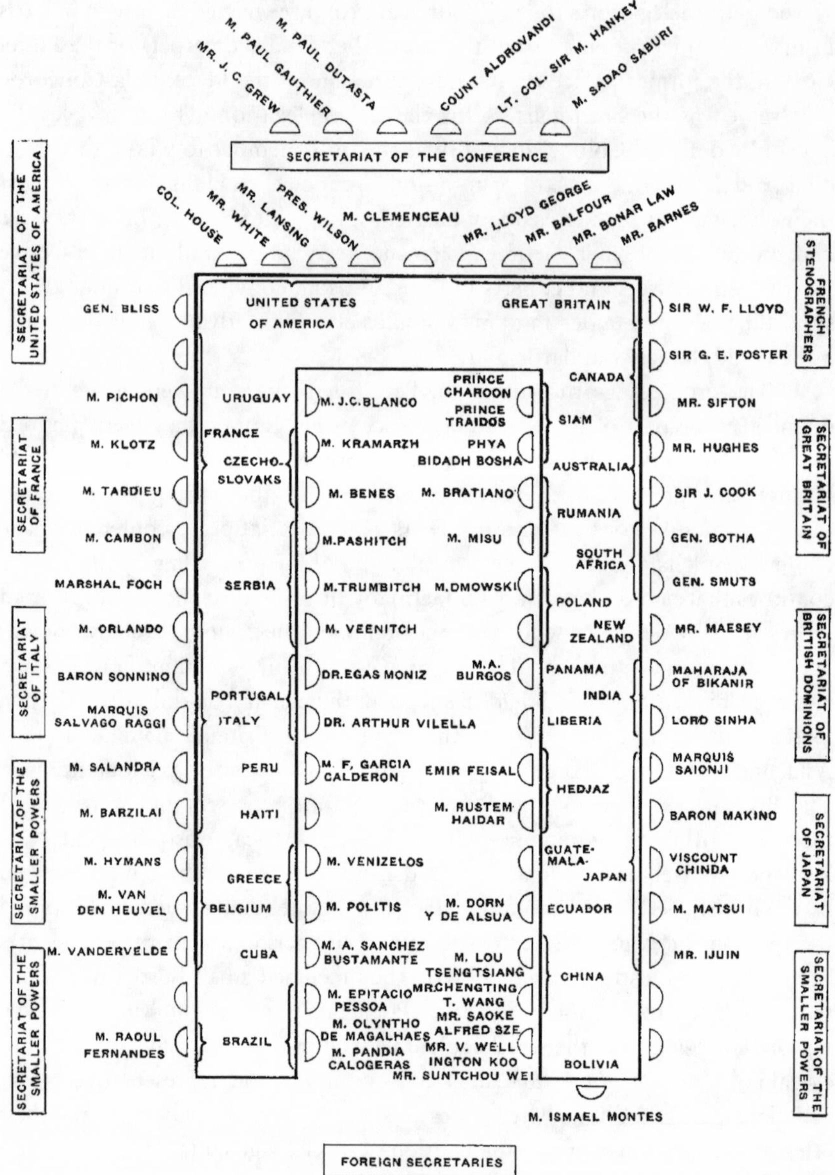

The number and location of the seats allotted to each delegation in the plenary of the peace conference reflected its relative power. The Chinese representatives protested in vain the decision to designate China a "small power" and allot it only two seats, while Japan was recognized as a great power and received five. *Charles T. Thompson,* The Peace Conference Day by Day *(New York: Brentano's, 1920), after p. 118.*

the Italian prime minister, Vittorio Orlando. Finally, in April, Orlando withdrew and there remained only the "Big Three"—Lloyd George, Clemenceau, and Wilson. They, in the end, decided all of the major questions alone.

Beyond the members of the official delegations—the plenipotentiary delegates who represented their countries and the long retinues that included hundreds of advisers, experts, and secretarial staff—there were thousands of others who streamed into Paris for the conference. They fell into several groups. The first group included hundreds of journalists, at least one hundred from the United States alone, who converged on the city to report on the historic proceedings of the peace conference to their readers back home. The second group, less easily defined but buzzing with activity and expectation, included hundreds of men and women who would in a later era be referred to as representatives of NGOs—non-governmental organizations—and who arrived, usually uninvited, to plead to the conference on behalf of a diverse range of causes and constituents. Labor leaders wanted the conference to promote the rights of workers; activists for female suffrage asked for recognition of their cause. Black leaders from the United States, led by the African-American scholar and activist W. E. B. Du Bois, joined with delegates from the Caribbean and from several African colonies to convene a Pan-African Congress that met in Paris in February and passed very moderate resolutions asking the peace conference to lay down regulations for good colonial governance in Africa.[3] More esoteric causes also had their advocates, such as the British Esperanto Association, which called on the conference to adopt that language as the medium of international communication, or Jerome Internoscia, an Italian-Canadian lawyer who wrote to propose himself for the job of secretary general of the nascent League of Nations.[4]

Most of all, however, there were dozens of representatives of oppressed nations who, either in person or by petition, demanded recognition of their right to self-determination. A few of them, like the Poles, Serbs, and Czechoslovaks, had their delegates officially admitted to the conference. Also present at the peace table was the Emir Faisal of the Hijaz, who was invited by the British and who asked the conference to establish a federation of Arabic-speaking peoples of the former Ottoman Empire under the leadership of his father, the Sharif Hussein of Mecca. Zionist leaders were also invited to speak before the conference, and they presented their claim for a Jewish national home in Palestine, which received the support of the British government and of Wilson himself.[5]

Most claimants for self-determination, however, never received an official hearing from the conference. Some were European: Albanians, Croatians, Estonians, Ukrainians, and others. Catalan nationalists petitioned Wilson for freedom from Spanish rule, and Sinn Fein leaders demanded independence for Ireland, quoting long excerpts from President Wilson's speeches in support of their demand even as the president's British allies were engaged in a brutal campaign to suppress the Irish movement.[6] Many petitioners, however, came from outside Europe, like the foreign minister of Persia, Moshaver al-Mamalek, who arrived in Paris to ask that the conference condemn the meddling of foreign powers in his country and recognize its right to full self-determination.[7] Delegations representing Georgians, Armenians, Syrians, Lebanese, and Assyrian Christians, among others, submitted petitions, laying before the conference their peoples' long histories of civilization and asking for self-determination.[8] Others who could not come in person sent their demands by cable, like the imam of Yemen, who wrote Wilson pleading for self-determination, and the Tunisian nationalists and Vietnamese revolutionaries who demanded freedom from French colonial rule.[9] All praised President Wilson's vision for a new world, noted the support that his principles gave to their claims, and often quoted at length from his speeches.

Wilson, however, made it clear early on that the specific territorial settlements to emerge from the conference mattered less to the United States than the establishment of an international mechanism that would prevent future wars and adjudicate claims that the conference could not. At his insistence, the League of Nations and its covenant dominated the discussions for the first four weeks. Wilson brought with him to Paris a draft of the covenant that he had written himself, which he kept secret to forestall any early opposition and which included a provision that explicitly established the principle of self-determination as a central instrument for adjudicating disputes that would come before the league.[10] General Bliss wondered incredulously when he saw this text whether it contemplated "the possibility of the League of Nations being called upon to consider such questions as the independence of Ireland, of India, etc., etc.?" David Hunter Miller, the U.S. delegation's expert on international law, warned the president that such a provision would make "dissatisfaction permanent," compelling "every power to engage in propaganda" and legalizing "irredentist agitation." For the British, too, it was unacceptable, challenging as it did the legitimacy of their imperial rule in India and elsewhere in Asia and Africa.[11]

For several weeks, Wilson, who headed the commission that drafted the league covenant, insisted on preserving the principle of self-determination in the covenant despite the opposition of his advisers and allies. By early February, however, as the work of the commission was drawing to a close, he was clearly growing more worried about the great expectations that his wartime emphasis on self-determination had aroused. On February 2, George Creel joined the president for a Sunday lunch and told him of his recent trip through the newly emerging countries of Central Europe, Poland, and Czechoslovakia. The people there, he told Wilson, had hung his portraits in many windows, considered him a "popular Saint," and told Creel that they wanted Wilson to "reign over them." All this, Wilson responded, made him "very nervous," fearful of the "revulsion" which would come when those people discovered he could not do all they hoped he would.[12] The next day, Wilson, perhaps with this fear still in mind, amended the draft of the covenant, deleting the clause that promised the application of the principle of self-determination to future claims for territorial readjustment. The final text consecrated the rights of existing states to "territorial integrity" and "political independence," but it offered little recourse for ethnic minorities or colonial populations that demanded self-government.[13]

When Wilson emerged on February 14 to present the text of the League of Nations covenant to the awaiting world press, the term "self-determination" was no longer there. The provisions that he outlined, however, were not entirely without promise for colonial nationalists. The long article in the covenant on the "mandate principle" for the governance of colonial possessions of the defeated powers did appear to envision their eventual independence, at least in some cases. The former Turkish possessions in the Middle East, deemed to be at "the highest stage of the development of the people," were declared in the text to be essentially independent nations subject only to the "administrative advice" of a mandatory power until they could "stand alone" in the "strenuous conditions of the modern world."[14] In subsequent years, with the league controlled by imperialist powers, the mandate system became not much more than a shadow of what it was intended to be.[15] At the time of its inception, however, it appeared that the league might exercise effective oversight over colonial territories and guarantee that they were governed according to the interests of their populations. When Wilson left Paris for a brief sojourn in the United States immediately after presenting the covenant, he was no longer the prophet of peace he was received as two months before, but he still cut a commanding figure in the international arena. To many colonial nationalists, he remained the world leader most likely to give effective support to their fight for self-determination.

The four chapters that comprise Part II narrate the responses to the Wilsonian moment of Egyptians, Indians, Chinese, and Koreans down to the beginning of March 1919, tracing in the process how anticolonial nationalism was internationalized during this period. Internationalization occurred in two distinct but related spheres, one of principle and the other of practice. First, the right of self-determination, which Wilson had advocated as a central principle of legitimacy in the new international order, was appropriated and interpreted by colonial nationalists as a challenge to the logic of imperialism in international relations, one that required the recognition of the international equality and sovereignty of hitherto "dependent" peoples. The principle of nationalism, which rejected the legitimacy of empire and took the self-determining nation-state as the sole legitimate entity in international relations thus became a central component of the new international order that anticolonial activists saw emerging. Second, taking the right of self-determination as now an established principle of international relations, colonial nationalists moved to leverage Wilson's rhetoric, his perceived power in the international arena, and the opportunities for international action presented by the peace conference to launch international campaigns for the recognition of their own right to national independence and sovereignty. In so doing, they brought the practice as well as the principle of anticolonial nationalism into the arena of international relations.

Once the peace conference began, however, the advocacy of self-determination for colonial peoples collided with the stubborn realities of the imperial international order, in which hierarchies of race and civilization defined the extents to which different peoples were accorded the right to self-government. At the center of the anticolonial nationalist wave of 1919 lay the claim that non-European, nonwhite peoples had an equal right to self-determination—not to be governed without their consent—as did the peoples of Europe, whom Wilson had largely in mind when he incorporated the principle enunciated by Lenin into his own wartime rhetoric. Unlike Wilson, Lenin did attribute the right to self-determination specifically to ethnically defined nations and used the term with the intention of asserting the right of immediate secession from imperial rule. But he, too, did not quite imagine that the implementation of self-determination would extend much beyond Europe for the time being. Colonial nationalists, however, saw clearly how the language of self-determination could be used to challenge the relationships between race, civilization, and sovereignty that underlay the prewar international order, and moved to do just that. It is to this story that we now turn.

3

President Wilson Arrives in Cairo

Some years after the event, Muhammad Husayn Haykal, a prominent Egyptian journalist and intellectual, wrote of an encounter he had with a friend on the streets of Cairo on a summer day in 1918. The texts of President Wilson's addresses had appeared in Egyptian newspapers over the previous months, and excited talk of postwar possibilities was in the air. "This is it, Sir!" exclaimed the friend. "We have the right to self-determination, and therefore the English will leave Egypt." Why did he think that Wilson's promises would be implemented? Haykal tells us he asked the friend. Could they not be yet more empty words from the mouth of a politician? "No!!" came the reply. "The United States is the one who won the war. She is not an imperialist country. She truly wants that there will not be another war. Therefore, she will enforce the right to self-determination and enforce the withdrawal." Egypt, the friend explained, now had a forum to make its case against England and a winning argument: its right, along with all other nations, to self-determination, a central tenet of the new international order that the peace conference would establish.[1]

Haykal's report reflected common sentiments among Egyptians who had learned of President Wilson's views on the postwar reorganization of international affairs. During the final years of the war, the Egyptian press reported widely on the U.S. leader's declarations. When Wilson came before Congress in April 1917 to ask for a declaration of war, the leading Arabic language newspaper, *Al-Ahram*, published an extended full-page summary of the president's speech, citing, among other quotes, Wilson's call to make the world safe for democracy and to fight to defend the rights of small nations. Over the next few days, additional articles appeared to analyze the meaning and impact of U.S. entry, emphasizing the "immense" potential contribution of the United States to the Allied war effort. America, the paper informed its readers, was in the process of conscripting as many as three million men to fight in the war, and its participation was bound to have a decisive impact on it.[2] Nine months later, Wilson's Fourteen Points address also received extensive coverage in the Egyptian press, with the full text of the points printed in Arabic translation, courtesy of the Reuters news service. The accompanying analysis put special emphasis on the positive reactions to the address in the U.S. and world press.[3]

Thus, although the Committee on Public Information had no branch or direct operations in Egypt, the public there hardly lacked information about the U.S. role in the war or its president's plans for the peace.[4] Wartime censorship, though in force, had little effect on such reporting; the censors focused on preventing criticism of the government, and they left the newspapers largely free to report on international affairs. Moreover, in addition to the Arabic-language press, educated Egyptians also had access to newspapers published in the country in European languages—especially French and English—for the large communities of Europeans resident in Egypt's major cities. Copies of European papers, especially from Great Britain and France, were also widely available.[5] News items reported not only on the situation in Europe and the United States but also on events in Asia, such as the desire of Chinese leaders to contribute to the war efforts and the development of the struggle of the Indian National Congress for home rule. Egypt, readers could see, was not alone in expecting the war to transform its international status.[6]

By the summer of 1918, with Allied victory on the horizon, the reporting on the United States and its leader in some of the Arabic-language press grew increasingly laudatory. That year, for example, the press reported extensively on an event that had not previously aroused much interested in Egypt, the Independence Day celebrations in the United States on the Fourth of July. A major item in *Al-Ahram* noted that while many nations marked their independence on a certain date, the American celebrations on the Fourth of July were unique. Other nations consecrated moments of conquest or violent upheaval, such as the storming of the Bastille or the taking of Rome, but Americans chose to mark the signing of the Declaration of Independence, an event characterized not by violence but by the affirmation of high principles. The implication was clear: The United States was a nation where high-minded ideals trumped mere force. Following an extended quotation from the Declaration of Independence itself, rendered into Arabic, the article noted that, only 142 years since their independence, the American people had come to lead all nations in freedom, prosperity, education, and culture. There were also separate items on Wilson's Fourth of July address at Mount Vernon, in which he reiterated the ideals for which the United States had gone to war, and on the Independence Day celebrations in European capitals.[7]

Such tributes to American exceptionalism were common in the Egyptian press during this period, as they were, we will see, in the press in India, China, and Korea. The United States, especially under Wilson's leadership, was often described as motivated by ideals rather than interests and, since it was less dependent on imperialism than other powers, as more supportive of the principle of self-determination. Egyptian nationalists, like many of their contemporaries the world over, noted the growing prominence of the United States and its president in the last months of the war and concluded that the peace settlement would have to conform to the ideals that Americans celebrated on the Fourth of July and that Wilson's wartime rhetoric reflected.[8] This perception gained further credibility when the other Allied leaders, as Egyptians noted with satisfaction, echoed Wilson's pronouncements. In early November, just before the armistice, a joint Anglo-French declaration on the Allied aims in the Middle East said that they would seek to "ensure the complete and final emancipation of all those peoples so long oppressed by the Turks, and to establish national governments and administrations which shall derive their authority from the initiative and free will of the people themselves." Though the declaration named only Syria and Mesopotamia in this context, Egyptians saw no reason that the same arrangements should not apply to them.[9] Egyptian leaders, who before the war focused on fighting for a larger role in the administration of their country, were now beginning to see as attainable a more ambitious aim: complete self-determination.

Already in September 1918, several prominent Egyptian politicians began to discuss Egypt's status in the postwar world in those terms. They included Sa'd Zaghlul, then the vice president of the Legislative Assembly and the future leader of the 1919 Revolution, and leading politicians and intellectuals such as the Oxford-educated Muhammad Mahmud, a member of the landowning elite; 'Abd al-'Aziz Fahmi, a liberal politician, jurist, and intellectual; and Ahmad Lutfi al-Sayyid, a famous lawyer, author, and reformist thinker. Perceiving a window of opportunity that would open in the wake of the war, they were determined, Lutfi al-Sayyid later recalled, to "fight for Egyptian independence." Others in the Egyptian elite shared this sentiment. Prince 'Umar Tusun, a Swiss-educated, cosmopolitan member of the Egyptian royal family, met several times with Zaghlul in the weeks before the armistice to discuss the possibility of Egypt sending a delegation to the peace conference to present its case for self-determination. The idea, he later wrote, had "occurred to him after the publication of President Wilson's famous Fourteen Points." In October 1918, even the Egyptian monarch, Sultan Fu'ad, told the British high commissioner, Sir Reginald Wingate, who represented British authority in Egypt, that he wanted "Home Rule for Egypt along the lines of President Wilson's Fourteen Points."[10] By the time of the armistice, leading Egyptians were determined to stake their claim in the new world order.

These claims, many Egyptian leaders believed, were in line with Wilson's principles and vision for the peace settlement and would therefore have not only his sympathy but also his support during the negotiations. On the day of the armistice, the top American diplomat in Egypt, the consul general in Cairo, Hampson Gary, filed a report that highlighted Egyptian expectations for such succor at the coming peace conference. "I have been made aware," he wrote, "of a tendency in all classes of Egyptians to believe that President Wilson favors self-government throughout all the world and that he will champion the right of the people of this country to govern themselves." Several "prominent officials" had already inquired whether the president did not mean his principles to apply to countries outside Europe, and he had heard a "persistent rumor" that a petition asking the president to support an Egyptian demand for self-determination was being circulated for signatures by the members of the Egyptian National Assembly. "All signs," he concluded, "seem to me to point to a definite movement to elicit the support of the American Government in behalf of their claims in the great international clearing house that is now in process of formation either by a general public appeal or before the Peace Congress soon to meet."[11]

This was an unsettling development for the British authorities in Egypt, where only a few years before, British rule, in place since the 1882 military occupation of the country, had seemed secure. Though Egypt had officially been a province of the Ottoman Empire since its conquest in the early sixteenth century by the armies of Sultan Selim I, the real power remained largely in the hands of its Mamluk elites, a self-perpetuating class of slave-soldiers. A French occupation led by Napoleon Bonaparte disrupted Mamluk rule between 1798 and 1801, and after the French retreat, the Ottoman sultan appointed Muhammad Ali, a military commander of Albanian origin, as governor of Egypt. Muhammad Ali gradually consolidated his rule, eventually destroying Mamluk power and even threatening to conquer Istanbul itself before British intervention checked his ambition. Impressed by Europe's power and prosperity, Muhammad Ali also instituted a series of modernizing reforms in military organization, industry, agriculture, and education, introducing into Egypt a variety of European techniques and ideas. After his death in 1849, his successors borrowed heavily from European bankers to finance modernization projects in education, industry, and transportation—including the Suez Canal, which opened in 1869—as well as the increasingly conspicuous consumption of the royal court. Egypt enjoyed a temporary economic boom during the American Civil War, when Egyptian cotton was in high demand in the world market to replace lost cotton exports from the American South.[12] But the boom soon turned to bust, and by 1878, Egypt's ballooning debt to European creditors led, in the usual imperialist practice of the time, to the imposition of Anglo-French control over Egyptian finances.

Modern ideas of Egyptian nationhood first emerged in the writings of intellectuals in the mid-nineteenth century, but for decades they remained confined to a thin sliver of urban intellectuals. In 1881–1882, growing dissatisfaction with the increasing foreign influence and court corruption ignited an uprising spearheaded by a group of disaffected army officers led by Colonel Ahmad 'Urabi, a man of relatively modest background. Leaders of the uprising used the slogan "Egypt for Egyptians," but they also proclaimed their allegiance to the

Ottoman sultan-caliph in Istanbul and couched their demands for increased political participation and their opposition to the royal court in Cairo and to the Europeans in terms that highlighted Egypt's Ottoman and Islamic identity. There were no demands made in 1882 in the name of an independent Egyptian nation and no claims for independence or self-determination. The uprising, however, exacerbated existing tensions between native Egyptians and the legions of foreign residents, who controlled much of Egypt's lucrative foreign trade. In Alexandria, a cosmopolitan port city of some 230,000 residents, a full fifth of the population was European. When tensions there erupted into anti-foreign riots in the summer of 1882, the British government, citing the need to defend Egypt's foreign residents, launched a military invasion that defeated units loyal to 'Urabi and established de facto British rule over Egypt.[13]

From 1882 to 1914, Egypt remained formally under Ottoman suzerainty, but Great Britain's diplomatic resident in Cairo, backed by the arms of British troops permanently stationed in the country, exercised decisive power. The British occupation aroused resistance and accelerated the development of Egyptian nationalism. Tensions came to a head in the Dinshawai incident of 1906, when British troops summarily executed a number of Egyptian villagers who got into an altercation with British officers. Widespread protests erupted, and the British, seeking to accommodate nationalist sentiments, implemented political reforms that gave more power to the Egyptian legislative assembly. Ultimate authority, however, remained in British hands. The founding of the National party in 1907 consolidated anti-British forces under the charismatic leadership of Mustafa Kamil, whose international horizons were reflected in a book he had written praising Japan as a model of modernization for other Eastern nations. But Kamil's untimely death the following year and the deportation of his successor, Muhammad Farid, effectively curtailed the National party's influence. In 1914, many Egyptian politicians and intellectuals still advocated a gradualist approach to building the nation, which called for cooperation with the British as educational and social reforms prepared Egypt for eventual independence. At the outbreak of the Great War, with the National party weakened and many leading figures supporting Anglo-Egyptian collaboration, British rule in Egypt appeared secure.[14]

In November 1914, three months after the outbreak of the war in Europe, the Ottoman Empire entered the war on the side of the Central Powers, and the sultan in Istanbul called on the world's Muslims to join him in *jihad* against the Western allies. The British authorities, who were concerned with the security of their position in Egypt, immediately declared martial law. The following month they declared that Egypt was now a protectorate of the British Empire, formalizing British control there and removing any remaining pretense of Ottoman suzerainty. The announcement presented the protectorate as a temporary wartime measure and even suggested that, with the Ottoman connection now severed, it was a step toward Egyptian self-government. Still, its new status as a protectorate did little to shield Egypt from the hardships of the war. The British, who wanted to defend the Suez Canal and establish a base for operations against the Ottoman territories in West Asia, stationed in Egypt a large contingent of troops that strained the country's resources. Runaway inflation, the requisition of provisions, and the forced conscription of labor made life increasingly difficult for much of the Egyptian population. Wartime attempts at land reform alienated landowners, and the urban population chafed under the restrictions of martial law. But these hardships, many Egyptians believed, were only temporary. As the armistice neared, they increasingly expected an imminent transformation of the Anglo-Egyptian relationship.[15]

On November 13, 1918, only two days after the armistice was announced, a delegation of political leaders visited the British high commissioner in Cairo, Reginald Wingate. The group, led by Sa'd Zaghlul, came to demand that Egyptian nationalist delegates be allowed to travel to London to discuss demands for independence. Zaghlul, about sixty years old at the time, was born in a village on the Nile delta to a prosperous family of local standing. His roots as a "true" Egyptian, not part of the Turkish aristocracy which had governed Egypt for centuries, were important in his subsequent popularity with the Egyptian people. His initial education was religious—there was no modern school in the village—but he later learned French and studied law in a French school in Cairo. He began his public career as a reform-minded administrator and served in several ministerial posts in Egyptian governments between 1906 and 1913. Like many of his associates he espoused liberal ideas, advocating educational reforms and the devolution of power from the Egyptian court to elected representatives in the Legislative Assembly.[16] When the British authorities resisted his reform proposals, Zaghlul resigned his cabinet post in protest. Elected to the Legislative Assembly, Zaghlul became its vice president and the leader of the opposition. He campaigned energetically for greater Egyptian representation and participation in government, but advocated progress through peaceful negotiations and reforms. Far from a revolutionary radical, Zaghlul was a veteran politician who had for decades worked within the British-controlled system. Wingate himself, reporting on his meeting with Zaghlul and his colleagues, described them as "politicians of advanced views."[17]

Their views, however, had now advanced further than what London was prepared to contemplate. The British government, beset with domestic concerns and preoccupied with preparations for the looming peace conference, was hardly in any rush to reconsider the British position in Egypt; a host of other issues seemed far more urgent. Wingate, who had no clear instructions

Sa'd Zaghlul (*seated on bench, second from right*) led the Egyptian nationalist uprising against British rule in 1919. Here he is shown with three colleagues in the nationalist leadership (*seated on bench, from left*): Hamad al-Basil, a prominent tribal leader; Isma'il Sidqi, a lawyer, wealthy landowner, and future prime minister; and the Oxford-educated Muhammad Mahmud, who would travel to the United States in late 1919 to advocate for Egyptian independence there. *Middle East Centre Archive, St Antony's College, Oxford. GB165-0005 Allenby Collection, Ref PA 5/8.*

from London, simply asked the Egyptian delegation that came to see him to exercise patience, given the "many important preoccupations of His Majesty's Government," but this response only increased the sense of urgency among the nationalists.[18] If officials in London were too preoccupied to see them, they would go to Paris to present the Egyptian case directly to President Wilson and the peace conference. Wingate, who had been the longtime commander of the British army in Egypt and the governor-general of the Sudan, urged the Foreign Office to show flexibility. But to the old imperial hands who made policy in London, Zaghlul appeared as a dangerous radical who threatened the core interests of the empire. British officials had long viewed the Suez Canal as an essential strategic lifeline for the empire, and they were determined to maintain full control of Egypt. In the following weeks, despite growing support for

Zaghlul's demands in both official and popular circles within Egypt, the British refused to recognize the delegation that he headed or to allow it to leave for Europe.[19]

The nationalists, however, were little inclined to sympathize with British priorities. Already intent on taking their case to the peace conference, their determination grew as they received news of the arrival in Paris of various delegations of oppressed peoples striving for self-determination, including an Arab delegation headed by Prince Faisal of the Hijaz. Several Egyptian commentators at the time noted that if even the desert Arabs were now candidates for independent statehood, how could Egypt, with its ancient civilization, possibly merit any less?[20] Within weeks, Zaghlul and his supporters organized themselves into a new political party called the Wafd, "delegation" in Arabic, whose platform defined Egyptian independence as its primary aim, and they launched a broad campaign to mobilize Egyptian public opinion behind their demands. They circulated petitions among provincial, municipal, and local councils, orchestrated a press campaign, and convened rallies, all urging that the British authorities allow the delegation to attend the peace conference to present Egyptian claims. Zaghlul, tall and distinguished in appearance, displayed his political charisma to good effect in a series of rallies that winter, announcing the Wafd's goal of Egyptian independence and declaring the party's faith in President Wilson's principles and support. Independence, the nationalists argued in many of the manifestos and petitions that they circulated during this period, had been declared "a natural right of nations." President Wilson's principle of self-determination prohibited the imposition of foreign rule on a people against its will, and Britain could therefore no longer claim legitimacy for its rule over Egypt.[21]

In the meantime, the Arabic-language press in Egypt reported in detail on the fanfare that accompanied President Wilson's landing on the shores of Europe. One celebratory item on the president's arrival, for example, listed a series of reasons that, in the writer's view, made the trip unprecedented. Wilson was the first sitting U.S. president to visit Europe, and the first to show Americans the extent of their economic and military power. He was the first statesman to formulate a plan for the world that looked to the future and left the past behind, and the first to guarantee all humanity its rights "without distinction between white, black, yellow, etc." Citing a comment attributed to the prime minister of Italy to the effect that Wilson's teachings would be the new bible of humanity, the writer nevertheless stressed the president's humility, noting that he arrived at the gates of Europe carrying a passport, just like a common citizen. What were his thoughts? the writer asked and, though admitting that no one knew for sure, expressed confidence that the words of the president's "great addresses" would guide his conduct at the peace conference.[22] In subsequent weeks, the Egyptian reading public could keep abreast of the schedule of the American president's triumphant European tour: visits to Paris, London, and Rome, even to his mother's ancestral village in the north of England, and stately receptions with the French president, Raymond Poincaré; King George V; and Pope Benedict XV, among others.[23]

The perception of Wilson's prominence and power in the international arena led Egyptian nationalists to turn directly to him for support in their campaign against British intransigence. Over the following months, the American legation in Cairo received dozens of petitions protesting the British refusal to allow Zaghlul's delegation to travel to Paris and calling on the United States to support Egyptian self-determination. This demand, petitioners noted, was based on the principles of the "illustrious president, who stands today in the eyes of the world for full justice for all nations, large or small."[24] A full cross-section of the Egyptian upper and middle classes signed the petitions: legislators, government officials, local political figures, merchants, lawyers, physicians, and military officers.[25] Egyptians, Hampson Gary reported from Cairo, were "basing their claims to independence on the president's self determination clause," and they would "endeavor to obtain an expression of opinion from him during his visit in Europe."[26] There was one dissenting petition, which Gary described as having been written by Egyptian Christians. It repudiated Zaghlul's leadership and called for continued British control in Egypt, arguing that the native Christians would not be safe under the rule of the Muslim majority. This was clearly a minority view, however. The petition, unlike those that supported Zaghlul, was unsigned, and Gary admitted that its authenticity could not be verified.[27]

The United States, Zaghlul reminded Gary in one note, intervened in the world war for no other purpose than "that of safeguarding the rights of the small nations," and the time had now come for the people of Egypt to control their own destiny. To ensure U.S. support, Egyptians would be willing, Zaghlul wrote, to place their independence under the supervision of the League of Nations proposed by the American president.[28] In a telegram that he addressed directly to Wilson in December, Zaghlul assured the president of the support of Egyptians for his vision. "No people more than the Egyptian people," he wrote, "has felt strongly the joyous emotion of the birth of a new era which, thanks to your virile action, is soon going to impose itself upon the universe." Wilson's leadership would "spread everywhere all the benefits of a peace" no longer "troubled by the ambitions of hypocrisy or the old-fashioned policy of hegemony and furthering selfish national interests."[29] Egyptians deserved to be heard at the peace conference in Paris—it was no more than their "natural and sacred right"—and the president should exercise his influence so that the British would permit it.[30]

A message composed by nationalist leaders in the Egyptian legislature to welcome President Wilson upon his arrival in Europe expressed similar sentiments even more emphatically:

> To the great and venerated President who led the people of the United States in their disinterested participation in the European conflict to save humanity and to preserve the world in the future from the horrors of war, we send our affectionate greetings.
>
> To the eminent philosopher and statesman who occupies today a preponderant place among the leaders of peoples, and whose high ideals are imposing themselves upon statesmen of all nations, we offer our homage and admiration.
>
> To the chief of the great American democracy, who left his country in order to bring about a durable peace based upon equal justice for all and guaranteed by the Society of Nations, we submit the cause of Egypt, which is subjugated to a foreign domination that Egypt unanimously rejects.
>
> Long live the United States! Long live President Wilson![31]

The message surely aimed to flatter the president and appeal to his sense of his own importance. But the tenor of the text echoed much of the writing on Wilson in Egypt during this time, and there is little evidence that would cast doubt on the sincerity of the sentiments expressed.

By January 1919, as the peace conference got under way, leaders of the Wafd grew increasingly anxious about missing the opportunity that a voice in Paris could provide. Representatives of numerous stateless and oppressed peoples, they noted, were arriving in Paris to present their cases, and self-determination seemed to be the order of the day, yet the British authorities continued to ignore their demands for representation and persisted in preventing them from leaving the country.[32] The injustice of the British position was all the more flagrant, Zaghlul noted, at a time "when every day brings its echoes of the claims presented to the conference by the representatives of the Hejaz, Armenia, Palestine, Syria and the Lebanon, but yesterday Turkish provinces," while Egyptians, with their long history of independence, had to "swallow our bitterness in silence and mourn for lost freedom."[33]

With the Egyptian public mobilized to support the Wafd in mass rallies and petition drives, Zaghlul quickly came to dominate the domestic political arena. The British authorities, however, remained obdurate. Arthur Balfour, the foreign secretary, was in Paris for the peace conference, and responsibility for Britain's Egyptian policy largely fell to the veteran imperial administrator and former viceroy of India, George Nathaniel Curzon. To Curzon, Zaghlul was a dangerous extremist with whom Britain could not negotiate; demands for Egyptian self-determination presented a strategic danger to the empire and had to be decisively suppressed. When the Egyptian prime minister, Husayn Rushdi, whom the British considered more moderate than Zaghlul, asked to travel to London to negotiate a compromise that would defuse tensions, the Foreign Office denied his request.

He would be welcome in London, they said, but only after the conclusion of the peace conference. For the nationalists, of course, this was precisely the point, since they saw the conference under Wilson as a potential ally against the empire. After this rebuff, Rushdi, under pressure from an irate public, tendered his resignation.[34]

The Foreign Office blamed the accommodating stance of the high commissioner, Wingate, for the mounting problems in Egypt; he should not even have agreed to see Zaghlul, let alone entertain his preposterous demands. His judgment in doubt, the dejected Wingate was recalled to London and soon replaced as high commissioner by the war hero and conqueror of Jerusalem, General Edmund H. H. Allenby.[35] Still, with the political crisis in Cairo deepening, the British found it impossible to replace the resigning Rushdi ministry in the face of opposition from the Wafd. Attempting to defuse an increasingly tense standoff and regain control, Whitehall backtracked and decided to permit a "moderate" delegation headed by Rushdi—though not Zaghlul and his "extremists"—to come to London for talks. By now, however, public sentiment against the British was such that Rushdi could no longer afford to appear to be collaborating with them. He would not go, he said, unless Zaghlul's delegation also received permission to travel.[36]

In the meantime, Zaghlul continued his campaign to enlist international support for his cause. He wrote Wilson again, beseeching him once more to apply his principles to Egypt, and he wrote to the French premier, Georges Clemenceau, who was president of the peace conference, to protest the British refusal to allow his delegation to travel to Europe.[37] The Wafd also circulated a detailed thirty-three-page memorandum, dated January 25, 1919, and signed by Zaghlul and the fifteen other members of his proposed delegation, to the foreign diplomats in Cairo outlining "The Egyptian National Claims."[38] Egypt, it argued, was perfectly suited for self-government, as evidenced by all of the characteristics of its history, politics, and society: its ancient civilization, its material development and progress over the preceding century, its "racial homogeneity, the high culture of her 'elite,' her sense of order, love of liberty and generous tolerance." British rule in Egypt was based on brute force alone and served interests "at utter variance with justice, not to mention civilisation." If the world was to be reorganized according to the principles of justice and equality, as Wilson had said, Egypt would have to assume its rightful place among nations.[39] The demand for self-determination, then, was placed squarely in the context of international developments. If before the war most of the liberal politicians who now led the Wafd could realistically envision no more than gradual reforms, the new international situation now made full and immediate self-determination the order of the day.

Even the leadership of the prewar National party, who had spent the war years in Europe hoping for a German and Ottoman victory that would destroy British rule in Egypt, were now eager to join the Wilsonian bandwagon.[40] In a message to the president from his exile in Switzerland, the party's leader, Muhammad Farid, lavished praise on the president, outlined the history of British oppression in Egypt, and made the usual appeal to the president's "noble principles" to argue that Egyptians should receive a hearing before the peace conference. Egyptians looked forward to "the dawn of a new era" in which Egypt would be an independent member of the League of Nations. As such, he added, it would welcome the good advice of powers that "entertain no imperialistic designs."[41] Farid also described Wilson as "that great man whose name is venerated by all Egypt as that of the champion of the liberation of nations."[42]

During this period, dozens of similar petitions arrived at the headquarters of the U.S. peace commission at the Hôtel Crillon from a diverse array of Egyptian groups both in Egypt and abroad. Most of these texts were similar in language and content, hailing, as one did, "with emotional joy" President Wilson's arrival in Europe "at one of the most solemn hours of the world's history" in order to serve "the cause of justice, right and liberty." All oppressed nations, the writers typically assured the president, were pinning their hopes on him in light of his declarations that all nations should control their own destiny.[43] Occasionally, lengthy memoranda and pamphlets also accompanied the petitions, explaining in detail the nationalist case for self-determination.

A thirty-one-page pamphlet entitled *Egypt and the Peace Congress*, prepared by an ad hoc group of activists living abroad who called themselves the Egyptian Committee in Geneva, recounted the country's modern history and outlined its demands for the future. The opening section, entitled "Egypt and the Wilsonian Principle," stated succinctly the nationalists' perceptions of the transformation that Wilson's emergence had effected in world affairs: "The principle of the rights of nations which, only yesterday, was in the eyes of many a chimera, has to-day become a reality." Arguing their case, the authors described Egypt's de facto autonomy prior to the British occupation as evidence that Egyptians were fit to govern themselves, and vigorously challenged the notions that British rule had made Egypt prosperous and that Egyptians acquiesced in it. Citing extensively from the president's wartime utterances as support for the demand for Egyptian independence, the document, like many similar ones, also tried to appeal to U.S. interests and assuage its fears, offering, for example, to submit the question of control over the Suez Canal to a decision by the League of Nations.[44]

In Paris, however, the British representatives worked assiduously to neutralize the Egyptian campaign for self-determination. The British delegation used its influence in the conference secretariat, run by the French, to ensure that it would simply file away Egyptian petitions addressed to the conference rather than circulate them among the delegations.[45] Petitions addressed directly to the American delegation, though not intercepted by the British, did not fare much better. The delegation's secretary, Joseph C. Grew, referred them for the consideration of "the proper persons in the Commission," who were ill inclined to favor the Egyptian demands.[46] The secretary of state, Robert Lansing, was a staunch Anglophile who strongly supported the British position in Egypt, and other U.S. diplomats generally agreed.[47] In one of the few official exchanges on the Egyptian demands, Allen Dulles, then at the State Department's Division of Near Eastern Affairs (and later director of the Central Intelligence Agency under President Dwight Eisenhower) suggested that communications from Egyptian nationalists "should not even be acknowledged." George Louis Beer, the Inquiry expert on African affairs under whose purview the Egyptian question fell, concurred: "Such a step would serve no good purpose," since it would only invite "similar appeals from factions in all parts of the world." Brief, polite acknowledgments from Wilson's private secretary, Gilbert Close, were the only direct replies Egyptian nationalists ever received from the president.[48]

In Cairo, the U.S. consul general, Hampson Gary, refused to receive Zaghlul or other Egyptian leaders at the legation and advised his superiors in Washington and Paris to reject out of hand Zaghlul's pleas for support against the British.[49] The nationalists, he opined, were not authentic representatives of the Egyptian people. Rather, they constituted a "native autocracy as foreign to the autonomous peasantry as the British," which was not "conversant with American and European ideals" and "incapable as yet of efficient government." The Egyptian masses, on the other hand, were "politically undeveloped," ignorant, and timid; having long suffered under the heavy hand of native officials, they "really prefer British protection to native autocracy." The application of the principle of self-determination to Egypt was therefore "manifestly impracticable," since its people were "as yet not fitted for self-government." It was best to support "the continued political education of the Egyptian people under British protection," which would protect the interests of the masses and those of foreign residents. The United States, Gary recommended, should recognize forthwith the British protectorate over Egypt.[50] But it had not yet done so, and Wilson, though remote and unresponsive, had not definitely rejected the nationalists' pleas. As long as the peace conference remained in session, there was still a possibility that it would take up their case. The Egyptian people, one nationalist pamphlet asserted, were entitled to decide their own destiny. "Are we to believe," it concluded, "that such a plain and natural aspiration can be deliberately put aside?"[51]

4

Laying India's Ailments before Dr. Wilson

The growing unrest in Egypt was by no means the only threat facing the British Empire in the crisis year of 1919. In India, the crown jewel of the empire, Wilson's call of self-determination had also found an audience. A few years later, in a preface to a collection of the president's wartime addresses published in India, the prominent liberal politician and intellectual V. S. Srinivasa Sastri noted the "unparalleled demonstration" that had met Wilson in Europe and added that he would have met a similar reception in Asia, had he come there. Sastri's description of Wilson as an ancient Asian sage, a "Christ or Buddha" returning to his ancestral home, was rather far-fetched, but his appraisal of the U.S. president's importance was not an unusual one in India and across much of Asia.[1] From early in the war, Indian nationalists, already mobilizing in the cause of home rule, had recognized the importance of the Wilsonian rhetoric of self-determination for their campaign, appropriated it in redefining the goals of their movement, and made concerted efforts to take advantage of the new opportunities and forums that emerged in the international arena to advance those goals.

Indian nationalists began to view the United States and its president as potential allies in their struggle for home rule in the spring of 1917, after Wilson announced that the United States would declare war on Germany in the name of democracy, popular government, and "the rights and liberties of small nations."[2] Wilson's "noble and moving utterance" received full and favorable coverage in India's leading nationalist dailies. In addition to a detailed summary of its contents and extensive verbatim excerpts, Indian readers learned that crowds outside the U.S. Capitol building in Washington "cheered frantically" as the president entered and left and that, inside the chamber, members of Congress, even the few "supposed Pacifists," greeted his words with "deafening" cheers. The speech, one paper reported, was also hailed abroad as "a new declaration of rights" and "a new gospel in the governance of mankind." Perhaps the most intriguing comment described the president's address as a "fitting sequel to the Russian Revolution," since both events were "bound to have the most profound influence on the destinies of nations." The revolution in question, of course, was the one that took place in March 1917, not the Bolshevik revolution, which was more than six months in the future. The rise of Wilson's principles and the democratic revolution in Russia both appeared as part of the advance of the same progressive spirit in world politics.[3]

The initial press reports on Wilson's address focused on the boost that American belligerency would give to the Allied war effort. But Indian home-rule activists also quickly saw that Wilson's rhetoric would be useful for India's own struggle against autocracy—not German, but British. One of the first to use Wilson's words for that purpose was Annie Besant, the Anglo-Irish advocate of Indian home rule. Besant, by then seventy years old and a veteran activist for radical causes, was president of the Theosophical Society, an international religious-philosophical movement heavily influenced by Hindu thought. She had moved to India in 1893 to propagate theosophy, settled near Madras, and in 1914, influenced by rising Irish resistance to the British, she began to work for Indian home rule. When Wilson's war message, in which he called for democracy, government by consent, and respect for the rights of all nations, appeared in the Indian press, Besant printed and circulated copies of the text as part of her campaign.[4]

When Besant was jailed soon thereafter for her "seditious" activities, her supporters launched a campaign for her release. A prominent Besant ally, Sir S. Subramanya Aiyar, decided to appeal directly to the U.S. president to intervene on her behalf. Aiyar, a retired Madras judge and the honorary president of Besant's All-India Home Rule League, warned Wilson that he, the president, had been "kept in ignorance of the full measures of misrule and oppression in India," of which Besant's arrest was but one example:

> At present we are a subject nation, held in chains, forbidden by our alien rulers to express publicly our desire for the ideals presented in your famous War Message. . . . It is our earnest hope that you may so completely convert England to your ideals of world liberation that together you will make it possible for India's millions to lend assistance in this war. . . . Honoured Sir, the aching heart of India cries out to you, whom we believe to be an instrument of God in the reconstruction of the world.[5]

In addition to the appeal to Wilson's religious sensibilities, Aiyar sought to convince the president that a free India would also help the Allied war effort: If India had home rule, he said, it would be able to contribute no fewer than ten million men to the Allied forces.

In order to circumvent the British censor, Aiyar gave the letter to a visiting American theosophist, Henry Hotchner, who brought it to the United States and delivered it in person to the White House. We even know that the president read it, since he instructed his personal secretary, Joe Tumulty, to check with the Department of State "whether anything properly can be done" in the matter of Besant's arrest. The department, however, advised that the writer be ignored, since the letter was clearly "an attempt to use the President to assist the propaganda" of the Indian nationalist cause.[6] Nevertheless, copies of the Aiyar letter circulated in Washington among lawmakers and journalists, and it was eventually published in full in the Hearst newspaper *Chicago Examiner* in October.[7] Hotchner also tried to smuggle copies past the British censors back into India, and in May 1918, it was finally published there and, shortly thereafter, in the *Times* of London. The publication aroused a great furor among the British political class. Aiyar's letter was roundly condemned in the British Parliament, where the secretary of state for India, Edwin Samuel Montagu, called it "disgraceful," a response that prompted, in turn, a wave of criticism and derision in the nationalist press in India.[8]

Nor did the "Aiyar affair" end there. When the viceroy of India, Lord Chelmsford, visited Madras with Montagu during the latter's tour of the subcontinent that year, he met the elderly judge and rebuked him for his impertinence in writing the letter to Wilson. Aiyar, in turn, defended himself with gusto and soon after publicly renounced his knighthood in protest.[9] The affair even came to the attention of King George himself, who inquired of the government whether Aiyar's pension could be terminated and his knighthood officially withdrawn as punishment for his actions. Both Montagu and Chelmsford, however, agreed that this would "make a martyr of this silly vain old man" and that the proper response was a display of "thinly veiled contempt" for his actions.[10] The unfolding of the Aiyar affair reflected the common perception among Indian nationalists that Wilson could be a potential champion for their cause. It also showcased British fears about the danger that Indian "propaganda" in the United States might harm the interests of the empire with a crucial ally, and, more generally, of the potential embarrassments that could come from the internationalization of the Indian struggle for home rule.

Internationalization threatened to reverse the gains the British had made in legitimating their rule in India since the eighteenth century. British influence in the subcontinent initially expanded under the semi-private aegis of the East India Company, but the British Crown assumed direct control after the great revolt of native troops in 1857, ruling through an appointed viceroy. The politics of an all-Indian national identity began to develop in the ensuing decades, and in 1885 a small group of Western-educated lawyers and professionals met in Bombay and established the Indian National Congress (INC). The INC was the first all-India political organization that had recognizably nationalist aims, but for the first two decades of its existence, it lacked a base of popular support and concentrated its efforts on defending and expanding the rights of Indians within the framework of the British Empire, rather than challenging the legitimacy of British rule itself.[11]

In their keynote addresses at the organization's annual gathering each winter, INC presidents—a new one was elected every year—often criticized the Raj for inefficiency and misrule. At the same time, they often reaffirmed India's loyalty to the British Crown. Their demands for reforms did not go beyond calling for a measure of self-government for India within the empire, asking for more "freedom" for Indians as "British citizens" under the "British flag," rather than for an independent Indian nation-state.[12] In his 1905 presidential address in the holy city of Banaras, Gopal Krishna Gokhale, perhaps the most prominent INC leader of the prewar era, described the ultimate goal of the organization as ensuring "that India should be governed in the interests of the Indians themselves, and that, in the course of time, a form of Government should be attained in this country similar to what exists in the Self-Governing Colonies of the British Empire."[13] During the prewar decades, then, the INC never attempted to challenge the legitimacy of the empire itself, and its aims were limited to modifying the terms of British rule rather than eliminating it.

The last years of the nineteenth century, however, saw a more radical sensibility emerge among some Indian intellectuals. Initially developing in local or regional contexts, this "extremist" position, as it was known at the time, burst onto the national all-India scene in 1905 with the Swadeshi movement—the term is usually rendered as "self-reliance" or "self-sufficiency." Occurring at around the same time of the Dinshawai incident that saw the intensification of resistance to the empire in Egypt, the Swadeshi movement erupted to protest the decision of the viceroy, Lord Curzon—who would later resist accommodating Zaghlul in Egypt—to partition the province of Bengal. The movement saw the rise to national prominence of radical leaders, known at the time as the "extremists," who unlike the INC "moderates" set out to challenge the very legitimacy of British rule in India. The trio who came to symbolize the movement reflected its national scope: Bal Gangadhar Tilak, popularly known as Lokamanya, or "revered by the people," a scholar and journalist from Poona (Pune) who had long been a prominent figure in the Marathi-speaking regions of western India; Lala Lajpat Rai, a Hindu lawyer from the Punjab; and the Bengali intellectual Bipin Chandra Pal. The three, often collectively known as Lal-Bal-Pal, mobilized Indians across the country against the Bengal partition, and the demonstrations, strikes, and boycotts of English goods that began in Bengal soon spread to other regions in a broader protest against the Raj.[14]

The British authorities, initially taken by surprise, met Swadeshi with an effort to divide the movement, combining limited concessions to INC moderates with the forcible suppression of the extremists. An open split in the ranks of the Congress in 1907 vindicated this policy, as the extremists, led by Tilak, broke off to form a separate party. With the moderates proclaiming their commitment to remain within the "constitutional" framework of the empire, the extremists were effectively curtailed by the deportation or imprisonment of several of their prominent leaders. Both Pal and Lajpat Rai went into prolonged exile, while Tilak, whom the British authorities saw as the ringleader of extremist agitation, was tried and sentenced to a six-year prison term for "sedition." Popular demonstrations over Tilak's arrest and conviction in Bombay and elsewhere were brutally put down by the police. Soon after, the reforms of the Indian Councils Act of 1909, implemented by the new Liberal government of Herbert Asquith, cemented moderate control of Congress. The Morley-Minto reforms, named after the Liberal secretary of state for India, John Morley, and the then-viceroy, Lord Minto, were hardly radical. They allowed for the increased participation of Indians in provincial legislative councils, but the councils had limited powers and executive authority remained firmly in the hands of the viceroy and the provincial governors, all British officials. Two years later, the new viceroy, Lord Hardinge, reversed the partition of Bengal province, which had been the original reason for the Swadeshi protests.[15]

By 1914, the rulers of the Raj, through a combination of co-optation and coercion, had largely managed to quell dissent. With the INC firmly in the hands of Gokhale and the moderates, Indian politics remained, as Jawaharlal Nehru later wrote, "very dull."[16] A scattering of revolutionary groups made sporadic efforts to attack British targets, and they found some support in Indian communities overseas, especially in North America. The revolutionaries, however, lacked arms and organization and failed to build a significant base of support within India itself, and the British security forces suppressed them without much trouble.[17] The customary Delhi *durbar* of 1911, where the new British sovereign, King George V, held audience for his Indian subjects, was a spectacular success, by some accounts marking the high point of British imperial authority in India. Prewar India, as historian Percival Spear has written, "was proceeding in growing trust between government and popular leaders, in increasing prosperity, and gathering self-confidence."[18] The British Raj, it seemed to most contemporaries, would last for many years to come.

The outbreak of war at first gave contemporaries little reason to revise this assessment. Despite the siphoning of British troops from India to distant battlefields—for a time, only 15,000 British troops remained in the country—few Indians tried to seize the opportunity to cast off the British yoke. Quite the opposite, in fact, occurred. In December 1914, only a few months into the war, the INC resolved "to convey to His Majesty the King-Emperor and the people of England [India's] profound devotion to the throne, its unswerving allegiance to the British connection, and its firm resolve to stand by the empire at all hazards and at all costs."[19] Indian support for the war effort, moreover, was not merely rhetorical: 1.2 million Indian men, 800,000 of them in combat roles, fought for the empire in France, Egypt, and Mesopotamia. Practically all prominent Indian politicians supported the military recruitment effort. One of its most enthusiastic advocates, in fact, was Mohandas K. Gandhi, then in his late forties and recently returned from twenty years in South Africa, where he had found renown as a fighter for the equal rights of Indians as subjects of the British Crown.[20]

Many nationalist leaders were vocal supporters of the efforts to recruit Indians into the military, since they saw it as an opportunity to prove the value and loyalty of Indians to the empire and thus establish their right to equality as its citizens. Tilak himself, released from Mandalay prison in June 1914 after serving his six-year sentence, publicly expressed in February 1917 his great satisfaction at the intention of the government to enroll Indians in the Defence of India Force and urged the people to respond wholeheartedly to this call to the defense of motherland and empire. Their status, he said, would have to be made equal to "European British subjects in India" and it would therefore have to remain so after the war.[21] A handful of revolutionaries attempted to organize violent anti-British uprisings in Bengal and the Punjab, but they failed to excite significant popular support. Their efforts were easily thwarted by the security forces, which were aided by the wartime measures of the 1915 Defence of India Act that gave them extraordinary powers of arrest and trial. By one estimate, forty-six revolutionaries were tried and executed under the provisions of the act during the course of the war, while sixty-four received sentences of life imprisonment.[22]

As the war drew on, the burden it put on the economic resources of the empire increased. While the virtual disappearance of European manufactured goods from Indian markets stimulated industrial growth in some sectors, most notably textiles, this development had immediate benefits only for a select few, while the effects of wartime inflation and economic dislocation were widely felt.[23] In India, as in Egypt, such wartime hardships fostered a general mood of restlessness and anticipation, and this, combined with the tremendous Indian contribution of men and materiel to the war effort, led many Indians to expect Britain to reward them, after the end of the war, with a greater voice in their own government. Already in 1916, one prominent moderate leader noted that the enormity of the war meant that the world was "on the eve of a great reconstruction," and "England and India will participate in that reconstruction."[24] The war, observed another leading politician, "has put the clock... fifty years forward." When it ended, Indians would have to begin "to take their legitimate part in the administration of their own country."[25]

Nothing was yet said of full independence or self-determination, but the position of the INC on India's place within the empire was clearly in flux. The deaths in 1915 of two of the most prominent moderate leaders, Gokhale and Pherozeshah Mehta, had cleared the way for the triumphant return of the extremists, led by Tilak, to the center of Congress politics. In 1916, Tilak began to organize the movement for Indian home rule, establishing a Home Rule league with branches across the country in order to mobilize the Indian masses around the goal of self-government. Annie Besant, who though not a native Indian served in 1917 as the INC president, also established a home rule league of her own, which sometimes collaborated and sometimes competed with Tilak's as it also set out to enlist grassroots support for self-government. But Besant stopped short of advocating Indian independence, asking only that India be a "Free Nation within the British Empire, under the Imperial Crown of His Majesty the King-Emperor George V and His successors."[26] Even as the demand for home rule was growing more urgent, the goal of most home rulers still remained reforms within the imperial system—Indian self-government within the empire—rather than challenging the legitimacy of empire itself.

Faced with this growing activism for home rule, London grew increasingly concerned with preserving the stability of British rule in India. In order to ensure the continued loyalty of INC moderates and defuse the demands of the extremists, the British cabinet decided that it would be prudent to declare Britain's intention to allow Indians a greater measure of self-government after the war. In August 1917, Secretary of State for India Montagu officially announced the government's policy to promote "the increasing association of Indians in every branch of the administration and the gradual development of self-governing institutions with a view to the progressive realisation of responsible government in India as an integral part of the British Empire." This was London's gambit to regain the initiative in Indian politics, and for a brief while it seemed to work. The Montagu declaration, as it came to be known, was initially well received by many of the INC moderates.[27]

As the rhetoric of the U.S. president echoed more loudly in the international arena over the following months, however, the Montagu declaration quickly began to appear inadequate in the new international environment that was taking shape. As in most other regions of the colonial world, the Indian press played a crucial role in informing Indians about world events. Newspapers first began to spread in India in the latter half of the nineteenth century. By the time of the war, they numbered in the thousands, published in English and in numerous Indian languages. An estimate on the reach of the Indian press reckoned that already in 1905 newspapers reached some two million subscribers as well as "an innumerable number who received them at second hand or heard them being read aloud."[28] The authorities tried to monitor and control the press to prevent the publication of writings that they considered politically inflammatory, and some journalists and publishers were jailed for "seditious" publications. There were simply too many publications, however, for the government to maintain full control of the information flows in India, and in any case, reports and discussions concerning declarations of Allied statesmen were not typically censored.[29]

Thus, though India, like Egypt, was not in any direct way a target of George Creel's propaganda operations, knowledge of Wilson's pronouncements was spread widely there by international news agencies, foreign and domestic newspapers, and political discussions. Indeed, one study of the Indian press during the war has concluded that native Indian editors and publicists saw Wilson's declarations of support for self-determination as the most significant wartime international development as far as India was concerned, and viewed the many other international concerns commonly voiced by British officials—threats to India's security from Afghanistan, Turkey, Germany, or the Bolsheviks—as excuses for tightening the British grip on the subcontinent.[30] The usefulness of Wilson's rhetoric for Indians was reflected in the response of Lala Lajpat Rai, the erstwhile Swadeshi leader, to the Montagu declaration. Welcoming Great Britain's willingness to move India toward self-government, he rejected its claim that the British government alone possessed the right to determine the nature and pace of political progress in India. The new principles of justice recently introduced in the international arena with "the declaration of President Wilson that every people must be free to determine their own form of government" rendered such claims untenable.[31] The declaration, though it promised more than Britain had ever done before, fell short of fulfilling the basic right of self-determination, destined to become a central tenet of the postwar international order. In this new world, London would have to do better.

With the emergence of the Wilsonian moment, Indian nationalists launched concerted efforts to enlist the support of "world opinion," and especially American opinion, on behalf of their cause. Besant's arrest for circulating copies of Wilson's war address helped their efforts, since it raised a furor among American theosophists, who launched a public campaign for her release and denounced Britain's "jailor's regime" in India. This campaign prompted Sudhindra Bose, an Indian scholar teaching in an Iowa college, to rejoice: "All America is now aware of India's demand for Home Rule . . . self-government for India has become the live subject of discussion in the American press."[32] The pro-Besant campaign also caused some consternation at the British embassy in Washington, which attempted to neutralize it by telling the U.S. authorities that Besant's support for Indian home rule was not genuine, but rather little more than a ploy calculated to attract Indians to the religion of which she was a "high priestess."[33] Though the condition of India never became a major topic of interest for the American public, the growing turmoil on the subcontinent toward the end of the war did spur Secretary of State Lansing to instruct the U.S. consul general in Calcutta in April 1918 to report "promptly and frequently" on the political developments in India.[34]

Indian revolutionaries, who advocated violent action to liberate India from British rule, also hoped that Wilson's international leadership would aid their cause. Ram Chandra, a leading activist in the revolutionary Ghadr ("Mutiny") party who resided in the United States, wrote the president shortly after the publication of his war address to note the applicability of Wilson's principles to India and express his hope that their implementation would quickly lead to the establishment of self-government there. "In view of the fact that the Allies have all accepted in principle your declaration of the purposes of the present war," he concluded, "we do not see how Great Britain can refuse [any] longer to grant self-government to India."[35] But though activists like Chandra operated in relative safety while the United States remained neutral, once it joined the war their German sympathies and contacts attracted official suspicion, and dozens of Ghadr activists, including Chandra, were arrested and prosecuted in what became known as the "Hindu conspiracy" trial. In May 1918, a federal jury in San Francisco convicted twenty-nine of the defendants for conspiring to foment revolution in India in violation of U.S. neutrality (since the acts in question occurred before the United States entered the war), and they received a total of twenty-three and two-thirds years in prison and $64,000 in fines. Chandra himself did not survive the trial: he was gunned down in the courtroom by a fellow Indian with whom he had a feud, who was in turn shot and killed by a U.S. marshal.[36]

Lala Lajpat Rai, however, rejected revolutionary methods and steered clear of German connections, and so was able to continue to propagate his message in the United States with some measure of success. Born in 1865 in a village in British-ruled Punjab, Lajpat Rai, unlike many Indian nationalist leaders of his generation, was not a Brahmin. His father belonged to a merchant caste and his family background epitomized the shifting, kaleidoscopic nature of religious and communal identities in the region. His paternal grandfather was a practicing Jain, but his father, influenced by a Muslim teacher, observed Islamic practices for much of his life. He encouraged his son to study Arabic, read the Quran, and fast on Ramadan. Lajpat Rai, however, was more strongly influenced by his mother, who, though born into a Sikh family, became a devout Hindu. A brilliant student, Lajpat Rai studied law at the Government College in Lahore, where he joined the Hindu revivalist movement Arya Samaj. During the Swadeshi struggles, he emerged as a national figure and he was briefly imprisoned, though never prosecuted. When Tilak, with whom he was closely associated, split away from the INC in 1907, Lajpat Rai joined him in the extremist camp. In England when the war broke out and unable to return to India, Lajpat Rai decided to sail for the United States, where he landed in November 1914.[37]

Like many nationalist leaders across the colonial world at the time, Lajpat Rai saw the struggle against imperialism as part of a broader quest to

The Indian nationalist leader Lala Lajpat Rai spent most of the war years in the United States, researching U.S. society as a model for reforms in India and promoting the cause of Indian home rule in U.S. public opinion. *Nehru Memorial Museum and Library.*

reform and modernize Indian society along progressive lines. In his writings on educational reform, he advocated an emphasis on science and foreign languages, the education of women, and the banning of corporal punishment, and called for making education Indian, rather than British, but also thoroughly modern.[38] The United States fascinated him as a model that, he thought, had much to teach Indian reformers, and his evolving views on it as he studied it during the war years can serve to illuminate common perceptions of the United States among anticolonial nationalists at the time. It was, he wrote upon his arrival, "the freest of all the countries of the world," a place "where equality, liberty and fraternity reigned and where people were inspired by goodwill and friendship for all peoples of the earth without distinction of colour, creed and caste." He wanted to study the workings of U.S. society and government so that India could "assimilate such of the American idea[s] and ideals as were likely to help her in her aspirations toward freedom, and in her efforts toward national efficiency."[39]

He set to work immediately upon arrival, traveling the country from Boston to New Orleans to Chicago to San Francisco. Armed with letters of introduction from the British social reformer Sidney Webb, Lajpat Rai visited with progressive intellectuals at Columbia, Harvard, Stanford, and the University of California, Berkeley, as well as with Indian émigrés in each locale. Lajpat Rai reported his impressions of the United States to readers in India in a book entitled *The United States of America: A Hindu's Impressions and a Study*, which was published in Calcutta in 1916. The book was received with acclaim in India, but it was also favorably reviewed in the United States. An extensive review in the *New York Times* noted that, though Lajpat Rai was already known to some readers, this book would probably make him "far better known to America." It judged the book to be "the scrutiny of a seeing man," which was "well worth the attention of American citizens." Going far beyond the expected "contrasts between East and West," it provided a "quiet, careful study" of the United States as a "great and growing nation, on the threshold of imperialism, to find her problems unique and difficult, to behold her as something complex and interesting in the present and full of strange promise and portent for the future, to study her thus as a thing worth studying." Still, the review found, the author's "observations on civilization remain Oriental, and somewhat depressing for Occidental readers." Lajpat Rai, though a committed reformer, found modern civilization too drawn to the pursuit of material things and neglectful of the spirit, and the book and the review both concluded with his lament: "I have not yet found a reply to the question, 'What is real civilization?' "[40]

Despite such occasional reflections, Lajpat Rai's first impressions of the country, he recorded, were that it was "beautiful, grand, and up-to-date, according to the best standards of modern life." The buildings were "magnificent," and everything was "on the grandest possible scale." But Lajpat Rai was not a mere tourist. He was an indefatigable researcher who wanted to glean from U.S. society useful lessons for Indian reformers. Long interested in educational reforms, he was keen to study American education, particularly its role in improving the condition of women and minorities, which was a task that he considered of central importance for Indian reform. He described the American educational system's achievements as "monumental" despite the many challenges before it, and found the system far more inclusive, in terms of class, than what he knew from Britain or India. He also reported favorably on the significant role played by women, both as teachers and students, and concluded that although the United States had as much "sin and immorality" as other communities, it had less poverty and physical degradation due to its emphasis on education and the physical welfare of children.[41]

Well aware of the problem of race relations in the United States, Lajpat Rai showed great interest in the education of "coloured people" in America and met with the leading African-American educators of the day, including Booker T. Washington at the Tuskegee Institute, President John Hope of Morehouse College in Atlanta, and W. E. B. Du Bois. In a lengthy section in his book on the condition of the "Negro" in the United States, Lajpat Rai drew parallels both to the status of the lower castes in Indian society and to the status of all Indians under British rule. At the same time, impressed with the "magnificent" black colleges he visited, such as the Tuskegee Institute and Spellman College in Atlanta, he concluded that, despite widespread discrimination, especially in the South, blacks in America were better off educationally than were Indians under British rule.[42]

Another topic of special interest for Lajpat Rai was U.S. rule in the Philippines, to which he devoted another chapter in his book. The initial U.S. conquest of Cuba and the Philippines, he conceded, was imperialistic, but it was an aberration. Cuba had since gained independence and the Philippines "have made wonderful progress politically and educationally." The U.S. rule in the islands, he emphasized, had "for its sole object the preparation of the Philippines peoples for popular Self-Government in their own interests and not in the interests of the United States."[43] Mindful that his book would have to muster the approval of the British censor in order to circulate freely in India, Lajpat Rai avoided explicit comparison to British rule in India, but his discussion of the details of U.S. rule in the Philippines left little doubt as to what he had in mind. He would leave it to the reader, he concluded, to compare the conditions just described to those in British India.[44] Here, too, Lajpat Rai found the American example useful for emphasizing the iniquities of British rule in India and outlining possible paths for progress.

Traveling across the United States, Lajpat Rai also met numerous Indian revolutionaries but found most of them, with a few exceptions, uncouth, misguided, or simply corrupt. He was especially critical of their efforts to establish contacts with German agents, who they hoped would supply them with funds and arms to organize resistance against the British. He had no faith in the Germans, Lajpat Rai wrote, and did not believe that they could help to liberate India from British rule.[45] The future of the Indian movement lay not in seeking support from reactionary regimes that happened to be at war with Great Britain, but in joining the rising global tide of resistance to colonialism. Indian nationalism was no longer merely an anti-British movement. It was becoming part of an international resurgence of subject peoples—Egyptians, Irish, Persians, and others—and "entering on an international phase which is bound to strengthen it and bring it into the arena of world forces."[46]

The United States, Lajpat Rai thought, had a leading role to play in this trend, and in October 1917 he established, in coordination with Tilak, the India Home Rule League of America in order "to spread correct knowledge of Indian affairs in America." The nationalist press on the subcontinent reported enthusiastically on this development: It was "bound to secure for the cause of Indian Home Rule the sympathy of America, which has always made common cause with those who are ready to fight for freedom."[47] During his wartime stay in the United States, Lajpat Rai wrote numerous books, pamphlets, and articles, often published with the help of his progressive contacts, including the *Nation*'s editor, Oswald Garrison Villard, and the journalist and presidential adviser Walter Lippmann.[48] Lajpat Rai and his right-hand man, N. S. Hardikar, went on speaking tours across the country, appearing before a diverse array of audiences at colleges, labor unions, women's groups, Fabian societies, and Unitarian churches. The league also worked in Washington, where it received sympathy from anti-imperialist and anti-British lawmakers, like the Democratic Speaker of the House, Champ Clark, and the Republican congresswoman and pacifist Jeanette Rankin.[49]

Initially, Lajpat Rai received ample exposure in mainstream media venues such as the *New York Times*, whose Sunday *Magazine* twice profiled him in full-page illustrated features as an effective advocate for Indian self-government.[50] After the United States joined the war, however, the *Times* banished Lajpat Rai from its pages. The British complained that his propaganda work in the United States was "seditious" and "mischievous" and asked the U.S. authorities to put a stop to them, and at one point in late 1917 Lajpat Rai received a letter from the U.S. Justice Department warning him not to circulate an anti-British pamphlet he had written.[51] He was otherwise left alone, however, and still found outlets for his writing in progressive publications like the *New York Evening Post* and the *Nation*, both owned at the time by his friend Villard, and in Herbert Croly's *The New Republic*.[52] In 1918, Lajpat Rai's Home Rule League of America also established its own monthly publication, *Young India*, much of whose content he wrote or edited himself until he returned to India the following year.

When Woodrow Wilson emerged as an eloquent spokesman for the expectations of a postwar transformation of international relations, Lajpat Rai was thrilled. Soon after the Fourteen Points address, he wrote in *Young India* that, reading the president's messages with their lofty principles, "one begins to wish that the whole world could be constituted into a single republic, with President Wilson as its head." The president's utterances "were bound to help all the subject peoples of the world in their fight for the right of self-determination" and so constituted a great step toward "real democracy" in international affairs and an educational and political tool whose value was "simply incalculable."[53] The following month, after Wilson declared that the war "had its roots in the disregard of the rights of small nations and of nationalities which lacked the union and the force" to determine their political lives, Lajpat Rai cabled the president personally to thank him for his words. They were bound, he said, to constitute "a new charter of [the] world's freedom" and "thrill the millions of the world's 'subject races.' " Wilson had "put the whole thing in a nut shell," and the future of the world depended on the willingness of the great powers to implement his principles.[54]

Lajpat Rai was not naive, and he knew well that India was not foremost on Wilson's mind when the president spoke of self-determination. But he argued that it mattered little, since the president's forceful statements of his vision for the postwar order would serve as a powerful tool for the advancement of Indian self-rule regardless of his intentions. Wilson said nothing, he noted, that suggested his principles were limited to Europe alone. Quite the opposite: The discussion among the Allies about applying the principle to the German colonies in Africa proved they were valid outside Europe. Even more important, the force of universal principles, once asserted and accepted, could not be confined only to certain regions for long:

> Ideas—universal ideas, have a knack of rubbing off all geographical limitations. It is impossible that the noble truths uttered by President Wilson in his War Message, could be limited in their application. Henceforth, his words are going to be the war cry of all small and subject and oppressed nationalities in the world. He has conferred a new charter of democracy and liberty on the latter and the people of Asia are going to make as much use of this charter, if not even more, as are those of America and Europe.

American participation in the war had thrown "the Imperial Powers of Europe into the shade," and they would have no choice but to go along with Wilson's plan for the postwar international order.[55]

Not all Indian activists shared Lajpat Rai's optimism about Wilson's importance for the Indian struggle. One who did not was Narendra Nath Bhattacharya, who had been active in the revolutionary movement in Bengal before the war. After its suppression, he escaped India and eventually arrived in California in the summer of 1916. Wary of British agents, he adopted the name M. N. Roy, and later fled to Mexico, then in the midst of its own revolution, and remained there for the duration of the war.[56] In an open letter addressed to Wilson from Mexico in late 1917, Roy chastised Wilson for describing Indian unrest, in an address in June 1917, as German-inspired, and detailed the brutal nature of British rule in India. Wilson's proclamations in favor of democracy and freedom, he noted, were at odds with the U.S. support for Britain and France, whose oppressive colonial regimes in India and Indochina ran contrary to the president's calls for government by consent. Only "the complete liberation of all dominated peoples and countries, not only in Europe but also in Asia and Africa" would cure the world's ills, and Roy hoped that Wilson would find the sincerity and courage to implement his ideas there.[57] Roy clearly saw the implications of Wilson's rhetoric for the Indian national struggle, but his letter suggests that, perhaps influenced by his Mexican revolutionary contacts, he was skeptical of Wilson's commitment to Indian self-determination.

However they estimated Wilson's intentions, Indian home-rule campaigners incorporated his principles into their rhetorical arsenal as they redefined their own goals and adjusted their expectations and demands to keep pace with the transformation they perceived in the international arena. In the summer of 1918, when the British government published a report that laid out its plans for implementing the promise of the Montagu declaration for political reform, it became clear that Indian expectations now went far beyond the gradual reforms proposed in the report. By now, INC leaders and the nationalist press frequently were raising the call for "the immediate grant of self-determination to India," and they condemned the British report as "inadequate, unsatisfactory and disappointing."[58] In a pamphlet about the reform proposals, INC leader Pandit Madan Mohan Malaviya noted that since the war had been fought for the rights of small nations to control their own destinies, Britain could not now deny the people of India those same rights. What was now needed was the "introduction of a substantial measure of responsible government in India, which would mark a clear recognition of her higher status and also of the principle of self-determination."[59]

Most Indian intellectuals, moreover, did not share Roy's skepticism of U.S. intentions at the time. The credibility of Wilson's pronouncements was bolstered by the common perception of the United States as a society that reflected a more progressive version of Western modernity than the aggressive imperialism of the European great powers. The Bengali poet and Nobel Laureate Rabindranath Tagore, a trenchant critic of European imperialism, wrote in 1913 that the United States was "rich enough not to concern itself in the greedy exploitation of weaker nations" and was therefore free, and perhaps ready, to "hold up the torch of freedom before the world."[60] The United States was "the best exponent of Western ideals of humanity" and had the potential of achieving "some higher synthesis" of the best of both East and West and holding up "the banner of Civilization."[61] During the war, Tagore professed great admiration for Wilson himself and even wanted to dedicate his 1917 book, *Nationalism*, to the president. When his publisher wrote to Wilson to obtain his permission, however, Colonel House ruled against it since Tagore, his British contacts told him, was involved with Indian revolutionaries in the United States. When news of this accusation reached Tagore, he was outraged, writing Wilson a long letter to protest against such "lying calumny." Officials at the Department of State received the letter and shuffled it around, but Wilson probably never saw it.[62]

Wishing to see in the United States a potential path away from imperialism and racism and toward the unity of humankind, Indian and other anticolonial leaders and intellectuals were willing to downplay even the most glaring contradictions between Wilson's avowed principles and U.S. practices at home and abroad. Tagore, who made extensive lecture tours in the United States during the war, noted the rampant presence of racial prejudice in the United States, but believed that it would eventually be alleviated. America, Tagore wrote, was "the only nation engaged in solving the problems of race intimacy" and could eventually solve "the problems of the human race, national, political, religious" to bring about "the nationality of man." And as we have seen, Lajpat Rai, too, held a hopeful view of the future of race relations in the United States, comparing the conditions of African Americans in U.S. society favorably to those of the lower castes in Indian society and of Indians in general under British rule. The United States, Indian readers of his book on his experiences there would have learned, was not free of problems and contradictions, but the progress that it had made toward solving them could show the way for reform in India.[63]

Like other colonial nationalists, Indians also commonly held up U.S. colonial rule in the Philippines at the time not as a blemish on the American record but as a model, which the British would do well to follow. Already in 1916, a review of Lajpat Rai's book on the United States published in Tilak's nationalist weekly, *Mahratta*, recommended that every patriotic Indian, as well as British colonial officials, study the chapter in the book that dealt with U.S. rule in the Philippines as an example of colonial benevolence. The reviewer, no doubt wary of the censor, added that the point did not need further elaboration, since it was already very familiar to "our readers."[64] And shortly after the armistice, Lajpat Rai wrote Wilson that India should be granted "at least such progressive measures of Home Rule as the present administration has established in the Philippines." If the United States could prepare the uncivilized Filipinos for self-government in less than twenty years, so went a common refrain in the nationalist press at the time, how could the British claim that an ancient civilization such as India was unfit for it after a century and a half of British rule? Surely, such a claim reflected most poorly on the British themselves.[65]

When the armistice came, therefore, Indian expectations for the coming peace conference were high. In congratulatory telegrams to President Wilson and to the British government, which Lajpat Rai reproduced in his journal, *Young India*, he expressed the hope that the victory would be followed by the "immediate grant of autonomy to India and other countries under the rule of the Allies."[66] In the following issue, in January 1919, he published yet another appeal that he had sent directly to Wilson, in which he succinctly laid out his hopes that the president would take up the role of a liberator of colonial peoples at the peace table. "Your deep historical learning," he wrote, "equips you most fully to understand India's problem," and "your moral outlook, the farthest and noblest of our generation, assures us of your sympathy; your position, the most commanding in the world to-day, gives you the power, as you have the right, to protect all who suffer under alien and undemocratic rule."[67]

Shortly after the armistice, Ganesh & Co., a well-known nationalist press, prominently published a collection of Wilson's addresses under the title *President Wilson: The Modern Apostle of Freedom*. Advertisements for the book in leading Indian papers described the president as "the most striking personality in the world" and a "man of destiny," whose addresses, "one of the finest and sweetest fruits of the deadly war," would bring "hope to small and weak nationalities" and "a new spiritual vision of human progress."[68] The publisher clearly considered the Wilson volume one of the most attractive items on its list. In numerous advertisements that ran in the Indian press in early 1919 the book prominently headlined an impressive selection of patriotic publications, which included books with titles such as *India for the Indians*, *India's Claim for Home Rule*, and *Heroes of the Hour*, a volume of biographies of prominent nationalist leaders, including B. G. Tilak and Gandhi. "The eloquent addresses of this great inspiring apostle of Modern Freedom," one Indian reviewer of *President Wilson* exclaimed, "must find a place in every household of a true patriot" and would "enormously help the itinerant Home Rule propagandist to advocate, in sober but clear and emphatic terms, the cause of liberty before his countrymen."[69]

With the peace conference looming near, Lajpat Rai began reminding the readers of *Young India* of their nation's stake in the new international order by adopting a new motto, printed on the penultimate page of every issue beginning January 1919: "Europe is not the only place that is to be made safe for

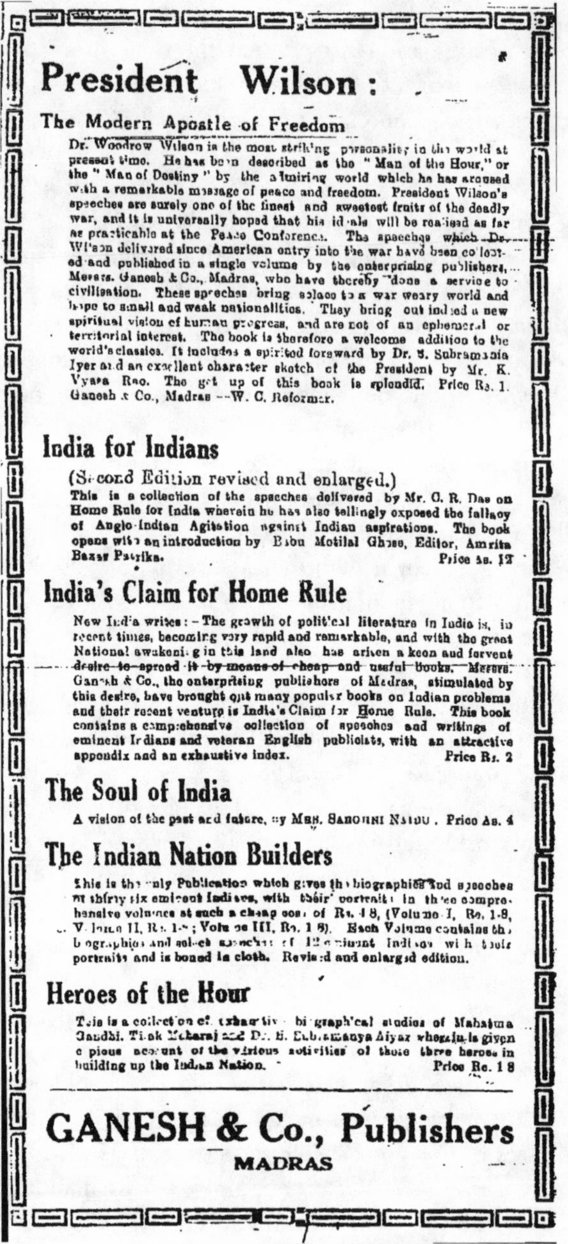

President Wilson:

The Modern Apostle of Freedom

Dr. Woodrow Wilson is the most striking personality in the world at present time. He has been described as the "Man of the Hour," or the "Man of Destiny" by the admiring world which he has aroused with a remarkable message of peace and freedom. President Wilson's speeches are surely one of the finest and sweetest fruits of the deadly war, and it is universally hoped that his ideals will be realised as far as practicable at the Peace Conference. The speeches which Dr. Wilson delivered since American entry into the war have been collected and published in a single volume by the enterprising publishers, Messrs. Ganesh & Co., Madras, who have thereby done a service to civilisation. These speeches bring solace to a war weary world and hope to small and weak nationalities. They bring out indeed a new spiritual vision of human progress, and are not of an ephemeral or territorial interest. The book is therefore a welcome addition to the world's classics. It includes a spirited foreward by Dr. S. Subramania Iyer and an excellent character sketch of the President by Mr. K. Vyasa Rao. The get up of this book is splendid. Price Rs. 1. Ganesh & Co., Madras.—W. C. Reformer.

India for Indians

(Second Edition revised and enlarged.)

This is a collection of the speeches delivered by Mr. C. R. Das on Home Rule for India wherein he has also tellingly exposed the fallacy of Anglo-Indian Agitation against Indian aspirations. The book opens with an introduction by Babu Motilal Ghose, Editor, Amrita Bazar Patrika. Price As. 12

India's Claim for Home Rule

New India writes:—The growth of political literature in India is, in recent times, becoming very rapid and remarkable, and with the great National awakening in this land also has arisen a keen and fervent desire to spread it by means of cheap and useful books. Messrs. Ganesh & Co., the enterprising publishers of Madras, stimulated by this desire, have brought out many popular books on Indian problems and their recent venture is India's Claim for Home Rule. This book contains a comprehensive collection of speeches and writings of eminent Indians and veteran English publicists, with an attractive appendix and an exhaustive index. Price Rs. 2

The Soul of India

A vision of the past and future, by Mrs. Sarojini Naidu. Price As. 4

The Indian Nation Builders

This is the only Publication which gives the biographies and speeches of thirty six eminent Indians, with their portraits in three comprehensive volumes at such a cheap cost of Rs. 4-8, (Volume I, Rs. 1-8, Volume II, Rs. 1-8; Volume III, Rs. 1-8). Each Volume contains the biographies and select speeches of 12 eminent Indians with their portraits and is bound in cloth. Revised and enlarged edition.

Heroes of the Hour

This is a collection of exhaustive biographical studies of Mahatma Gandhi, Tilak Maharaj and Dr. S. Subramanya Aiyar wherein is given a pious account of the various activities of those three heroes in building up the Indian Nation. Price Re. 1-8

GANESH & Co., Publishers

MADRAS

One indication of the popularity of Wilson's wartime addresses in India was a collection, entitled *President Wilson: The Modern Apostle of Freedom*, produced by the Madras publishing house Ganesh & Co. The volume, billed in this January 11, 1919, advertisement as "a welcome addition to the world's classics," headlined the publisher's list of patriotic publications. New India *(Madras), January 11, 1919, p. 11.*

democracy." To illustrate this vision in detail, the same issue also displayed on its first page a world map entitled "Here Are the Oppressed Nations of the World; What Will the Peace Conference Do for Them?" which showed the status of every territory in relation to the ideal of self-determination. The map designated East-Central Europe, Ireland, and practically all of Asia and Africa as "oppressed nations." China was described as "nominally independent, really dependent," and southern Africa was marked as "nominally republics. Whites free; natives dependent." India, together with Ireland, Korea, Southeast Asia (excluding Siam), and much of Africa was shaded black and marked simply as "dependencies."[70] The Indian struggle against Britain, the map clearly suggested, was an integral part of a global struggle against imperialism, a struggle in which the peace conference was now expected to play a pivotal role.

The Indian nationalist press often reminded is readers that India's expectations at the peace conference were intimately tied to the recent ascendancy of

HERE ARE THE OPPRESSED NATIONS OF THE WORLD; WHAT WILL THE PEACE CONFERENCE DO FOR THEM?

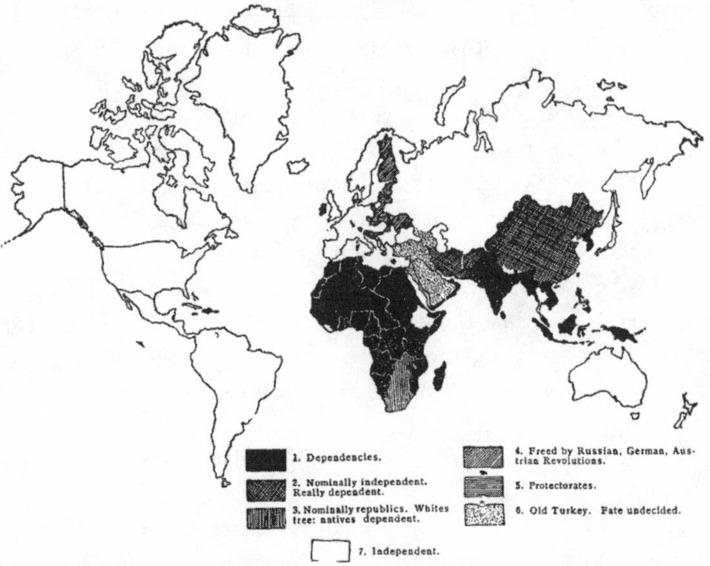

This map, which the India Home Rule League of America published in January 1919, illustrates how broadly many anticolonial nationalists viewed the mission of the peace conference in liberating dependent peoples. It includes nations that were nominally sovereign, like China, and those subjugated within other self-governing entities, like the native populations in the republics of southern Africa. Young India, *Vol. 2, No. 1 (January 1919), p. 2.*

the United States and its president in world affairs. If Wilson's declaration that the war was about "nothing but the freedom of nations, their right of self-determination" was to provide the basis for the conference, then England had "no other go but to frame her policy of governing India in accordance with them."[71] Some commentators noted with concern that Wilson's specific attitude toward Indian demands for self-determination remained unclear, and that the president never explicitly mentioned India in his calls for the establishment of democracy all over the world despite naming "petty States" such as Serbia and Romania as eligible for it. Perhaps this could be remedied if delegations of Indian leaders headed to England and America to "apprise the British and the American public of India's demands," wondered one writer.[72] Despite such uncertainties, however, on one thing there was general agreement: A window of opportunity was now open, and Indians had to stake their claim. "We should put forward our demands," declared another editorial. "It will be a sin if India does not lay her ailments before Dr. Wilson."[73]

In December 1918, when the Indian National Congress convened in Delhi for its annual session, it adopted a resolution that called for the application of the principle of self-determination to India. "In view of the pronouncements of President Wilson, Mr. Lloyd George, and other British statesmen, that to ensure the future peace of the world, the principle of Self-Determination should be applied to all progressive nations," the INC demanded that India be recognized by the powers as "one of the progressive nations to whom, the principle of self-determination should be applied." The Congress further urged that elected delegates represent India at the peace table, and it proceeded to nominate Tilak, Gandhi, and the Muslim leader Syed Hasan Imam as its delegates to the conference.[74] Other organizations involved in the home-rule movement, such as Annie Besant's All-India Home Rule League, also joined in the call, congratulating the British sovereign on the Allied victory and demanding as "absolutely essential" the immediate implementation of home rule in India.[75]

The Muslim League, too, though established in 1906 as a counterweight to the Hindu-dominated INC and hitherto generally a staunch supporter of the Raj, now declared in favor of Indian self-determination. "In view of the announcements of President Wilson and the British and Allied Statesmen... India's right to Self-Determination [should] be recognised by the British government and the Peace Conference," and India should have the "immediate opportunity of freely exercising that right." The league also welcomed the proposal to establish a League of Nations for deciding international questions through arbitration and urged that India receive its proper place in it. "The rights of the non-White races," it added, should receive equal consideration at the hands of the League of Nations "as those of the White races."[76] This Muslim demand for racial equality in the League of Nations reflected not only concern for the international rights of India. It also echoed the rising indignation among Indian Muslims about the rumors that the victorious European powers intended to dismantle the Ottoman Empire and dethrone the sultan in Istanbul, whom many Indian Muslims saw as the symbolic head of the Islamic world.[77]

British officials were gravely concerned about the effect that U.S. influence at the peace table would have on the future of British rule in India. It would be very difficult for the British, Montagu had noted even before the armistice, not to "fall in line" with the U.S. program at the war's end given Wilson's preponderant power. "We have been so long accustomed to dictate to the world... our position," he wrote, that it was "rather galling now that we find ourselves playing second fiddle to the autocratic ruler of the United States."[78] Privately, Montagu thought that Britain would eventually have to move India toward significant self-government, but he still rejected as extreme the INC demands that its elected delegates represent India in Paris. In the Congress, he wrote to the viceroy, there was no longer, as there had been before the war, a division between moderates and extremists. Now, there were only "Extremists and super-Extremists," since both factions wanted to move much further, and much faster, toward self-government than the British were willing to concede.[79] Chelmsford, who was more conservative than Montagu was and unenthused even about mild reforms, was quick to agree that the session in Delhi was an unqualified triumph for the most extreme elements in the Congress.[80]

In India, as in Egypt, then, the battle lines between the empire and its nationalist opponents were drawn by the time the peace conference began meeting in Paris in January 1919. For nationalist leaders, the gathering in Paris presented an opportunity they could not miss for advancing their cause. They hoped that Wilson's influence there, and his apparent determination to reconstruct the world according to the principles of self-determination and the equality of nations, would force the hand of the British and other imperialists and compel them to give their colonial possessions, if not complete independence, then at least a much greater measure of self-government. British officials, on the other hand, remained determined to prevent any discussion of issues related to their empire at the peace conference, where the United States and its president could meddle with them. Wilson, they would all soon discover, was neither as powerful in Paris nor as committed to the universal application of self-determination as his popular image suggested.

5

China's Place among Nations

As the Great War ended in November 1918, many Chinese, too, contemplated the opportunities that the postwar world would hold. Though China was not ruled by any one power, its sovereignty was severely circumscribed by a web of unequal arrangements with foreign powers. China had become, as Lala Lajpat Rai's map frankly put it, a "nominally independent, really dependent" state, and like Egyptians and Indians, Chinese nationalists looked to the U.S. president to usher in a new era of international equality. Wilson, wrote the veteran journalist Hollington K. Tong, respected both abroad and at home, was "the best qualified statesman to assume the role of champion of human rights generally and of the rights of China in particular." Tong informed his readers that Wilson was equal to the task, quoting the impressions of a former Chinese prime minister:

> [President Wilson] is a wonderful man, having a firm grasp of the world situation and knowing exactly how to deal with it. That is why he is to-day heading the movement to make the world safe for democracy. President Wilson is kind hearted in dealing with a weak and oppressed nation; just in his relationship with a strong power; and extremely severe in his treatment of predatory countries. I have not met him, but his picture as thrown on the screen or shown in the magazines—serene, resolute, fearless, and yet gentle, reasonable and friendly—shows that he is not a man who temporises. On the contrary, he is spiritual, fair-minded and firm in his determination.[1]

This image of Wilson was widespread in China at the time. During the war, the Chinese-language press published Wilson's important speeches, often verbatim, and their credibility was buttressed, as among Egyptians and Indians, by an indulgent view of the United States and its motivations. When a major Shanghai daily reproduced the full text of the Fourteen Points in January 1918, it appended an editorial comment reflecting this exceptionalist view. The U.S. president's ideas for peace were "a beacon of light for the world's peoples." The United States already had enough economic and military resources to become the most powerful nation in the world, and therefore Wilson could not be promoting these ideals for ulterior motives. He had only the good of the world in mind.[2] Another writer lamented that China had suffered through countless civil wars and political turmoil during the past three thousand years, and not once did a Chinese visionary raise a notion akin to Wilson's ideal of permanent peace. Chinese politicians should, therefore, abandon their struggle for power and personal gain and instead work to create a society ruled by law.[3] This was a dig at China's corrupt, squabbling political class; as we will see, other writers took a different tack, locating Wilson's ideas on world peace squarely within Chinese tradition and even comparing them to those of Confucius.

Unlike in territories under the direct control of other Allied powers, in China George Creel's Committee on Public Information did launch direct propaganda operations, though only in the last months of the war. The CPI's foreign propaganda efforts were initially concentrated in the European arena, and the U.S. minister in Beijing,[4] Paul S. Reinsch, along with several resident American journalists, complained to Washington that all the news about the United States was coming to China through the British agency Reuters and its Japanese ally, the Kokusai news agency. They felt that their reporting, though not unfavorable to the United States, did not sufficiently highlight the American contributions to the war effort and the president's vision for the postwar world. At first, Reinsch and the CPI tried to fix the problem cheaply by using Reuters to distribute copy from the CPI wireless service. That method, however, was soon judged to be inadequate, and in the summer of 1918, Creel authorized the establishment of a full-fledged CPI branch in China.[5]

In order to compete with the direct subsidies that the British, French, and Japanese propaganda operations paid to Chinese-language newspapers to print their materials, the CPI concluded that the United States needed its own news service, which would employ Chinese journalists and solicit Chinese-language newspapers as clients.[6] Reinsch obtained the necessary funds from Washington in June 1918, and the CPI recruited Carl Crow, a veteran China hand and former muckraking journalist, to lead its China branch.[7] Upon arrival in Shanghai, Crow began by studying the British propaganda operation there. The British consulate in the city had set up its own Chinese-language paper to publish British war news and had pressured British businesses to pull their advertising from the Chinese papers and move it to their official gazette instead. This method, Crow concluded, was "stupid," since the British paper, as a quasi-official organ, had little credibility with Chinese readers. In addition, the operation antagonized the local Chinese press by cutting into its advertising revenues.[8]

Crow decided to do things differently. Rather than setting up his own organ, he would translate American news dispatches and offer them to the Chinese press. Charging a nominal fee for the service, he decided, rather than providing it free of charge, would help present it as "real" news rather than propaganda. The Chinese-American News Agency, also known as the

Zhong-Mei News Agency, was established under CPI's aegis that fall. The news dispatches, broadcast by the U.S. Navy to the French wireless station in Shanghai, were translated into Chinese, and by October, the agency was supplying news and articles to dozens of Chinese-language newspapers. "American news," Crow boasted, "now predominates in the Chinese papers, and this American agency... is now supplying the bulk of foreign news and comment published in the Chinese press."[9] It was a wide field: In 1919, there were some three hundred daily newspapers in China. Not everyone, of course, could read them, since only about ten percent of the Chinese population was fully literate at the time. This group, however, represented the most influential segment of public opinion.[10]

The print medium, moreover, was only one venue for CPI propaganda. Borrowing from the techniques of American election campaigns, Crow ordered some twenty thousand large photographs of Wilson to distribute and display in sympathetic institutions such as missionary schools, as well as buttons and engravings sporting the president's image.[11] He recruited hundreds of volunteer agents throughout China, usually representatives of American corporations or Christian missionaries, who helped to distribute CPI news summaries, newsreels, posters, maps, and other materials. Window and wall posters were plastered on the local branches of American companies, such as Standard Oil, Singer Sewing Machine, and British-American Tobacco, and in churches and schools. Crow also compiled mailing lists of some twenty-five thousand prominent Chinese—intellectuals, local politicians, officials, and business leaders—to whom he sent articles and pamphlets extolling the progress and successes of American society and industry. In order to achieve the maximum impact, Crow had the texts, selected from the stock of CPI propaganda material, rendered in the literary Chinese idiom that would appeal to such a well-educated audience.[12] In addition, American propaganda movies, such as *Pershing's Crusaders*, were shown in Shanghai and other Chinese cities, though the audiences seemed to include many more foreign residents than native Chinese.[13]

For the CPI efforts in China, as elsewhere, Wilson's wartime speeches served as central texts. Already in mid-1917, more than a year before CPI operations in China officially began, Reinsch had recruited missionary volunteers to translate the speeches into Chinese so they could be distributed to the press or published in pamphlet form. Later, shortly after the armistice, Crow arranged the publication of the full texts of Wilson's wartime speeches translated into Chinese and used the royalties to advertise the volume widely.[14] The venerable Commercial Press in Shanghai published two editions of the book: one in Chinese translation only and a second, more costly edition containing both the original English texts and their Chinese translations side by side. The collection was widely advertised in the Chinese-language press as a "must-read book" for everyone who wanted to know "how the world's most important problems are to be settled." The volume became something of a best seller, going through several printings.[15]

The English-language Shanghai weekly *Millard's Review*, in its November 23 issue, reported this publishing event on its front page:

> One of the most timely publications of the hour is an edition of President Wilson's principal War Addresses which has just been issued by the Commercial Press of Shanghai. They have printed in one volume all of the addresses in which President Wilson interpreted the Allied policy and laid down the principles on which a permanent peace could be secured. One edition contains these addresses in Chinese with explanatory notes and the other edition, which is intended for use in Chinese schools, contains the addresses in both Chinese and English. The translation was done by Mr. Monlin Chiang [Jiang Menglin], who has done the work so well that little of the eloquence of President Wilson's utterances have been lost in the Chinese version. If the Chinese are to understand the causes of the Great War which has just ended they will find this understanding through reading the addresses of President Wilson.

The writer recommended that Americans in China purchase these books as gifts for Chinese friends.[16]

Crow attributed the volume's success partly to his vigorous advertising, but added that the book would have probably done well in any case because the "Wilsonian philosophy" had great appeal for the Chinese "who, while utilitarians in practice, take great pleasure in discussions of high ideals and finely spun theories of ethical conduct." Crow sent the volume directly to his mailing list of influential Chinese, with a cover letter suggesting that, if readers wished to communicate with President Wilson, they should send their messages to Crow, and he would have them translated and relayed to the president. Some five thousand letters soon poured in, expressing "an air of confidence in the future, a faith in the idea that President Wilson's words would prevail and that China, as well as all other oppressed nations, would be liberated." Many also wrote to order more copies of the book. The powerful warlord Feng Yuxiang, a convert popularly known as the "Christian General," bought five hundred copies, which he distributed among his officers as required reading.[17] Some missionary schools used the bilingual edition, which printed the original English text side by side with the Chinese translation, as a textbook for English instruction. By the time the peace conference in Paris opened in January, many Chinese students could recite the Fourteen Points by heart.[18]

Thus, when Crow reported that the U.S. president had become "one of the idols of the Chinese" and "the most popular and revered man in China," it was not entirely the empty boast of a seasoned ad man.[19] The CPI's efforts to disseminate Wilson's message in China, moreover, were helped by the dominance of pro-Allied news agencies, especially Reuters, in supplying international news to the Chinese press. With Reuters as the primary source of international news for the vast majority of Chinese readers during the war, most of the news items that they read were sympathetic to the Allied cause. At the same time, the Bolsheviks and their revolution, which might have competed with Wilson for the attention of Chinese intellectuals trying to discern the direction of international developments and the opportunities they held for China, appeared through the Reuters lens as anarchic and menacing. Though interest in socialist ideas in general was common among Chinese intellectuals even before the war, it was not until the consolidation of the Bolshevik regime in Russia and the beginnings of the outreach efforts of the Third International in the early 1920s that Chinese nationalists began to look to Lenin for inspiration and assistance.[20]

In the fall of 1918, Chinese interest was still focused squarely on the American president and his plans for the postwar world, especially as Allied victory grew imminent and news arrived that Wilson's Fourteen Points would serve as the basis for peace. Upon the announcement of the armistice, the Beijing government declared a three-day celebration and some sixty thousand people took part in the victory parade in the city. Participants carried signs calling for the world to be made "safe for democracy," and throngs of students gathered in front of the American embassy to chant: "Long live President Wilson!"[21] Over the following weeks, the fanfare of Wilson's arrival in Europe was reported in the Chinese press on a daily basis and in detail.[22] A Western journalist reported that an "intelligent Chinese gentleman" in Shanghai told him that "all the Chinese in Shanghai are greatly excited over President Wilson's speech on the fourteen principles on which peace is to be based." When the journalist noted that Wilson's points referred to Europe, his Chinese interlocutor countered that this did not matter since "the principle is there."[23] Pictures of George Washington, Abraham Lincoln, and Woodrow Wilson were on display in many schools in the city, and Lincoln and Wilson especially were "well known among the students of China, and by many . . . ranked above their own heroes and leaders."[24] The British minister in Beijing, Sir John Jordan, reported that the Chinese were eager to use the opportunity to carve a place in the world for their country: "They are waiting for a sign from the allies as to whether their declared principles will be applied to China."[25]

China in 1919 was not under the colonial rule of a single power, as Egypt and India were. Since the mid-nineteenth century, however, a growing list of foreign powers had inflicted upon it a long string of defeats and humiliations and increasingly encroached on and diminished its sovereignty. China's defeats

A crowd in Beijing celebrated the announcement of the armistice in November 1918 with banners that carried Wilsonian slogans. They proclaimed support for a League of Nations and for making the world "safe for democracy." *Sidney Gamble Collection, Rare Book, Manuscript, and Special Collections Library, Duke University.*

in the First (1839–1842) and Second (1858–1860) Opium Wars resulted in a series of "unequal treaties" that gave foreign powers—Britain, France, the United States, and somewhat later Russia, Germany, and Japan—increasing control over Chinese trade, industry, resources, and infrastructure, as well as of patches of territory in designated "treaty ports" and around mining and rail concessions.

After the ruling Qing dynasty barely escaped collapse in the great Taiping Rebellion of 1851–1864, a group of reform-minded officials launched a "self-strengthening" program that sought to empower the Chinese state by adopting Western techniques, first in arms manufacturing and later in other branches of industry and communications. This approach, however, suffered a serious blow when China lost a war against France in 1884–1885 and was finally exposed as an utter failure when, to the horror of Chinese officials, their new army and navy were crushed by a rising Japan in the Sino-Japanese war of 1894–1895.[26]

This humiliating defeat by a people whom Chinese elites had long considered to be inferior was a significant turning point. When they learned the terms of the Treaty of Shimonoseki, imposed by Japan at the war's end, a group of several thousand young literati submitted a long memorial to the throne to protest its terms and urge the implementation of a series of economic and administrative reforms to strengthen the state.[27] It was, historian Andrew J. Nathan has noted, the first instance in which significant elements of Chinese society outside the official bureaucracy "began to claim a regular right to influence government policies" on a national level, constituting an incipient public opinion concerned with both domestic and international affairs.[28] At the same time, telegraph technology spread across China, and the burgeoning press printed increasingly up-to-date news, both national and international, in tandem with the expansion of literacy beyond the official classes.[29] Though the literate audience still represented a small percentage of the overall population, it was a far broader and more diverse group than ever, comprising not only intellectuals and university students but also members of the expanding mercantile and professional middle classes. They became a nationally aware, articulate public interested in questions of foreign relations and China's position in the world.[30]

The imperial bureaucracy ignored the protest memorial, but the group's leader, the accomplished Confucian scholar Kang Youwei, continued his campaign for reform. By 1898, Kang, who came from a prominent family of scholar-officials from the southern Guangdong Province, had managed to convince the young Guangxu emperor to issue a series of edicts promulgating reforms similar to those Kang and his group had advocated in 1895. Conservative elements in the court, however, soon quashed the experiment, known as the "Hundred Day Reform." The young emperor was sidelined, and the intellectuals and bureaucrats who had supported the reforms were either arrested and executed or forced to flee. Kang barely managed to escape to Japan, as did his most prominent student and supporter, Liang Qichao.[31] The imperial court finally implemented some reforms after the failed Boxer Uprising against foreign encroachment in 1900, but failed to satisfy those who were now calling for a more radical approach: not reform, but revolution. To many of the revolutionaries, the Qing emperors were foreign tyrants responsible for China's backwardness and its failure to achieve "wealth and power."[32] In 1905, several revolutionary groups joined to form the Revolutionary Alliance under Sun Yat-sen, China's future "Father of the Nation," a Christian convert who was educated in British Hong Kong and had spent much of his life abroad as an itinerant revolutionary.[33]

The dynasty finally fell to a military insurrection in late 1911, and China became a republic in early 1912. However, Sun and his band of revolutionaries, now known as the Guomindang (Kuomintang), or Nationalist party, failed to hold national power for long. Yuan Shikai, a top general under the Qing, seized control of the Beijing government, and Sun established a rival government in the southern city of Guangzhou (Canton) in his home province of Guangdong, supported by the local military commanders. Control of much of the rest of China fell to numerous regional warlords. At the same time, new cultural, social, and intellectual trends spread, and the rapidly expanding press, which had been instrumental in setting the stage and defining the aims of the 1911 revolution, continued to play a central role in the nationalization and politicization of China's literate, educated elites.[34] The widening horizons of educated Chinese shaped a new consciousness of both national and international spaces, and the spread of nationalism among Chinese elites at the time marked a shift from the traditional perception of China as *the* civilization—"China as the world"—to imagining it as one of numerous, notionally equivalent "national" units: "China in the world," aspiring to become an equal member in the family of nations.[35]

For many Chinese, the United States appeared to hold a unique position within this world of nations, and the political classes of the fledgling republic generally held a positive, though not uncritical, view of the United States. The American record toward China was not unblemished. Chinese had long deplored and protested the ill treatment and exclusion in the United States of Chinese migrants, which had already in 1905 led to a movement to boycott U.S. goods. The U.S. conquest of the Philippines, too, was well known in China and often criticized by Chinese writers. Even here, however, the tone was sometimes ambivalent, with criticism of U.S. practices framed in the context of perceptions of the country's high ideals and relative benevolence. Discussing U.S. rule in the islands, Kang Youwei wrote that if even the United States, with its long tradition of "equality" and "justice," could do such things, what could one expect of other imperialist powers?[36] The United States, went another analysis, was a colonial power, but it had far fewer colonies than did others, ruled them more liberally, and did not depend on them economically; therefore, it could remain a plausible champion of colonial freedom.[37]

Chinese intellectuals often cited the American Revolution and American political and economic institutions as models for China. In addition, they thought that the United States under Wilson, alone among the major powers, wanted to help the nascent Chinese republic overcome decades of defeat and humiliation and achieve a position of respect in the international community.[38]

The rhetoric and policies of the Wilson administration seemed to bear out this view. In March 1913, only two weeks after taking office, Wilson hailed the "awakening of the people of China to a consciousness of their possibilities under free government" as "the most significant, if not the most momentous event of our generation." When, in order to attract foreign support for his fledgling regime, Yuan Shikai publicly asked Christians in the United States to pray for China, Wilson and his cabinet responded with unbridled enthusiasm.[39] Several years later, as the Wilsonian rhetoric of self-determination and the equality of nations echoed around the globe, this view of the United States and of Wilson in particular as friends of China bolstered the president's credibility among Chinese nationalists.

By the time of the armistice, then, the mood among Chinese opinion leaders was one of excitement and anticipation. China had declared war on Germany in August 1917, after a long and contentious internal debate, in the hope that joining the winning side would improve its international status, and though the country saw little combat it contributed some 200,000 laborers to the Allied war effort in the European theater.[40] Now that the war was won, they hoped, the powers would no longer treat China as a second-class citizen in international society. The feuding governments in Beijing and Guangzhou, though they agreed on little else, both saw the moment as one of opportunity, and newspapers across the country carried editorials in praise of the new international order and its prophet. A Guangzhou newspaper exclaimed that "during the present time, no words of any person would carry such great weight" as those of President Wilson, and in Beijing, the recently inaugurated president of the republic, Xu Shichang, called on his countrymen "to help realize the consummation of President Wilson's scheme of world peace."[41]

Many leading Chinese intellectuals saw an unprecedented opportunity for China in the coming world settlement. Cai Yuanpei, president of Beijing University and one of the most influential intellectual figures of the period, welcomed the armistice as marking the end of the age of inequality and the coming of a new era of openness in international affairs.[42] His colleague Chen Duxiu, dean of letters at the university, wrote at the time that the American president stood poised to transform the nature of international affairs. Chen, who a few years later would cofound the Chinese Communist party with Li Dazhao, explained that the meaning of Wilson's principles was the triumph of right over might, both in relations between states and in relations between peoples and their governments; this was the connection between domestic and international progress that colonial leaders like Zaghlul and Lajpat Rai, and Wilson himself, also saw as crucial. For his achievement, Chen hailed the president as the "number one good man in the world."[43] Even the veteran reformist Liang Qichao, a prolific and influential public intellectual who had long been skeptical of America's good will toward China, was caught up in the spirit of the time. Allied victory, he wrote, would augur a "new age" and help bring about "permanent peace for the world."[44]

Perhaps the most ardent Wilsonian among China's intellectual leaders was Hu Shi, a philosopher and educator best known as the foremost champion of Chinese literary reform, who called on intellectuals to abandon the classical style and write in a more accessible, spoken idiom. Hu, a Shanghai native, received a classical Chinese education before traveling to the United States to continue his studies. He graduated from Cornell University and went on to receive a Ph.D. from Columbia University, where he studied under the celebrated pragmatist philosopher John Dewey, who was a strong supporter of Wilson during the war. Hu, who believed passionately in the classical Confucian ideal of the scholar-official who combined high principles with practical politics, thought that Wilson could achieve that ideal on a global scale. The American president was a man who made "philosophical ideas the basis of politics, so that although he enters into the political arena, he maintains his uprightness and stresses humane principles in all things." Indeed, Hu's admiration for the president's "idealistic" and "humanitarian" approach to politics was such that he characterized Wilson, in a phrase that unintentionally echoed Rabindranath Tagore's view of the United States, as "the supreme product of Western civilization."[45]

Kang Youwei, the leader of the reform movement in the 1890s, was also fascinated by the possibilities of the moment. Early in the war, Kang had believed that Germany would win, and advocated that China should remain neutral, since it was too weak to gain anything from joining the fray.[46] By the time of the armistice, however, Kang had grown intrigued with the potential of Wilson's peace plan, especially Wilson's plan for the League of Nations. The league, he thought, would unite all of humanity under its covenant, and thus promote the realization of the traditional Confucian notion of *datong*, a utopian vision of universal peace, on which Kang had elaborated in a manuscript he had written some years earlier.[47] This connection was hardly unique to Kang, and other Chinese who wrote about the League of Nations at the time also typically rendered it into Chinese using the term *datong*. Kang believed that through Wilson's global leadership, his own *datong* vision could now be on the verge of fulfillment. The United States had "achieved a great victory, and sponsored a peace conference based on right and justice," where it "would support the weak and small countries." China should consider itself fortunate to participate in this conference, an opportunity "of one thousand years" to recover its lost sovereignty and to achieve equality among nations. "I have never dreamed of the good luck to see the formation of a League of Nations in my own days," Kang wrote to his son-in-law in early 1919. "The impossible is about to happen. You can't imagine my happiness."[48] Thus, Kang and others hoped that Wilson's vision would transform the conduct of international

Veteran reformer and scholar Kang Youwei believed that the world in 1919 was on the cusp of far-reaching transformation. He likened Wilson's plan for a League of Nations to the traditional Confucian ideal of *datong*, or universal peace. *Library of Congress*.

relations and bring about, through the League of Nations, a just and peaceful community of nations in which China would be an equal member.

Chinese students living and studying abroad were among the loudest voices advocating for China in the international arena. Intensely political and closely attuned to world affairs, overseas student groups swung into action as the peace conference drew near. A number of Chinese student organizations in Britain and France, for example, addressed a lengthy petition to Wilson upon his arrival in Europe, making clear that the president's principles would have to apply universally, rather than be limited to a specific geographic region. Since "the principles of humanity and justice for which the allies have fought are now securely established," issues relating to European and non-European matters alike should be resolved according to "the principles of self-determination and the right of every nation, great or small, to work out its own destinies unmolested. East or West, the same doctrines must hold good." The United States, therefore, must support China's claims at the peace conference. Only this would bring about the "millennium," when China, the United States, and all the other countries would "join hands in true brotherhood in the onward march of civilization." Echoing a common notion among Chinese intellectuals—and, more generally, among Asian intellectuals at the time—the petition called the League of Nations a "meeting point of the Western and Eastern civilization" and therefore a sound basis for a comprehensive world peace.[49]

Even at the height of Wilson's popularity in Chinese public opinion, some remained skeptical. Li Dazhao, the head librarian at Beijing University, who a few years later would co-found the Chinese Communist party together with Chen Duxiu, had earlier praised the American president for "his deep love of world peace."[50] But by late 1918 he was far more impressed with the rise of Bolshevism in Russia and, it seemed at the time, elsewhere in Europe, and saw Lenin, not Wilson, as the true visionary of the future. Li was critical of his compatriots' celebration of the war as a victory of the Allied powers over Germany. It was not, he argued, Allied power that had defeated German militarism, but rather the power of the German people and German socialism. Victory, therefore, belonged not to Wilson but to revolutionary leaders like Lenin and Trotsky, Karl Liebknecht and Philipp Scheidemann.[51] Over the next several months, the cutting-edge literary magazine *New Youth* published a number of articles, most of them authored by Li himself, which analyzed various aspects of Marxist theory or offered translations of key Marxist texts. Still, though Li celebrated the spread of socialism in Europe and predicted that "the world of the future" would be "a world of red flags," he did not yet relate these developments explicitly to the future of China.[52]

Li's position on these issues, however, remained at the time at the margins of Chinese public discourse. For the mainstream Chinese press and the great majority of opinion leaders, Wilson, not Lenin, was the world figure who appeared to offer the most promising path for China's future in international affairs.[53] Wilson seemed to offer China an escape from the Darwinian logic that had dictated China's relationship with the world in the previous decades. In the prewar period, many intellectuals in China and elsewhere thought of international relations as an arena of Darwinian struggle in which only the "fittest" nations would survive. This logic had propelled the reform efforts designed to bring China "wealth and power," so that it could compete and win in the struggle for national survival. As Chinese opinion leaders were painfully aware, however, China had done poorly in this arena, and the removal of the Qing dynasty and the establishment of a republic had failed to change its course. Wilson's principles offered an escape from this dilemma, since they stated that, as a matter of right, all nations, "those that are powerful and those that are weak," should be equal in international affairs. Wilson had said that the postwar settlement must reflect "the principle of justice to all peoples and nationalities and their right to live on equal terms of liberty and safety with one another, whether they be strong or weak."[54] If this were so, and full international sovereignty and equality were no longer a prize to be won or a privilege to be earned but a basic right that any nation could claim, China would no longer have to wait until it was strong and prosperous in order to enjoy it. It could do so immediately.

Such expectations among Chinese for a revolutionary transformation of international affairs left Paul Reinsch, the American minister in Beijing, with a growing sense of trepidation. Before his appointment to Beijing, he had been a professor of political science at the University of Wisconsin at Madison, a leading expert on international affairs in East Asia, and among the founders, together with Woodrow Wilson himself, of the American Political Science Association. A devout Christian and long-standing critic of European imperialism on moral grounds, he believed strongly in the righteousness of the Wilsonian mission in the world, and in China in particular, and in his public declarations he remained steadfast in promoting the Wilsonian gospel in China.[55] "Perhaps in all the world," he told a Chinese journalist around the time of the armistice, "President Wilson is the only man who will raise a strong voice in pleading for international justice and individual rights. . . . I am proud that I work in China chiefly because of the propagating of the gospel which I rightly call 'Wilsonism.' "[56]

In his correspondence with Washington, however, Reinsch sounded notes of alarm. Wilsonian principles, he reported, had "found a deep response throughout China" and entered "deeply and directly into the hearts of the Chinese people."[57] As a result, the Chinese were pinning their hopes on Wilson and the United States to help them erase the humiliations of the past and to gain acceptance and equality among nations. Should these hopes be disappointed, he warned Wilson, the consequences would be dire:

> The eager attention which has been paid to your words, the trust and confidence which the Chinese feel in your policies and aims, are evidence of a spontaneous desire to follow along the path of American action and aspiration which you have made so clear to the world. If China should be disappointed in her confidence at the present time, the consequences of such disillusionment on her moral and political

> development would be disastrous, and we instead of looking across the Pacific towards a Chinese Nation sympathetic to our ideals would be confronted with a vast materialistic military organization under ruthless control.[58]

Reinsch knew that many U.S. officials, including Wilson himself, harbored a genuine if somewhat condescending sense of sympathy toward the young Chinese republic. He was clearly worried, however, that its problems and hopes would receive low priority compared to the pressing issues of Europe and in the face of competing U.S. interests in East Asia, particularly its relationship with the regional power, Japan. Achieving China's goals at the peace conference, he suspected, would prove more elusive than the heady mood of the moment implied.

As the Chinese prepared to stake their claim for a place in the new world order, they enjoyed a distinct advantage over other marginalized groups in the international arena. Koreans, Egyptians, Indians, Vietnamese, and many others who rushed to Paris to stake their claims were simply turned away at the gates of the peace conference, and their claims, petitions, and requests for audiences were rejected or ignored by its principals. China, on the other hand, seemed to have a much stronger position. As a sovereign state that had fought in the war on the Allied side, surely it would be entitled to reap the fruits of victory. For much of the war, Chinese diplomats had been worried that the powers would exclude China from the general peace conference and considered, as an alternative, proposing a separate conference that would deal only with the settlement of Far Eastern questions. In the last months of the war, however, when it appeared that President Wilson and his principles would dominate the peace conference, Chinese confidence in their chances for success in the negotiations increased substantially.[59]

Hoping that Wilson's leadership at the conference meant that a thoroughgoing revision of international practice was imminent, China's diplomats formulated far-reaching goals for China's participation in the peace conference, drawing up memoranda containing sweeping claims for the application of Wilson's ideals of self-determination and equality to China. They called for the abrogation of all of the unequal treaties that had been concluded with foreign powers and that abridged Chinese sovereignty. They proposed the phasing out of the system of extraterritorial jurisdiction, which exempted foreigners in China from prosecution by the local legal system. And they asked for the return to Chinese hands of leased territories and foreign concessions in Chinese railroads, mines, and communications. Such a restoration of China's sovereignty, territorial integrity, and economic independence, they argued in the documents they submitted to the conference, would fulfill "the great design set forth by President Wilson," which guaranteed "political independence and territorial integrity to great and small nations alike."[60] In the new world order, they expected nothing less.

The Chinese delegation in Paris comprised five plenipotentiary representatives and several dozen support staff, including advisers and secretaries. At its head was the Beijing government's foreign minister, Lu Zhengxiang. Lu, a veteran diplomat with long experience in foreign capitals, has sometimes been depicted as "a product of the classical training of the Chinese Empire" who represented the "conservative point of view" on the delegation. His background, however, was far removed from that of the traditional Chinese official.[61] Born in 1871 in Shanghai to a father who worked for Protestant missionaries, Lu was educated in special foreign-language schools in Shanghai and Beijing. In 1899, while working as an interpreter at the Chinese legation in St. Petersburg, he met and married a Catholic woman from Belgium, and in 1911, he joined the Roman Catholic church himself. An advocate of modernization, he supported the 1911 revolution, and, as minister to Russia, he was the first Chinese minister abroad to advise the emperor to abdicate. He then held a number of top posts in the new republican government, including foreign minister and, briefly, prime minister.[62] Lu was fluent in French and other European languages and believed fervently in China's need to modernize and join the family of nations.[63]

The other Chinese plenipotentiaries included Sao-Ke Alfred Sze (Shi Zhaoji), the minister in London and a graduate of Cornell University, and Suntchou Wei (Wei Chenzhou), the Chinese minister in Brussels. The two delegates who were most active and influential in Paris, however, were V. K. Wellington Koo (Gu Weijun), the youthful but highly regarded Chinese minister to Washington, and Chengting Thomas Wang (Wang Zhengting). Wang was close to the Guomindang regime in the south and was named to the delegation in order to present a united front in Paris and advance the efforts to achieve unity at home.[64] Though Koo and Wang represented rival regimes and frequently clashed personally, they shared similar aspirations for China's future and agreed on their overarching goal in Paris: the establishment of China as a fully sovereign, equal member of international society.

Koo was a rising star of China's diplomatic corps. Born into a prosperous family in Shanghai, he had studied at St. John's College, an American missionary school in the city, before moving to the United States to continue his education. Matriculating at Columbia University in New York City, he received a bachelor's degree in 1908 and a doctorate in international law in 1912, having studied under the renowned scholar John Bassett Moore. At Columbia, Koo was a master debater, a skill he would display when presenting China's case at the peace negotiations. Upon graduation, Koo was immediately recruited into the foreign service of the fledgling Chinese republic. By 1919, he had already

V. K. Wellington Koo (Gu Weijun), a Columbia Ph.D., was the Chinese minister to Washington and a leading member of China's peace commission in 1919. He was the most eloquent advocate for Chinese self-determination at the peace negotiations in Paris. *Library of Congress.*

become one of China's leading diplomats and had received honorary doctorates from both Yale and Columbia universities. Barely thirty-one years of age at the time of the conference, he was described by one American expert as "eloquent . . . polished, diplomatic, tactful, amiable, and of keen intelligence." Shortly before he left for Paris, Koo's wife died in the influenza pandemic that swept the globe in the fall of 1918, leaving him with two infant children. In his grief, he asked to resign his post, but stayed on at the urging of Beijing officials, who asked him to consider his country's need for his talents. Wang, too, had been educated in the United States. A 1910 graduate of Yale College with highest honors, he spoke English fluently "in the American manner."[65]

Despite—or perhaps due to—their cosmopolitan backgrounds, both Koo and Wang were ardent Chinese nationalists. Acculturated and accomplished in both the Chinese and Western worlds, they wanted to see China accepted as a full member of a broader international society in which they themselves moved comfortably, and imagined Wilson's League of Nations as the ideal vehicle to achieve this goal. In a pamphlet entitled *China and the League of Nations* that Koo and Wang coauthored during their time in Paris, Koo, echoing Kang Youwei's view of the league as embodying the classical Confucian ideal of *datong*, drew a parallel between Wilson and the ancient sage:

> Confucius saw, just as the illustrious author of the present League of Nations has seen, the danger to civilization and humanity involved in the continued existence of such a sad plight [of constant war], and therefore spared no effort in emphasizing the need of creating and preserving a new order of things which would ensure universal peace. Although his appeals to the princes and the people did not succeed in bringing about many concrete results in his own age, his ideals and principles have survived him from generation to generation, and been deeply inculcated on the minds of the Chinese people.[66]

Wilson's project of fashioning a more harmonious international order, Koo suggested, was in fact the culmination of thousands of years of Confucian teachings, and the establishment of a League of Nations would be the fulfillment of Confucian ideals.

From the outset, however, such aspirations came up against the realities of power and the persistence of the old international regime, dominated by the great powers. The first disappointment for China came at the preliminary discussions in Paris, when the great powers decided that it would have the status of a minor power. It could seat only two representatives at the conference plenary and would only participate in sessions that dealt with questions that directly concerned it. This, the Chinese delegates noted with dismay, put China, with its vast territory and population, on the same level as Greece, Poland, and Siam and below Brazil, Serbia, and Belgium, which received three seats each. The issue was merely symbolic, since the real decisions would be taken by the great powers and not in the plenary, but for the Chinese the symbolism was significant, since it meant that China would remain inferior at a forum that they had hoped would institute the recognition of their equality on the international stage.[67] The decision was even more insulting since Japan, China's nemesis in Asia and in Paris, was recognized as a great power, allotted five plenary seats, and invited to participate in all sessions of the conference.[68]

Internal conflict and dissension further exacerbated China's weakness in the international arena. The regime in Beijing was the internationally recognized government of China, but domestically its legitimacy was contested by Sun Yat-sen's rival government in Guangzhou. Its writ was limited to north and central China, and even there it was dependent on fragile alliances with numerous regional warlords. Xu Shichang, the new president who came into office in Beijing in October 1918, was determined to end the north-south split, and he called for an internal peace conference to restore national unity that would run in tandem with the international peace conference in Paris. The internal peace conference met intermittently in Shanghai from February until May 1919, but the possibility of success of the negotiations depended on the general atmosphere of optimism and possibility for China's international future in the immediate postwar months.[69] Intimately tied to China's struggle for self-determination in the international arena, the efforts at internal unity would not survive its failure.[70]

The factionalism and indecision that plagued their putative political masters left the peace delegates in Paris largely lacking clear instructions for shaping Chinese strategy at the conference.[71] This did not mean, however, that the delegates did not face external pressures in their work. In stark contrast to the feebleness of official Beijing, many Chinese civic groups both at home and abroad, some long-standing organizations and others established ad hoc, displayed passionate commitment and fiery activism on the issues related to China's goals at the peace conference. Chinese student groups overseas, notably in Britain, France, and the United States, led the charge, but other types of organizations also followed the negotiations closely and worked to influence their outcome: merchant associations, chambers of commerce, local and provincial assemblies in China, and a range of nationalist organizations in Chinese communities around the world. All frequently cited Wilson's principles and were anxious to see their implementation for China. They followed the news that emerged from the negotiating chambers and prodded the Chinese delegates to take a firm stand in demanding that China enjoy full sovereign rights under the new order.[72] At the same time, they sought to bring China's case before world opinion, producing a stream of petitions and pamphlets that explained China's position and demanded the application of the principles of self-determination and national equality to it. The Chinese delegates in Paris made frequent use of this public mobilization to show popular support for their demands, at one point producing and circulating a pamphlet that compiled some one hundred of the messages they had received from such Chinese organizations across the world.[73]

Many of the petitions warned the Chinese delegates to stand firm for China's rights. Others addressed the leaders of the great powers directly—Clemenceau, as president of the peace conference, Lloyd George, and, of course, Wilson himself. A typical text, signed by "the European and American returned Students of China," asserted that "during the period of the war there has grown up throughout the world a new sense of the equality of nations." This sentiment "has become more and more dominant," and "it is now axiomatic that the final peace treaty shall be framed so as to give the world, as far as is humanly possible, a just settlement."[74] Another petition, signed by a number of Chinese student organizations in Britain and France, called for "the establishment of a new international order" based on "the exalted ideas inspiring the immortal message of President Wilson."[75] In many of these texts, Wilson appears not as a flesh-and-blood politician but as a prophetic icon of the coming new era in international relations, with his words, often cited verbatim, serving as a central reference point in their articulation of China's rightful place in the international arena. One group of Chinese students in Britain established a League of Nations Society, complete with an elaborate charter stating its rules and goals, to study and promote the president's brainchild. The league, they emphasized, must not be "a League of great Nations with smaller Nations as satellites, but a League of all Nations with equality of rights before the Law."[76]

As the negotiations proceeded, such groups of patriotic Chinese kept a vigilant eye on developments. When Liang Qichao, the veteran reformer and public intellectual, arrived in Paris to observe the peace proceedings, some Chinese students in Europe were alarmed. Liang had spent many years in exile in Japan before the 1911 revolution and had ties with pro-Japanese factions in Beijing. Could he be an agent of pro-Japanese interests, sent to Paris to watch over the Chinese delegates and prod them to compromise? Leaders of the Chinese student union in the United Kingdom sent Liang a sharply worded message in February 1919, soon after his arrival, warning against such an attempt. The world, they reminded him, was now "completely different from that of the past." Russian and German "tyranny" had collapsed, and the "righteous United States" had, along with democratic Britain and France, established the League of Nations. Hereafter no treaties could stand that did not pass muster with the league, and the Chinese must do all in their power to advance their claims: "If this opportunity is lost, the political evils will be firmly established [with] no hope for repeal." They called on Liang to use his influence to convince public opinion that all previous Sino-Japanese treaties, which gave the Japanese various concessions in China, were unjust and had to be voided.[77] At the peace conference in Paris, Chinese nationalists demanded that the infrastructure of imperialism in China be dismantled and that China's full membership in the expanding family of nations be recognized. As winter turned to spring in 1919, they remained confident that, with the influence of President Wilson on their side, they would succeed.

6

Seizing the Moment in Seoul

In the spring of 1919, as Chinese nationalists in Paris and across the world worked in the international arena to establish China's place among nations, patriotic Koreans were also stirred to action. The Korean peninsula had been under increasingly oppressive Japanese rule since 1905, and during the war the censors tried to keep the language of self-determination out. But during the last months of the war, Koreans seized on Wilson and his principles as they began to contemplate the possibilities of the postwar world. As the peace conference began, they resolved to ensure that Korea would be part of the transformation that Wilson's declarations promised. On the morning of March 1, 1919, thirty-three prominent religious and civic leaders in Seoul gathered to sign a document they called Korea's Declaration of Independence. The declaration, which adopted Wilsonian language to assert Korea's right to liberty and equality within the world of nations, launched a broad popular movement against Japanese rule. Over the following months, more than a million people across the peninsula participated in demonstrations and protests for independence, which involved Koreans of every province, religion, education, age, and occupation. The March First movement, as it came to be known, was an unprecedented manifestation of Korean nationalism as a mass phenomenon, no longer limited to intellectual elites, and it marked a watershed in the evolution of the Korean movement.[1]

Unlike in Egypt, India, and China, the war had little direct impact on the population of the Korean peninsula. Koreans did not participate in the fighting in any sizable numbers, nor did the war cause them significant economic hardship. For the Japanese empire, of which Korea was a part, the war years were a period of relative prosperity and, indeed, opportunity. But if Japanese leaders wanted to use the war to expand Japan's power in Asia and raise its standing in world affairs, Korean nationalists hoped it would help them to throw off Japanese rule. Early in the war, when Japan declared war on Germany and launched attacks on German colonial possessions in Asia, some Korean nationalists, like their Chinese counterparts, entertained hopes that the Central Powers would win and so help Koreans throw off Japanese rule. After the United States entered the war, however, and especially after Korean nationalists learned of President Wilson's Fourteen Points address and his subsequent declarations, they adopted the Wilsonian vision of a new international order as an unprecedented opportunity for Korea to emerge—or to reemerge, as they saw it—as an independent, equal member in the expanding community of nations.

The March First uprising was the culmination of several decades of rapid political and social change in Korea, which followed its "opening" by Japanese forces in 1876. For centuries, the Korean peninsula had been largely isolated from the external world, with no formal relations with other states except for the annual tribute missions that the kings of the Yi (Choson) dynasty, in power since 1392, dispatched to the imperial court in Beijing to pay obeisance to the Son of Heaven.[2] By the mid-nineteenth century, the dynasty was in perceptible decline and peasant revolts broke out frequently in the outlying provinces, but the Korean court, which learned of China's difficulties with "Western barbarians" following its defeats in the Opium Wars, resolved to repulse any attempts at foreign encroachment. In 1866, when the *General Sherman*, an American trading vessel, attempted to sail upriver to Pyongyang, the local population attacked and burned it, killing all twenty-four members of its crew. In response, Washington ordered the U.S. Asiatic Squadron to dispatch an expeditionary force to retaliate for the outrage and incidentally to open Korea to American trade, as Commodore Matthew C. Perry had famously done in Japan in 1853. Five U.S. warships arrived on the Korean coast in 1871 but met with stiff resistance and eventually returned to their base in China without achieving their purpose.[3]

Such minor clashes notwithstanding, the Western powers paid little attention to Korea during this period, focusing their efforts of commercial expansion in the Far East on China. Thus, it was Japan rather than one of the Western powers that opened the "hermit kingdom" to the external world a few years later. Japan, then in the midst of the Meiji Restoration, sought opportunities for territorial and commercial expansion to build up its national power and prestige and saw Korea as a natural target. Taking a page from the British imperial playbook in Asia, the Japanese provoked a naval incident with Korean forces, and their victory in the ensuing conflict resulted in the conclusion of the Treaty of Kanghwa on February 22, 1876. The treaty, modeled closely on the unequal treaties that the Western powers had earlier forced on China and on Japan itself, opened several Korean ports to foreign trade and allowed for the establishment of extraterritorial Japanese settlements in those ports. Japan, seeking to pry the peninsula loose from its traditional place in the Chinese orbit, also inserted an article that declared Korea to be an independent nation possessing full sovereign rights.[4] The Japanese would ignore that declaration three decades later, when they annexed Korea to their expanding empire.

Beijing, concerned with the rise of Japanese power in its traditional sphere of influence, encouraged Seoul to seek bilateral treaties with the Western powers in order to balance them against Japan. The first such treaty was signed with the U.S. representative Commodore Robert W. Shufeldt in 1882, followed closely by treaties with Britain, Germany, Italy, Russia, France, and Austria. The 1882 U.S.-Korean treaty recognized Korean sovereignty and promised to provide the "good offices" of the United States if Korea became the target of the aggression of another nation, and in 1919 Korean nationalists demanding self-determination would cite these clauses in their appeals to Wilson.[5] Despite the recognition of Korean sovereignty that these treaties suggested, however, Korea remained an arena of contestation between foreign powers, especially China and Japan. In 1884, Chinese troops helped suppress a Japanese-supported reformist coup against the conservative Korean court, escalating Sino-Japanese tensions. The decade that followed also saw the growth of Russian influence there as the Romanov empire sought to expand eastward, as well as the arrival of Protestant missionaries, many of them American, who began to work in the peninsula around that time and would play significant roles in its subsequent history.[6]

Tensions reached a breaking point in 1894, when followers of Tonghak (literally "Eastern learning"), a syncretic religious movement that had recently emerged in the Korean countryside and combined elements of Eastern religions with Roman Catholicism, launched a popular uprising that threatened the stability of the Yi regime. The Tonghak uprising gathered force on the wave of peasant discontent with worsening economic conditions, corrupt officials, and foreign encroachment. Both China and Japan rushed significant military forces to the peninsula to protect their interests and extend their influence there. Fighting soon broke out between them, quickly escalating into a full-fledged war. Japan's decisive victory in 1895 put an end to centuries of Chinese suzerainty over Korea, though the intervention of European powers led by Russia frustrated Japanese attempts to wrest far-reaching concessions from China in the wake of the war. With China no longer a significant force in Korea, rising Russo-Japanese competition became a central feature of its politics for the next decade.

In 1896, soon after the Sino-Japanese war ended, a group of Western-educated Korean intellectuals and professionals established the Independence Club, the first Korean organization to espouse a recognizably modern nationalist ideology. Members of the club were frustrated with Korea's weakness in the face of increasing foreign pressures and advocated political and economic reforms along Western liberal lines in order to strengthen Korea against further encroachment and launch it on the path to modernity. The club's founder, Philip Jaisohn (Sŏ Chaep'il), was an early convert to Christianity and a veteran reformer who had been one of the leaders of the reformist coup attempt of 1884 and went into exile in the aftermath of its failure. Settling in the United States, Jaisohn studied medicine and eventually became a naturalized citizen by marriage, the first U.S. citizen of Korean extraction. Another prominent club member was Syngman Rhee, later the first president of the republic of South Korea from 1948 to 1960. Rhee, born in 1875 to a family of scholar-officials, studied the Confucian classics before entering an American missionary school in 1894.[7]

To help propagate the program of the Independence Club, Jaisohn founded a Korean-English bilingual newspaper, the *Independent* (Tongnip Sinmun). In the period between 1896 and 1898, the club and its paper advocated modernization and "self-strengthening" reforms in education, government, and the economy, citing both Japan and the United States as models for Korean development. Conservatives in the court, who feared that reforms would undermine their power, strongly opposed the club and its agenda and soon banned the club and its paper. Jaisohn left Korea once again for the United States, and Rhee was arrested and imprisoned for six years, during which he converted to Christianity. The Independence Club episode was similar in many respects to the contemporaneous "Hundred Days" reform movement in China, led by Kang Youwei, which also advocated modernizing reforms and which was suppressed in 1898 by court conservatives. The Korean movement, however, was more radical in its ideas and more directly influenced by Western, and specifically American, ideas of popular sovereignty and economic progress, which Jaisohn had absorbed during his time in the United States.[8]

By 1904, Russo-Japanese tensions finally exploded into full-scale and brutal war, often seen, with its widespread use of defensive trenches, barbed wire, and machine guns, as a dress rehearsal for World War I. Japan's surprising victory in the war cemented its power in Korea and increased its sway in China. But it also echoed more broadly in the colonial world, where many saw it as a challenge to Europe's claim to superior civilization, a claim that underlay the imperial order in international affairs. The sense of an "awakening East" that the victory produced helped spur the challenges that appeared around that time to the legitimacy of empire and its embedded assumptions of Western superiority. The Swadeshi movement in India, the founding of the National Party in Egypt, and the constitutional movements in China, Persia, and Turkey, all occurred within a few years of 1905.[9] But the Japanese victory, though it undermined the legitimating claims of Western imperialism in the eyes of colonial nationalists, offered no new levers or venues that could help them to challenge imperialism in practice. Efforts to adopt the Japanese model in order to construct stronger, wealthier, more "modern" societies, while potentially attractive, were long-term projects. And Japan itself—as an actual state rather than as a model—showed little interest in using its growing international clout to challenge the logic of the existing order. On the contrary, it strove to join it as an imperial power itself.

This was made plain in the Russo-Japanese negotiations to end the war, in which U.S. president Theodore Roosevelt provided his good offices as mediator. In the resulting Portsmouth Treaty, named after the Maine naval shipyard in which it was signed in September 1905, the Russians effectively recognized Korea as a Japanese protectorate. Korean groups in the United States tried to forestall the protectorate through diplomatic action, and expatriate organizations based in Hawaii collaborated to send emissaries to petition Roosevelt for the preservation of an "autonomous government" in Korea. Roosevelt gave the two emissaries—Syngman Rhee, recently released from prison in Korea, and P. K. Yoon (Yun Pyŏnggu), a Protestant minister—a hearing in New York City, but told them that he could do little to help them. If they wanted to attend the peace conference themselves, he said, they would have to take the matter up officially with the Korean minister in Washington. When they did, the minister pleaded a lack of instructions from Seoul and refused to take action.[10]

The Rough Rider later defended his failure to support the preservation of Korean independence despite the U.S. commitments in the U.S.-Korea treaty of 1882 by noting that, if Koreans were unable to protect their own independence, "it was out of the question to suppose that any other nation without any interest of its own at stake would attempt to do for the Koreans what they were unable to do for themselves." This statement of foreign policy realism would return to haunt him during the world war, when, as a fierce opponent of Wilson's neutrality policy, he exhorted the administration to intervene in the war immediately in order to defend the independence of Belgium, so callously trampled on by the Germans. Clearly, chuckled Wilson's supporters in the press as they compared this statement with his earlier one on Korea, Roosevelt had one standard for Belgium and another for Korea.[11]

In conjunction with its role in negotiating the Portsmouth Treaty, the Roosevelt administration, concerned with containing the rise of Japanese power in East Asia, also helped to secure Japanese control over Korea with the secret Taft-Katsura agreement, signed in July 1905. In the agreement, signed between William Howard Taft, who was then Roosevelt's secretary of war, and the Japanese prime minister, Katsura Taro, the United States effectively acknowledged Korea as a Japanese protectorate in return for Japanese recognition of its own rule over the Philippines. The U.S. legation in Seoul, along with the other foreign missions there, closed its doors soon after as the Japanese government took over the conduct of Korea's foreign relations, though the fact that the full text of the memorandum did not become public until 1922 helped keep alive the hopes of Korean nationalists for U.S. support. Koreans continued to argue that Roosevelt's recognition of the Japanese protectorate in Korea, as well as the Taft administration's subsequent recognition of Korea's annexation to the Japanese empire in 1910, contravened the 1882 U.S.-Korea treaty, which had recognized Korea as a sovereign state and promised American "good offices" in the case of aggression against Korea by a foreign power. The official position of the U.S. State Department, however, employed a piece of circular logic similar to Roosevelt's: once Korea ceased to be a sovereign state with the Japanese annexation, all previous treaty obligations that might have required the United States to defend its sovereignty became moot.[12]

The years after 1905 saw the rapid spread of nationalist consciousness and activities in Korea, as its people came under increasingly repressive Japanese rule. Armed groups engaged Japanese forces in guerrilla warfare in the countryside, while in the cities patriotic societies were established and then disbanded by the Japanese in quick succession. This period also saw a sharp rise in the activity and success of Protestant missionaries in Korea, mostly from the United States. Although the missionaries themselves were careful not to offend the Japanese authorities by showing open support for Korean nationalism, an increasing number of Korean Christians became prominent in nationalist activities as new ideas about progress, modernity, and nationhood spread among the growing ranks of intellectuals and professionals. Korean Buddhists and adherents of Ch'ondogyo, or "heavenly way," as the Tonghak sect was now known, were also prominent in nationalist organizations and activities. A modern discourse of Korean national identity, which had begun to emerge in the 1890s borrowing from Western models, continued to expand and develop in those years. Korean intellectuals studied Korean language and mythology, as well as world history, in their quest to develop their ideas on the nature and significance of the nation. They often concluded, as was typical in other emerging national movements in Europe and elsewhere, that the Korean nation was born in the ancient mists of time and that it possessed a well-defined and homogeneous ethnic character.[13]

In the meantime, Korean nationalists continued their efforts to appeal to international opinion in order to resist Japanese rule. In 1907, as the Second International Peace Conference was convening at the Hague (the first had occurred in 1899), the Korean emperor Kojong secretly sent envoys to the conference to ask for the restoration of Korean independence.[14] The envoys were admitted to the conference through the good offices of the Russian representative, who, naturally enough, was more than happy to use them to embarrass Japan in an international forum. The envoys claimed that the Japanese-Korean protectorate treaty of 1905 was void since Korea had signed it under duress and asked that the powers intervene to restore Korean sovereignty. The Korean representatives, however, failed to sway the diplomats at the Hague. They were quickly ejected from the conference under Japanese pressure, and the head Korean envoy, devastated by this failure, committed ritual suicide. Still, the episode caused great embarrassment to the Japanese authorities in Korea, and when Kojong's role in it was discovered he was forced to abdicate. Far from advancing Korean independence, the Hague affair led the Japanese to tighten their hold over Korea and set the stage for the full annexation of the peninsula to Japan three years later, in August 1910.[15]

Korean historiography often describes the period of direct military rule that lasted from 1910 to 1919 as the "Dark Period" of Korean history. The Japanese authorities, adopting a policy that called for the complete assimilation of Koreans into the Japanese nation, suppressed all political and cultural activities. The Korean press, hitherto relatively free, came under heavy censorship, and all nationalist organizations were outlawed. The discovery in 1911 of a plot to assassinate the Japanese governor general, General Terauchi Masatake, led to dozens of arrests, including most of the nationalist leaders still in Korea. In this repressive environment, religious organizations remained one of the sole venues for organized activities, and the influence of the Protestant churches continued to grow.[16]

With a complete ban in place on nationalist activities within Korea, many activists left the country, spurring the growth of patriotic organizations in Korean expatriate communities, especially in Russia, China, Japan, and the United States. Japan, ironically, became a major incubator for Korean national sentiments in this period, since Korean students, encouraged to attend Japanese universities as part of the assimilation policy, had access to literature promoting liberal ideas and criticizing Japanese rule that the military authorities had banned from Korea itself. One of the most important expatriate nationalist organizations emerged in 1909, when two existing groups merged to form the Korean National Association (KNA), under the leadership of An Ch'angho. An, a tireless organizer and a major figure among Korean activists abroad, had been educated by missionaries and immigrated to the United States in 1902, settling in California but traveling extensively to expatriate Korean communities in Hawaii, Mexico, and China. Syngman Rhee, who had remained in the United States following his failed mission to Theodore Roosevelt to pursue graduate studies at Harvard and then at Princeton, also began to play a leading role in the KNA after 1912.[17]

The presence of so many Korean patriots abroad mattered, among other things, because during the war years they had easy access to information that the Japanese censors worked hard to prevent from circulating in Korea itself. Though the KNA had begun to try to propagate the cause of Korean independence in American public opinion even before the war in Europe began, Korean activists in the United States recognized early the potential usefulness of Wilson's rhetoric for their cause and took the lead in preparing to present the Korean claim for self-determination before world opinion. The Korean community in the United States, including Hawaii, was small, numbering only about six thousand at the time. It was, however, well educated, politically active, and well organized, and its role in the Korean response to the Wilsonian moment was therefore disproportionately large. (This was also true for the small groups of educated Koreans in Shanghai and Tokyo, each no more than seven or eight hundred strong, which played, as we will see, an important role in the nationalist movement.[18]) In December 1918, the KNA published an open letter to Korean residents in the United States and Mexico, calling for unity in the fight for national independence. A "unity meeting" then convened in San Francisco and resolved that, in light of Wilson's vision for the postwar settlement, Koreans should submit a petition to the peace conference after the war and make an appeal to the United States and to Wilson himself to recognize Korean independence.

The meeting elected Syngman Rhee, Min Ch'anho, an ordained Methodist minister, and Henry Chung (Chŏng Hangyŏng) as delegates for this task. Chung, who was twenty-nine at the time, was born, like Rhee, into a scholarly family and trained in classical Chinese texts and Confucian classics. Under the influence of the stories about the wonders of the West that he heard from a local teacher who had returned from the United States, however, he cut off his traditional topknot at fourteen and decided to emigrate, on his own, to the new world. He arrived on the West Coast and soon thereafter accepted an invitation from a sympathetic American couple in a small town in Nebraska to come live with them. Though there were few other Koreans living in the area, Chung did well in his studies, graduating from his Nebraska high school as valedictorian. He later studied at Northwestern University and received a Ph.D. from American University in Washington, D.C. Even in Nebraska, he had already begun his involvement with the Korean national cause; like many Korean and other colonial nationalists at the time, Chung's opposition to colonialism was rooted in a worldview that was both liberal and cosmopolitan, part of a broader vision of bringing progress and modernity, as he saw them, to his land of origin and integrating it as an equal member within a progressive international order.[19]

Rhee and the others set out for Washington in December 1918 to apply for passports and prepare for the trip to Paris. In a message addressed to President Wilson, they informed him of their appointment to the peace conference as representatives of the 1.5 million expatriate Koreans living in America, Hawaii, Mexico, China, and Russia, and attached a memorandum, which they intended to present to the peace conference upon arrival in Paris. The text told the story of the Japanese conquest of Korea and the subsequent suppression of the local economy, culture, and religion, including, the document emphasized, Christianity. They expected Wilson, as "a champion of equal rights for all peoples, strong or weak," to help them get justice at a time when, as he had said, "the particular purposes of individual States are about to submit to the common will of mankind." The text also noted the contributions of Korean expatriates to the Allied effort: some had joined the U.S. military, others fought against the Bolsheviks in the Russian East. Japanese aggression in Asia threatened not only Korea but also U.S. interests, and the world could not be made "safe for democracy" as long as the 15 million Koreans on the peninsula remained under "alien yoke." Citing, like so many petitioners at the time, Wilson's words back to him, the text assured the president that the Korean movement met the standard of "well-defined national aspirations" stated in his February 11, 1918, address, since Koreans were an ethnically and linguistically distinct people and had a long history of civilization. Therefore, they should have the opportunity to "choose the government under which they wish to live."[20]

As with other anticolonial activists, Korean perceptions of Wilson and their hopes for his support drew on long-standing views of the United States as an exemplar of modern civilization and the power most sympathetic toward colonial aspirations for independence.[21] Among Korean nationalists, moreover, such perceptions of the United States were more common and more deeply entrenched than among other colonial peoples, given the impact of Protestant missions in Korea and the prominence among expatriate activists of men who studied and lived in the United States. Like many educated Egyptians, Indians, and Chinese, they considered the United States wealthy and powerful enough not to depend on colonial exploitation, and Wilson's rhetoric seemed to confirm this impression. Even after the Japanese annexed Korea with U.S. acquiescence, Korean nationalists, encouraged by resident American diplomats and missionaries, continued to believe that the United States supported their independence. Wilson's declarations on the establishment of new universal principles for international relations, they thought, would apply to Korea as well.[22] Eager to seize the opportunity, Koreans moved to frame their demands for independence in the new Wilsonian language and to take them before the president himself in Paris.

Shortly after the armistice, a group of Korean activists wrote to Wilson to help convince him that his wartime rhetoric applied to Korea. The president, they wrote, had "said very truly that all homogeneous nations that have a separate and distinct language, civilization and culture ought to be allowed independence."[23] Wilson, of course, had never defined the prerequisites of nationhood in such a detailed fashion in his wartime rhetoric. The authors of the petition read into his advocacy for self-determination the characteristics that Koreans and other nationalists commonly considered as defining national identity—ethnicity, language, cultural tradition, history—and sought to make the case that Korea met the standard. While this approach implied that not all claimants deserved satisfaction if they did not meet the criteria, other petitioners were less circumspect. A group of Koreans residing in New York City, for example, treated Korean nationhood as self-evident and simply asked that the postwar settlement grant Korea the same rights promised to other small nations. The United States and its allies have "endorsed the grand principle of self-determination of weaker and smaller nations, so nobly advocated by president Wilson," and Korea, like other small nations, had the right "to regulate her national life according to her own standards and ideas." The United States, therefore, should work to secure for Korea the right of self-determination.[24]

Koreans living in China and Japan, in the meantime, also paid close attention to the wartime developments in the international arena. For them, an important watershed came in the summer of 1918, when news reached them of Wilson's Independence Day address. In it, he had said explicitly for the first time that his principles would apply not only to the peoples actually engaged in the war but to "many others also, who suffer under the mastery but cannot act; peoples of many races and in every part of the world." Korean students in Japan understood this reference as a direct assault on Japanese rule of the peninsula and decided that it was time for them to act.[25] Chang Tŏksu, a Korean student leader in Japan, traveled to Shanghai that summer and, together with Yŏ Unhyŏng, the principal of a Korean school in Shanghai, founded the New Korea Youth Association (NKYA) and began to plan their campaign.[26]

When Charles R. Crane, an American businessman and Wilson confidant, arrived in Shanghai in November, the two thought they had found their opportunity. Crane, the heir of a plumbing supplies fortune, was an amateur diplomat and backroom political operator whom Wilson sent on various fact finding missions, most famously the King-Crane commission to the Middle East the following year. In Shanghai, Crane received the VIP treatment from both the local Chinese authorities and the foreign diplomatic corps, and he gave numerous speeches praising Wilson and his principles and hailing in rousing terms the coming new era in world affairs. Yŏ, who attended a reception in Crane's honor, was "inspired by Crane's speech on the principle of self-determination." He approached the American after his speech and, he later testified, had an exchange with Crane that encouraged him to believe that the principle of self-determination would be applied to Korea at the peace conference.[27] Excited, Yŏ and his colleagues quickly drafted a petition calling for Korean independence and gave a copy to Crane to deliver to Wilson personally. A second copy was handed to Thomas Millard, publisher of the popular English-language Shanghai magazine *Millard's Review*, who was leaving for Washington and then Paris, to deliver personally to the peace conference.[28]

In addition, the NKYA selected Kim Kyusik (Kim Kiusic), a young Korean Christian, to travel to Paris in person as their official representative to the Paris Peace Conference.[29] Kim was an orphan who had been raised by a well-known American missionary to Korea, Horace G. Underwood, and later traveled to the United States to attend Roanoke College in Virginia and Princeton University. He returned to teach at several Christian schools in Korea, but left for China in 1913 to escape Japanese rule. Kim's first challenge on his mission was transportation, since all boats from Shanghai to Paris were fully booked until March. After considerable effort, he managed to arrange passage with members of the Chinese delegation to the peace conference, making the trip with a Chinese passport and under a Chinese name in order to evade the Japanese police. The Chinese, of course, were eager for the opportunity to embarrass Japan at the international forum, and several top Chinese leaders at the time, including Sun Yat-sen, told U.S. diplomats that the peace conference should take up the question of Korean independence.[30] Beyond that, however, the Chinese, themselves locked in a struggle against Japanese designs in China, could do little for Korea.

As the delegates assembled in Paris and the peace conference opened over the winter, a group of Korean students in Tokyo, who organized themselves as the Korean Youth Independence Association, decided they must do something dramatic to bring Korean claims to the attention of "those nations of the world which have secured victory for Freedom and Justice." The method, they decided, would be a "declaration of independence" in the name of Koreans everywhere. Yi Kwangsu, a young novelist who would become a pioneer of modern Korean literature, was asked to draft the declaration. Yi himself believed that independence required the gradual evolution of Korean "national character," and confessed privately that he was unsure whether Korean society was actually ready for independence, but he concluded that Koreans could not pass up the opportunity that Wilson's presence at the peace conference offered.[31] The declaration was prepared in Korean, Japanese, and English versions, and the students dispatched copies to Wilson, Clemenceau, and Lloyd George in Paris, to politicians, scholars, and newspapers in Japan, and even to the governor general of Korea. On February 8, the declaration was read with much fanfare before a large crowd at the Tokyo YMCA. In the name of "the twenty million Korean people," it declared "before those nations of the world which have secured victory for Freedom and Justice, the realization of our independence." Soon after, the Japanese police broke up the meeting, arresting twenty-seven of those present.[32]

Within the peninsula itself, even the strict Japanese censorship—banning, for example, the showing of a foreign film on the grounds that it included some images of President Wilson—could not prevent the spread of

Kim Kyusik was the representative in Paris of the newly declared Provisional Government of the Republic of Korea, which operated in exile since Korea was then part of the Japanese empire. Kim labored to bring Korean demands for self-determination before the peace conference. *Seomoondang*.

interest in Wilsonian principles. Korean exiles living in Shanghai, who were headquartered in the French concession to stay outside the reach of the Japanese police in the city, sent the news and texts of his addresses to nationalists inside Korea through a network of couriers who crossed the border from China on foot. One young schoolteacher who was active in the nationalist underground in Korea remembered the excitement she felt when the message came from Shanghai: "President Wilson of the United States has proclaimed a fourteen point program for world peace. One of those points is the self-determination of the peoples. You must make the most of this situation. Your voice must be heard. President Wilson will certainly help you."[33] Though the term "self-determination" was actually nowhere to be found among the Fourteen Points, this technicality mattered little at the time, since the term "Fourteen Points" had come to stand for the sum total of Wilson's vision, as it was perceived through the eyes of Koreans and others.

By year's end, with news of the international situation trickling into Korea through such clandestine contacts with Korean nationalists abroad as well as with Westerners living in Korea, anticipation for the application of the doctrine of self-determination to Korea became increasingly widespread, especially among the young and the educated.[34] The American consul general in Seoul reported in January 1919 on the new mood among Koreans:

> There can be no doubt that the present general movement throughout the world looking towards the self-determination of peoples, and particularly of the subject races, has produced its effect on the thought of the people in this country. At the outset of the war there was a strong undercurrent among the Koreans of hostility to the Allies, a feeling that arose from a not unnatural antagonism to Japan, one of the Allies. As the war progressed, however, and the ultimate aims of the Allies were more carefully and fully stated, those Koreans who are accustomed to look beyond immediate conditions in their own country and to view affairs here in light of world conditions began to see that they might also be affected in no adverse manner by the victory of the Allies.[35]

By now, activists inside Korea had also begun contemplating action. Since the colonial authorities had outlawed all political groups, religious organizations, which remained the only venues for community action, were prominent in these activities. Religious leaders, who had a broad following among the populace, could help mobilize Koreans against colonial rule, and nationalist activists therefore worked to convince them that they must follow the lead of the Tokyo students and launch a campaign for independence on the peninsula itself. Both Christian and Buddhist leaders were prominent in the movement, as was the leadership of Ch'ondogyo. Upon learning of the student declaration of independence in Tokyo, Son Pyŏnghi, the Ch'ondogyo supreme leader, reportedly said: "At a time when young students are carrying out this kind of righteous action, we cannot just sit and watch."[36] At the same time, the Shanghai group dispatched Sonu Hyok, a Protestant Christian, to Korea to help convince Christian leaders to hold peaceful demonstrations in support of Kim Kyusik's mission in Paris. Such demonstrations, they said, would show the world that the Korean population, despite Japanese propaganda to the contrary, was unhappy under Japanese rule and was rallying to the cause of independence.[37]

In the meantime, an unexpected event occurred that afforded the nationalist activists an unprecedented opportunity to mobilize the masses around the call for self-determination. On January 22, the former emperor Kojong, whom the Japanese had deposed in 1907 in the wake of the failed Korean mission to the Hague, died suddenly. Rumors quickly spread that the Japanese had poisoned the former emperor because of his opposition to their rule. As the preparations for the royal funeral procession began, the military authorities felt compelled to relax restrictions on travel, and as many as 200,000 people streamed from the provinces into Seoul to pay their respects to the departed monarch. As the people gathered, nationalist leaders debated whether they should petition the Japanese for independence or simply declare it unilaterally, and finally decided on the latter course. They would draft a declaration of independence and hold nonviolent demonstrations across the country to show the world their desire for self-determination. They would also present petitions to the representatives of foreign powers in Tokyo, and send a letter to President Wilson himself asking for his support. To circumvent the Japanese censors, the petitions addressed to Wilson and the peace conference were to be smuggled across the border to Manchuria and sent by the Chinese postal system to Shanghai and thence to Paris.[38]

The date of the proclamation was set for March 1, to take advantage of the crowds gathered for the imperial funeral proceedings in Seoul scheduled for that day. On that morning, a group of thirty-three eminent religious leaders—Christians, Ch'ondogyo, and Buddhists—gathered in a Seoul restaurant to sign and proclaim the Declaration of Independence. To emphasize the pacific nature of their movement, they sent a copy of the declaration to the governor general and notified the colonial police of their intentions to stage nonviolent protests.[39] The text of the declaration, which recounted the history of Japanese injustice in Korea, drew heavily on Wilsonian imagery as the authors associated themselves "with the worldwide movement for reform," which was "the central force of our age and a just movement for the right of all peoples to determine their own existence." A new dawn, they said, was upon the world, and justice would henceforth replace force as the arbiter of international affairs. This offered Koreans "a great opportunity" to recover their country and "move with a new current of world thought," with "the conscience of mankind" on their side.[40]

That same morning, copies of a second manifesto, also calling for Korean independence, were posted along the main streets of the city. This manifesto, whose authors remain obscure, was not the work of the same leaders who had signed the declaration of independence, but rather was most likely prepared and circulated by a group of students who had learned of the plan to issue the declaration and wanted to show their support for it.[41] Its style was very different from the official declaration, far sharper and more confrontational, but its message was similar: A new age of self-determination had come in world affairs, and Koreans must have their independence. Reflecting the rumors that had been circulating since the emperor's death, the text blamed the Japanese for poisoning him in order to subvert the efforts of Korean nationalists to make their case in the international arena. "As we advocated the national independence in the Paris Peace Conference, the cunning Japanese produced a certificate stating that 'The Korean people are happy with Japanese rule and do not wish to be separate from the Japanese,' in order to cover the eyes and ears of the world." When the Japanese submitted this statement to the emperor for the affixation of his royal seal, the student manifesto speculated, he refused to sign it, and the Japanese therefore decided to assassinate him. The text concluded with a rousing call to action that placed Korean aspirations squarely within the context of recent international developments:

> Since the American President proclaimed the Fourteen Points, the voice of national self-determination has swept the world, and twelve nations, including Poland, Ireland, and Czechoslovakia, have obtained independence. How could we, the people of the great Korean nation, miss this opportunity? Our compatriots abroad are utilizing this opportunity to appeal for the recovery of national sovereignty.... Now is the great opportunity to reform the world and recover us the ruined nation.[42]

With copies of the student manifesto posted in the streets, the "official" declaration of independence was read aloud in Pagoda Park in the heart of downtown Seoul before a large cheering crowd. When the reading ended, the masses poured into the streets, with many shouting "Long live Korean independence!" One young participant recalled how he learned of the movement at his school on the morning of March 1, when the student representative rose to address his fellow students: "Today we Koreans will declare our independence," he told them. "Our representatives have gone to the Paris Peace Conference. To show our desire for independence to the world we must shout 'manse' [long live] for Korean independence."[43] For the organizers of the movement, then, the most important audiences for their declarations and demonstrations were not the Japanese authorities but the world leaders gathered at the other end of the Eurasian land mass. With this audience in mind, one of the signatories of the declaration of independence asked a Canadian missionary and amateur photographer, Dr. Frank Schofield, to take photographs of the reading in Pagoda Park so that they could be sent to the peace conference. Schofield, alas, was stampeded by the throng of excited demonstrators that came streaming out of the park and failed to carry out his mission, though he followed the demonstrators with his camera in hand and managed to take some photos later that day.[44]

Over the following months, more than one million Koreans participated in the March First protests as they spread over the entire peninsula. Store owners closed their shops and workers went on strike in shows of support for the movement.[45] The uprising was also fueled by the spread of rumors—a major source of information since Japanese censorship largely prevented the circulation of more reliable news—that the United States and President Wilson himself supported the Korean demands for self-determination. Among other things, rumors circulated that "President Wilson was to come to Korea by airplane to assist Korean independence; that scores of United States battleships had been dispatched for Korea; that American troops had already landed at Inchon; that the peace conference had recognized the independence of

These Korean women marching in Seoul were part of a mass movement for independence that erupted across the Korean peninsula in March 1919. Many organizers and participants believed that once the powers in Paris, led by Wilson, learned that the people of Korea rejected Japanese rule, they would grant Korea independence. *Seomoondang.*

Korea."[46] Another widespread story was that shortly before Wilson left for Paris, he was approached by a Korean who asked him if Korea would be discussed at the peace conference. The president, the rumor went, replied that if Koreans remained quiescent they would not be heard, but if they protested they would get a hearing.[47] An American missionary in Pyongyang reported that, with Wilson's advocacy of self-determination well known among "educated Koreans," they believed that they had to act immediately. The peace conference would hear and rectify "every political 'sore' and difficulty throughout the whole world." After it adjourned, no further adjustments would be possible.[48] But even as Koreans moved to seize the opportunity they perceived in Paris, Wilson's own fortunes there were beginning to wane.

Part III

The Failure of Liberal Anticolonialism

Wilson in Paris was like an ant on a hot skillet. He didn't know what to do. He was surrounded by thieves like Clemenceau, Lloyd George, Makino, and Orlando. He heard nothing except accounts of receiving certain amounts of territory and of reparations worth so much in gold. He did nothing except to attend various kinds of meetings where he could not speak his mind. One day a Reuter's telegram read, "President Wilson has finally agreed with Clemenceau's view that Germany not be admitted to the League of Nations." When I saw the words "finally agreed," I felt sorry for him for a long time. Poor Wilson!

—Mao Zedong, July 1919

Wilson left Paris for a few weeks in the United States immediately after presenting the league covenant on February 14. He landed in Boston on the twenty-third to a thunderous reception, but the cheers were deceptive. Wilson's visit was a difficult one. A new Congress, which his Republican opponents would control, was about to come into session, and Wilson's nemesis, Massachusetts senator Henry Cabot Lodge, was set to become chair of the Senate Foreign Relations Committee. In that role, Lodge, a leading Republican critic of the president and his plans for the peace, would have a decisive influence on the Senate deliberations on the ratification of the peace treaty, including Wilson's crowning achievement, the League of Nations covenant. On March 3, just before midnight, Lodge made his move, introducing on the Senate floor his famous "round robin" resolution. Signed by thirty-seven senators—enough to block the required two-thirds majority for ratification—the resolution declared that the United States should reject the covenant of the League of Nations "in the form now proposed." Though the league still appeared to have strong support among the American public, the president's domestic opponents were clearly gaining ground, and this development was not lost on his negotiating partners back in Paris.[1]

The president arrived back in France on March 14. He again landed in Brest, but in a reflection of the precipitous decline in his international stature since his last landing there only three months and one day earlier, this time "there was little or no ceremony connected with his return."[2] During his absence, the focus of the negotiations had moved away from the abstract ideals of the league covenant to the hard details of territorial changes, reparation payments, and limitations on German rearmament. Indeed, Wilson, whose health was already beginning to fail under the great strain of his task, was so concerned that the league had been cast aside in his absence that his first act upon his return was to announce that the covenant remained an inseparable part of the peace treaty. Still, sharp disagreements among the Allies over the terms of the peace with Germany continued to drag the discussions on, and in late March a full-fledged crisis broke out in Paris over the Italian demand for the city of Fiume (now Rijeka), on the eastern coast of the Adriatic Sea. Wilson, citing the largely Slavic population of the surrounding region, rejected the demand as contradictory to the principle of self-determination and insisted that the area should be part of the new Yugoslav state. The president, hoping to call on the support of the cheering crowds that had greeted him during his Italian sojourn less than three months earlier, released a public statement making his case to the Italian people over the heads of their leaders. The main result of his public plea, however, was to make the Italian delegates livid. Prime Minister Orlando and his foreign minister, Sidney Sonnino, withdrew from the conference and left Paris in protest. They did not return for several weeks.[3]

By late April, an atmosphere of general crisis engulfed much of the continent. Armed conflicts had broken out across Eastern and Central Europe as the new states that were emerging from the ashes of the Habsburg and Romanov empires jockeyed for territory, and radical governments had recently come to power in Bavaria and Hungary amid the general chaos in the defeated countries. Deprivation and hunger were growing in much of the region, and the peace treaty with Germany was still not ready. It was not until May 4, several months later than the original projections, that the Big Three managed to resolve their final differences on the most difficult issues, including the territorial settlements in Europe and the question of German reparations, and to submit the treaty to the German delegates. By then, it was clear that the preliminary consultation among the Allies, which was to have lasted only several weeks at most, had become the peace conference itself, and the conditions on the continent left little time or desire among the Allied leaders for substantial negotiations with the defeated enemy. The German representatives who arrived at Versailles, led by the foreign minister Ulrich von Brockdorff-Rantzau, were presented simply with the treaty as the Allied leaders had prepared it. They objected strenuously that it was not the Wilsonian peace that the terms of the armistice had promised, but their objections were brushed aside. On June 28, 1919, with their country near collapse and under the threat of an Allied invasion if they rejected the treaty, the Germans had little choice but to sign.[4]

In much of the colonial world, too, the spring of 1919 was a time of crisis. The uprising that had erupted in Korea on March 1 was still a hopeful one, predicated on the belief that if Koreans rose to claim their right to self-determination, the peace conference, under Wilson's influence, would grant it to them. But at the same time, Egyptians and Indians both found Britain adamantly opposed to any attempt to bring their claims before the peace conference, and saw the British moving to tighten rather than loosen their grip on their lands. The promise of self-determination appeared to grow increasingly distant, and Wilson, the hero of the Fourteen Points, appeared unable—or unwilling—to help. The Chinese, who, unlike the Korean, Egyptian, and Indian nationalists did have representation at the peace table, held on the longest to hopes of success, but they, too, could not sustain the mood of high optimism with which they arrived in Paris. With the peace conference in profound crisis and Wilson so clearly weakened and isolated, the prospects that right would triumph over might at the peace table began to look increasingly distant. Before the treaty was signed, upheaval would break out among all of these groups.

Wilson left Paris immediately after the signing ceremony in June, but he could have very little satisfaction in a job well done. Even the League of Nations covenant, the last, deeply compromised remnant of the great Wilsonian promise of the previous fall for a new international order, was in danger. In his efforts to find a progressive middle ground between the forces of revolution and the forces of reaction, the president had made no one happy. Liberals and radicals thought he had not gone nearly far enough to implement the ideals of international equality and justice, while conservatives and imperialists thought he had gone much too far, with Europeans blaming him for fomenting upheaval in the colonies and Americans for compromising the sovereignty of the United States and dragging it into the swamp of European intrigue. Moreover, Wilson's own physical fate that fall seemed to mirror that of his ambition to transform the world. On October 2, after months of straining to convince the American people to support the treaty, he suffered the incapacitating stroke that effectively ended his political career, though his wife and a few close aides did manage to keep up the appearances of presidential competence until the end of his term in office in March 1921.

The Versailles Treaty was now before the U.S. Senate, which needed to ratify it by a two-thirds majority, and with Wilson's Republican opponents at the helm it was bound to be a difficult struggle. As the Senate debates on ratification continued over much of the next year, Wilson's political opponents occasionally pointed to the demands that colonial peoples had raised for self-determination and attacked the treaty for failing to stem the power of imperialism, accusing Wilson of collusion with the imperialist interests of the British and the French. In these discussions, as we will see, the unmet claims of Egyptians, Indians, Chinese, and even Koreans were raised, and the senators heard a number of representations on their behalf. But for the vast majority of senators, as for Wilson himself and for most Americans, the fate of the colonial world was never a central issue in 1919. For the colonial nationalists who had responded to the call of self-determination, however, nothing was more important. The liberal anticolonial vision that Wilson had conjured was rapidly fading, but anticolonial movements had now emerged as a force in international affairs, with the right of all peoples to self-determination as their rallying cry.

7

The 1919 Revolution

By March 1919, as Koreans rose in protest against Japanese rule, events were coming to a head in Egypt as well. With tensions rising in Europe and across the empire, the British authorities in Egypt grew increasingly anxious over the Wafd's success in mobilizing the Egyptian public behind its program of resistance to British rule. It was time, they decided, to move forcefully against its leadership. On March 6, the commander of the British forces in Egypt, General Watson, summoned Zaghlul and several of his lieutenants for an interview and warned them to stop their campaign against the British presence in Egypt. Martial law, he reminded them, had been proclaimed in 1914 at the outset of the war and remained in effect. If they persisted in their attacks on the legitimacy of the protectorate and continued to block efforts to put together a new Egyptian cabinet to replace the resigning Rushdi ministry, they would face serious consequences. Zaghlul began to protest, but Watson would not let him speak. "No discussion," he said, and immediately left the room.[1]

This imperious display, no doubt designed to impress the Wafd leaders with British resolve, only served to strengthen the nationalists' determination. Conspicuously ignoring Watson's warning, Zaghlul shot off a defiant telegram to Lloyd George immediately after this encounter. In the telegram he again condemned the protectorate as "illegal" and reiterated his mission to secure complete independence for Egypt. For the British, this was the last straw. Two days later, a contingent of British troops arrived at Zaghlul's house and placed him under arrest, together with three of his leading colleagues in the Wafd leadership: Oxford-educated landowner Muhammad Mahmud; the tribal leader Hamad al-Basil, who was prominent in organizing Wafd propaganda in Egypt; and Isma'il Sidqi, also a wealthy landowner and a future prime minister. The next morning, March 9, the four were loaded onto a British steamer and deported to the Mediterranean island of Malta. According to one biographer, a search of Zaghlul's person upon his arrest turned up a clipping from a British newspaper, the *Daily Express*, which listed Wilson's Fourteen Points.[2]

The arrests were a fateful move, sparking a massive wave of popular demonstrations and strikes across Egypt and precipitating a period of violent clashes known in Egyptian historiography as the 1919 Revolution. Over the next several months, Egyptians of all classes took part in the upheaval: students and urban laborers, middle-class professionals and Delta peasants.[3] Members of religious and ethnic minorities, in particular leaders of the Christian Coptic Orthodox minority, expressed their solidarity with the movement and, in a conspicuous departure from tradition, Egyptian women also took to the streets. The protests began with peaceful student demonstrations but quickly deteriorated into violence as British troops tried to suppress the uprising. As railway and telegraph lines were sabotaged, the British countered with strict enforcement of martial law. Some eight hundred Egyptians and sixty British soldiers and civilians died in the clashes that spring, and thousands more were wounded.[4]

The 1919 Revolution was a major watershed in the development of the Egyptian national struggle, forming, according to the prominent Egyptian historian 'Abd al-Rahman Rafi'i, "the basis for all the developments that followed."[5] Zaghlul himself noted in his diary on April 2 that "the events that occurred in Egypt following our departure" were "more cataclysmic than anyone could ever have predicted. They have turned the tables against the colonizing power and alerted the entire world to the fact that there is an oppressed nation calling out for justice." It was the first truly popular revolution in Egypt, which included all regions, age groups, classes, and religious communities. It augured, another Egyptian historian, 'Abd al-'Azim Ramadan, has written, "a new age in Egyptian history—the age of Egyptian nationalism—which replaced the idea of the Islamic community that made Egypt part of the Ottoman state."[6] The violent clashes of that period escalated Anglo-Egyptian tensions and fostered mutual fear and mistrust. They hardened attitudes and positions on both sides and cast a long shadow over all subsequent attempts at negotiation.

As the revolution unfolded in the streets, Egyptian protesters strove to obtain the support of the United States for their cause. One group of demonstrators attempted to march to the U.S. legation in Cairo with an American flag at its head, but British troops dispersed the crowd and confiscated the flag.[7] A wide variety of organizations, professions, and religious groups within Egyptian society, as well as Egyptian organizations and individuals abroad, produced the telegrams, letters, and petitions that poured into the U.S. legation. Most of the messages shared a similar thrust: They protested strongly the arrest of Zaghlul and his followers, who only wished "the Egyptian people to take its place among the free nations of the earth," and decried the violent suppression of peaceful demonstrations, appealing to "the public opinion of the world" to intervene on behalf of Egypt. They declared their faith in President Wilson and his Fourteen Points and called on the United States to come to their aid: "Long live America, liberator of the world," concluded one, signed by some fifteen notables from Alexandria.[8] Petitioners also sought to dispel concerns about the possible impact of Egyptian independence on foreign interests in the country. Egyptians, asserted many of the messages, were a peaceful and tolerant people, and Egyptian self-government would pose no danger to foreign lives, property, or interests.[9]

To emphasize the unity and tolerance of Egyptian society, many of the authors also took pains to highlight the participation of Egyptians of all classes and of religious minorities and women in the nationalist movement. Leading Egyptian Copts wrote to express their solidarity with the movement, and the Egyptian Association, a group formed soon after Wilson's arrival in Paris to advocate independence, adopted a flag displaying the symbols of Egypt's three main religious communities—a crescent, a cross, and a star of David— on a red background to signify the unity of Egyptians of all faiths in the national struggle.[10] The brutality of British rule was also emphasized. A widely distributed pamphlet that recorded the results of the suppression of protests in one Nile Delta village displayed graphic photographs of Egyptian men with whip marks on their exposed torsos. The name and social position of each man—peasant, student, religious scholar, notable—was noted below each photograph to provide evidence of the broad support for the independence movement.[11] A group of Egyptian women, appealing to a presumed American sensitivity to the mistreatment of women, testified that British troops "leveled their weapons at us and kept us standing thus for two hours under a burning sun." The women suggested that "this fact alone without commentary of any sort shows clearly the persistence of the British in employing brute force even toward women, in order to stamp out our unanimous movement."[12] The participation of women in the movement was unprecedented, and historians have often cited the 1919 Revolution as a transformative moment in the place of women in Egyptian society, taking them, as one Egyptian historian put it, from the harem to the public arena and the labor market.[13]

Though the British authorities attempted to quell the revolt by military force, they also realized that their earlier obstinacy in the face of Zaghlul's demands had been ill advised and was partly to blame for the conflagration.[14] The high commissioner, Reginald Wingate, in London since January, had tried to impress upon the British government the severity of the Egyptian situation, but he was out of favor with the Foreign Office bureaucracy and had been largely ignored. With the eruption of large-scale upheaval in March, however, officials in London began to appreciate the seriousness of the situation. In late March, General (soon to be Lord) Edmund Allenby, commander of the Egyptian Expeditionary Force during the war and the conqueror of Palestine and Syria, was named as the new high commissioner. Allenby arrived in Egypt determined to restore order and reestablish British control, but he was prepared to make some concessions to the nationalists in order to do so, and invested his prestige in order to overcome Curzon's continued opposition to

This woman, addressing a crowd in a main street in Cairo in May 1919, called for cheers for country, for liberty, and for President Wilson. Women played an unprecedented public role in Egypt's 1919 Revolution, and they often tied the liberation of women in society to the liberation of the nation from foreign rule. *Corbis*.

any concessions. One of Allenby's first acts was to announce, on April 7, that the deportees would be freed from their internment on Malta and permitted to travel as they wished.[15] Egyptians greeted the announcement with demonstrations of joy, and hundreds of thousands filled the streets calling nationalist slogans. A group of some twenty Wafd members left immediately for Malta, where they planned to meet Zaghlul and the others and proceed immediately to Paris to put their case before Wilson and the peace conference.[16]

Finally, it seemed, Egypt's representatives would have the opportunity to bring their case for self-determination before the U.S. president. Zaghlul had been preparing for this task during his four weeks on Malta, taking English lessons with an instructor he met there. The Egyptian leader, fluent in French, wanted to improve his English-language skills in anticipation of a possible meeting with Wilson, though he noted that the instructor, a German, did not speak very good English himself.[17] Zaghlul had also been following the news from Paris during his exile, and he was well aware of the troubles that mounted there by early April. Wilson had recently returned from a difficult trip to the United States and found only more conflict upon his return, as tensions rose among the Allies over the terms of the German treaty and a crisis erupting over the Italian demands for Fiume. On April 8, Zaghlul recorded in his diary his concern with the impact that Wilson's difficulties might have on the Egyptian mission: "The voice of President Wilson, on whose words we counted and whom we saw as a prophet in his own time, has weakened, and he has been accused by his people of deferring to the British! Only Allah knows what will happen!"[18] Soon after, just as Zaghlul received word that he would be able to travel to Europe, news spread that a severe crisis had overtaken the conference and that Wilson was threatening to leave Europe immediately. "Will he be back?" Zaghlul wondered. "If he does not intend to return, will an Egyptian trip to Paris have any benefit? . . . Should we fear that the Egyptians were allowed to go only after the future of Egypt was agreed upon? I do not believe so! If anything like that had been done, it would have been reported and heard everywhere!"[19] Though Zaghlul tried to remain optimistic, the collusion he feared was in fact well in the making.

As Zaghlul waited in Malta and worked on his English-language skills, British officials worked to ensure that his mission in Paris would fail by securing American recognition of their protectorate in Egypt. Though the protectorate had been declared in November 1914, the Wilson administration, then still pursuing a policy of neutrality, did not formally recognize it and persisted in this policy even after the United States joined the war to emphasize his distance from the expansionist war aims of the Allies. This, General Allenby wrote from Cairo, now had to change. The Egyptian public still hoped that the Wafd would secure the support of the peace conference for the nationalist position, and they must be disabused of this notion by clear statements from "responsible Allied statesmen" to the effect that the great powers agreed to leave Egypt in British hands.[20]

The Foreign Office concurred with the general's position. The situation in Egypt, Balfour, the foreign secretary, wrote in an April 17 memorandum to Sir William Wiseman, a British intelligence official and confidential liaison to the American leadership, was "daily becoming more serious." The "extreme nationalists"—whom he implausibly described as both "chiefly paid agents of the revolutionary party in Turkey and Bolshevists"—claimed to have President Wilson's support "in their attempts to stir up a Holy War against the Infidels." Having invoked the specters of Egyptian chauvinism, Bolshevism, and Islamic fanaticism in one fell swoop, Balfour concluded that it was of the utmost importance that the United States recognize the protectorate immediately. Only this, he wrote, could "remove from Egyptian politics the dangerous religious and Bolshevist appeal" that was gaining force there.[21] Balfour's argument reflected the suspicion, common among British officials at the time, that Bolshevik agents had a hand in the upheavals that erupted in Egypt as well as in India. In fact, there were no organized communist or even socialist parties in either place at the time, and there is no evidence that the Russian Bolsheviks were involved in instigating the protests or even served as a significant source of inspiration for them. But for effect, if not for veracity, Balfour's characterization was quite apt.[22] Wiseman transmitted this memo to his close friend and Wilson confidant Colonel House, along with the request that the president recognize the protectorate in Egypt without delay. Only this, Wiseman warned House, could "steady native opinion and avoid the terrible consequences which would follow a Holy War."[23]

Most American officials shared the British assessment of the situation in Egypt. The U.S. delegation's Africa expert, George Beer, had already recommended in August 1918 that the United States recognize the protectorate.[24] Hampson Gary, the consul general in Cairo, who had from the outset warned against American recognition of nationalist claims, dispatched a string of increasingly alarming reports after the eruption of violence in March. The situation in Egypt was "very critical" and American lives and property there could be in danger. American missionary societies active in Egypt had already written him asking for the safeguarding of their property and activities in any new arrangement made in Paris.[25] Gary blamed the "indefiniteness of the political status of Egypt" for the volatile situation and echoed Allenby's position by recommending that an "authoritative source" in Paris clarify the U.S. position on the future government of Egypt immediately. A few days later, he warned that the British authorities refused to negotiate with the nationalists and were intent on suppressing the upheaval by force, and suggested that a discussion of the issue in Paris might help to avert a bloodbath.[26]

In March, Secretary of State Lansing handed Wilson one of Gary's frantic telegrams, which described the situation as "exceedingly grave." The disturbances in Egypt were "rapidly developing into Bolshevism" and exhibiting "an animus against all foreigners and their property." The acting high commissioner, Milne Cheetham—Allenby had not yet arrived—had called on Gary to ask that the United States help to restore order, since "the warm relationship that all Egyptians feel for the United States" guaranteed that "an announcement by the American representative here would have great influence." Even the nationalist leaders, he said, had become alarmed, and they were trying to help the British restore order; indeed, at least some among the Egyptian elite were growing concerned about the possible consequences of a broad popular upheaval on their own fortunes.[27] Although Gary had earlier described the nationalists as an "autocratic elite," he now admitted that their demands were "largely representative of the Egyptian people in their present state of mind," which had "steadily progressed to extreme degree during the past four disastrous months" since the war ended. For the first time, the Copts and the peasants had joined politically with the Muslim nationalists. "Nearly all Britons in Egypt," Gary wrote, "attribute present chaotic condition here to what they describe as pernicious American theory of self-determination." Egyptians had seen the demands of Syria and Mesopotamia come before the conference and failed to understand why their claims should not also be considered there. A decision regarding Egypt at the peace conference would therefore be necessary to "solace Egyptian pride" and would be "the only decree susceptible of carrying moral weight here."[28]

House took the British request for recognition of the protectorate to Wilson immediately. Judging by the few lines that House devoted to this matter in his diary, the decision did not require much deliberation. Among the plethora of pressing issues that stood before the president at the time, the Egyptian question had low priority, and when presented with the British request and the recommendations of his advisers, Wilson quickly agreed to it, though, he stressed, "with certain limitations." The United States still supported the principle of self-determination for Egypt, but wished see it implemented through an orderly, gradual process of reforms rather than by revolution against the established order. This was good enough for the British, and Wiseman reportedly commented with satisfaction that the British request, raised at breakfast, was granted by lunchtime.[29] When the Egyptian question came up in September before the Senate Foreign Relations Committee, Senator Philander Knox, himself a former secretary of state under President Taft, commented upon hearing that the decision to recognize the protectorate took only a few minutes: "We never chewed them up that fast."[30]

On April 19, just as Zaghlul and the Egyptian delegation, who had left Malta a few days earlier, landed in Marseilles on their way to Paris, House replied to Balfour that the president had agreed to recognize the protectorate. The president also had "no objection to this decision being made public, as he understands that it may help in the restoration of order and in the prevention of further bloodshed in Egypt." The American announcement, however, qualified its recognition of the protectorate by reiterating its support for self-determination achieved through a peaceful, orderly process. "The President and the American people," it read, "have every sympathy with the legitimate desires of the Egyptian people for a further measure of self-government, but they deplore the effort to obtain such rights by anarchy and violence."[31] The announcement of recognition was officially released on April 21, prompting Balfour to thank the president profusely for his act "of friendship and of humanity." The next day, the note was communicated to Allenby in Egypt, who was reportedly "highly pleased thereby." Wilson's recognition of the protectorate, Gary rejoiced, met a wholehearted welcome in "official circles" and "has practically insured the collapse of the Radical Nationalist program."[32]

British officials were naturally delighted with the American decision. Curzon believed that such a "severe rebuff" in Paris, most especially one that came from the president of the United States, was a crucial step in neutralizing Zaghlul's dangerous extremism: Wilson's recognition, he said, was "a very important step in the right direction."[33] George Lloyd, who would serve as the British high commissioner in Egypt in the late 1920s, later remarked with undisguised glee that the United States' recognition of the protectorate had meant that "Zaghlul's last hope of effective action in Paris disappeared," a statement that revealed the depth of British concern with the possibility that Wilson would give Zaghlul a hearing in Paris.[34] The British authorities ensured that the American announcement received wide publicity in Egypt. The foreign-language press that served the European residents in the country gave it fulsome praise, and even some of the Arabic-language papers accepted it, reflecting the concerns of some Egyptian elites about the growing disorder. One editorial recommended that Egyptians "be content with the sympathy of President Wilson and the American nation for their legitimate aspirations" and advised the nationalist leaders to work to restore order and advance peacefully to achieve those aspirations.[35]

Reporting on the responses in Egypt, Gary was in a congratulatory mood. He reserved special praise for the final paragraph of the American note, which expressed American sympathy for the goals of Egyptian nationalists but excoriated their violent methods. This paragraph, he reported, succeeded in fostering "a slightly diverse interpretation by the European and Arabic press" in Egypt, with the former commending its rebuke of nationalist violence and the latter comforted by its sympathy for Egyptian aspirations. The announcement thus managed cleverly to attain the "dual end" of vindicating British policy in Egypt and rejecting nationalist excesses while at the same time sparing the nationalists "an immoderate discomfiture which might have entailed considerable bitter feeling directed against the United States." In order to better achieve this effect, Gary inserted some modifications in the text of the note, such as substituting "view with regret" for "deplore" and eliminating the reference to "anarchy." The final text of the paragraph published in Egypt read: "The President and the American people have every sympathy with the legitimate desires of the Egyptian people for a further measure of self-government, but they view with regret any effort to obtain the realization thereof by a resort to violence."[36] The U.S. government, then, would not help the Egyptians in their struggle for independence, but it did hope, to the extent possible, to retain their good will and preserve its own image as a supporter of liberty and self-determination everywhere.

As the public in Egypt learned of the U.S. decision to recognize the British protectorate, the nationalist delegation, which had landed in Marseilles a few days earlier, was on its way to Paris to present its case before President

Wilson and the peace conference.[37] According to the memoirs of several members of the delegation, they were "shocked" when news of the recognition reached them, and "despair began to seep into their hearts" about the prospects of their mission.[38] The nationalists had pinned their hopes on Wilson's support for their cause, and the American decision left them with a lingering sense of betrayal. In his memoirs, Muhammad Haykal recalled that the American decision fell upon the nationalists "like a bolt of lightning":

> Here was the man of the Fourteen Points, among them the right to self-determination, denying the Egyptian people its right to self-determination and recognizing the British protectorate over Egypt. And doing all that before the delegation on behalf of the Egyptian people had arrived in Paris to defend its claim, and before President Wilson had heard one word from them! Is this not the ugliest of treacheries?! Is it not the most profound repudiation of principles?![39]

"No one could imagine," said delegation member 'Abd al-Rahman Fahmi, "that this decision could come from President Wilson, who had entered the war to destroy colonialism, to abolish the authority of the strong over the weak, and who proclaimed before the armistice those famous principles of liberty and justice."[40]

In Switzerland, National party leader Muhammad Farid at first did not believe the news of the recognition. After receiving confirmation, he noted bitterly that the United States had left the protectorate unrecognized for almost five years since 1914, but acknowledged it now just as the Egyptian delegation was arriving in Paris. It was as if the U.S. intention was "to kill the hope in the hearts of Egyptians." This was "a policy of betrayal and perfidy by Wilson" in the service of British interests. He worried how the news would affect the movement in Egypt, but also asserted that the recognition did not change anything in principle, "since the nation's right to independence is a natural right that could not be revoked even if the whole world recognized the British protectorate in Egypt."[41] Wilson may have betrayed his own principles, but the principles themselves remained valid. The president's failure to uphold and implement his vision may have dented the faith of Egyptian nationalists in Wilson, the United States, and the new liberal international order that he had championed, but they remained committed to self-determination as the ultimate goal of their movement.

Despite this serious setback, the Wafd representatives arrived in Paris in April and set to work advocating for Egyptian independence. Though some members saw the U.S. recognition of the protectorate as a fatal blow to Egyptian aspirations in Paris, others, including Zaghlul himself, decided to persevere in their mission. The Egyptian people, Zaghlul wrote in his diary, have become a "revolutionary people determined to achieve independence and willing to pay a price for it," and they would not accept failure.[42] Concerned that they would face tighter British restrictions on their freedom if they returned to Egypt in the midst of a popular upheaval there, Zaghlul and most of the others remained in Paris for almost a year to try to gain support for Egyptian independence. As conflicts unfolded in the streets of Egypt and the halls of Versailles, the Wafd organized a campaign to propagate the Egyptian cause in the French press and among the hundreds of foreign journalists present in Paris. They had some minor successes, especially in socialist circles and with sympathetic American journalists, though not, as the British ambassador in Paris noted with satisfaction, with any "prominent persons."[43] One delegation member recalled that upon arrival in Paris Zaghlul visited the headquarters of all of the official delegations and left his calling card, but only the Italian premier, Orlando, even bothered to acknowledge the courtesy.[44]

The nationalists also continued their petition drives, dispatching dozens of messages to members of the diplomatic corps in Cairo and to the peace delegations present in Paris. Many Egyptians continued to address petitions to Wilson himself, noting the contradiction between his declared principles and his recent decision on the protectorate. The recognition of the protectorate, a petition from the Egyptian Association in Great Britain reminded him, was "a complete violation of his well known principles of justice and fair play to the weak as well as the strong nations," and the United States must therefore reverse it and aid Egyptians in their struggle.[45] Another letter, signed by seventy-two Egyptian physicians, called upon America, as the "recognized champion of Right and Justice to the weaker members of the great family of the Human Race," to offer Egyptians not only rhetorical sympathy, as the last section of the U.S. announcement had tried to do. It must also provide them with "real and active help to realize their legitimate national aspirations."[46]

Quite a few messages reflected the conviction that President Wilson, the prophet of self-determination, could not have willingly betrayed the Egyptian cause and must therefore have been duped by the wily British—a view that, given Balfour's implausible characterization of the forces behind the Egyptian movement, was not entirely without basis. A group of Egyptian university students presented a lengthy memorandum that called the U.S. decision on the protectorate "a thunderbolt from a clear summer sky" but emphasized continuing faith in the president's "fidelity to his principles." His decision to recognize British rule in Egypt, they assumed, was taken because he was ill acquainted with the true nature of the Egyptian movement and had therefore "allowed himself to be hustled into a course of action," which despite appearances was "obviously well-meant and honourably inspired." Seeking to correct the president's misapprehensions, the students assured him that the Egyptian national movement was "neither religious, nor xenophobe" and "far from being bolshevist in any sense." They were certain that the president and the people of the United States, upon gaining a correct understanding of the nature of Egyptian nationalism, would not "withhold their moral weight and political influence from the side of Right in the present test between Might and Right."[47]

Despite the stream of protests, the British authorities in Egypt reported that Wilson's recognition had contributed to calming the situation, and U.S. diplomats in the country shared their optimism. In Cairo, Gary recognized that the decision came as a shock and shattered Egyptian hopes, but added that rather than leading to despair it had met "a surprising lack of resentment" and "had a most salutary effect upon the general situation," even pleasing a large number of "responsible Egyptians." Even Sultan Fu'ad himself, he said, while regretting the necessity for the president's announcement, welcomed it "as affording a practicable solution of the impasse which had been reached here" between the British and the Wafd.[48] The American consul in Alexandria, where anti-British protests had also been widespread, reported that the recognition caused "dismay among the natives" and a "revulsion of feeling toward the United States." But he agreed that the "better class natives" were glad that the declaration had dispelled any illusions on the part of the nationalists that the United States was backing their violent actions against British rule.[49]

In Paris, Zaghlul disagreed with these sanguine evaluations. Failure to apply the principle of self-determination to Egypt, he wrote to Lloyd George, would only fuel greater despair and unrest in Egypt.[50] Still hoping to change Wilson's mind, he dispatched a series of emphatic messages requesting an audience with the president. Like the Indian leader Tilak, however, the only replies he received were terse notes from Wilson's private secretary, Gilbert Close, acknowledging his missives but rejecting his request due to the president's preoccupation with other pressing matters.[51] In a letter to Wilson in June, Zaghlul acknowledged receipt of Close's replies, noting rather optimistically that though they did not grant his request for an interview with Wilson, neither did they exclude such a possibility in the future:

> We wish to impress upon you what would be the despair of the Egyptian people if their delegation failed to get even a hearing before the Exponent of International Right and Justice.
>
> We do not believe you wish Egypt to be condemned unheard. And we do not feel that you can form a judgement on the Egyptian situation without giving a hearing to the Egyptians themselves.
>
> We believe you purposely left open the possibility of a future audience with us, and we respectfully request that this be granted us as soon as possible, in order that history may reflect honour on you in this affair, as in all others connected with the Conference.[52]

Wilson, however, never found the time to meet with the Egyptian leader. Ten days after this letter was sent, immediately after the signing of the peace treaty with Germany, he left Paris to return to the United States.

Even after the signing ceremony at Versailles and the departure of Wilson and the other leading statesmen from Paris, the Wafd members abroad continued to try to advance the Egyptian nationalist cause in the international arena. Among other efforts, they published and distributed a collection of documents related to the nationalist campaign, including telegrams sent to various world leaders and detailed reports about British atrocities in Egypt.[53] In an open letter to the British House of Commons published in July, Zaghlul protested the peace treaty's recognition of the protectorate and repeated his plea for the internationalization of the Egyptian question. He demanded that the peace conference, which remained in session after June 28 to work on the treaties with the other defeated powers, send a commission of inquiry to Egypt.[54]

At the same time, the Wafd, though disappointed with Wilson, launched a campaign to enlist support in the U.S. Congress and in American public opinion, writing to various politicians and journalists for support. These efforts, one Egyptian paper reported in the summer, were bearing fruit: American public opinion, once wholly ignorant of the situation in Egypt, had been enlightened. Some six hundred newspapers across the United States, it claimed, were now publicizing and defending the Egyptian case against Britain.[55] In Congress, too, the nationalists thought they had scored a success. In August, the Committee on Foreign Relations of the U.S. Senate, debating the Egyptian request to put their case before it, ruled that Egypt was not under Turkish or British authority but rather "self-governed." The committee, therefore, could hear its case without fear of intervening in the internal affairs of another power.[56]

Zaghlul announced this decision with much fanfare to the Egyptian public, and the prospects of having their case heard in the Senate ignited a furor of discussion and speculation in the press, with many commentators stressing the importance of the decision for the national struggle. One paper celebrated the news of the committee's decision, noting that it "produced profound emotion in Egypt" and "filled Egyptians with joy." Another editorial, reflecting the complexity of the views that some anticolonial nationalists held regarding the basis on which the right to self-determination could be claimed and recognized, concluded that the decision indicated that Americans recognized the status of Egyptians as a civilized people, which was a prerequisite for self-determination. The decision was

> proof that the Egyptian Question has attracted the attention of the New World, and that Egypt has won the sympathy of the supporters

> of liberty. This is the first time our case has ever crossed the Ocean, and the first time the Americans have come to realize that there are inhabitants in Egypt who are not barbarians or negroes or red-skinned, but are rather the heirs of an ancient civilization who are demanding to occupy their due place under the sun.[57]

Such implied assumptions of racial and civilizational hierarchy were hardly unusual among Egyptians and other colonial peoples at the time, and help explain how they could hope for U.S. support despite its well-known record of discrimination and imperialism. Even if Americans mistreated "negroes and red-skinned" peoples, went this logic, they would surely recognize that Egyptians—or, for that matter, Indians, Chinese, and Koreans—were "civilized" and therefore deserved their "place under the sun" in the new world order. While 1919 saw the principle of self-determination begin to emerge as an inalienable right in international affairs and a powerful claim to international legitimacy, at the time many liberal anticolonialists in the West and elsewhere still accepted that its application in practice depended on what International Relations scholar Gerrit W. Gong called the "standard of civilization" in international affairs. Sovereign rights, they held, could only be conferred on peoples that were deemed fully "civilized." What such nationalists disputed, then, was not the perception that hierarchies of race and civilization existed or that they conferred differential rights depending on a group's location within the hierarchy, but only the place of their own groups within those hierarchies. The notions of racial and civilizational hierarchies that served as a central legitimating tenet of the imperial order in international affairs were not at the time limited to Europeans alone.[58]

The perception that the Senate's finding that Egypt was "self-governed" amounted to recognition that Egypt was "civilized" and therefore implied the recognition of its right to self-determination, helps explain the enthusiastic reactions to it among Egyptian nationalists. According to one press report, various Egyptian groups and individuals sent more than fifteen hundred telegrams of thanks to the Senate for its support. Nationalist Egyptians still pinned their hopes for undermining the protectorate on the international influence of the United States, though no longer on Wilson himself. If the Senate rejected the peace treaty as it stood, they hoped, the rejection could lead to a full reconsideration of its terms, including its recognition of the British protectorate over Egypt. Egyptians who, until recently, had cheered for Wilson's victory in Paris were now hoping for his defeat in Washington.[59]

The Egyptian case, in fact, did come before the Senate Committee on Foreign Relations that summer in the course of the hearings it held on the Treaty of Versailles. Since only U.S. citizens could appear officially before the committee, the Wafd contracted with Joseph W. Folk, a long-time progressive who had served as the Democratic governor of Missouri from 1905 to 1909, to represent them there. Folk had been recommended to the Egyptian delegates in Paris by Frank Walsh, a leading Democratic labor lawyer and chair of the National War Labor Board under Wilson who was also the head of the Irish-American delegation that had come to Paris in 1919 to advocate for Irish self-determination. Folk, known as "Holy Joe" for his uncompromising crusades against corruption, earned a reputation as a reformer but also the enmity of many in the political establishment, even within his own party.[60]

In the statement he gave before the Senate committee on August 23, Folk emphasized the Egyptians' faith in Wilson's liberal internationalist principles: They had fought in the war on the Allied side in order "to make, as they believed, the world safe for democracy, and for the right of national self-determination." When the war ended, he said, Egyptians rejoiced because they thought it would mean independence for Egypt, and they "did not doubt that they would have the right of self-determination." Since Great Britain still persisted on denying Egypt that right, Egyptians wanted the U.S. government to recognize their right to independence, or at least to rescind its recognition of the British protectorate so that Egypt could bring its claim before the League of Nations and have it adjudicated there.[61] Zaghlul, after reading a translation of the testimony, concluded that Folk was an "open-minded, intelligent, professional, and perceptive fellow" who had studied the issue well and done a good job. British diplomats had a rather different view, describing Folk as "a radical theorist, with very bad judgement and a disappointed man" who "does not now enjoy much consideration."[62]

Not content to have their case presented in the United States by a hired hand, the Wafd decided to dispatch its own high-level delegation to the United States to advocate for their cause. Initially, Zaghlul wanted to go to the United States himself, telling his advisers: "I must travel there because my conscience demands it, my responsibilities demand it, and I feel that if I did not do it I would be letting my people down."[63] Zaghlul prepared to make the trip with a small party of aides. He even visited an American eye doctor in Paris to receive certification that he was free of trachoma, a highly contagious eye infection that can cause blindness, as required by U.S. immigration regulations, though upon arrival he discovered that the doctor was out. But a few days later, news came that the British government had decided to send to Egypt a commission of inquiry led by the colonial secretary, Alfred Milner, to investigate the uprising, and Zaghlul decided to cancel his American trip in order to prepare his response to the commission. Still, he continued to try to enlist U.S. opinion in support of his cause, asking an Egyptian Copt living in London to compile for him summaries of remarks in the American press on the situation in Egypt, especially anything critical of the Milner commission that he could use to attack it. He also wrote to Folk in the United States, asking him to send relevant clippings from the U.S. press.[64]

The Oxford-educated Wafd member Muhammad Mahmud was chosen to head the delegation instead, and the Egyptians arrived in Washington in November after the State Department initially delayed their visas for fear that the delegation "might have a harmful effect upon Anglo-American relations."[65] They presented petitions to the secretary of state and to members of Congress, arguing that American recognition of the protectorate notwithstanding, it was clearly not the intention of the U.S. government to allow the British to rob Egypt of its independence. They emphasized Egypt's contribution to the war effort and, echoing Wilson's own language, they asked: "Is Egypt to continue to be ruled by might, or are we really in the dawn of a new day when justice and right shall reign?"[66] They received some expressions of support from the anti-imperialist Left and from some Irish-American activists eager to attack Britain, but these had little effect on U.S. policy.[67] In November, Senator Robert Owen, a progressive Democrat from Oklahoma, proposed that the Senate make its ratification of the treaty conditional on a demand that Great Britain recognize Egyptian independence. To this, Secretary of State Lansing replied that the U.S. recognition of the protectorate was already predicated on British promises of eventual Egyptian independence. In any case, the Senate rejected Owen's proposal out of hand.[68]

By the end of 1919, the hopes of Egyptian nationalists for any effective support from the United States were clearly waning. In November, Zaghlul, still in Europe attempting to get a hearing for his case, sent Wilson yet another telegram, imploring the president "not to leave Egypt alone in her fight against England the implacable." But in the same message, he also revealed the Egyptians' bitter disappointment and disillusionment with Wilson. The Egyptian people, he wrote:

> hailed you more than any other people as the Chief of a new doctrine which was to have assured peace and prosperity to the world. This era which your principles promised would indeed have given satisfaction to all, to the great as well as the small, the strong as well as the feeble, and the powerful as well as the oppressed. For having had faith in your principles . . . the Egyptian people . . . see themselves today suffering under the most barbarous treatment on the part of the British authorities.[69]

By December, Zaghlul had clearly given up on American support. In his diary, he noted that "Egypt's position vis-à-vis England has become delicate and precarious, since all the governments—even America—have washed their hands of this region!" The Egyptian nation had relied on the support of foreign governments to rescue Egypt from British rule, but this approach, "if it has not already failed, is bound to fail—at least until there is a transformation in [their] general policies!" Taking a page from Gandhi's ongoing campaign against the British in India, Zaghlul concluded that Egyptians must adopt "passive resistance," like general strikes and avoidance of taxes.[70]

Despite the failure to gain American support, Zaghlul, with strong backing from Egyptian public opinion, refused to compromise on his demands for independence, a fact that Lord Milner discovered to his detriment when he arrived in Egypt in December 1919 to study the crisis there and suggest possible remedies. The commission's mandate, predicated on the well-worn British practice of pacifying colonial disturbances by combining firm treatment of "extremists" with negotiations with "moderate" elements, was to devise an arrangement that would promote peace and prosperity in Egypt "under the Protectorate," but it was ill prepared for the new challenges posed by the Wafd. Zaghlul had rejected the protectorate and insisted on full independence ever since his initial meeting with Wingate the previous November. He was hardly willing to settle for minor British concessions that would leave the protectorate in place, and the commission was met in Egypt with widespread strikes and protests and effectively boycotted. Given Zaghlul's exalted status among the Egyptian public, even those Egyptian officials who were privately inclined to negotiate with Britain could not afford to be seen cooperating with Milner against his wishes.[71]

Zaghlul's arguments against the Milner commission reflected his sense of the transformation that the Wilsonian moment had produced and the importance of the opportunity it presented to internationalize the nationalist struggle. The commission's mandate implied that Egyptian demands for independence were an imperial issue that should be negotiated between colonized and colonizer, rather than, as the Wafd contended, a conflict between equals that should be adjudicated by the international community on the basis of Wilsonian principles. The Milner commission, he said, was "purely English, and to negotiate with it would make the question of Egypt one purely between us and England, while the Delegation depends on the question being an international one." The commission wished to settle Egypt's internal affairs under the protectorate rather than discuss the Egyptian demand for independence, and therefore it could not possibly satisfy nationalist aspirations.[72]

Zaghlul's language revealed his conviction that a radical transformation had come about in the international discourse of legitimacy, one that transformed the relationship between the colonizers and the colonized and rendered obsolete the old justifications for colonialism. Writing in December to Lord Curzon, who had recently formally replaced Balfour as foreign secretary, Zaghlul denounced the protectorate as violating "the spirit of the age," which dictated that "every people shall have the right to self-determination." It was nothing but annexation, which was formerly accepted in international affairs but "is now condemned, and has given way to the right of nationality." Mocking the British claim that their interests in Egypt justified the protectorate, Zaghlul wanted to know, echoing Wilsonian language, "[w]hen it has been considered that the interests of the strong justify the humiliation and subjugation of the weak?" Quoting directly from Wilson's Fourteen Points speech, Zaghlul proclaimed that "the recent magnificent development in the outlook of mankind towards right, justice, 'political independence and territorial integrity of great and small states alike' is now so overwhelming that such a thinly-veiled annexation bearing the name of 'protectorate' can no longer deceive anybody."[73] Even after the collapse of the Wilsonian moment and the disappearance of any hope for American support, Egyptian nationalists continued to draw upon Wilsonian language in defining and defending their aims.

8

From Paris to Amritsar

The men that the Indian National Congress appointed to represent India at the peace conference—Tilak and Gandhi among them—were not in attendance when the conference convened in January. The government of India did send a delegation to Paris, which could participate, the powers agreed, in deliberations that touched upon Indian interests. The delegation, however, was headed by the Secretary of State Montagu, and its Indian members, Sir (soon to be Lord) S. P. Sinha and Ganga Singh, the Maharaja of Bikanir, were handpicked by the British and represented their interests. Bikanir, the ruler of a small state in northwest India, represented the nominally autonomous Indian princely states. He apparently "said very little but gave nice dinner parties."[1] Sinha, who represented British India proper, was a veteran imperial administrator who would soon become the first native Indian to rise to the peerage and the first to serve as undersecretary of state for India in the British cabinet. A prominent member of the Indian National Congress, Sinha even served as its president in the 1915 session. By 1919, however, the movement had so changed with the rise of the home rule leagues and the return of Tilak's extremists that Sinha's support for India's imperial connection marginalized him within it. The nationalist press criticized Sinha and Bikanir as unrepresentative and demanded that the conference admit Tilak and the other INC delegates.[2] With Tilak's admission unlikely, some in the nationalist press argued that "the entire hope of India" lay in President Wilson: "May he strive for the application of his doctrine of self-determination to India," exclaimed a Madras newspaper, "and thereby proclaim to the world the sincerity and inviolability of his law!"[3]

As the deliberations in Paris began, others were more skeptical about India's status and chances of success in the halls of international power. One Delhi paper accused the conference of continuing the practice of racial exclusion in international affairs: "The black Indians," it reported, "will not be allowed to impurify [*sic*] by their colour the sacred hall where the Peace Conference will assemble." Bikanir and Sinha would "only be allowed to sit at the entrance and not to enter the house."[4] Montagu, as the official head of the Indian delegation, took umbrage at this "infamous statement," retorting: "Indian delegates are, in every respect, on exactly the same footing as delegates of the Powers represented and have the same authority and rights."[5] The secretary of state further reported that Bikanir distinguished himself at the conference by securing for India representation in the new League of Nations, winning the point and, Montagu added with unconcealed delight, "even bearding and obtaining the necessary answer from the great President Wilson himself." The maharaja apparently capped his triumph by inviting the French premier, Clemenceau—widely known as "the Tiger"—to join him on a tiger hunt. "That amazing septuagenarian has that one ambition, and you may find him in your jungles next cold weather," Montagu wrote the viceroy, Lord Chelmsford. "The whole proceeding appears to have concluded by Bikanir displaying to the Big Five the tiger tattooed on his arm, which was inspected and approved not only by Clemenceau, but by Orlando and Wilson. Thus, we make peace with Germany!"[6]

While Sinha and Bikanir, then, did little to give voice to the demands of Indian nationalists, the presence at the international forum of a separate representation for India was symbolically significant. In one of his letters to the viceroy, Montagu, the scion of a banking family who was given to lengthy, often melancholy musing, contemplated the presence at the conference of separate delegations for the British dominions and for India. He pondered "the profound, irretraceable changes that have been made in the constitution of the British Empire during the last few months" and concluded:

> It would seem to me that we are riding two constitutional horses. From the back of the first we proclaim the unity of the Empire.... From the back of the other horse we proclaim that the British Empire should be represented by something like fourteen representatives to everybody else's five on certain matters; and the British Empire Delegation agreed yesterday that the Dominions and India might, if they so chose, on matters of interest to them, put in memoranda to the Inter-Allied Conference separately from the British Imperial Delegates, although they took part in the deliberations which led to the decisions of those delegates. As regards India, I would only make this observation. Ex-Pro-Consuls and others are holding up their hands with horror at any substantial efforts towards self-government, and at the same time we have gone—shall I say lightly?—into a series of decisions which puts India so far as international affairs are concerned on a basis wholly inconsistent with the position of a subordinate country.[7]

For Montagu, the presence of separate Indian representation at an international forum such as the peace conference meant that India's international status had "soared far more rapidly than could have been accomplished by any of our reforms." India's admission to the conference as an entity apart from the empire reflected the tension at the center of the imperial discourse of legitimacy between the unity of the empire, on the one hand, and the emergence of its constituent parts as international actors in their own right, on the other. In May 1919, noting that the conference had decided that India would be a "State Member of the League of Nations," Montagu added that "the constitutional position which she [India] has achieved for herself in the last few months is amazing and is wholly inconsistent with an attitude of ascendancy on our part, either economic or governmental." India's representation in international forums, he worried, was at odds with its autocratic governance and would ultimately render untenable the British insistence on denying India self-determination. In the terms used later by international legal scholars, Montagu was concerned that India's achievement of "external" self-determination, or recognition as an international actor, would eventually compel Britain to grant it "internal" self-determination, or the right to choose its own rulers.[8] As the gap between India's international status and its domestic condition grew larger, Indian nationalists moved to redefine the goals, means, and timetable of their movement as they strove to liberate it from the confines of British colonial policy and bring it into the international arena.

When Tilak was elected by the Delhi Congress as one of its representatives to the peace conference, the long-time leader of the extremists was already in London working to internationalize the Indian struggle. He had arrived there in October 1918, shortly before the armistice, and would have been there even sooner had the government not refused him a passport earlier that year in order to prevent him from spreading "mischievous propaganda" in Britain. In order to circumvent this refusal, Tilak asked to go to London to pursue a libel suit against the British author Sir Valentine Chirol, who had described Tilak as the "father of Indian unrest" in a book he had published in 1910.[9] And though he did pursue that case—without success—his main purpose in the trip, according to his close confidant N. C. Kelkar, was "to impress upon the world leaders the need for applying the principle of self-determination to India."[10] He worked assiduously at this task through the spring, when he was joined in England by a number of other leading nationalist figures. The peace conference might not go into details, he reasoned, but it would lay down the principles of international relations in the postwar world, and Indians must therefore inform it of their demand for self-determination.[11]

Initially, Tilak had faith in the good will toward India of Lloyd George and his government, and he saw the Liberal prime minister as a potential ally in the struggle against the opponents of Indian self-government in England. He accused the opponents of Indian self-determination in the Tory press of hypocrisy. The *Times* of London and other conservative papers, while granting the importance of the principle of self-determination in general, claimed that it

Indian nationalist leader Bal Gangadhar Tilak had long advocated an uncompromising stand against British rule. During the Wilsonian moment, he traveled to London and worked to bring the case for Indian self-determination before "world opinion" and the assembled leaders in Paris. *Nehru Memorial Museum and Library, New Delhi.*

did not apply to India because "she is not a nation, or she is unfit, or that all progress must be made 'step by step.' " This was a good summary of the common arguments against extending self-determination to the colonial world: colonial peoples were not nations, or not sufficiently civilized to exercise self-determination, or they required gradual reforms rather than immediate home rule. But these were "invented arguments," Tilak said. Did not those very papers call for self-determination for the German colonies in Africa, which were clearly less advanced than India? Even if India needed progress, self-determination was now a precondition for it rather than its ultimate destination. It was imperative, Tilak wrote to his supporters back in India, that Lloyd George should be informed forthwith, through "hundreds of messages from all parts of India," that India wanted self-determination.[12]

When, in the preliminary discussions that preceded the conference, the great powers agreed that India should have separate representation at the peace table, the nationalists' hopes for effective action in Paris increased. The appointment of Sinha to the position of undersecretary of state for India in January 1919, and his subsequent entry into the House of Lords, further stoked Indian optimism about the intentions of the Lloyd George government. Lajpat Rai described the appointment as "of sufficient importance to justify the hope that a radical change is coming over the spirit of British imperialism,"[13] and Tilak, too, believed that these developments signaled London's willingness to have the Indian nationalist view put before the conference.[14] Writing to Lloyd George directly, Tilak congratulated him on his recent election victory and asked that the prime minister grant him an interview, as the elected representative of the INC and the Home Rule League, in order to present and explain India's claim for self-government.[15] He also wrote to Clemenceau, as president of the peace conference, to demand for India "her birth-right . . . the principle of self-determination."[16] Tilak reserved the most effusive missive, however, for Wilson. "The world's hope for peace and justice is centered in you as the author of the great principle of self-determination," he wrote to the president in January, and the peace conference must apply the president's "principles of right and justice" to India.[17] Tilak enclosed a copy of his letter to Lloyd George, hoping no doubt that Wilson would put additional pressure on the premier to do right by India.

Tilak's letter to the president also included a handsomely illustrated pamphlet entitled *Self-Determination for India*, which was published by the India Home Rule League's London office. This pamphlet, part of the international propaganda campaign spearheaded by Tilak during this period, made an eloquent case for India as a nation that was fully deserving and prepared to govern itself. The pamphlet opened with an illustration that depicted a steamship, the *Self-Determination*, boarding numerous passengers for its journey on a "new route from autocracy to freedom." The passengers, identified by their "Oriental" dress and features, come from all corners of the non-Western world—there are Jews and Armenians, Chinese and Arabs, and many others. Only India, represented as a young woman in a sari, is prevented from boarding by a "passport officer" in the image of Lloyd George. Standing on the deck, "Captain Wilson" calls out "What about India?" "No passport, Captain," comes the reply. A second illustration in the same pamphlet depicted Montagu, dressed as Father Christmas, offering India, again shown as a young woman in a sari, a cake labeled "Indian reform," which India declines as insufficiently appetizing: "No Thanks. No sugar in it."[18]

The pamphlet was widely distributed not only in Britain but also in the United States, and despite the criticism that the illustrations leveled at the British policy on India, the text itself was a model of reason and moderation.[19] The task of the peace conference, the pamphlet opened, was to establish durable peace by extending the "rule of right throughout the globe," and President Wilson had asserted that this could not happen unless powerful nations were "ready to pay the price, and the price is impartial justice, no matter whose interest is crossed." The British approach as laid out in the Montagu declaration contradicted this principle, since it denied India's right to self-determination and left it to London to decide the scope and pace of Indian reforms. The declaration, however, had been issued before the principle of self-determination was announced by President Wilson and accepted by the government and people of Great Britain as the basis for the postwar settlement. In the new international order, therefore, the declaration should be considered null and void. It was no longer enough that India should have reforms toward self-government; Indians must play a central role in deciding the pace and extent of the reforms.[20]

The pamphlet then moved to describe the Indian demands of the peace conference. Emphasizing the moderation of the Indian claims, it noted that Indians did not demand the "dismemberment" of the British Empire, but rather wanted home rule along the lines enjoyed by the white dominions. This, it pointed out, was no more than the "autonomous development" promised to the various peoples of the Ottoman and Habsburg empires in Wilson's Fourteen Points, which the government of Great Britain had accepted. The "ideals and rights" of self-determination, nationalism, freedom of nations, national dignity, and self-respect were "immortal principles" that had "infused a new life into India during the war," and without their implementation, the world could "never be made safe for democracy." What Indians wanted, the pamphlet continued in an explicit gesture to Wilson's own sensibilities, was a "Monroe Doctrine for India." Just as that doctrine "saved the South American Republics for self-development," so should Great Britain do by India. Indeed, the same principle should apply to all of Asia and Africa, removing their peoples from the "pupilage" of the imperial powers for "the common welfare of all mankind." This rendering of the intent and impact of the Monroe Doctrine, of course, elided the long history of U.S. interventions in Latin America, but the elision is hardly surprising in light of the efforts of Indian nationalists to enlist Wilson's support for their cause.[21]

CAPTAIN WILSON: Hullo! What about India?
PASSPORT OFFICER (Ll--d G----e): No passport, Captain.

This cartoon, representing the world situation from the perspective of Indian nationalists, appeared in a pamphlet entitled *Self-Determination for India*, published by Indian Home Rule League in late 1918. It depicts President Wilson as the captain of a ship, the *Self-Determination*, which is boarding numerous non-European passengers headed for freedom. Only India is held back by a figure representing British prime minister David Lloyd George. Self-Determination for India *(London: Indian Home Rule League, 1918). Pamphlet found in Library of Congress, Woodrow Wilson Papers, Series 5F, Reel 446.*

The text next took up the common Tory refrain that self-determination did not apply to the Raj because India was not a nation, but rather a collection of many different nations: Bengali, Marathi, Punjabi, and so forth. Even if that were so, were not each of these nations entitled to its own self-determination rather than being forced under British rule? Moreover, India might be diverse along lines of race, region, and religion, but its underlying unity in terms of geography, history, and culture, as recognized by numerous Western scholars, meant that it was in fact one nation. The idea that a nation as ancient as India, "the eldest brother in the family of man," should be put under the sort of indefinite trusteeship envisioned by London was both counter to the principle of self-determination and a "deep wound inflicted on Indian sensitiveness."[22] Indians were quite capable of settling their own affairs, and if the peace conference did not grant India immediate self-determination, it should at least fix a definite time limit—no more than fifteen years—to British trusteeship in India, within which Parliament would have to enact a democratic constitution for India. Each province would enjoy internal autonomy, and together they would be federated as the United States of India, with democratically elected central executive and legislative bodies, and incorporated as a self-governing unit of the British Commonwealth with full and equal rights.[23]

The moderation of the Indian claims, however, failed to move the great power leaders in Paris. There is no evidence that Clemenceau ever replied to Tilak's letter, and President Wilson, the prime target of the arguments made in the Indian text, did only slightly better. His private secretary, Gilbert Close, wrote back to Tilak: "I am instructed by President Wilson, to acknowledge your letter and express to you his high appreciation of your kind thought of him and to assure that the matter of self-determination for India is a question which will be taken up in due time by the proper authorities."[24] Though there is little direct evidence of the president's thoughts on India, we know that he was in accord with the great power decision that the conference would consider only questions emanating directly from the war. The League of Nations, he said, would sort out the rest in due course. Once organized, he wrote in response to Irish demands for independence, the league would "afford a forum not now available for bringing the opinion of the world and of the United States in particular to bear on just such problems."[25] For the time being, therefore, British officials were not much concerned that the president might support Indian demands. Upon receiving news of Wilson's exchange with Tilak, a Foreign Office official commented tartly that its text did not actually commit the president to support India's claims and concluded that "not much attention need be paid to Pres. Wilson's acknowledgement."[26]

Tilak and his supporters tried to present the president's brief, vague reply in the best light, as an indication of U.S. support for bringing Indian claims, after the conclusion of the peace treaty, before the League of Nations.[27] Indeed, throughout the early months of 1919, Tilak and his entourage in London remained buoyant about their chances of success in Paris. He was doing his best, Tilak intimated to an aide, to have the subject of self-determination for India brought before the conference:

> I feel *sure* that we shall succeed therein. ... The Peace Conference will not consider the details of the scheme. It is too big a body for that. But there is a good chance that it may assert the principle of Self Determination for India. And if this is done our purpose is served any how. I am sure the question of India will not go unnoticed in the present sitting of the Conference. It is for us to see that the decision is in our favour. Government may not like the idea of our appealing to the Peace Conference. But that is no reason why we should not do so.

Analyzing British domestic politics, Tilak concluded that, in matters related to India, Parliament would pass whatever Whitehall wished. The difficulty, then, would be to bring the Lloyd George government to adopt the Indian view, and the only way to do so would be to have the matter publicly discussed at the peace table.[28]

To this end, Tilak mobilized a broad campaign to bring Indian demands to the peace table. Dozens of organizations at the local and provincial levels in India—branches of Tilak's Home Rule League, various provincial committees of the INC—dispatched petitions to the peace conference and its principals. They all repeated a similar coordinated message: India wants self-determination in accordance with President Wilson's principles.[29] Tilak also wanted to work hard to propagate the Indian nationalist cause among the leading powers, pressing the INC to set up permanent propaganda bureaus in a number of locations, including England, France, America, Germany, and Japan. Praising the work of Lajpat Rai's Indian Home Rule League of America as a model for such activity, Tilak said that "a favourable opinion of the civilised world towards Indian aspirations is a valuable asset in our struggle for freedom. We cannot afford to neglect world opinion except at our peril."[30] Tilak oversaw the production of a series of pamphlets advocating Indian self-determination that were circulated in England and India, and in the spring, he joined other prominent figures in the Indian nationalist movement who had arrived in England on lecture tours to promote Indian home rule.[31]

Early on, Tilak, citing his appointment by the Delhi Congress as its delegate to the peace conference, applied for a passport to travel to Paris, but the British authorities summarily denied his application. "The idea of our going to [the] Peace Conference is not relishable to them, and any deputation coming here after the Peace Conference is over will be ... not of much use."[32] Weeks passed without a substantial success, but Tilak did not lose hope. He was doing all he could, he wrote in early February, to have India's question brought up before the League of Nations, and he remained confident "that it will be so brought provided we keep up the cry." In the meantime, he instructed his followers back home to do all they could to keep the nationalist camp united behind the demand for self-determination. If the conference took up the issue and pronounced upon it favorably, he was convinced, the British government and Parliament would have no choice but to follow suit.[33]

But Lloyd George and his cabinet were less favorably disposed toward Indian home rule than Tilak had imagined, and the petition campaign failed to achieve the desired effect. The British delegation at the conference largely ignored it, and the petitions that arrived at its headquarters were simply filed away into oblivion. Indian efforts to circumvent the British by appealing directly to the peace conference itself also came to naught. When Paul Dutasta, the French chief of the conference secretariat, received the petitions, he took the trouble to inquire with the British delegation what should be done with them. Should they be copied and circulated to other delegations, asked Dutasta, or merely registered and filed away? The British, not surprisingly, chose the latter option, thanking Dutasta for his "friendly action in this matter."[34] Still, even in April, when Tilak already knew that the conference would not take up the Indian question in any formal fashion, he wrote that "even a suggestion from the Conference—a hint—would be of great value and I have not yet grown hopeless about it."[35] That hint, however, never came.

Within India, the tensions that had been rising since the armistice reached a breaking point in the spring. It came when the British authorities, concerned with the growing agitation for home rule, moved to enact a series of bills that extended the government's wartime powers of internment without trial. The bills were based on a committee report, submitted in July 1918, which made recommendations for legislation that would allow the government to continue to suppress "conspiracy and political outrage" once the war was over. The report was put before the Imperial Legislative Council in early February 1919 and made into law on March 21, 1919. As historian Judith M. Brown has noted, the Rowlatt bills—named after the judge who headed the committee—which dealt with an issue that had "very limited political appeal" and "barely impinged on the lives of ordinary people," would seem a curious trigger for the launching of a broad popular movement against British rule.[36] But the response to the Rowlatt bills must be understood in the context of the anticipation of far-reaching change that had built up among Indians during the war years, which now quickly gave way to bitter disillusionment.

The transition is evident in the nationalist press at the time. While the gathering of the peace conference and the Indian campaign for self-determination were the most prominent topics in the headlines in December and January, by early February there was a stark shift to outraged reporting on the Rowlatt bills.[37] Indians, who had expected an immediate push toward self-government after the war, were incensed, and Mohandas Gandhi, who had until then remained "only a peripheral figure in the politics of nationalism," now moved to the forefront. Gandhi had been cutting his teeth in Indian politics through involvement in local issues since his return in 1914 from South Africa, where he had begun his public career leading the struggle of Indians there for equal rights as imperial subjects. For Gandhi, this was a moment of transformation, both in his private views and in his public stature. Throughout the war, he had been a staunch supporter of the empire and had worked hard to assist in the recruitment of Indians into the military. Now, however, he realized that his hopes of achieving equality for Indians within the empire had been in vain, and emerged for the first time as a figure of national stature to lead the movement to oppose these "black acts." Denouncing the Rowlatt bills as a "symptom of deep-seated disease among the ruling class" of the empire, Gandhi announced his intentions to launch a campaign of nonviolent resistance, or *satyagraha*, against the bills, calling for civil disobedience and a nationwide *hartal*, or general strike.[38]

The response to his announcement was unprecedented. Strikes were declared in many of India's cities, and, despite Gandhi's call for the observance of nonviolence, clashes between protesters and police occurred in several places. The British officials in India, many of whom saw the movement as the prelude to revolution in India and across the empire—the Egyptian protests against Zaghlul's deportation had broken out almost simultaneously—often responded, as they did in Egypt, with the harsh enforcement of martial law, setting curfews and prohibiting public gatherings. The most infamous incident of the Rowlatt Satyagraha occurred on April 13, 1919, when forces under General Reginald Dyer opened fire on a large gathering in Jallianwala Bagh, a walled park in the Punjab city of Amritsar, inflicting hundreds of casualties. That bloody episode, remembered as the Amritsar Massacre, quickly became a symbol to Indians of the oppressive nature of British rule and marked a new stage in the Indian movement. As happened in Egypt, the violence that erupted in the spring of 1919 dealt a blow to Indians' faith in British intentions to move India expeditiously toward self-determination and sealed their disillusionment with the promise of the Wilsonian moment.[39]

Both the British and Indians at the time made the connection between the rhetoric of the Wilsonian moment and the Indian campaign against the Rowlatt bills. The All-India Congress Committee president, Madan Mohan Malaviya, wrote shortly after the events at Amritsar that a complete understanding of Indian discontent and its causes must realize how "cheered and encouraged" Indians had been by Allied declarations that the aims of the Great War were self-determination for all. Now, Indians felt betrayed by the widespread opposition of the official and nonofficial British communities in India even to Montagu's "mild recommendations" for political reforms, which were "regarded as inadequate by the bulk of Indian opinion." The Government of India itself agreed. A 1920 report on the violence in the Punjab and across India in the spring of 1919 noted: "The utterances of European and American statesmen regarding the ideals for which the Allies have fought, the principles of democracy and self-determination, have been widely discussed and naturally adopted by enthusiastic Indians as no less applicable to themselves as to other countries." The atmosphere in India, "as elsewhere has been affected by the doctrine that the war was to inaugurate a new era of greater freedom and happiness for all." Another British report on these events concluded that "the desire for a larger say in the government of the country was greatly fostered by the dissemination in the press and otherwise of the doctrine of self-determination which formed so prominent a subject of discussion at the Peace Conference in Paris."[40]

Gandhi himself made almost no mention of Wilson in his voluminous writings, either at the time or later. Wilson's progressive ideals, which sought the improvement of modern society, would have held little attraction for the Mahatma, whose philosophy involved, as he wrote himself, "a severe condemnation of 'modern civilization' " *in toto*, and who sometimes argued for the abolition of all its manifestations, such as railroads, hospitals, medicine, law, and government. In his 1908 book *Hind Swaraj*, or Indian self-rule, Gandhi enjoined representatives of modern civilization—doctors, lawyers, industrialists—to give up their professions and take up the handloom.[41]

At the same time, there is little doubt that the opportunities that Wilson's proclaimed support for self-determination seemed to offer India were well recognized within Gandhi's circle. C. F. "Charlie" Andrews, a British missionary and a long-time friend of the Mahatma, told the leading liberal politician Srinivasa Sastri shortly after the armistice that the reform schemes previously proposed by the British had become moot, since the charter of Indian nationalism was now Wilson's doctrine of self-determination. It would allow Indians to demand the right of entry not only into the peace conference but also into the future League of Nations, and thus introduce India as an independent, sovereign entity in international affairs. Sastri, who thought that India should remain firmly within the empire, was appalled. "The idea that this move on the part of the Indian politicians is nothing short of asserting India's independence of the British Empire," he commented, "does not deter him." Andrews got the idea, Sastri speculated, from Gandhi when he stayed with him at his ashram at Sabarmati.[42]

Sastri's conjecture aside, Gandhi himself was clearly aware of Wilson's rhetoric and international stature. But the few recorded comments he made about the president were critical of the latter's failure to go far enough in the promotion of world peace. Shortly after Wilson presented the League of

Nations covenant publicly on February 14, 1919, the Mahatma wrote to Andrews: "Have you noticed an unconscious betrayal of the true nature of modern civilization in Mr. Wilson's speech? . . . Saying that if the moral pressure to be exerted against a recalcitrant party failed, the members of the League would not hesitate to use the last remedy, viz., brute force."[43] He repeated that same point again a few weeks later, in a speech he gave on satyagraha in Madras:

> The message of the West which the Government of India, I presume, represent[s], is succinctly put by President Wilson in his speech . . . : "Armed force is in the background in this programme, but it is in the background, and if the moral force of the world will not suffice, the physical force of the world shall." We [satyagrahis] hope to reverse the process, and by our action show that physical force is nothing compared to the moral force, and that moral force never fails.

Gandhi, however, neglected to cite the sentence that came immediately after the words he had quoted. "But that [physical force] is a last resort," Wilson had added, "because this is intended as a constitution of peace, not as a league of war."[44]

Wilson himself, unaware of Gandhi's rebuke, used the fact of Indian representation in Paris to defend the peace treaty and the League of Nations to an American public wary of foreign entanglements. In the very last speech he gave in the fall of 1919, just before he suffered the debilitating stroke that marked the practical end of his public career, Wilson presented India's representation in the League of Nations as a move toward the goal of bringing non-European peoples into the folds of international society. "For the first time in the history of the world," he told a crowd in Pueblo, Colorado, "that great and voiceless multitude, that throng hundreds of millions strong in India, has a voice among the nations of the world." And it was a good thing, too: some of the "wisest and most dignified figures in the peace conference at Paris . . . came from India." They "seemed to carry in their minds an older wisdom than the rest of us had, whose traditions ran back into so many of the unhappy fortunes of mankind," and so "seemed very useful counselors as to how some ray of hope and some prospect of happiness could be opened to its people."[45] Such musings, though tinged with exoticism, suggest that Wilson saw eventual Indian self-determination "among the nations of the world" as within the scope of his vision for the new international order, even if he left unclear how, or how quickly, that goal would be achieved.

As the struggle in the U.S. Senate over the ratification of the Versailles Treaty raged in the fall of 1919, Indian nationalists, like their Egyptian counterparts, continued to work to enlist American public opinion in their favor, often with the support of anti-imperialists and anti-British activists. To advance the cause of Indian self-determination, a group of American activists joined Lajpat Rai and several other Indians resident in the United States to establish an organization called Friends of Freedom for India. The group's president was the University of Chicago English professor and long-time social activist Robert Morss Lovett. Its general secretary was the twenty-seven-year-old Agnes Smedley, a radical feminist and anti-imperialist activist. Smedley had ties to M. N. Roy and other Indian revolutionaries in the United States—ties which Lajpat Rai, concerned for her safety, warned her against—and she was arrested and indicted in 1918 under the wartime Espionage Act for abetting rebellion against British rule in India, though she was not convicted. The roster of the national council of the Friends of Freedom for India also boasted such luminaries as W. E. B. Du Bois, whom Lajpat Rai had met numerous times during his study of American race relations; Franz Boas, a Columbia University professor and the founder of modern anthropology; and the author and social reformer Upton Sinclair.[46]

Irish-American advocates of Irish independence were especially prominent among American supporters of Indian and Egyptian claims against Britain. Appalled by London's suppression of the Irish independence movement since the Easter Rising in the spring of 1916, they wanted to advance the cause of Irish self-determination by opening a broad front against British imperialism and saw the Indian and Egyptian nationalists as natural allies in that fight.[47] When the president of Sinn Fein, Eamon De Valera, arrived in the United States in June to a hero's welcome after a daring escape from a British prison, they arranged for him to meet Lajpat Rai in New York.[48] Though little came of that meeting, or of the Irish-Indian connection more broadly at the time, Lajpat Rai's "pernicious activities" and the contacts of Indian nationalists with other anti-British elements in the United States were nevertheless sources of irritation for British journalists and diplomats. One report to London warned of the danger of Indian propaganda in the United States, supported as it was by "Hun sympathizers," "irreconcilable Irish," and the "long-haired and high-brow people."[49] This prompted the India Office to suggest that Indian students wishing to study abroad should be encouraged to forgo American schools for Canadian universities, where they would get a more "truly British point of view."[50]

As the Senate Committee on Foreign Relations began its hearings on the peace treaty, Lajpat Rai approached Dudley Field Malone, a prominent Irish-American and Democratic party activist, to present the case for Indian self-government before the committee. Malone, a New York attorney who was known as a forceful public speaker, had been a close supporter of Wilson, but fell out with the president in 1917 over the administration's lack of support for female suffrage, throwing his support behind the Socialist party.[51] In his testimony on August 21 before the committee, which Lajpat Rai and his aide N. S. Hardikar had prepared, Malone pointed out that the Indian delegation present in Paris was not a representative one, since the British government had handpicked its members while denying the delegates that the INC had selected permission to attend. This ran counter to the spirit of the League of Nations, and the covenant should therefore be amended to require that every signatory provide democratic institutions to the peoples subject to their rule.[52] Malone also presented the Senate committee with a memorandum, composed by Lajpat Rai, which laid out the arguments for Indian self-determination based on its long history, the high level of its civilization, and the new principles of international legitimacy.

Like Zaghlul in Paris at the time, Tilak followed the Senate deliberations closely from London. The Indian appearance there, he thought, was another step in the campaign to internationalize the struggle for Indian home rule. The Senate appearance, he wrote, was an important follow-up to his own efforts to bring the Indian case before the peace conference, and should in turn be followed by an appeal to the League of Nations, once it begins its sessions.[53] Upon receiving the news that the Indian memorandum was entered into the official Senate protocol, one of Tilak's aides wrote: "We may thus have the satisfaction" of "having entered the case of India's claim for Self Determination on the official records of the United States."[54] The senators themselves, however, showed little interest in the Indian claims that Malone presented to them. Though the persistence and the brutality of British rule over India, as well as Ireland and Egypt, was used by some American opponents of the treaty to denounce it as fig leaf for empire, such denunciations were usually little more than rhetorical posturing, part of the domestic political struggle within the United States. Neither the Wilson administration nor the Senate had the intention, and even less the power, to influence British policy in India in the direction of self-determination.

Tilak returned to India in November 1919, after more than a year abroad trying to achieve international recognition for the Indian demands of self-determination. Despite his failure to gain a hearing for the nationalist cause in Paris, he continued to exhort the Indian National Congress to try to advance its claims in the international arena and work to bring them before the League of Nations, even if no immediate results could be expected. "The most important point" to be urged on the upcoming INC session in Amritsar, Tilak's weekly magazine declared in December 1919, was "the arrangement to be made to represent India's case before the League of Nations and to put before it the question of the application of self-determination to India." India's position was "hopelessly anomalous." As a member of the league, India could vote on the appeals of others for self-determination, but it could not apply the same principle to itself. The claim of the Montagu declaration that the time and manner of India's progress toward responsible government could only be determined by Parliament was "just the opposite of self-determination" and had been rendered illegitimate, since "President Wilson has plainly said... that all claims to self-determination" could be brought before the League of Nations.[55] Echoing almost precisely Zaghlul's argument against the legitimacy of the British protectorate over Egypt, Tilak believed that in the postwar international order, these newly established principles of international legitimacy would trump the logic of empire and allow, indeed require, the eventual emergence of national independence for colonial possessions.

Tilak would not live to see this come about. Soon after his return, he fell ill with pneumonia and died on August 1, 1920, at the age of sixty-four. His funeral procession ran a mile and half long on the streets of Bombay, and in his tribute, Gandhi, who had replaced Tilak as the most prominent leader of the nationalist movement, called him "the maker of Modern India."[56] But Tilak's emphasis on internationalizing the Indian struggle did not die with him. Lajpat Rai, too, believed that the war had transformed the problem of India from "a domestic problem of the British Empire" into "an international problem on which hinges, more or less, the future peace of the world.... The world cannot be made safe for democracy without India being democratic."[57] He called repeatedly on Indian leaders to emphasize propaganda work abroad, including the publication of books and the establishment of information bureaus, news agencies, and academic exchanges.[58]

At the same time, by late 1919, Lajpat Rai, like other colonial intellectuals, began to view events in Russia, rather than in the United States, as standing at the forefront of the movement for global progress. The fall of autocracy in Russia, he noted, "has given birth to a new order of society aglow with the spirit of a new and elevated kind of internationalism. This internationalism must have for its foundation justice and self-determination for all peoples, regardless of race or religion, creed or colour," and be based on cooperation among peoples rather than exploitation of the weak by the strong. But even with his turn toward Russia, Lajpat Rai remained a Wilsonian, endeavoring to chart a middle way between imperialism and revolution. The only alternatives to self-determination, he warned, were "reaction, with the certainty of even greater wars in the near future, or Bolshevism," and they could be averted only if "the different peoples of the earth, now being bled and exploited," were conceded their rights. India would have to "come into its own soon or else not even the Himalayas can effectually bar the entry of Bolshevism into India," he wrote in December 1919.[59]

Finally receiving a visa allowing him to return to India, Lajpat Rai departed New York City in late 1919. The farewell dinner, organized by Malone and his League of Oppressed Peoples, hosted numerous anticolonial activists, including Oswald Garrison Villard, U.S. socialist leader Norman Thomas, an Irish representative, and a Chinese delegate who gave a speech hailing Sun Yat-sen.[60] When he arrived in India in February 1920, Lajpat Rai told the *Bombay Chronicle* that there was strong support for India in the United States and a desire to learn more about the situation there. Work in England was important, but "we must supplement this work by an extensive propaganda elsewhere, particularly in America." Lajpat Rai remained a prominent figure in the nationalist movement until his death in 1928, at the age of sixty-three, of wounds received in a severe beating from police while leading an anti-British demonstration in Lahore in his native Punjab. Upon his death, Gandhi eulogized him as one of the heroes of the Indian national struggle. Lajpat Rai's work for his nation, he said, had to be understood in a broader, global context: "His patriotism was no narrow creed. He loved his country because he loved the world. His nationalism was international."[61]

By that time, the Indian nationalist movement had adopted goals and means that were far more radical than most Indian leaders, including Tilak and Lajpat Rai, could have imagined as feasible prior to the war. The INC, a pillar of the empire until 1914, was now its determined enemy. In 1920, it officially adopted Gandhi's policy of noncooperation, thus abandoning its long-standing status of a "loyal opposition" committed to protest only through constitutional means, and instead set out to undermine British rule through extralegal campaigns of resistance.[62] The INC moderates, who as late as 1915 had been in control, practically disappeared as a significant political force by the early 1920s, and even some erstwhile extremists found themselves out of step with the new, radical tone of the Gandhian Congress.[63] The newfound contempt for the empire was promptly reflected in the nationwide protest that met the visiting Prince of Wales in 1921, a striking contrast with the spectacle of imperial loyalty and pomp that had greeted King George V in Delhi only a decade earlier. To be sure, debates and dissent in the Congress about its goals and means continued in subsequent years, and another decade would pass before it adopted *purna swaraj*, or complete independence, as its official aim in 1929.[64] The spring of 1919, however, remained a crucial watershed, in which the national movement swung decisively toward the goal of terminating British rule in India.

9

Empty Chairs at Versailles

On November 26, 1918, shortly before Wilson left the United States for Europe, Wellington Koo, as the Chinese minister in Washington, came to see the president at the White House. He wanted, Koo tells us in his memoirs, "to ascertain the American attitude toward China's hopes at the conference." Secretary of State Lansing had already assured him of U.S. sympathy, but he wished "to get a direct reaction" from the president.

> When I was received at the White House, President Wilson in reply to my question confirmed the sympathetic attitude of the U.S. towards China's desiderata. He was delighted that I was going to Paris and he hoped that I would keep in touch with the U.S. delegation. But evidently he was more preoccupied with his program for the peace conference. He talked at length about his hopes in the Conference and he reiterated what he had already stated in his famous Fourteen Points; if the world was to have permanent peace, he said there must be a new order.

The Chinese people, Koo told Wilson, had the greatest faith in his principles, which "had given expression to the ideals of the world and kindled the hearts of all." Wilson admitted that applying his principles to the Far East would be difficult, but added that "mere difficulty was no good reason for not applying them there." The meeting was congenial, and though the president gave him no specific assurances, Koo nevertheless left the meeting convinced that the president would support China at the peace conference.[1]

After their arrival in Paris, however, the Chinese delegates discovered that the political realities there were considerably less accommodating than they had hoped. In its preparatory work for the conference, the Chinese delegation had planned to use the international forum to challenge the full gamut of privileges enshrined in the "unequal treaties" that China had signed with foreign powers over the preceding decades and demand the abolition of such provisions as legal extraterritoriality and limitations on its tariff autonomy. These practices abridged China's political and economic sovereignty, and if the new international order were to be based on justice and self-determination these arrangements could not remain in place. Such demands, however, were quickly put aside by the great powers in Paris, which were not inclined to forgo the territorial and commercial advantages that the unequal treaties gave them. They had already agreed at the outset that only issues directly emanating from the war would be on the table at the conference, and the broad Chinese claims for the abrogation of the unequal treaties did not. Any discussion of comprehensive readjustments to China's international status, Clemenceau later informed the Chinese delegation, did not fall within the province of the peace conference. China, if it wished, could bring them up later for adjudication at the League of Nations.[2]

The Chinese demands for a general readjustment of China's international status toward full sovereignty were accordingly shelved for the time being. The issue that moved to the top of the Chinese agenda in Paris was the one territorial question that was a direct result of the war: the disposal of the German-controlled territory in Shandong (Shantung) Province, which Japanese forces had captured early in the war.[3] In 1897, Germany had compelled the Qing government to lease it the territory around Jiaozhou (Kiaochow) Bay in the south of Shandong Province, a peninsula in northern China jutting into the East China Sea. The Germans made the territory into their major outpost in the Far East and a showpiece of their expanding imperial ambitions. The village of Qingdao (Tsingtao), located within the concession, quickly grew into an industrial port city that served German business interests in China.[4] When Japan joined the war, one of its first acts was to seize the territory from the German contingent that defended it, and Tokyo then proceeded to try to induce the feeble government in Beijing into recognizing Japan as the rightful heir of German rights there. In January 1915, the Japanese government issued an ultimatum to China that listed twenty-one demands, which included the recognition of special Japanese rights in Shandong, and which President Yuan Shikai accepted in May that year in the face of popular uproar. This recognition was later confirmed in a secret exchange of notes that Tokyo extracted from Beijing in September 1918, shortly before the armistice.[5]

The question of Shandong came for the first time before the Council of Ten on January 28, 1919, and the Chinese representatives were invited to present their case. Wellington Koo rose to speak on behalf of China. Reminding his audience that he spoke for some 400 million people, one-quarter of the human race, Koo said that China asked for the full restoration of the Shandong leased territories to its control. Germany had taken them under the threat of force, and their entire population and history were Chinese. The region not only had great economic and strategic significance for China; it also contained the birthplace of the sage Confucius and it was therefore considered by many Chinese as the "cradle of Chinese civilization." While China was grateful, he said, for the heroic services of the Japanese and other Allied forces in liberating the territory from Germany, it could not repay them by "selling the birthright of their countrymen" and sowing the seeds of future discord. Makino

Nobuaki, the Japanese delegate, responded. There had been an exchange of notes between Beijing and Tokyo in September, he said to the surprise of the Chinese delegates, who had been kept in the dark by their government, and the exchange recognized Japanese possession of the German rights in the territory. Would the Japanese government object to laying these notes before the council? President Wilson asked. Makino responded that he did not think so, but he would have to return to his government for instruction.[6]

Makino's surprise announcement notwithstanding, Koo's appearance before the council won plaudits from most observers. Edward T. Williams, a veteran American Sinologist who served as an expert adviser to the U.S. peace commission in Paris, had no doubt as to who had made the stronger case at the meeting. Koo, the Columbia Ph.D., "spoke in perfect English, and in a cool, lucid and logical argument which carried the members of the Council right along with him." Makino's English, on the other hand, was "poor and his delivery bad" as he "floundered" and "stumbled" in his presentation.[7] The press back in China also celebrated Koo's performance in the halls of international power. A major Shanghai daily noted that his defense of Chinese rights at the international forum meant that China no longer only obeyed the dictates of other powers, but had now stood up for its own demands. And those demands had a good chance of acceptance, the article further noted, since Great Britain, Japan's closest ally, would follow the lead of the United States, and the power of Wilson's Fourteen Points would block Japanese ambitions in China and elsewhere.[8] After this initial performance at the peace table, both the Chinese delegates in Paris and Chinese public opinion back home continued to expect that, with U.S. support, China would win acceptance as an equal member of the new community of nations and reclaim its lost territory in Shandong.[9]

Throughout the months of the peace conference, the Chinese representatives in Paris remained in continuous and friendly contact with members of the American delegation, including Wilson himself. The United States, long wary about the rise of Japanese power in the Pacific, had its own reasons to oppose Japan's expansionist plans in Shandong, and several advisers for the U.S. delegation even helped the Chinese representatives to draft their memoranda and petitions to the peace conference. Secretary of State Lansing, no friend of self-determination, assured the Chinese delegates of U.S. support on strategic grounds, as did Williams, the U.S. delegation's expert on East Asian affairs.[10] Williams, a progressive and mild-mannered Midwesterner, already had a long career in China behind him. He first arrived there as a Protestant missionary in 1887, and later worked as a diplomat. He had lived in China for more than twenty years, during which he learned the language and became a noted scholar of classical Chinese philosophy and literature. During the war years, he served as chief of the Division of Far Eastern Affairs at the State

Department. He retired from the foreign service in 1918 and accepted a chair in Oriental languages and literatures at the University of California at Berkeley, only to be pressed back into service a few months later to serve as an expert adviser to the American peace commission in Paris.

During his time in Paris, Williams, along with the second American expert on East Asian affairs in Paris, the Inquiry staffer Stanley K. Hornbeck, remained steadfast in his support for the Chinese claims in Shandong. When he forwarded to the U.S. peace commissioners the dozens of petitions from various political and civic bodies in the province—the Shandong Provincial Assembly, Chamber of Commerce and Agriculture, Educational Association, Industrial Association—asking for U.S. support in transferring German rights there back to China, he added his own favorable recommendation. The United States, he reminded the commissioners, was not only legally bound to support China under the 1858 U.S.-China treaty of "good offices," it also had a "moral obligation" to do so if it was to fulfill Wilson's declared principles. Japan's claim to the territory had no merit, he said, since it was based on force and conquest. China had been "encouraged by our attitude" to expect that its claim would be allowed. "To disappoint her," he warned, "will mean irreparable injury to our good name in the Far East and [will instill] in the hearts of the Chinese a burning sense of wrong endured which will make impossible any lasting peace."[11]

Beyond their apparent agreement on the issue of Shandong, the American and Chinese delegates also had warm social relations. Koo, who had received his doctorate from Columbia only seven years earlier, enjoyed singing old university songs with a Columbia professor who was in Paris as an adviser to the U.S. delegation.[12] The chief Chinese delegate, the Beijing foreign minister Lu Zhengxiang, recalled later that amid the general "moral obtuseness" of the major powers in Paris, the American delegates stood out in their understanding, helpfulness, and "sincere friendship" for China. Most members of the U.S. delegation returned the sentiment. Ray Stannard Baker, Wilson's ubiquitous press secretary, explained that the Chinese in Paris "were practically all American and British educated and spoke English fluently. They were much more open, outright, and frank than the Japanese."[13] The Chinese delegates were, as it were, their kind of people.

But if the Chinese in Paris had personal affinities and moral principle on their side, Japan countered with international law and the realities of power. The revelation of the secret agreements with the Beijing government appeared to weaken the legal basis for the Chinese demands on Shandong. The agreements, the Japanese argued, proved that the sovereign government of China consented to the transfer of the German rights in Shandong to Japan, and they were valid under prevailing international law and norms. Koo and his supporters retorted, however, that such logic belonged to a previous age, when imperial powers extracted agreements under the threat of force from weak states like China in order to legitimize acts of military aggression. This had been the pattern of China's relationship with the European powers, and later with Japan, since the First Opium War in the 1840s. If, however, the Paris conference wished to augur a new and righteous international order in which nations weak and strong treated each other equally and treaties could not be extracted under duress, such practices would have to end. The Japanese claims in Shandong, they said, were born of the old diplomacy of imperialism, whose time had passed. The principles of self-determination and government by consent were the new measure of justice in international affairs, and no one could dispute that Shandong, historically and demographically, was Chinese. Wilson's principles, therefore, dictated its restoration to full Chinese sovereignty. The secret agreements should be nullified.[14]

Initially, it appeared that President Wilson shared this conviction. In February, when the U.S. minister Paul Reinsch reported from Beijing that the Japanese were pressuring Chinese officials to instruct their delegates in Paris to adopt a more cooperative attitude toward Tokyo's demands, the president told him to encourage the Chinese government to "stand firm." Koo, he added, should be advised "to follow the course that he thinks right."[15] But the Japanese, too, had some powerful supporters. In the course of the conference, it emerged that Japan had not only managed to obtain from the Beijing regime recognition for its rights in Shandong. More important, Tokyo had also reached secret wartime agreements with both the British and the French governments, in which the latter recognized Japan's seizure of Shandong in return for its participation in the Allied war effort. Such agreements were normal practice in the wartime diplomacy of the European Allies, and similar treaties promising territorial gains had been made with Italy and with czarist Russia. But the Allied treaties with Japan were the only case in which the promised territories belonged to an allied rather than an enemy power; though the rights in question were German, the territory itself was indisputably Chinese. Still, Clemenceau and Lloyd George showed little inclination to renounce their promises to the Japanese. Both powers, after all, also had significant interests in their own Chinese "leased territories" obtained through unequal treaties.[16] Thus, while Clemenceau complimented Koo on his eloquence before the council, he also intimated that France could not support China in contravention of its wartime agreements with Japan.[17]

Another episode that complicated matters for the Chinese occurred in early April, when the League of Nations Commission rejected the Japanese proposal to add to the league covenant a "racial equality clause"—language guaranteeing the equality of all nations and the fair treatment of their nationals, regardless of race. The proposal, first advanced by Japan in

February, had aroused fierce opposition from representatives of the British dominions that wished to preserve practices of racial exclusion in immigration. The Australian premier, Billy Hughes, was an especially vociferous opponent of the clause, since he feared that it would lead to a flood of Japanese immigrants and jeopardize his policy of a "white Australia." Wilson himself did not think very highly of Hughes, referring to him contemptuously as a "pestiferous varmint." But Wilson, too, faced similar domestic opposition to any clause that affirmed the principle of racial equality, especially from politicians and labor unions in the western United States, where there was long-standing and virulent opposition to Asian immigration.[18]

After delaying the vote on the Japanese proposal for several weeks, Wilson, who chaired the League of Nations commission, finally pronounced it rejected for lack of unanimity despite the majority support it had received among the members of the commission. The rejection, a blow to Japanese national pride, was widely decried in the Japanese press as exposing the hypocrisy and emptiness of Wilson's slogans on the equality of nations.[19] The episode exacerbated U.S.-Japanese tensions, already high over Japanese suspicions that U.S. missionaries and diplomats, not to mention Wilson himself, were providing succor to the March First protesters in Korea. A further clash with Japan over Shandong, the president feared, would lead it to withdraw from the peace conference and jeopardize the success of his most cherished achievement—the League of Nations.[20]

After several months of postponements, the Supreme Council finally took up the Shandong issue once more in late April. Koo, who appeared before the council on April 22, was again eloquent in defense of Chinese rights. Beijing had signed its wartime agreements with Japan under duress, he argued, and they were therefore invalid. At the outset of the discussion, however, both Lloyd George and Clemenceau left no room for doubt: Britain and France had promised the Shandong concessions to Japan, and they did not intend to rescind these promises.[21] Williams reported that both leaders, and especially the British prime minister, knew little of East Asian affairs and cared even less, and that the Japanese were uncompromising. One of the Japanese delegates told Secretary of State Lansing that it was "ridiculous for a nation of 400 millions to go around complaining that they had signed a treaty under duress." If their claims were not met, the Japanese vowed, they would not sign the treaty.[22] Wilson, in a last attempt to finesse the problem, shifted the issue to a committee of experts and sent Williams to plead with the Chinese to accept the transfer to Japan of the German rights in Shandong in return for a verbal assurance that these rights would revert to China at a later date.[23] The Chinese asked that this assurance be incorporated into the treaty, or at least be given to them in writing. But the Japanese professed to find such a requirement humiliating, since it implied that they could not be trusted to keep their word, and it was summarily rejected.[24]

By the last days of April, Williams reported bitterly that his peace conference "barometer" now "points to storms" and may be headed to a "complete shipwreck." The crisis over Wilson's adamant refusal to accept the Italian demands for Fiume had just erupted in full force, and Williams noted that the president's "bombthrowing" over the matter had especially worried the Japanese, who feared that Wilson's tough stand against territorial demands that contravened the principle of self-determination was aimed at them also. The Shandong question, Williams continued, was the last major issue that remained unsettled, but the Anglo-French commitments to the Japanese made an "unjust settlement" of the issue almost inevitable, and the recent refusal to give Japan some "harmless declaration" on racial equality had made matters even worse. When Williams met with Wilson in late April, he found the president distressed over the Shandong question, calling it "the most difficult and perplexing problem that had thus far been presented." Since the war had been fought largely to enforce respect for treaties, Wilson asked him, should not the agreements that the Japanese obtained from Beijing, however "unconscionable in character," be respected? When Williams noted that those treaties were extorted by force, the president countered that the Japanese might not admit that to be the case. Do the documents not prove it? Williams wondered. "Well," the president replied, " 'if the documents show it, of course they would not deny it.' He left the main question unanswered," Williams concluded, "and I was filled with anxiety."[25]

The support for China within the U.S. delegation was broad, but it was not unanimous. Colonel House, always solicitous of the need to preserve smooth relations among the principal allies, advised Wilson to relent on Shandong. England, France, and Japan ought to get out of China in principle, he said, "and perhaps they will later if enough pressure is brought through public opinion." For the time being, however, a compromise with Japan would allow the conference to "clean up a lot of old rubbish with the least friction," leaving it to the League of Nations and "the new era" to do the rest. China, House knew, was the weaker side in this diplomatic tug-of-war, and its interests could most easily be ignored.[26] On April 30, the Big Three, discussing the Shandong question one last time, agreed to accept the Japanese claim for the former German concessions in Shandong in return for a verbal assurance—the Japanese delegates would not agree to include it in the treaty in any form—that Japan would restore these rights to China in due time.[27] "Thus China was betrayed in the house of her friends," a despondent Williams recorded in his diary that night, "and militarism is put at a premium." Many years later, Stanley Hornbeck recalled that he thought Wilson bowed in the end to "considerations of what appeared to be immediate practical political necessity," but that the president continued to hope and believe that the League of Nations would right the errors of the conference once it began its work.[28]

When the members of the Chinese delegation learned of the decision the following day, they were utterly shocked. "Little has been heard here of the famous fourteen principles," Koo wrote to one of his former professors at Columbia shortly afterward, "and still less has been noted in practice."[29] Williams went to see C. T. Wang soon after the decision and found the Chinese delegates depressed and contemplating withdrawal from the conference. It is too soon, he told them; they should appeal the decision to "the sense of justice" of world opinion. But Wang disagreed: There was "no hope now for China save in revolution," he said.[30] Lu, the head of the Chinese delegation, sent the Council of Three an official communication expressing China's deep disappointment. China, he wrote, had relied on Wilson's Fourteen Points and on "the spirit of honourable relationship between states which is to open a new era in the world," but the result had been great disappointment.[31] A subsequent press release by the Chinese delegates protested the decision but struck a rather resigned if disillusioned tone: "If the Council has granted the claims of Japan in full for the purpose of saving the League of Nations, as has been intimated to be the case," China "would have less to complain, believing as she does that it is a duty to make sacrifices for such a noble cause." It might have been more in keeping with the spirit of the league, they suggested bitingly, "to call upon strong Japan to forgo her claims animated apparently only by a desire for aggrandizement, instead of weak China to surrender what was hers by right."[32]

The American peace commissioners, who, apart from House, had been kept in the dark by Wilson about this as well as most other important questions, were equally distressed.[33] General Tasker Bliss sent Wilson a strongly worded memo explaining in detail his opposition to any concession to the Japanese on Shandong. His explanation echoed the Chinese arguments: Both the German lease in Shandong and the Sino-Japanese wartime agreements were born of coercion and were therefore invalid. "It can't be right to do wrong even to make peace," he concluded.[34] Bliss, an army general who was the chief military liaison to the Allies during the war, had been an enthusiastic supporter of Wilson's wartime policies. Now he threatened to resign his commission in protest, though in the end he stayed put. Secretary of State Lansing penned a sharp critique the next morning in his diary: "China has been abandoned to Japanese rapacity. . . . I am heartsick over it, because I see how much good-will and regard the President is bound to lose. I can offer no adequate explanation to the critics. There seems to be none." When he met with Koo that day, Lansing promised to do all he could to rectify the "great wrong" that had been done. Long sidelined and little respected by Wilson, however, he could do nothing.[35]

Perhaps no one among the Americans in Paris was distressed more than the two experts on Far Eastern affairs, Williams and Hornbeck. The two had worked together closely to advocate for the acceptance of the Chinese claims over those of the Japanese. It was the right thing to do, they believed, and it would also serve U.S. interests in the region, dealing a blow to dangerous Japanese ambitions. Now, they saw all their work come to naught. In the days following the decision, Hornbeck produced a stream of memoranda, laying before the American delegates a whole litany of arguments against the Shandong decision. It would, he predicted, strengthen militarism in the region, destroy any confidence in the peace conference among the Chinese people, and drive the country either to anarchic violence or, in desperation, into the arms of Japan. Japanese promises to restore the Shandong concessions to China in the future, Hornbeck argued, meant little, since they were informal and Japan could easily ignore them later. Japan had long enjoyed a higher status than its actual power warranted in the international arena, and this decision, a great diplomatic victory, would strengthen the militarists in Japanese domestic politics and weaken the liberals. And it contravened the great principles of the conference. It must, he concluded, be reconsidered.[36]

Williams was even more distraught. "The very worst possible has happened," he wrote. The decision gave Japan more than it could have hoped for, violating in the process most of the main principles the United States was supposed to stand for in Paris: antimilitarism, self-determination, no annexations. As a consequence, U.S. prestige in Paris, which had risen somewhat after Wilson's principled stance on the Fiume issue, was now lower than ever. The glaring contradiction between the U.S. position on Fiume, on the one hand, and on Shandong, on the other, went a long way toward convincing observers that it could not possibly be principle driving U.S. decisions, but rather no more than "mercenary motives" dictated by self-interest. The consequences for American prestige in the East would be even more baleful, and the decision would surely propel China down a dangerous path. It would be, said the former missionary, "like the man out of whom a devil was cast only to make room for seven more devils worse than the first." A sense of personal failure haunted him: "I did the best I could in the matter but failed. I feel as if I had wasted six months of my life. I am ashamed to look a Chinese in the face." President Wilson had promised to stand behind China and "he did, and pushed her over head first. My one desire now is to get away from here just as soon, and just as fast and just as far as I can."[37] Within two weeks, Williams had left Paris and returned to the United States, where, in an uncharacteristic departure from his usual diplomatic composure, he publicly criticized the Shandong decision. The injustice of the decision was so glaring, he explained to a State Department official, that he could not respect himself if he did not protest against it.[38]

When news of the decision reached China on May 2, it caused widespread shock and anger there as well. Reinsch reported from Beijing that people and officials were "deeply depressed" and felt "utterly helpless," faced with the rejection by the peace conference of their "fundamental rights and the approval of the most iniquitous, ruthless and corrupt acts of aggression." Chinese officials, expressing disbelief, told him that they did not see how China could affix its signature to a treaty that sanctioned such an outrage. Such a diplomatic disaster, he warned, could very well mean the collapse of the peace negotiations in Shanghai between the competing regimes in Beijing and Guangzhou and augur a prolonged period of internal turmoil. The failure to admit China into the international community on equitable terms, he warned, could lead to a veritable civilizational clash: Chinese indignation could cause the Chinese to lose confidence in the power, justice, and principles of the nations of the West and lead to "a violent anti-Foreign movement." The disillusionment that would follow the realization that China's demand for justice at the peace conference had been futile would open the way for "organizing the forces of the Asiatic mainland in cynical hostility to Western civilization."[39] The hope of many leading Chinese intellectuals that Wilson's principles and his league would serve as bridges between East and West would give way to a growing sense of estrangement from the Western-dominated international society.

The next day, Reinsch again reported that the people in China, and particularly in Beijing, Shandong, and Shanghai, were greatly agitated and planned to stage large protest rallies. The government, the protesters insisted, must instruct the Chinese delegation not to sign the treaty. Could the United States, they wondered, really stand up to the Italian demands for Fiume and yet sign a treaty that allowed Japan to despoil China?[40] In his memoirs, Reinsch lamented the blow that the Shandong decision delivered to the Chinese confidence in Wilson, whose words had reached the "remotest parts" of the country: "It sickened and disheartened me to think how the Chinese people would receive this blow which meant the blasting of their hopes and the destruction of their confidence in the equity of nations." The decision would cause "a revulsion of feeling against America," not because it was more to blame for it than others, but because "the Chinese had entertained a deeper belief in our power, influence and loyalty to principle" than in those of any of the other powers. Reinsch, who had worked hard to build Chinese good will toward the United States during his tenure in Beijing, now saw his efforts collapse. Disheartened by Wilson's abandonment of China in Paris, he tendered his resignation to the president soon after in a long, bitter letter.[41]

Students in Beijing, who had hailed Wilson as a hero only six months earlier, were outraged at the decision. As one student recalled:

> When the news of the Paris Peace Conference finally reached us we were greatly shocked. We at once awoke to the fact that foreign

> nations were still selfish and militaristic and that they were all great liars. I remember that in the evening of May 2nd very few of us slept. I and a group of my friends talked almost the whole night. We came to the conclusion that . . . we could no longer depend upon the principles of any so-called great leader like Woodrow Wilson. . . . we couldn't help feel that we must struggle![42]

In an emotional mass meeting on May 3, student participants agreed that the Shandong problem had arisen out of corruption and injustice and swore to show to the world that "might should never be right." They decided to send telegrams to the Chinese delegates in Paris demanding that they refuse to sign the treaty; to contact provincial leaders around the country and ask them to declare a National Humiliation Day to mark the event; and to gather the following day at Tiananmen Gate in central Beijing to express their anger.[43]

On Sunday, May 4, 1919, some three thousand students, representing thirteen colleges and universities, had gathered in front of Tiananmen Gate in the heart of the city by half past one in the afternoon. At two o'clock, they began marching toward the nearby foreign legation quarter, carrying signs that read "Give Us Back Qingdao!" "Refuse to Sign the Peace Treaty!" "Oppose Power Politics!"[44] Stopped at the gates of the legation quarter by its police guards, the demonstrating students selected representatives to enter the quarter to meet with the American minister; finding him absent they left a petition instead. Similar results met efforts to see the British, French, and Italian ministers to protest the decision. Frustrated, the marching students turned toward the houses of several high government officials identified with pro-Japanese policies, shouting slogans that branded the officials as traitors. One was discovered at his home and beaten. Another, who managed to escape in disguise through a window, had his house ransacked and set on fire. The police, who at first had been reluctant to intervene, dispersed the demonstrations by force in the end and made several dozen arrests.[45]

The students now called the U.S. president a liar, his promise of a new world exposed as a mere illusion. A leading Chinese newspaper, reporting on the protests the following day, noted that China had suffered a tremendous defeat: "To have Shandong gone is to ruin Chinese soil, to demolish China's nationhood. Therefore, the intellectuals have been congregating at the embassies to demand that other countries uphold justice."[46] Over the next several weeks, the student protests and strikes that began in Beijing spread to numerous other cities in China, including Tianjin, Nanjing, Wuhan, and Shanghai, and to Chinese student communities abroad in Europe, Japan, and the United States. Activists launched a movement to boycott Japanese goods and formed numerous new patriotic organizations, such as the People's Self-Determination Society, to organize protests against Japan and the other

Protesters in front of Tiananmen gate in late 1919. The May Fourth protests, sparked by the great power rejection of the Chinese demands at the peace conference, began among university students in Beijing but quickly spread to other regions and social groups. *Sidney Gamble Collection, Rare Book, Manuscript, and Special Collections Library, Duke University.*

powers. The movement spread beyond university students by early June, after a number of violent clashes with police left many casualties among the students and sparked outrage among broad constituencies in Beijing and elsewhere—legislators, merchants, industrialists, workers—who now joined the protests themselves.[47]

A pamphlet published by the Shanghai Student Union summed up the prevailing sentiments:

> Throughout the world like the voice of a prophet has gone the word of Woodrow Wilson strengthening the weak and giving courage to the struggling. And the Chinese have listened and they too have heard. . . . They have been told that in the dispensation which is to be made after the war un-militaristic nations like China would have an opportunity to develop their culture, their industry, their civilization, unhampered. . . . They looked for the dawn of this new Messiah; but no sun rose for China. Even the cradle of the nation was stolen.[48]

Such sentiments, of course, were not limited to young, excitable university students. One of the most ardent Wilsonians among leading Chinese intellectuals, Hu Shi, was no less distraught: "The 'New World Order' was no more!" he wrote. "This disillusionment was followed by a conviction: China must not rely upon the wishes of other nations for settling our own affairs."[49] The anger and frustration that spread throughout Chinese society in the wake of the May Fourth incident helped to galvanize the myriad discontents that had built up over the preceding decades of political, social, and cultural turmoil into a movement that would mark a watershed in the evolution of Chinese nationalism.[50]

As protests spread around China, Chinese who were living or studying abroad also vented their anger and dismay at Wilson's betrayal. In a gathering in Paris on May 5, under the joint auspices of the Chinese Society for International Peace and the French Ligue des Droits de l'Homme, Chinese students interrupted and heckled American speakers and sharply condemned President Wilson. One speaker, a female art student, declared defiantly that since peace had failed, the use of force was now the only hope remaining for China. Stephen Bonsal, Wilson's interpreter in Paris, who attended the rally, remarked that the hostility that Chinese students directed at Wilson was such that he feared that one of them might try to assassinate the president.[51] Chinese students in Tokyo also held demonstrations against the decision on Shandong and, like the Korean students who had declared independence there in February, were violently dispersed by the police. The students protested Japanese brutality to the representatives of the Western powers in Tokyo, expressing their hope that "those wild beasts who treated a good number of our girl-fellows badly and rudely, be punished quickly." Their protests, however, went unheeded.[52]

As Reinsch had feared, the crisis that the Shandong decision created in China also delivered a decisive blow to the ongoing efforts to achieve internal political unity. President Xu had launched what he hoped would be a "great enterprise" of uniting China through talks among the rival factions in Shanghai. The May Fourth crisis, however, caused the collapse of these talks and doomed the efforts to reach a negotiated agreement between the northern and southern regimes, and China remained weak and divided for another three decades.[53] The failure of the Chinese effort at the peace conference in Paris discredited the Beijing government, with which it was associated, and encouraged the Guomindang regime in the south to reject compromise, while at the same time emboldening the northern militarists who opposed the civilian government. The rise of the politics of mass mobilization and protest after 1919 precipitated the collapse of the precarious constitutional system created after the 1911 revolution and augured a period that was marked by internal division and conflicts during the 1920s and 1930s.[54]

The prominent intellectual and journalist Liang Qichao, who had arrived in Paris in February to observe the peace proceedings, delivered his own evaluation of the Shandong decision and its implications for the future. Few in Europe, he noted, realized how "momentous" the council's decision on Shandong was: "Without exaggeration, we say that it exceeds in importance all the other territorial adjustments made by the Conference because of the area and population affected. No well-informed man can have any doubt that it will profoundly modify the history of the Asiatic continent, if not that of the whole world." The reasons behind the decision, Liang continued, were no mystery. Great Britain and France, which each had an interest in China's continued weakness, were determined to keep their wartime promises to Japan, and President Wilson feared that the threatened Japanese withdrawal would jeopardize his League of Nations. But though it might appear inevitable in retrospect, the decision had a dramatic impact on China. "Rightly or wrongly," Liang noted, "the Chinese people believed seriously that the downfall of Germany meant also the end of militarism all the world over and the Peace Conference [would be] a unique opportunity for redressing our wrongs." They put their case before the peace conference thinking it would receive a sympathetic hearing and were thoroughly disappointed. China's "only crime," he concluded, had been "her weakness and her belief in international justice after the war. If, driven to desperation she attempts something hopeless, those who have helped to decide her fate cannot escape a part of the responsibility."[55]

As the Chinese protests continued, Hornbeck, still hoping that Wilson would reconsider or at least amend his decision, assiduously gathered the dozens of Chinese petitions received at the delegation headquarters and forwarded them to the peace commissioners with a cover letter urging that they receive serious consideration. The frantic activity among overseas Chinese, especially though not exclusively students, was reflected in a memorandum Hornbeck produced on May 9, only ten days after the Big Three made their decision on Shandong. The document included petitions demanding reversal of the decision from numerous community and student organizations, both national and local, in France, Britain, and the United States. They included the Chinese Society for International Peace in Paris, the Chinese Patriotic Committee in New York City, the Chinese American Citizens Alliance, the Chinese Association of Oregon, the Chinese University Club of Hawaii, the Chinese Press Association of America, the China National Defense League in Europe, the Chinese Democratic Committee in France, and the Central Union of the Chinese Students in Great Britain. One petition was signed by a group of eighty-three Chinese students from universities in the northeastern United States. The students, hailing from Harvard, MIT, Princeton, Yale, and Tufts College, had gathered in Thayer Hall in Harvard Yard to call on Wilson to reverse the Shandong decision.[56] Loy Chang, a Harvard graduate student and president of the Chinese Student Alliance, which included more than eight hundred Chinese students enrolled in U.S. educational institutions, chaired the meeting.[57]

Perhaps the most active overseas group was the Chinese Patriotic Committee in New York City, which expatriate Chinese activists set up on Manhattan's Upper West Side at 510 West 113th Street. It produced a flood of publications explaining China's position in Paris and expressing its disillusionment with the results. The China Society in America, established in 1911 in order, according to its motto, "to promote, foster, and perpetuate the friendly relations between the United States and China," distributed these pamphlets widely across the country. A representative publication, entitled *Might or Right?* began:

> The year 1918 marked the beginning of an [era]... when President Wilson on January 8, 1918, voiced the sentiment of all mankind in his address to Congress, embodying the famous fourteen principles.... Power politics was adjourned, for justice, justice that knew not the weak nor the strong was to be the guiding principle in international relations. Peoples hitherto submerged under the domination and oppression of an alien power were promised the right of self-determination.... Such being the case, all human beings irrespective of race or nationality were filled with joy. They were inspired... to believe that, at last—The New Order Cometh.
>
> The New Order does not come to China, however. The principles enunciated are admittedly sound, but up to the present all that China has received is the vibration of the sound but not the application of the principles.[58]

The Shandong decision was a "flagrant injustice" and meant that "the gentlemen at Paris are merely postponing the funeral service Japan has planned for her neighbor."[59] There was still a chance to remedy the situation, however. Japan's promise to return the province to China in the future was worthless, but the United States, "the greatest example of democracy" and "the most powerful nation in the world," a defender of justice and an enemy of imperialism, could still right the wrong.[60]

Eight and a half weeks passed between the decision on the Shandong question on April 30 and the signing ceremony of the peace treaty on June 28 in the Hall of Mirrors at Versailles. During this time, Chinese around the world continued to make their positions known to the men they saw as their representatives in Paris. Student groups, chambers of commerce, provincial and local assemblies, and overseas Chinese patriotic groups from Peru to Mexico,

Java to Manila, and many places in between, dispatched hundreds of urgent telegrams to the Chinese delegates in Paris. They condemned the Shandong decision and demanded that the delegates refuse to sign the peace treaty unless the decision was revoked.[61] This widespread campaign of public diplomacy was encouraged by the delegates themselves. They disseminated information on the demands that China made at the peace conference and circulated the protocols of the relevant peace conference sessions to expatriate communities in order to mobilize their support for the delegation's efforts to convince the great powers to modify the provisions of the treaty pertaining to Shandong before the signing ceremony.[62]

During those weeks, both the Chinese and American delegates were engaged in a desperate scramble to mollify Chinese opinion and negotiate a solution that would allow China to sign the treaty. After Williams left Paris in disgust, it remained for Stanley Hornbeck to coordinate the effort on the U.S. side. First, he urged, it was crucial to ask the Japanese for more concrete commitments concerning the eventual restoration of Shandong to China, including definite dates for troop withdrawals and the relinquishment of preferential economic rights. Wilson, influenced by Hornbeck's recommendations, asked Lansing to see Makino, the Japanese delegate, and impress upon him strongly "the desirability, not to say necessity, of quieting opinion in China and making the fulfillment of the Treaty provisions possible without serious friction." Continued unrest in China, he added, "will certainly ensue unless the most explicit reassurance is given," and it "might not only immediately but for a long time to come disturb the peace of the East and might lead to very serious international complications."[63] The Japanese, however, assured of the support of the other major powers, would not budge.

In a last-ditch attempt to reach a compromise, the Chinese delegates proposed that China would sign the treaty but enter a formal reservation to the articles in it dealing with Shandong.[64] Only days before the signing ceremony, the Chinese proposal came before the Big Three. Wilson voiced his support but met with the adamant opposition of Clemenceau and Lloyd George. The French and the British were eager to have the Chinese sign the treaty but were unwilling to countenance formal reservations. Other states, Clemenceau pointed out, did not have the option of signing with reservations, and Lloyd George complained that if China signed while rejecting the articles of the treaty that pertained to itself, its signature would be meaningless.[65] On June 27, on the eve of the signing ceremony, Koo made a last-minute appeal to Wilson to exercise his "friendly influence" to enable the Chinese delegates to sign the treaty "without sacrificing their sense of national honour and pride." The Chinese offered several alternatives: If they could not note their reservations on the treaty itself, next to their signature, perhaps they could attach them as an annex or as a separate letter entirely? The French secretariat of the conference, however, rejected all of these proposals out of hand.[66]

In the meantime, the faction-ridden government in Beijing could not decide whether China should sign the peace treaty, dispatching a string of vague and contradictory directives to its delegates in Paris. Public opinion across China was vehemently against signing, and the Guomindang government in Guangzhou issued fiery declarations to that effect.[67] But refusal to sign, Beijing worried, might completely exclude China from the emerging institutions of international community, including the League of Nations, and might also expose it to Japanese retaliation. Some officials in Beijing were also worried about the possible dangers of the upheaval that was growing in Chinese communities overseas. Were the groups behind the petitions that denounced the Shandong decision and opposed the Chinese signing of the treaty, the Foreign Ministry anxiously inquired of its consuls in New York, San Francisco, Ottawa, and other cities, supporters of the Guomindang opposition? the bureaucrats in Beijing wondered. No, came the replies from Chinese diplomats abroad; the protesters were not radicals but patriotic Chinese, and the government should make a public statement to console them and win their allegiance.[68] But the collapse of the cabinet in the wake of the May Fourth protests and its replacement with an even feebler caretaker government only exacerbated Beijing's indecision. As the signing ceremony neared, it appeared that the responsibility for the decision would rest on the shoulders of the delegates in Paris themselves.[69]

Even on the day of the ceremony, the Chinese delegates were still unsure what to do: Should they attempt to sign with reservations, or not at all?[70] By then, however, events had overtaken them. As they considered whether to emerge from their Left Bank headquarters at the Hôtel Lutetia for the trip to the signing ceremony, they found themselves besieged by outraged Chinese students determined to prevent them from signing the treaty. On the afternoon of June 28, when all the delegations gathered, with the appropriate pomp and circumstance, to attend the signing ceremony at the Hall of Mirrors in the palace at Versailles, the two seats reserved for the Chinese delegates were the only ones that remained empty. The Chinese failure to appear at the ceremony surprised the other delegations. Clemenceau, who as president of the conference had summarily dismissed all of the Chinese requests to enter formal reservations, had apparently believed that their resolve would weaken at the last minute.[71] In the summer of 1919, however, neither the feeble government in Beijing nor the delegates in Paris fully controlled Chinese policy in the international forum. It was rather the mobilized Chinese nationalists around the world who had heard the call of self-determination and were determined that China, too, would have it. Largely due to their firm opposition, China became the only state represented at the conference that did not sign the treaty.

In the heated debates over the treaty that raged in the United States in the following months, the Shandong decision became the focus of public controversy, and both disillusioned progressives and anti-league conservatives attacked it as epitomizing the iniquity of the treaty. George W. Norris, a Republican senator from Nebraska and a vigorous opponent of the league, cited the Shandong decision, along with the abandonment of Korea to Japanese rule, as the most egregious examples of "the greed and avarice" of the great powers that had shaped the treaty. Other league opponents, like Henry Cabot Lodge and Idaho Senator William Borah, also offered sharp critiques of the Shandong decision.[72] Lansing, in his Senate testimony, agreed that the decision violated the principle of self-determination, and Wilson himself admitted to the Senate Foreign Relations Committee that Lansing and Bliss both disagreed with the decision but argued that, given the previous commitments that the British and French had made to Japan, it was the "best that could be accomplished out of a dirty past."[73] Among the fourteen amendments that the Senate Republicans wanted to attach to their ratification of the treaty was one that demanded the reversal of the decision, giving the former German rights in Shandong to China rather than to Japan. But the Senate failed to ratify the treaty at all, and this amendment, like the others it proposed, became moot.[74]

In China, protests against the treaty continued well after the signing ceremony, accompanied by street demonstrations and boycotts against Japanese goods.[75] Beyond the anger at their humiliation in Paris, Chinese responses to the collapse of the Wilsonian promise showed an acute consciousness, even in China's more remote provinces, of the similarity of the Chinese experiences at the time with those of other emerging national movements. Shortly after the Chinese delegates failed to appear at the signing ceremony at Versailles, a student activist in the inland province of Hunan noted that China was hardly alone in having entertained high hopes for a new era in which it would have a place in a community of nations, only to be thoroughly disillusioned. "India has earned herself a clown wearing a flaming red turban as representative to the Peace Conference," he wrote, referring to the Maharaja of Bikanir, but "the demands of the Indian people have not been granted." Korea, the young student continued, also "bewails the loss of its independence ... but it was simply ignored by the Peace Conference. So much for national self-determination!" He exclaimed, "I think it is really shameless!"[76]

For this young activist, whose name was Mao Zedong, the summer of 1919 was a formative period, the "critical point in the evolution" of his views about China, its internal problems, and its place in the world. Mao, who was twenty-five years old at the time, closely followed press reports about the course of the war and the developments at the peace conference, and he took part in the May Fourth demonstrations in Changsha, the provincial capital. His reflection on these dramatic developments ignited the first of "those bouts of concentrated and focused activity that would characterize his later career." Mere weeks after the incident, he founded a short-lived journal, the *Xiang River Review*, which he furiously filled with his thoughts and observations on both domestic and international questions. These reflections testify that Mao, like many of his contemporaries, came to see China's problems, as historian Michael H. Hunt has concluded, "not as unique or isolated but rather global in nature and solution."[77] The Chinese protest against international injustice, Mao discovered, was part of a wider pattern of uprisings of marginalized groups in international society striving for the recognition of their rights to self-determination and equality. Only the transformation of the norms and practices of international relations would allow China to attain its rightful place among nations.

Mao was scornful of the Allied leaders in Paris, calling them "a bunch of robbers bent on securing territories and indemnities," who "cynically championed self-determination" while denying it in practice.[78] But with Wilson and his ideals now defeated and no longer captivating the imaginations of Chinese nationalists, Mao spied another force rising to rally the people of Asia. The "Russian extremist party," he wrote, had made headway in India and Korea, spreading revolution, and its ideas could not now be dismissed out of hand: "Each of us should examine very carefully what kind of thing this extremist party really is."[79] Although Mao, like the British and the Japanese, had an exaggerated view of the Bolshevik influence on the upheavals in India and Korea, this statement was nevertheless significant. It was Mao's first published reference to Bolshevism as a movement that China and other oppressed nations in Asia should study and perhaps even emulate. Shortly thereafter, the local warlord shut Mao's journal down, and the young student moved back to Beijing. There, he would join the nascent Chinese Communist party, cofounded in 1921 by his intellectual mentor Li Dazhao.

Historians have long viewed May Fourth as a major turning point in the history of Chinese nationalism, but most studies have framed the movement in the context of domestic Chinese history, focusing on its cultural, intellectual, and literary aspects. Studies that examine the international context of May Fourth often focus on the impact of the Bolshevik revolution and of socialist ideas more generally on the transformation of Chinese nationalism and on the early development of Chinese communism, and Mao himself claimed years later that May Fourth erupted "at the call of the Russian Revolution and Lenin."[80] In fact, however, the impact of the Russian Revolution on the organization and ideology of Chinese nationalists became significant only after May Fourth—indeed, in many ways as a consequence of it. From 1917 to 1919, most Chinese intellectuals were much more familiar with Wilson than with Lenin, and the influence of his rhetoric on them far eclipsed the influence of the Russian revolutionaries. With the collapse of the Wilsonian promise in mid-1919, disillusioned nationalists like Mao began seriously to examine Bolshevism as an alternative path for resisting imperialism and attaining international equality and dignity for China.[81] The new Soviet government helped this process along when, in 1920, it renounced imperial Russia's treaties with China and earned widespread praise from Chinese intellectuals, who contrasted the gesture to the abject failure of the Western Allies to fulfill the promise of Wilson's ringing declarations.[82]

The Chinese experience at the Wilsonian moment reveals the imbrication of international processes and national construction in the colonial world at the time. Events in the international arena ignited the May Fourth protests, as they did the contemporaneous movements in Egypt, India, and Korea, and shaped the expectations, actions, and frustrations of many Chinese. The Wilsonian discourse of legitimacy influenced their perceptions of what dependent nations like China could do, and what they could *be*, in the international arena. The language of international equality and self-determination that emerged at the Wilsonian moment opened a space for political action in which networks of nationalist activists could pursue in the international arena the goal of unqualified self-determination for their nation, implied in Wilson's declarations on the "equality of all nations, whether they be big or small, strong or weak." Wilson and the United States proved to be a fragile reed upon which to rely at the time, but as the expectations gave way to disillusion, Chinese and other anticolonial nationalists remained committed to the pursuit of self-determination and equality in international society. The rise of communism in China and elsewhere in the early 1920s was part of that quest, as the failure of the liberal anticolonialism of the Wilsonian moment to fulfill its promise sparked a search for alternative ideologies that could support the goals that came to the forefront then.

10

A World Safe for Empire?

Even as the young Mao counted the uprising in Korea as part of the broad upheaval against empire in the spring of 1919, the Japanese colonial authorities engaged in a harsh campaign of suppression that left thousands of casualties in its wake.[1] As in India, the protests had begun with an emphasis on nonviolence, but they soon turned bloody. Police clashed with stone-throwing demonstrators, and protesters tried to storm police stations and other symbols of the colonial regime. In the course of the next several months, the colonial police arrested thousands, many of them students. They were often subjected to rough treatment, sometimes resulting in death, to try to compel them to divulge information, sign confessions, or make declarations repudiating the independence movement. Reports of torture and humiliation, many relayed to the outside world by missionaries, were widespread. Detainees were beaten, spat upon, denied food and water, forced to squat for long hours, and deprived of sleep. Many female detainees also testified to acts of sexual humiliation and molestation by the colonial police, including being stripped naked and paraded, hung by the thumbs or hair, and subjected to beatings and other humiliations.[2]

From the outset, the colonial authorities and the Japanese press blamed U.S. influence for inciting the Koreans, and President Wilson was a frequent target of attack. The U.S. leader, wrote one Japanese newspaper in April, was simply an arrogant "second Kaiser" who preached to others about morality but failed to uphold it himself, as his rejection of the Japanese racial equality proposal proved. Wilson's hypocrisy, another paper contended, was also revealed by his demand to make provisions in the league covenant to protect the Monroe Doctrine—a demand Wilson raised to try to improve the covenant's chances of passage in the U.S. Senate—while at the same time seeking to resist the Japanese claims in Shandong. This was little more than great power bullying of Japan, and showed the League of Nations to be simply a cover for "British and American selfishness." Even Japanese liberals who had "worshipped across the Pacific at Mr. Wilson as a living God of the world's peace," the paper claimed, now saw that he was "an angel in rhetoric and a devil in deed."[3]

American missionaries in Korea were another frequent target of Japanese ire during the spring of 1919. Sixteen of the thirty-three signatories to the March 1

Declaration of Independence were Korean Christians, and the Japanese police suspected the hidden hand of the missionaries behind the uprising.[4] The missionaries, it charged, spread subversive Wilsonian propaganda in Korea, encouraging revolt, and it even suspected President Wilson of direct complicity in the uprising. One police report noted that an American missionary, Shannon McCune, whom the Japanese authorities had long suspected of opposing their rule in Korea, had gone to the United States in October 1918 and met with President Wilson, reaching an "understanding about the future of Korea." Upon his return, the report continued, McCune told Korean Christian leaders that Korea could soon become independent in line with Wilson's principles, but he as an American could not be seen as publicly assisting the movement. The Koreans themselves would have to demonstrate to foreign countries that they rejected Japanese rule, and if they did so, the peace conference might approve their demand for independence. This, concluded the report, "was the secret viewpoint of the 'mystical president.' "[5]

The U.S. minister in Tokyo, who followed closely the Japanese press coverage of the upheaval in Korea, reported that Japanese opinion saw the "secret instigation of American missionaries" and the "inspiration of the principle of self-determination" as the principal causes of the uprising against their rule. What Koreans failed to understand, the Japanese press argued, echoing the position of the Tory papers in Britain on India, was that the principle of self-determination was "only applicable to races capable of it." The "sin of the American missionaries" lay in erroneously applying Wilson's statements to people who were "not fully civilized," thereby "stirring up of the mind of the Koreans."[6] At the same time, Japanese papers also contended, somewhat incongruently, that due to the material development of Korea under Japanese rule and the "racial kinship" between the two peoples, the Japanese annexation of Korea in fact represented "the perfection of the principle of self-determination of races."[7] The Japanese authorities in Korea quickly moved against the perceived Christian threat, persecuting converts and working to disrupt missionary activities.[8]

With accusations multiplying in the Japanese press and anti-American sentiment in Japan on the rise, officials in Washington grew concerned.[9] For the State Department, Japan's annexation of Korea was a fait accompli, one that the U.S. government had already recognized. It therefore took great care to distance the United States from any appearance of support for, or involvement with, the Korean protests and instructed its diplomats to warn missionary leaders against any such involvement.[10] Thus, when a group of Korean refugees in eastern Siberia approached the U.S. consul in Vladivostok asking for protection against persecution by the Japanese and Russian authorities and for assistance in transmitting telegrams to Korean delegates in Paris, they were rejected on both counts. At the same time, Washington warned the Japanese government against the dangers of "undeserved hostility to Americans" that resulted from "the campaign of falsehood being conducted by the Japanese press." The "misunderstanding" between the two countries should be cleared up by a "frank exchange of views" on the subject between the United States and the Japanese Foreign Office.[11]

Under pressure from their own government, American missionaries in Korea vehemently denied any charges of complicity in the uprising. Although Korean Christians were prominent in the uprising, foreign missionaries claimed that they did not know about the plans for the uprising and were thoroughly surprised when it erupted. Initially, they sought to maintain a neutral position to avoid antagonizing the Japanese authorities and risking expulsion.[12] But as reports of Japanese atrocities against unarmed protesters multiplied, some missionaries declared they could no longer remain on the sidelines. Adopting the slogan "No Neutrality for Brutality," they appealed to the Japanese authorities to cease the violence against unarmed demonstrators. When these appeals met with little success, the missionaries began to report stories of purported atrocities to the press back home, aiming to produce a public outcry that would put pressure on the Japanese government.[13] One report, for example, described how security forces attacked demonstrators with pickaxes, lances, iron bars, and hardwood clubs, as well as firearms, causing numerous casualties. The reports were widely disseminated in the United States and Europe despite the efforts of the Japanese authorities in Korea to censor outgoing correspondence. This created, historian Timothy S. Lee has observed, a "public relations nightmare" for the Japanese and played a part in Tokyo's decision in the summer of 1919 to overhaul the colonial administration of Korea along less oppressive lines.[14]

The popular uprising inside Korea further energized Korean nationalists abroad, and in the weeks following March 1, a string of declarations of Korean independence were proclaimed in various overseas Korean communities.[15] In April, activists in Shanghai decided that the time had come for the next move toward independence, and they announced the establishment of the Provisional Government of the Republic of Korea. Syngman Rhee, still in the United States trying to obtain permission to travel to Paris, was appointed president in absentia, and Kim Kyusik, already in Paris attempting to get a hearing at the peace conference, was named foreign minister in the new government.[16] Cut off from Korea and lacking a significant following in China—the Korean community in Shanghai numbered only about seven hundred at the time—the provisional government governed little. Its establishment was largely a symbolic act, and its members saw bringing the cause of Korean independence before world opinion as their main task for the time being. One of the few decisions immediately taken by the new cabinet was to intensify those efforts. They established an information office in the French concession in Shanghai to advocate their cause in the Chinese and foreign press and sent to Kim Kyusik in Paris official credentials as ambassador plenipotentiary to the peace conference.[17] They spared no effort in the attempt to get the message to Wilson himself. Korean nationalists in Shanghai even approached Carl Crow, who headed the China branch of the Committee on Public Information, to enlist his help. Crow, however, wanted no part of the "Korean revolution," which he considered "dangerous business."[18]

Korean nationalist groups in the United States also intensified their efforts to enlist the support of the U.S. government and public opinion to their cause. Copies of the Seoul Declaration of Independence, translated into English, were dispatched to President Wilson in Paris and to various other officials, informing them that the Korean people wanted independence and calling on the United States to help. Building on the common notion that self-determination was intended only for "civilized races," one petition pointed to the "thousands of Koreans [who] have been educated abroad in recent years" and were "trained in the best thought of the Western world" as proof of the Korean capacity for self-government.[19] The "new Korea" was part of the civilized world and shared its values, and should therefore become an equal member in the community of nations that the peace conference was bringing into existence.

Back on the peninsula, delegates representing the various regions of Korea convened secretly in Seoul on April 23 and announced the establishment of the Republic of Korea and the promulgation of its constitution. Thus, a second independent Korean government was established along similar lines to the one in Shanghai, this one, too, with Syngman Rhee named as its head. Rhee, signing himself as the President of the Republic of Korea, quickly informed the State Department of this new development. Korea, he reported, was now "a completely organized, self governed democratic State," and he hoped that the friendly relations that had long existed between the United States and Korea would continue. Rhee addressed a copy of this announcement to President Wilson himself, but like most other communications from Korean nationalists, Wilson almost certainly never saw it. His White House secretary, Joseph P. Tumulty, received it and routed it directly to the Department of State, where it was filed away with the notation: "Do *not* acknowledge."[20] The official position of the U.S. government remained constant throughout this period. The leading powers, including the United States, had already duly recognized the annexation of Korea to the Japanese empire. The matter was therefore settled, and the American peace commissioners in Paris need not even bother considering it.[21]

Rhee's disappointment with Wilson's lack of response had a personal dimension. Rhee, who had received his bachelor's degree from George

Washington University and a master's degree from Harvard, was enrolled in the doctoral program at Princeton University from 1908 to 1910, when Wilson was the university's president. Rhee had met Wilson there and, according to one account, he was among the Princeton students who were occasionally invited to the president's home on campus to attend the songfests that the Wilsons sometimes held around the family piano. Rhee, the first Korean to receive a doctoral degree from Princeton, was already then a veteran independence activist, and Wilson sometimes introduced him around campus, presumably half in jest, as "the future redeemer of Korean independence." In a letter of recommendation that he had written for Rhee, Wilson had described him as a man "of ability and high character" who possessed "strong patriotic feeling" and "great enthusiasm for his people," and predicted that he would "prove very useful to them." At Rhee's graduation ceremony, Wilson, as university president, handed him his diploma.[22]

By April 1919, however, it had become clear to Rhee that his acquaintance with the president would not do him much good. The State Department denied the requests that he and his co-delegate, Henry Chung, filed to receive U.S. passports that would allow them to travel to the peace conference in Paris. The department's Washington staff, initially unsure how to handle the request, cabled Secretary Lansing in Paris, asking for instructions. Lansing replied that since the United States had already recognized the Japanese annexation of Korea, it would be "unfortunate" to have the Korean representatives in Paris demanding independence. The department then advised Rhee and Chung that since they, as Koreans, were considered subjects of Japan, they would have to request passports from the Japanese authorities. Such a request, it was clear, would never be granted.[23]

In lieu of traveling to Paris, the Korean delegates tried to get an interview with Wilson on his brief stateside visit in late February and early March, but they failed to get past his secretary. In an effort to appeal to the president's sensibilities, Rhee even proposed publicly in March that Korea forgo complete independence for now and accept the status of a League of Nations mandate until the league decided that it was "fit for full self-government."[24] For this suggestion, Rhee was condemned as a traitor by some of the more radical Korean nationalists, and he later repudiated it himself. In any case, it, too, received no response from Wilson, who wanted to have the cooperation of Japan on the League of Nations and, like the rest of his administration, viewed Korea's annexation to Japan as fait accompli.[25] According to his biographer, Rhee was "thunderstruck to discover that his friend and hero, the architect of peace based upon justice, was planning to sacrifice Korean independence for the sake of power politics."[26]

With his travel plans derailed, Rhee joined Korean National Association leader Philip Jaisohn, with whom he had worked during the Independence

Club episode in the late 1890s, to organize a congress of Korean organizations in the United States. The main purpose of the event was to attract support for the Korean struggle in U.S. public opinion.[27] The city of Philadelphia was selected as the location and the event was dubbed the First Korean Congress, partly in order to evoke associations with the First Continental Congress, which the American colonists had convened in the same city some 145 years earlier in order to throw off their own colonial bondage.[28] Twenty-seven expatriate Korean organizations from the United States and Mexico sent representatives. "We called the Korean Congress," Jaisohn declared at the opening session, "because we want America to realize that Korea is a victim of Japan.... We believe that America will champion the cause of Korea as she has that of other oppressed people, once she knows the facts."[29] If U.S. officials would not help Korea, perhaps public opinion would.

One of the first acts of the congress, which convened on April 14 in the Little Theatre on 17th Street and Delancey near Philadelphia's famed Rittenhouse Square, was to approve a document entitled "An Appeal to America," prepared by a committee that Rhee headed. The appeal, echoing Wilsonian language, described the Korean cause as antimilitaristic and democratic and also rendered it as a Christian mission: "Our cause is a just one before the laws of God and man. Our aim is freedom from militaristic autocracy; our object is democracy for Asia; our hope is universal Christianity."[30] In a separate appeal to Wilson and the peace conference, the congress asked that Korea be allowed to enjoy its "inalienable right of self-determination."[31] But what shape would a self-determining Korea take? Rhee, the newly appointed president of the Korean provisional government, declared that free Korea would not stand for a "heathen autocratic government" like that of Japan. Korea's leaders, trained under "American Christian influence" and imbued with "American democratic ideas," would assure freedom of religion, free commerce, free speech and press, education and health, and liberty of action. Their government would derive its powers from the consent of the governed and be modeled after the United States, "as far as possible, consistent with the education of the masses." At first, he admitted, centralized power might be necessary, but as the education of the people improved, their direct participation in government would increase as well.[32]

Like Egyptians, Indians, and Chinese, Korean nationalists wanted to prove to U.S. public opinion that they met the standard of civilization and therefore deserved self-determination. "Clever" Japanese propaganda, Jaisohn pointed out, had managed to convince many Americans that Koreans were "on a par with the American Indians," a "weak and spineless" people who needed "nurses and guardians" because they had "no common sense" and could not help themselves. To combat this view, he called for organizing an information campaign that would bring the truth about Korea to the American public.[33]

A demonstration for Korean independence in Philadelphia, Pennsylvania. The Korean community in the United States, though small, played a major role in the independence movement of 1919. One of its main goals was to appeal to U.S. and world opinion for support. *Seomoondang.*

Koreans, he said, should refrain from using the term "propaganda," which had acquired negative connotations by its association with Germany during the war, but rather describe their campaign as "spreading the true facts about Korea."[34] A monthly periodical, *Korea Review*, published in the United States starting in March 1919 and edited by Jaisohn, was an important element of this campaign. Its advertised goal was "to bring to light the hidden grievances and the forbidden claims of Korea under Japan and thus to obtain the world's sympathy with and interest in her."[35] It contained news about Korean nationalist activities, documents and speeches by Korean nationalist leaders, letters from Korean students abroad, and articles and news items by and about American supporters of Korean independence—scholars, clergy, and others.[36]

Syngman Rhee and Henry Chung, their mission to Paris aborted, were appointed to spearhead the Korean public relations effort. Rhee went on speaking tours across the United States throughout the fall of 1919, and Chung wrote and published several books advocating the Korean cause.[37]

Both also published letters and op-ed pieces in the press to parry claims that Koreans were incapable of self-government and were better off under efficient Japanese rule. In March, the *New York Times* published an editorial that discussed the simultaneous uprisings in Egypt and Korea, arguing that, while the right of all peoples to self-government was fine in principle, its implementation in practice would have to depend on evidence that the people in question had the actual "capacity" for self-government. Did not Egypt and Korea both fall under foreign rule in the first place due to the weakness of their "native governments"? Even if intellectuals from the "upper classes" agitated for self-rule, they did not really speak for the masses, who were presumably content under the respective colonial regimes. To this, Chung replied that Koreans would never have a chance to prove their capacity for self-government as long as they remained under oppressive Japanese rule. Koreans "of all classes," he noted, supported the appeal to the peace conference and to public opinion in the West for a chance to prove their capacity for self-determination.[38]

Rhee, too, mounted a spirited defense of the Korean capacity for independence against those who impugned it. In one such instance, he replied to an article by George Trumbull Ladd, a well-known philosopher and professor emeritus at Yale, in which Ladd described Koreans as unfit for self-government. Attacking the ignorance of the "learned Professor" of Korean society and history, Rhee proceeded to ridicule his arguments against the capacity of Koreans for self-rule. "No incident is too trivial to suit the Professor's purpose," he noted:

> He drags in a story of a Korean who, he says, after having fallen into the clutches of a Japanese usurer, squandered some trust money upon a sweetheart. Of course such a thing could never happen in America! But let us strain our imagination and suppose that it did; would any person of sound mind advance that incident in support of the contention that the Americans are unfit for self-government?

Rhee attacked Ladd's reliance on Japanese propaganda and asserted that Korean "morality" was "superior to that of any other Oriental nation and infinitely higher than that prevailing in Japan." If Japan would only leave Koreans to govern themselves, they would show their fitness to be part of the modern, civilized world.[39]

Numerous other Korean activists in the United States also took part in the efforts to win over opinion in the press, government, and academia. David Lee, head of the KNA in San Francisco, wrote to the famed Harvard history professor and Boston Brahmin Archibald Coolidge to present the Korean case for independence and ask for his support. He enclosed copies of a number of Korean nationalist proclamations of independence and a KNA pamphlet advocating the need for Korean self-determination, which was authored by an American supporter of the movement, J. E. Moore. In their efforts to appeal to the American public, Korean nationalists and their American supporters often repeated the analogy between the Japanese conquest and occupation of Korea and the German invasion of Belgium in 1914. The "rape of Belgium" had caused much outrage in U.S. public opinion and held up as an important justification for the U.S. intervention in the war. Korea, its supporters argued, was the "Belgium of the Orient," and its condition under Japanese rule should excite the same condemnation that the German treatment of Belgium did.[40] Clearly, however, it did not. As Lee wrote indignantly to Coolidge:

> The very same Americans who worked themselves up into frenzies of rage and pity over Belgium have never even taken notice of Japan's savage treatment of Korea.... What does all this fine talk about making the world safe for democracy really amount to, so long as poor, helpless Korea is ground under the heel of Japanese autocracy without even a protest coming from any government, including our own?[41]

The First Korean Congress in Philadelphia convened for three days, April 14–16. During that time, messages from Korean communities in Hawaii and elsewhere that celebrated Korean independence as if it had already been attained were read aloud to the assembled delegates. The gathering discussed various texts of appeals to world opinion, including one addressed to the "thinking people of Japan," and it heard supportive speeches from a number of non-Korean academics and religious leaders, including Rabbi Henry Berkowitz of Philadelphia, who spoke eloquently of how the Jewish heart rejected oppression everywhere. The gathering culminated with the delegates marching through the streets of downtown Philadelphia, brandishing Korean and American flags, to Independence Hall. There they heard a presentation from the site's curator explaining its significance in American history as the location of the signing of the Declaration of Independence and the U.S. Constitution. Syngman Rhee then ceremoniously read the text of the Korean Declaration of Independence to the assembly. As they exited the hall, each delegate walked by the Liberty Bell and touched it reverently with his right hand. Before leaving, Rhee had his photograph taken sitting in the chair from which George Washington had presided over the Constitutional Convention 132 years before.[42] The symbolism was unmistakable: The Korean movement against colonial rule was akin to, and drew inspiration and legitimacy from, the history and ideals of the United States.

With Rhee and Chung stranded on the other side of the Atlantic, Kim Kyusik, with a small group of advisers and secretaries, remained the only Korean representation in Paris. His instructions from the provisional government were to seek interviews with peace delegates and other influential

Korean nationalist leader Syngman Rhee, later the first president of South Korea, had himself photographed sitting in George Washington's chair in Philadelphia's Independence Hall in April 1919 as part of the effort to associate the Korean struggle for independence with the American Revolution. *Seomoondang.*

individuals in Paris, explain the dire condition of Korea under Japanese rule, and convince them that an independent Korea was the key to lasting peace in the Far East. He was to work to "create worldwide opinion regarding the necessity of Korea's liberation" and, having laid the groundwork, make a formal demand for recognition by the peace conference and present it with a petition calling for the liberation of Korea. A document he carried with him from Shanghai laid out the reasons that Korea should have self-determination: "If the civilized world has any regard for the principles for which they have made the immense sacrifices," it read in part, "they must press on Japan to liberate Korea at once." This, after all, was the spirit of the new age: "If the allies have restored the Czecho-Slavs to independence after so many centuries of slavery and forced Germany to vacate Belgium, Serbia, etc., why should poor Korea's case be neglected?"[43]

Kim worked diligently in Paris to carry out his instructions. Upon his arrival, he established a Korean Information Bureau that would compile and distribute press summaries of events in Korea. He also tried to approach the U.S. delegation directly to seek support. His first contact was with Stephen Bonsal, a close aide and interpreter to Wilson and House, who had served in Korea as a diplomat before its annexation to Japan and knew the country and its people well. Bonsal met with Kim and was sympathetic to his plea for help, but when he brought the issue up with House, the colonel replied that Korea could not be discussed at the conference: "If we attempt too much we may fail to accomplish anything." House, however, did not rule out the possibility that the Korean question might come before an international forum later on, suggesting that the League of Nations might be able to curb Japan "when it has less pressing matters nearer at hand to deal with." Bonsal recalled that, when he relayed House's reply back to Kim, the young Korean took the news well and appeared confident that the league would eventually hear Korea's case.[44] His optimism turned out to be misplaced: The Korean question did not come before the international forum in subsequent years, and in any event, Japan officially withdrew from the league in 1933, after the league condemned the Japanese military occupation of Manchuria that occurred two years earlier.

Stanley Hornbeck, the East Asia expert on House's Inquiry commission, was also sympathetic to the Korean claims, as he was toward the Chinese demands over Shandong. In March, Hornbeck forwarded a petition he had received from Korean nationalists in Shanghai to Joseph Grew, the secretary general of the U.S. delegation, and suggested that the U.S. peace commissioners consider hearing the Korean representative in person or at least accepting a written statement from him. Grew referred the question to E. T. Williams, who, like Hornbeck, was sympathetic to the Korean claims against Japan. But Williams also knew there was little the U.S. government was likely to do for them. "Since you refer this to me," he responded ruefully, "I can only say that in view of the fact that the U.S. has recognized the annexation of Korea, the representative ought not to be received." With this, the hopes of Korean nationalists for gaining any official U.S. support at the peace table were dashed.[45]

Unable to enlist the support of the U.S. delegation, Kim nevertheless ventured to petition the peace conference to recognize the right "of the Korean People and Nation for liberation from Japan." In making the case for Korean independence, he echoed Chinese arguments over the Japanese seizure of Shandong, citing the tenets of international law as well as President Wilson's wartime declarations. The 1910 Treaty of Annexation which made Korea part of the Japanese empire, Kim wrote, was concluded under "fraud and force" and should be nullified. If the postwar settlement was to be based on Wilson's Fourteen Points, including the right of "all peoples . . . to live on equal terms of liberty," then Korea had no less a right to self-determination than other peoples whose sovereignty was being restored as part of the peace:

> In virtue of rights founded in International Law and of the New Justice which is to redress the wrongs of nations, the Korean people have a just claim for the Reconstitution of Korea as an Independent State unless, indeed, they are excluded from the scope of the principles which have already found expression in the reconstitution of Poland after almost one and a half centuries of partitions and annexations and the dis-annexation of Alsace-Lorraine after nearly half a century of Prussian rule.[46]

The logic was impeccable, but it floundered on the shoals of power politics. Poland and Alsace-Lorraine were wrested away from empires that were defeated or had collapsed in the war, while Japan had emerged as a leading power among the victors. In the case of Korea, as in others outside Europe in 1919, the force of principle could not overcome the realities of power.

Kim sent copies of his petition, with personal cover letters, to the leaders of the major Western powers, carefully tailoring each letter to address what he thought might be important to each leader. In Wilson's case, he tried to appeal to the president's sensibilities as a man of faith, drawing his attention to the Japanese hostility toward Christianity in Korea, and as a scholar, hoping to "tempt" Wilson's "intellectual curiosity" by detailing the Japanese plan to use Korea as a base to dominate China and turn the Pacific Ocean into a "Japanese lake."[47] This combination of religious and strategic appeal, Kim hoped, would prove effective with the U.S. leader. Like other Korean petitions, however, and like the petitions of dozens of other oppressed and stateless peoples at the time, it did not elicit the desired response. Wilson's private secretary, Gilbert Close, wrote to Kim politely to say that his letter had been "called to the attention" of the president. When Hornbeck again attempted to bring the Korean question before the American delegation, Close replied that the Korean petitions had already been "acknowledged on behalf of the president" and sent "for the consideration of the proper authorities at the Commission."[48]

Kim's letter to Lloyd George, a man considerably less devout than Wilson, made no mention of the Japanese treatment of Christians and emphasized the strategic argument, but it added a specific reference to the danger posed to Australia by the rise of Japanese power in the Pacific.[49] On May 24, Kim circulated another letter to the delegations of all the great powers, this one signed by Syngman Rhee as "the President of the Cabinet of the Provisional Government of Korea." Asking the conference to recognize the newly established republic of Korea and its government, Rhee expressed the "unanimous and passionate desire" of Koreans for independence, so they can "develop themselves as a free and responsible people among the civilised nations of the world." The principle of self-determination rendered Japanese attempts to suppress the Korean movement "illegal, immoral and invalid." The indefatigable Hornbeck tried to bring this petition as well to the attention of the president but had no more success than before.[50] And the British, as Japan's main allies in Paris, were even less inclined than the United States to entertain Korean claims for independence. Lloyd George's private secretary, Philip Kerr, forwarded Rhee's note to the Foreign Office in London marked: "For Information—The Prime Minister has taken no action in the matter." Korean efforts to interest the French delegation in their predicament under Japanese rule met with a similar fate.[51]

Though Kim was the only "official" Korean representative who managed to make it to Paris, he was not alone in his efforts to present Korea's case before the conference. As was the case with Chinese, Egyptians, and Indians around the world, a wide array of Korean patriotic organizations, most of them based outside the peninsula, petitioned Wilson and the other world leaders in Paris to take up the Korean question. One petition to the peace conference, signed by Young L. Park of the United Asiatic Society of Detroit, Michigan, laid out once again the history of Japanese oppression in Korea and, citing Wilson's wartime rhetoric, demanded that the peace conference recognize Korean independence. The "loftiest declaration of human rights proclaimed by America's statesmen," he pleaded, should "become the law of the world."[52] Another petition, from the Methodist minister and nationalist activist Hyun Soon, gave further details of Japanese brutality against Korean protesters and beseeched Wilson to save Korea from its despoilers "in the name of God." By the time he returned to the United States, Hornbeck's files bulged with numerous other letters from Koreans and their supporters; none of them received a substantial response.[53]

In June, with the conclusion of the German treaty approaching, Kim was growing desperate. Might he possibly, he asked Hornbeck, have a brief interview with Wilson, or House, or even Lansing, "even in an unofficial way," to put the Korean plight before them? Hornbeck continued to try to find some way to help, asking if perhaps Commissioners Henry White or Tasker Bliss, who in any case had little to keep then busy, could find time to see Kim, merely to signal U.S. sympathy for an oppressed people. No such meeting, however, ever materialized. Kim dispatched another note to the various peace delegations reminding them of the Korean claims and begging them "not to overlook the plea of the Korean People," but even his efforts to gain the attention of the Chinese delegation failed. The Chinese, though they had earlier helped to transport Kim to Paris, were losing their own diplomatic battle against Japanese expansion and could do little more for Korea.[54]

Having failed in his mission to bring Korean claims to the peace table, Kim departed from Paris late that year. But he did meet one more time with his friend Bonsal to muse dejectedly on the irony and injustice of the moment. The world now counted Japan, which in the past had learned the ways of civilization from Korea, as a great power, while Korea itself remained utterly subordinated and excluded from international affairs. "How can anyone in his sense," he asked Bonsal plaintively, "imagine that these swashbucklers will help to make the world safe for democracy?"[55] Still, Kim, like Tilak, Zaghlul, and Koo at the time, did not give up on the efforts to bring the case of Korea before the international community. "Our next court of appeal," he wrote to one of his assistants, "is the League of Nations, which ... shall and must decide upon the invalidity of the treaty of annexation of Korea by Japan."[56]

Kim's suggestion that the Japanese government was hostile to the Wilsonian vision for a new world order was not off the mark. Japanese leaders perceived Wilson's ideas as a serious challenge to their country's role in world affairs, since they implied that the imperial state that the Meiji reformers had labored to construct since 1868 was no longer legitimate. "The tidal wave of world thought today," Japanese prime minister Hara Takashi warned at the time, "may destroy all order and damage the essence of our National Polity." Japan had joined the international system in the late nineteenth century, a time when a nation's international status was measured by its military prowess and the acquisition of colonies. But Wilson had argued that this imperial order was a major cause of the war and called for excluding authoritarian, militaristic states like Germany from membership in the reconstructed international society. Meiji Japan had been modeled after Europe's imperial nation-states and after Prussia most of all, a model that Japan's leadership, as historian Frederick Dickinson has noted, had consciously adopted as standing at the "vanguard of modern civilization." Wilson and his supporters, however, now condemned it as militaristic and autocratic, a danger to world peace and an impediment to the progress of makind.[57]

Wilson's articulation of self-determination as a universally valid ideal inspired both domestic and foreign opponents of the imperial Japanese government. "The great tide of democracy," declared one Japanese reformer, "is overwhelming the entire world at this moment." The prominent liberal thinker Yoshino Sakuzō, a political theorist and Tokyo University professor who led the liberal-democratic "mass-awakening" movement in Japan in 1919 and openly sympathized with Korean aspirations for independence, noted in January 1919 that the "trend of the world" was, in matters of domestic policy, "the perfection of democracy" and in foreign policy, "the establishment of international egalitarianism."[58] Organized labor, students, and other domestic opposition groups in Japan rallied to the Wilsonian vision, invoking the new "spirit of the League of Nations" in their critique of their government even as Koreans were marching for their own liberation.[59] Events in Korea, in turn, served as an example to other opponents of Japanese imperial expansion. Chen Duxiu, the Chinese intellectual and future cofounder of the Chinese Communist party, described the March First protests as "grand, sincere, and tragic" and lamented that with "this glory manifesting in the Korean race, the embarrassment of the decay of the Chinese race is all the more apparent." Despite Japan's diplomatic victories in Paris, then, the Wilsonian wave in Asia—in Korea, China, and Japan itself—posed a threat to the empire and a serious challenge to the government in Tokyo.[60]

Like the British in Egypt and India, the Japanese authorities in Korea did not anticipate the full effects that the postwar atmosphere of expectation and the rhetoric of self-determination would have on Koreans, and the March First protests caught them off guard.[61] Moreover, the efforts at violent repression that followed proved insufficient and in some ways even exacerbated the problem: The atrocity reports that proliferated in the Western press acutely embarrassed the Japanese government, which continued to justify its rule in Korea in terms of a civilizing mission.[62] Even as the efforts at military pacification in Korea continued, Tokyo therefore moved quickly to reform its rule over the peninsula. In August 1919, the Japanese government announced the passage of a reform act, the Revised Organic Regulations of the Government General of Korea. The reform act abandoned the radical assimilation policies of the previous regime. It inaugurated a new "cultural policy," which promised to give Koreans some measure of self-rule and relaxed some of the controls on cultural and political life imposed by the military rule of the period between 1910 and 1919. The new policy was aimed both at Koreans and at international opinion, seeking to improve the image of Japanese rule in Korea abroad as well as to induce and co-opt more Koreans to acquiesce in it. Admiral Saitō Makoto, a former naval attaché in the United States and navy minister and a future prime minister, was appointed to be the new governor general of Korea to implement the reforms, and he remained in that position until 1927.[63]

Saitō's reforms, however, fell far short of the aspirations of many Korean nationalists, who, like their Chinese, Egyptian, and Indian counterparts, had come to see anything less than full self-determination as inadequate. Immediately after the Japanese government announced the reforms, Kim, by now in the United States, and Rhee issued declarations rejecting them and demanding "absolute independence" in line with the principle of self-determination.[64] Rhee and his colleagues also continued their efforts to rouse U.S. public opinion against Japanese rule in Korea. They received support in this task from American church groups and missionary boards, which produced dozens of petitions to their government and letters in the press protesting Japanese brutality, advocating Korean self-determination, and calling on Washington to take action. The pastor of a congregation in Beloit, Kansas, for example, wrote to the White House to protest the "bloodshed and horror" in Korea and to ask that Koreans receive the right to self-determination. The Federal Council of Protestant Evangelical Missions wrote to Saitō directly to make the same request. And there were many others.[65] The State Department's position, however, remained the same: Korea was part of the empire of Japan and therefore a domestic Japanese matter about which the United States could do little.[66]

When the focus of debate about the postwar settlement shifted from Paris to the U.S. Senate in late summer, Koreans, like Chinese, Indians, and Egyptians, wanted to have their case heard there. Fred A. Dolph, an American who served as a legal adviser to the Korean provisional government, successfully petitioned Senator Selden P. Spencer, a Republican from Missouri, to raise the issue of Korea on the floor of the Senate, but Spencer's resolution was referred to the Foreign Relations Committee and never heard of again.[67] Senator George Norris, the Nebraska Republican and irreconcilable opponent of the Versailles Treaty, used the press reports of atrocities in Korea to attack the treaty in the Senate debate. The situation in Korea, Norris argued, proved that Japan could not be trusted, and the concessions made to it in the treaty, not least over Shandong, belied Wilson's claims to be fighting for world democracy, self-determination, and civilization. The treaty, he concluded with flair, put back "the clock of civilization a thousand years."[68] Such condemnations of the wrongs done to Korea, like similar rhetoric attacking the Shandong decision or the British practices in Egypt and India, may have helped to defeat the treaty in the Senate; they did little, however, to advance the cause of Korean self-determination. Korean nationalist activists in the United States and their missionary supporters continued their efforts into the 1920s, but they had little success in influencing American or Japanese policies toward Korea.[69]

As occurred in China and elsewhere, the collapse of the program of liberal anticolonialism that many colonial nationalists adopted at the Wilsonian moment sent Korean patriots on a search for alternative ideologies and allies on the road to national liberation. In August 1919, a memorandum composed by Korean socialists and submitted to the conference of the Second International in Lucerne stated: "Not even one of the 14 Wilsonian promises is realized. It is then quite natural that the oppressed peoples should stretch their hands to us socialists for help."[70] Soon after, Korean nationalists active in the Russian Far East turned to the consolidating Bolshevik government for assistance, and the support that they received led to the establishment of the Korean Communist Party in 1925. In subsequent years, some North Korean and other Marxist historians would claim that the March First movement was itself inspired by the October Revolution in Russia. But the testimonies of the movement's leaders and participants themselves provide "ample proof that the Declaration of Independence and the appeal to the Peace Conference were inspired by Woodrow Wilson and his doctrine of self-determination" rather than by the events of the Bolshevik revolution, which were little known or understood in Korea at the time.[71]

The Provisional Government of the Republic of Korea, established in Shanghai in 1919 to seize the opportunity presented by the peace conference, continued to exist in the interwar years. Though it had little influence on events in Korea itself and was riven by internal strife, its members did not give up their hope for attaining international recognition, and it reemerged during the Second World War to renew its demand for recognition from the U.S. government and then from United Nations Conference that gathered in San Francisco in 1945. After the Allied victory in the Second World War, several of the leading figures of 1919, Syngman Rhee chief among them, would return to Korea to play significant roles in Korea's subsequent fortunes, and they would make the March First movement a founding event in the official historical narrative of the Republic of Korea. The centrality of March First to Korean national history was challenged by official histories in the north, where it was dismissed as a failed effort of bourgeois intellectuals, and more recently by revisionist historians in the south, who have emphasized the role of other popular resistance movements such as the Tonghak.[72] Nevertheless, at the dawn of the twenty-first century, the preamble to the South Korean constitution, first adopted in 1948, still declares: "We the people of Korea, proud of a resplendent history and traditions dating from time immemorial," uphold "the cause of the Provisional Republic of Korea Government born of the March First Independence Movement of 1919."[73]

Like other contemporaneous anticolonial uprisings, the March First movement could easily be seen as a failure. It did not achieve its aspiration of international recognition for Korean independence, nor even the more modest goal of raising the question of Korea officially at the peace negotiations. Still, even if it failed in its proclaimed objectives, the movement played a pivotal role in the history of Korean nationalism. In the immediate term, it prompted the replacement of the harsh military rule of 1910–1919 with the more accommodating "cultural policy" of the 1920s. More broadly, it changed the character and scope of the Korean nationalist movement, mobilizing Koreans against Japanese rule and constituting, as the historian Lee Chong-sik concluded, "the beginnings of the era of modern nationalism" in Korea.[74] Like the contemporaneous uprisings in other parts of the colonial world—the 1919 Revolution in Egypt, the Rowlatt Satyagraha in India, and the May Fourth movement in China—did in those societies, March First transformed the Korean national movement and helped to shape its subsequent identity and development.

Conclusion: Toward a "Family of Nations"

The violent conflict between East and West, between imperialism and self-determination, between slavery and freedom, between darkness and light; this violent conflict, which began on the day that the Great War ended and will continue until light triumphs and right prevails—is it not the consequence of these great principles, that some today see as illusions? They are not illusions. They are a force which has built up over the ages, created by general suffering and hopes, by individual dreams and yearnings, by the ideas of philosophers and the words of poets, by all the power, feeling, and desire of the human soul. And then, fate chose President Wilson to be their translator and spokesman.... Wilson has died, but his ideas remain, and they will no doubt triumph.

—Muhammad Husayn Haykal, 1924

When I gave utterance to those words [on the right to self-determination], I said them without a knowledge that nationalities existed, which are coming to us day after day.... You do not know and cannot appreciate the anxieties that I have experienced as the result of many millions of people having their hopes raised by what I have said.

—Woodrow Wilson, June 1919

On August 6, 1919, shortly before he left Paris, Kim Kyusik threw an evening banquet for friends and supporters of the Korean cause at the Foreign Press Association quarters on the Champs Élysées. The guests, some eighty in all, included editors and correspondents for numerous French, American, British, and Italian newspapers, as well as a smattering of midlevel officials and diplomats sympathetic to Korea's plight. Several Chinese were present, including the consul general in Paris. The hall was decorated with the French tricolor and the Korean national flag, and at their seats, each guest found several souvenirs: a handsomely printed copy of the Korean Declaration of Independence in French, a small Korean flag, and a copy of a slim book, *Pauvre et Douce Corée*, by the French journalist Georges Ducrocq. In his keynote address that evening, Kim summarized the history of Korea and its contributions to civilization since ancient times. He then turned to describe the "unforeseen repercussions" in the Far East of those "principles so often reiterated during the entire war—Liberty, Justice, the rights of the peoples." Koreans, he assured his audience, had taken to heart the declarations of European and American statesmen calling to uphold such principles. President Wilson had said that the treaty recently signed at Versailles puts "an end to the right of conquest and rejects the policy of annexation" and guarantees that peoples "will no longer be subjected to the domination and exploitation of a stronger nation." The people of Korea, Kim concluded, wished to be included in that process to become part of the "family of nations of the world."[1]

The Chinese in 1919 shared the same aspiration. They had envisioned the coming of a new era of self-determination and equality in international relations, and though their faith in Wilson crumbled when he failed to apply his principles to China, the experience left its mark. Sun Yat-sen, the icon of Chinese nationalism, suggested a few years later the far-reaching implications of this process, which he, like Mao, viewed within a broad global context:

> Wilson's proposals, once set forth, could not be recalled; each one of the weaker, smaller nations . . . stirred with a great, new consciousness; they saw how completely they had been deceived by the Great Powers' advocacy of self-determination and began independently and separately to carry out the principle of the "self-determination of peoples."[2]

China had failed to win its case in Paris, but the failure was only temporary. The Japanese had won Wilson's agreement to their claims in Shandong only by promising to return the territory shortly to China, and in fact they did so, under U.S. pressure, on the margins of the Washington Naval Conference of 1921–1922. By then, however, it was too late to reverse the broader consequences of the Paris decision, and in any case, Chinese nationalists now wanted nothing less than a complete abrogation of the unequal treaties. That goal, too, was largely achieved by 1928, as China, newly reunited under the Guomindang leader Chiang Kai-shek, renegotiated its treaties with foreign powers, achieving tariff autonomy and doing away with legal extraterritoriality.[3] But this successful self-assertion was quickly overshadowed by the Japanese encroachments of the 1930s, which began with the conquest of Manchuria in 1931 and culminated in the outbreak of all-out war between China and Japan in 1937. When Mao Zedong, now head of the victorious Chinese Communist Party, announced in 1949 that the Chinese people had "stood up," he declared the attainment of the goal that Chinese nationalists had pursued for the better part of a century.

Even as Mao, in 1919 still a twenty-five-year-old activist in a remote Chinese province, analyzed the international events from Changsha, the urbane, Cambridge-educated twenty-nine-year-old Jawaharlal Nehru made similar observations in Allahabad. Penning a review of the philosopher Bertrand Russell's 1918 book, *Roads to Freedom*, Nehru suggested the turn away from the Wilsonian millennium with the quote from Karl Marx with which he chose to preface his review: "A spectre is haunting Europe, the spectre of communism." "Much was expected of the war," Nehru lamented. "It was to have revolutionised the fabric of human affairs, but it has ended without bringing any solace or hope of permanent peace or betterment. President Wilson's brave words have remained but words, and the 'fourteen points,' where are they?" Nehru noted Russell's observation that "the Millennium is not for our time. The great moment has passed and for ourselves it is again the distant hope that must inspire us, not the immediate breathless looking for the deliverance." Russell, Nehru continued, argued for a combination of anarchism and guild socialism as the ideal regime for the present times. Nehru had some doubts about this formulation, but recommended that Indian politicians pay close heed to them. Indians must first struggle for representative government, but in time perhaps "some form of communism will be found to suit the genius of the people better than majority rule."[4]

The Wilsonian moment had encouraged Indian and other nationalists to formulate their claims for self-government in language that resonated with a wider, international discourse of legitimacy. Veteran nationalists like Tilak and Lajpat Rai left the confines of the British Empire, physically and conceptually, to take their case before world opinion. The principle of self-determination supported both Indian demands for home rule and their claim for representation in the international arena, and though India's colonial masters denied those demands, they could not deny their legitimacy. The new radicalism of the Indian National Congress under Gandhi was reflected in its continued rejection of postwar reforms as insufficient, as it boycotted the elections for new provincial councils in 1921 and the visit of the Simon Commission, sent to propose further reforms, in 1928. Indian nationalists were no longer willing to accept the measured, piecemeal process that London wanted. In 1929, at the annual gathering of the INC in Lahore, Nehru, now presiding over the session, officially announced the Indian goal as *purna swaraj*, or complete independence. "The brief day of European domination is already approaching its end," he declared in his presidential address. "The future lies with America and Asia. . . . India today is part of a world movement."[5] And so it was: a movement away from empire and toward the self-determining nation-state as the organizing principle of governance in the non-European world.

In Egypt, too, Wilson's rhetoric led nationalists to expect immediate independence after the war and helped to shape their demands and the ways they pursued them as they prepared for the postwar world. Like Koreans and Indians, Egyptian nationalists believed that with Wilsonian principles on the ascendant, the formation of the League of Nations would allow demands for self-determination to come before a tribunal of the world community, shifting the balance of power in colonial relationships away from the colonial powers. Egyptian nationalists saw the numerous representatives of subject nations who rushed to Paris to present their demands and could see little reason that they should be excluded from that opportunity. The violent clashes that erupted in response to British intransigence escalated Egyptian resistance to their rule, broadened the social base of the movement, and hardened Egyptians' commitment to nationalist goals. When Wilson died in 1924, Muhammad Husayn Haykal, the Egyptian intellectual, could easily recall the striking impression his appearance had made: "We all know Dr. Wilson. We all remember the time when we gazed at the Fourteen Points in awe. We all remember the great hopes built upon those principles, hopes which still grip the world." The emergence of the Wilsonian moment had heralded the end of a great conflict, the European war, but its dissipation gave rise to a greater one still, one "between East and West, between imperialism and self-determination."[6] The new era of self-determination had come, but it was one of conflict rather than cooperation.

The ad hoc alliance that Zaghlul had created to bring Egyptian claims to the peace conference became a political party that dominated Egyptian politics for nearly three decades. Zaghlul himself, who returned from his European sojourn in 1920, remained the most popular political figure in Egypt. He served as prime minister for ten months in 1924 following a landslide election victory for the Wafd, and when he died in August 1927 he was widely hailed in Egypt as the "Father of the Nation." The British, attempting to accommodate nationalist sentiment while preserving their interests, ended the protectorate and granted Egypt limited independence in 1922, but the nationalists found it inadequate and continued to demand full sovereignty. They won a greater measure of independence in 1936, but the struggle against British influence in Egypt continued until 1956, when the last of the British forces evacuated Egyptian territory in the wake of the Suez crisis. By then, however, Egyptians no longer imagined the United States as a benevolent and well-intentioned force in international affairs as they had in 1919. In 1958, when tensions between the United States and a newly assertive Egypt were at a peak, Egyptian president Gamal Abdel Nasser—who was born on January 15, 1918, exactly one week after Wilson's Fourteen Points address—accused the United States of forgetting "the principles invoked by Wilson."[7]

In November 1918, on the deck of the *George Washington* en route to France, Woodrow Wilson ruminated on the task ahead of him and the unsettled state of much of the world. His chief propagandist, George Creel, recalled the president's trepidation about the hopes and expectations that his words had raised. Disillusionment, Wilson feared, was inevitable:

> One evening, as we walked the deck, I spoke to the President of the tremendous help that his addresses had been to us in our work—of the wholehearted response of the people of the earth, their gladness in his words, the joyful liberation of their thought....
>
> The President stood silent for quite a while, and when he turned to me at last his face was as bleak as the gray stretch of sunless water.
>
> "It is a great thing that you have done," he said, "but I am wondering if you have not unconsciously spun a net for me from which there is no escape. It is to America that the whole world turns to-day, not only with its wrongs, but with its hopes and grievances. The hungry expect us to feed them, the roofless look to us for shelter, the sick of heart and body depend on us for cure. All of these expectations have in them the quality of terrible urgency. There must be no delay. It has been so always. People will endure their tyrants for years, but they will tear their deliverers to pieces if a millennium is not created immediately. Yet you know, and I know, that these ancient wrongs, these present unhappinesses, are not to be remedied in a day or with a wave of the hand. What I seem to see—with all my heart I hope that I am wrong—is a tragedy of disappointment."[8]

The events that unfolded in much of the colonial world over the next several months—indeed, over the next several decades—bore out Wilson's apprehensions, as the language of self-determination became a central component of the nationalist challenge to the imperial order in international relations. Partly through the efforts of Creel and his crew, Wilson's words had been disseminated around the world, far beyond the primary audiences in Europe and the United States for whom they were intended. By the time of the armistice, many in the colonial world expected Wilson to lead a transformation of international affairs and mold an international society in which the right to self-determination would be recognized and the equality of nations guaranteed. The credibility of Wilson's pronouncements among colonial nationalists was bolstered by a prevailing image of the United States as a nation that represented a more benign version of Western modernity when compared with the practices of imperial aggression associated with the European powers. This perception was reflected in the views of intellectuals like Rabindranath Tagore and Hu Shi and of political activists like Lajpat Rai, Zaghlul, and Syngman Rhee. Many colonial intellectuals during this period saw the American Revolution as a pioneering movement of national liberation from imperialism and admired American political, social, and economic institutions as models for the progressive, "modern" society and popular government to which they aspired.[9]

The millenarian, quasi-religious renderings of Woodrow Wilson—Sastri's description of Wilson as "Christ, or Buddha," Aiyar's rendering of him as an agent of "salvation," or Kang Youwei's hope that the president could be the purveyor of *datong* utopia—reflected a powerful if fleeting sense in the immediate wake of the war that a historical moment had arrived in which humanity could transcend the logic of Darwinian competition and long-established power relationships and found an international community in which all nations would enjoy recognition and dignity. Wilson, as the leading icon of the moment and its possibilities, appeared to colonial nationalists to be poised to take international society beyond the dichotomies that hitherto governed the relations between colonizer and colonized: powerful versus weak, advanced versus backward, material versus spiritual, might versus right. Hu Shi's view of the president as a leader who could remain uniquely pure and unworldly even while wielding political power in the world depended on imagining Wilson as at once bridging and transcending these poles, which in the past had seemed inescapable.

Such views of Wilson, of course, hardly reflected the man himself. A supporter of the U.S. conquest of the Philippines, Wilson thought that non-European peoples needed the trusteeship of more "civilized" powers in order to develop the capabilities for self-determination. Though his wartime rhetoric did not explicitly exclude non-Europeans from self-determination, he never specified how that principle would apply to them beyond a vague promise, perfectly compatible with the reigning theory of colonial trusteeship, to take into account the "interests of the populations concerned." Moreover, Wilson's background and approach was well known to some colonial leaders, who noted and criticized the injustices of American society and foreign policy. Lala Lajpat Rai had carefully studied and documented the state of American race relations, and Chinese intellectuals had long deplored and protested the ill treatment and exclusion in the United States of Chinese migrants. During the height of the Wilsonian moment, however, the deficiencies of the United States and its president as champions of freedom seemed to be overshadowed by Wilson's image as a vigorous advocate of international justice.

In the fall and winter of 1918–1919, such perceptions of Wilson and the United States reinforced the sense that a window of opportunity had opened and thrust the issue of colonial liberation to the fore. The proliferation of demands for self-determination put before the peace conference created a domino effect that drew in more claims still. As some new nations achieved recognition in Paris, representatives of others doubled their efforts to stake their own claims to independent nationhood. Self-determination became the order of the day. Leaders such as Zaghlul, who were previously willing to accommodate empire as an instrument of progress and reform, now came out decisively against it; old opponents of empire, such as Tilak, moved from the margins of the movement to its center and often quickly came to be seen as too moderate as popular sentiment rushed past them.

In the campaigns that they launched to claim the right to self-determination for their own peoples, anticolonial nationalists appropriated Wilsonian language to articulate their goals and mobilize support for them both at home and abroad. Western-educated nationalists like Syngman Rhee and Wellington Koo and expatriate communities more generally played central roles in speaking for their nations in international society, reflecting their geographic, intellectual, and cultural proximity to the arenas of power and influence in international society. But diverse groups back home—religious communities, local councils, professional organizations, and women's groups—also mobilized to ask the peace conference for self-determination. In thousands of petitions, pamphlets, declarations, and memoranda, they adopted Wilson's language, refracted it through the lenses of local conditions and sensibilities, and harnessed it to claim their rights in international society.

The simultaneous eruption of anticolonial upheavals in the spring of 1919 occurred in this context. In Korea and Egypt, the protests initially broke out as part of the campaigns to bring demands for self-determination to international attention. In China and India, the upheavals reflected the collapse of the expectations for change, as the peace conference rejected Chinese claims and the promulgation of the Rowlatt acts signaled that Britain had little intention of loosening its grip on the empire's crown jewel. By the spring of 1919, as the contours of the peace settlement began to emerge, it became clear that the leading powers, including the United States, had little intention of applying the principle of self-determination significantly beyond Europe. The faith in Wilson's commitment to a more just international order, or in his ability to fashion one, began to ebb, and disenchantment with the Wilsonian promise spread.

Still, the experiences of the Wilsonian moment cemented ideological and political commitments to anticolonial agendas, and the movements launched then did not disappear with its demise. The colonial authorities moved to stem the anticolonial wave, and the popular momentum of the spring of 1919, driven by international events, could not last indefinitely. In its wake, however, political programs and organizations committed to self-determination became more powerful and more pervasive than before. Moreover, the upheavals of the spring of 1919 themselves created narratives of colonial violence and popular resistance that quickly became etched into collective memories and that came to symbolize each nation's striving for liberation. These movements—the 1919 Revolution, the May Fourth movement, the Rowlatt Satyagraha and Amritsar, and the March First movement—became focal points in the construction of national identity and inspired continued commitment to nationalist agendas. The language of self-determination as a central norm of legitimacy in international relations remained central in the rhetoric of anticolonial movements, useful in mobilizing public opinion and action both at home and abroad and in rejecting any accommodation with empire.

Wilson himself did acknowledge that the peace conference failed to deal with colonial claims, especially those related to the possessions of the Allied powers, in accordance with his much-advertised principles. In Paris, he said shortly after his return to the United States, there were numerous delegations clamoring to be heard, and though the conference, limited to issues that arose directly from the war, could not take up their demands, it did lay the institutional groundwork for dealing with them. Now that the League of Nations was established, oppressed peoples would receive justice in the court of world opinion.[10] Soon after, however, the president suffered the stroke that ended his career, and on March 19, 1920, the U.S. Senate finally rejected the Treaty of Versailles and with it the League of Nations covenant.[11] The United States never joined the League of Nations, and even if it had, it is hard to imagine that the league, controlled as it was by the major imperial powers, would have been sympathetic to colonial demands for self-determination. In the end, the Wilsonian moment did alter the relationship between colonizer and colonized, but it did not do so in the consensual, evolutionary manner that Wilson had envisioned.

Framing the Wilsonian moment in the colonial world as an international and transnational event is not merely an analytical device or an expression of a particular historical method. Rather, it reflects the perceptions and actions of historical actors at the time, and much of what they saw and did at the time is rendered incomprehensible, even invisible outside that framework. The moment was inherently international in that it played out in an arena defined by the interactions between sovereign nation-states and in which such states were the primary actors. It was also transnational, meaning that the perceptions and actions of the actors regularly transcended and crossed existing political boundaries; indeed, in many cases such crossings—for example, in order to travel to Paris or to Washington—were among the primary purposes of their activities at the time. Moreover, the Wilsonian moment in the colonial world operated both internationally and transnationally in a number of related but distinct fashions that were juxtaposed and overlaid upon each other in various combinations at different times and places during the unfolding of events.

First, individuals and groups that participated in the events of 1919 in the colonial world were located across the globe rather than confined to specific national or imperial territories, and they interacted with each other intensively across the boundaries of such territories as they launched their respective movements. Koreans from Shanghai to Philadelphia were integral to the March First movement; Chinese in Paris, Peru, and Cambridge,

Massachusetts, took part in the May Fourth protests; Egyptians in Manchester and Geneva joined the 1919 Revolution; and Indians in London and New York City were crucial to the campaign for Indian self-determination. Moreover, the very "national" character of the territories they each claimed to represent—the Korean peninsula, the Indian subcontinent, the British protectorate in Egypt, a Chinese subcontinent ruled by a patchwork of warlords and at least two governments vying for legitimacy—was at the time a central point of contestation, though we have since come to take it for granted. An important goal of nationalist activists was precisely to achieve international recognition that these territories were in fact "national" territories in the first place, and therefore deserving of a sovereign status in the new international society.

Moreover, even those anticolonial nationalists in 1919 who were based within their respective national territories—and they certainly played crucial roles in the events—saw their own conditions as embedded within a broader global order that was now on the cusp of change. Egyptians noted the arrival in Paris of Arab representatives who were promised self-determination and concluded that Egypt deserved no less, and Indians published maps that located India within a world of dependent nations yearning for liberation. Chinese placed their desire to recover the former German territories in Shandong in the context of changing norms of international behavior, and Koreans stressed the similarity of their plight as a Japanese colony to that of Belgium under the German occupation and asked for similar redress. In the fall of 1918, they all carefully followed the gathering in Paris of representatives of the "small nations" of Europe—Poles, Czechoslovaks, Yugoslavs—that were emerging from the fallen empires of the Habsburgs and the Romanovs. And in the spring of 1919, they each looked to the simultaneous revolts that broke out across much of the colonial world as evidence that their own movements were part of a global wave and that their claims were both just and timely.

As they laid their plans, therefore, anticolonial activists in 1919 sought explicitly to operate on an international stage. They organized broad information campaigns designed to influence "world opinion," preparing thousands of telegrams, letters, and petitions that were dispatched across national or imperial boundaries and aimed at an international audience. They also initiated and took part in missions that traveled, or sought to travel, abroad to Paris, Washington, and London. Indeed, the preparation and execution of such missions formed a core element of the nationalists' plans at the time and an important lever of popular mobilization behind those plans. The Anglo-Egyptian struggle over Zaghlul's demand to go to Paris ignited the 1919 Revolution in Egypt, and the refusal of the peace conference to admit Tilak and the other INC delegates fueled the disillusion that found expression in the protests of the Rowlatt satyagraha. The March First movement was launched to communicate Korean nationalist goals to an international audience, and much of the effort of those involved in it was directed toward admitting a Korean delegation to the peace conference and putting the case of Korea before "world opinion." And Chinese nationalists, too, launched campaigns that were international in their conception and purpose and transnational in their operation and audience.

Finally, the aspirations expressed by the anticolonial movements of 1919 were international in their scope and ambition. They aimed to bring into existence a vision of international relations in which hitherto dependent nations would obtain recognition of their equality and sovereignty and join a League of Nations where they would enjoy equal status regardless of size or power. The great majority of the petitioners that tried to make themselves heard on the international arena, whether political leaders, civic organizations, or simply individuals who were moved to communicate directly with the powerful foreign leaders they read about in newspapers, had this image of a new international society in mind. They anticipated a transformation of international relations along liberal anticolonial lines, which would render illegitimate the suppression of national claims within imperial structures, and they wanted to see the national entity with which they identified recognized within a broader community of nations constructed on Wilsonian principles. Within this new order, moreover, reforms toward liberal, democratic goals in each emergent national society would proceed in a mutually reinforcing relationship with international norms.

The nationalist leaders of 1919 pursued an anticolonial agenda and sought to challenge an international order in which the groups they represented were subordinated, but, as their perceptions of Wilson suggest, their aims and sentiments were not anti-Western as such. Most of the leaders of the anticolonial campaigns of 1919—men like Sa'd Zaghlul, Lala Lajpat Rai, Wellington Koo, and Syngman Rhee, many of them with a Western education—were reformers who proclaimed their ambitions to remake their societies along the lines of liberal democratic models. The campaigns they led in 1919 did not set out to tear down the existing international order but rather to join it as members of equal status. When the quest to achieve self-determination through the peace conference failed, however, many anticolonial activists, disillusioned with the results of Wilson's liberal internationalism, began to seek alternative ideological models and sources of practical support in their struggles for self-determination. The "revolt against the West," to use Geoffrey Barraclough's term, that was launched after 1919 emerged not from the experiences of the war; rather, it came from the failure of the peace to break the power of imperialism and allow colonial peoples a voice as full-fledged members in international society.[12]

The history of the Paris Peace Conference is often read as a tragic failure to fashion a European settlement that would bring lasting peace. But the story of the Wilsonian moment in the colonial world illuminates another, no less important facet of that central turning point in twentieth-century international history. From the perspective of the periphery, rather than the center, of international society, the conference appears as a tragedy of a different sort, as the leading peacemakers, Wilson foremost among them, failed to offer the populations of the non-European world the place in international society that Wilson's wartime speeches had implied that they deserved. At the Wilsonian moment, Egyptians, Indians, Chinese, Koreans, and others glimpsed the promised land of self-determination, but enter into it they could not. That experience, inasmuch as it shaped the formative stages of major national movements in the colonial world, helped to displace the liberal, reformist anticolonialism that failed in 1919 in favor of the more radical, revisionist nationalism that became an important force in the subsequent history of the twentieth century.

Human agency, John Hall has noted, can matter greatly in international affairs because "international orders are often the result of conscious strategy."[13] At least as often, however, rhetoric in the international arena has unintended audiences, and actions beget unintended consequences. The Western powers in Paris ignored the demands and aspirations of non-Western peoples, but their struggles for sovereignty, equality, and dignity as independent actors in international society continued. The Wilsonian moment marked the beginning of the end of the imperial order in international affairs, precipitating the crisis of empire that followed the war and laying the foundations for the eventual triumph of an international order in which the model of the sovereign, self-determining nation-state spread over the entire globe. The Wilsonian moment saw the right to self-determination vault from the musings of obscure theorists into the center of the international discourse of legitimacy, and though colonial powers—including the United States itself—resisted its implications during the interwar years, it became an integral part of the political agendas of colonial elites. As Wilson faded from the international arena in defeat, anticolonial movements embraced the language of self-determination that he brought to prominence, refashioning their goals and identities in its image even as they recast its meanings in theirs. Their struggles for recognition as fully sovereign actors in international society would shape the history of the succeeding decades.

NOTE ON SOURCES AND ABBREVIATIONS

Sources in Chinese and Arabic are rendered in pinyin and IJMES transliterations, respectively. For Arabic sources, full diacritics are given in the bibliography only.

Abbreviations

ABP	*Amrita Bazar Patrika*
AICC	All-India Congress Committee
BDFA	*British Documents on Foreign Affairs* (series)
CPI	Committee on Public Information, U.S. government (1917–1919)
DOS	U.S. Department of State
FO	Foreign Office
FRUS	*Foreign Relations of the United States* (series)
INC	Indian National Congress
IOR	India Office Records, British Library, London
KNA	Korean National Association
KP	G. S. Khaparde Papers, National Archives of India, New Delhi
LOC	Library of Congress, Washington, D.C.
MAE	Archives du Ministère des Affaires Etrangères, Quai d'Orsay, Paris
MFA	Ministry of Foreign Affairs (China)
NAI	National Archives of India, New Delhi
NAUK	National Archives of the United Kingdom, Kew, England
NMML	Nehru Memorial Museum and Library, New Delhi
PCC	Provincial Congress Committee
PHS	Presbyterian Historical Society, Philadelphia, Pennsylvania
PID	Political Intelligence Department, British Foreign Office
PPC	Paris Peace Conference
PWW	*The Papers of Woodrow Wilson*, 69 vols.
RG	Record Group
SHAT	Service Historique de l'Armée de Terre, Vincennes, France
USNA	U.S. National Archives, College Park, Maryland
WJB	Waijiaobu (Chinese Foreign Ministry) Archives, Academia Sinica, Taipei
WWP	Woodrow Wilson Papers, Library of Congress, Washington, D.C. (microform)

NOTES

Preface

1. Erez Manela, "Good Will and Bad: Rethinking US-Egyptian Contacts in the Interwar Years," *Middle Eastern Studies* 38:1 (2002), 71–89.

2. Writing on the peace conference began immediately with accounts from some of the participants. Two of the most influential works, both written by junior members of the British delegation to the conference, were John Maynard Keynes, *The Economic Consequences of the Peace* (London: Macmillan, 1919); and Harold Nicolson, *Peacemaking 1919* (New York: Harcourt, Brace, 1939). Subsequent scholarship on the peace conference has been vast. A few examples are H. W. Temperley, ed., *A History of the Peace Conference of Paris*, 6 vols. (London: Frowde and Hodder & Stoughton, 1920–1924); Seth P. Tillman, *Anglo-American Relations at the Paris Peace Conference of 1919* (Princeton, N.J.: Princeton University Press, 1961); Arno J. Mayer, *Politics and Diplomacy of Peacemaking: Containment and Counterrevolution at Versailles, 1918–1919* (New York: Knopf, 1967).

A good summary of many of the key historiographical debates can be found in Manfred F. Boemeke, Gerald D. Feldman, and Elisabeth Glaser, eds., *The Treaty of Versailles: A Reassessment after 75 Years* (Cambridge: Cambridge University Press, 1998). A recent and richly detailed history of the peace conference is Margaret MacMillan, *Paris 1919: Six Months That Changed the World* (New York: Random House, 2002).

3. See, for example, David Fromkin, *A Peace to End All Peace: Creating the Modern Middle East, 1914–1922* (New York: Holt, 1989).

4. MacMillan, *Paris 1919*, is actually better than most on this count. Still, in nearly five hundred pages that tell the story of the peace negotiations, the efforts of Indian and Egyptian nationalists together are discussed in five pages (pp. 400–404), and those of Koreans are mentioned only in one parenthesized sentence (p. 311). MacMillan's book is framed around the perspectives of the leaders of the major powers—British, French, and American—so this is neither surprising nor detrimental to her achievement. It does, however, reflect the approach of much of the literature on 1919.

5. For U.S. wartime diplomacy and politics, see Thomas J. Knock, *To End All Wars* (Princeton, N.J.: Princeton University Press, 1995); and Lloyd Ambrosius, *Wilsonian Statecraft: Theory and Practice of Liberal Internationalism during World War I* (Wilmington, Del.: Scholarly Resources, 1991). Works on the U.S. role in Paris include still useful firsthand accounts, such as Edward Mandell House and Charles Seymour, eds., *What Really Happened at Paris: The Story of the Peace Conference, 1918–1919, by American Delegates* (New York: Scribner's, 1921); and Robert Lansing, *The Peace Negotiations: A Personal Narrative* (Boston: Houghton Mifflin, 1921). The most comprehensive recent study is Arthur Walworth, *Wilson and His Peacemakers: American Diplomacy at the Paris Peace Conference, 1919* (New York: Norton, 1986). On Wilson's treaty fight with the Senate, see John Milton Cooper, *Breaking the Heart of the World: Woodrow Wilson and the Fight for the League of Nations* (New York: Cambridge University Press, 2001); Lloyd Ambrosius, *Woodrow Wilson and the American Diplomatic Tradition: The Treaty*

Fight in Perspective (New York: Cambridge University Press, 1987); Herbert F. Margulies, *The Mild Reservationists and the League of Nations Controversy in the Senate* (Columbia: University of Missouri Press, 1989). For a survey of recent scholarship on Wilson, see David Steigerwald, "The Reclamation of Woodrow Wilson?" *Diplomatic History* 23:1 (1999), 79–99.

6. For British perspectives on Wilson, see Laurence W. Martin, *Peace without Victory: Woodrow Wilson and the British Liberals* (New Haven, Conn.: Yale University Press, 1958); G. R. Conyne, *Woodrow Wilson: British Perspectives, 1912–1921* (New York: Macmillan, 1992). His impact on Central Europe is covered in, e.g., Victor S. Mamatey, *The United States and East Central Europe, 1914–1918: A Study in Wilsonian Diplomacy and Propaganda* (Princeton, N.J.: Princeton University Press, 1957). Also see Betty Miller Unterberger, *The United States, Revolutionary Russia, and the Rise of Czechoslovakia* (Chapel Hill: University of North Carolina Press, 1989).

7. Frank Ninkovich, *The Wilsonian Century* (Chicago: University of Chicago Press, 1999); Tony Smith, *America's Mission: The United States and the Worldwide Struggle for Democracy in the Twentieth Century* (Princeton, N.J.: Princeton University Press, 1994), 7. The description of Wilson as "the hinge" of U.S. foreign policy comes from Henry Kissinger, *Diplomacy* (New York: Simon & Schuster, 1994), chap. 2 title.

8. Frank Ninkovich, "The United States and Imperialism," in *A Companion to American Foreign Relations*, ed. Robert Schulzinger (Malden, Mass.: Blackwell, 2003), 90.

9. Steigerwald, "Reclamation," 97–98.

10. See, for example, the essays in Thomas Bender, ed., *Rethinking American History in a Global Age* (Berkeley: University of California Press, 2001); Akira Iriye, "The Internationalization of History," *American Historical Review* 94:1 (1989), 1–10; Michael H. Hunt, "Internationalizing U.S. Diplomatic History: A Practical Agenda," *Diplomatic History* 15:1 (Winter 1991), 1–11; Brenda Gayle Plummer, "The Changing Face of Diplomatic History: A Literature Review," *The History Teacher* 38:3 (May 2005), 385–400.

11. The impact of the wider world on U.S. political, social, and intellectual history is explored, e.g., in Daniel T. Rodgers, *Atlantic Crossings: Social Politics in a Progressive Age* (Cambridge, Mass.: Belknap, 1998). For cultural aspects of this relationship see, e.g., Kristin Hoganson, "Stuff It: Domestic Consumption and the Americanization of the World Paradigm," *Diplomatic History* 30:4 (2006), 571–594. Recent studies that view the history of U.S. politics and foreign policy in a broader international context include Fredrik Logevall, *Choosing War: The Lost Chance for Peace and the Escalation of War in Vietnam* (Berkeley: University of California Press, 1999), and Mark Atwood Lawrence, *Assuming the Burden: Europe and the American Commitment to War in Vietnam* (Berkeley: University of California Press, 2005). There are also a number of works that have placed the history of U.S. race relations in an international framework, e.g., Thomas Borstelmann, *The Cold War and the Color Line: American Race Relations in the Global Arena* (Cambridge, Mass.: Harvard University Press, 2001), and Carol Anderson, *Eyes off the Prize: The United Nations and the African American Struggle for Human Rights, 1944–1955* (Cambridge: Cambridge University Press, 2003).

12. See Alan McPherson, *Yankee No!: Anti-Americanism in U.S.–Latin American Relations* (Cambridge, Mass.: Harvard University Press, 2003); Ussama Makdisi,

"'Anti-Americanism' in the Arab World: An Interpretation of a Brief History," *Journal of American History* 89:2 (2002), 538–557.

13. Among the few recent works that explore this theme are Mark Philip Bradley, *Imagining Vietnam & America: The Making of Postcolonial Vietnam, 1919–1950* (Chapel Hill: University of North Caroline Press, 2000).

14. This is seen most prominently in the works on Indian history of scholars connected to the Subaltern Studies collective, e.g., Partha Chatterjee, *The Nations and Its Fragments: Colonial and Postcolonial Histories* (Princeton, N.J.: Princeton University Press, 1993). Also see Prasenjit Duara, *Rescuing History from the Nation: Questioning Narratives of Modern China* (Chicago: University of Chicago Press, 1995). Duara and another historian of China, Rebecca Karl, have done pioneering work that relates the construction of nationalist identities and claims to international events and norms. See Prasenjit Duara, *Sovereignty and Authenticity: Manchukuo and the East Asian Modern* (Lanham, Md.: Rowman & Littlefield, 2003), and Rebecca E. Karl, *Staging the World: Chinese Nationalism at the Turn of the Twentieth Century* (Durham, N.C.: Duke University Press, 2002). An important call for integrating the insights and methods of subaltern studies and diplomatic history is Matthew Connelly, "Taking Off the Cold War Lens: Visions of North-South Conflict during the Algerian War for Independence," *The American Historical Review* 105:3 (2000), 739–769.

15. Prasenjit Duara, ed., *Decolonization: Perspective from Now and Then* (London: Routledge, 2004), 7.

16. On the functioning of the mandate system in the interwar period, see Michael D. Callahan, *Mandates and Empire: The League of Nations and Africa, 1914–1931* (Brighton, England: Sussex Academic Press, 1999); Michael D. Callahan, *A Sacred Trust: The League of Nations and Africa, 1929–1946* (Brighton, England: Sussex Academic Press, 2004); and Susan Pedersen, "The Meaning of the Mandate System: An Argument," *Geschichte und Gesellschaft* 32 (2006), 1–23. The usefulness of the international arena for the advancement of anticolonial nationalist claims in the postwar period is the central argument in Matthew Connelly, *A Diplomatic Revolution: Algeria's Fight for Independence and the Origin of the Post–Cold War Era* (New York: Oxford University Press, 2002).

17. Geoffrey Barraclough, *An Introduction to Contemporary History* (New York: Basic, 1964), 2, 16, 115.

INTRODUCTION

1. Ho's original petition, dated 18 June 1919, is in U.S. National Archives, College Park, Maryland [USNA], RG 256, 851G.00/1. On Ho's petition and its consequences, see Mark Philip Bradley, *Imagining Vietnam & America: The Making of Postcolonial Vietnam, 1919–1950* (Chapel Hill: University of North Carolina Press, 2000), 10–11; Hue-Tam Ho Tai, *Radicalism and the Origins of the Vietnamese Revolution* (Cambridge, Mass.: Harvard University Press, 1992), 68–69; Loren Baritz, *Backfire: A History of How American Culture Led Us into Vietnam and Made Us Fight the Way We Did* (New York: Morrow 1985), 36.

2. Hedley Bull and Adam Watson, eds., *The Expansion of International Society* (New York: Oxford University Press, 1984); also see Geoffrey Barraclough, *An Intro-*

duction to Contemporary History (New York: Basic, 1964), 151–155. For a sociological perspective on the prevalence of the nation-state model in world society, see John W. Meyer, John Boli, George M. Thomas, and Francisco O. Ramirez, "World Society and the Nation-State," *American Journal of Sociology* 103:1 (1997), 144–181.

3. Arno Mayer, *Wilson vs. Lenin: Political Origins of the New Diplomacy, 1917–1918* (Cleveland, Ohio: World, 1964). The assignment of a central role to the Bolshevik Revolution in explaining the transformative impact of 1919 is a common move. For example, Eric Hobsbawm's *The Age of Extremes: A History of the World, 1914–1991* (New York: Pantheon, 1994) conceptualizes the global transformation that was launched in 1919 in terms of the rise of the Bolshevik "world revolution."

4. This aspect of self-determination in Paris has been extensively studied, though again largely from the standpoint of the great powers. One partial exception is Mamatey, *The United States and East Central Europe*. In the settlements in the Middle East and Africa, the idea of self-determination was incorporated, though in much diluted form, in the mandate system. For an interpretation of the post-Ottoman settlement and its consequences, see Fromkin, *Peace to End All Peace*. For the mandates in Africa, see Michael D. Callahan, *Mandates and Empire: The League of Nations and Africa, 1914–1931* (Brighton, England: Sussex Academic Press, 1999).

5. On Irish expectations for Wilson's support, see Ronan Brindley, "Woodrow Wilson, Self-Determination and Ireland, 1918–1919: A View from the Irish Newspapers," *Éire-Ireland* 23:4 (1988), 62–80. On African-American expectations and activities, see Jonathan Rosenberg, "For Democracy, Not Hypocrisy: World War and Race Relations in the United States, 1914–1919," *International History Review* 21:3 (Sept. 1999), 592–625; and Rosenberg, *How Far the Promised Land: World Affairs and the American Civil Rights Movement from the First World War to Vietnam* (Princeton, N.J.: Princeton University Press, 2005), chap. 2.

6. For a detailed treatment of the faith that progressives in the United States and Great Britain had in Wilsonian ideals, see Knock, *To End All Wars*; for details on the Wilsonian hopes of the Left in Germany, see Klaus Schwabe, *Woodrow Wilson, Revolutionary Germany, and Peacemaking, 1918–1919: Missionary Diplomacy and the Realities of Power* (Chapel Hill: University of North Carolina Press, 1985). A useful account of the rise and fall of liberal expectations in the United States during the war is Stuart I. Rochester, *American Liberal Disillusionment in the Wake of World War I* (University Park: Pennsylvania State University Press, 1977).

7. These are the regions and populations that, with Latin America, would later become the "Third World" and, still later, the "developing world." Like these other phrases, the term "the colonial world" is problematic. It does, however, retain analytical usefulness since the regions and peoples included in it shared elements of historical experience. For a similar use of the term, see, for example, Partha Chatterjee, *Nationalist Thought and the Colonial World: A Derivative Discourse?* (Minneapolis: University of Minnesota Press, 1986), 10.

8. For the process of formation of national identities in colonial societies, see Benedict Anderson, *Imagined Communities: Reflections on the Origin and Spread of Nationalism*, rev. ed. (London: Verso, 1991); Chatterjee, *Nationalist Thought and the Colonial World*; Elie Kedourie, *Nationalism*, 4th ed. (Oxford: Blackwell, 1993).

9. For extended treatments of these events, see Janice J. Terry, *The Wafd, 1919–1952* (London: Third World Centre for Research and Publishing, 1982).

10. Judith M. Brown, *Gandhi's Rise to Power: Indian Politics, 1915–1922* (Cambridge: Cambridge University Press, 1972).

11. On the importance of the May Fourth movement in modern Chinese history, see, e.g., Rana Mitter, *A Bitter Revolution: China's Struggle with the Modern World* (New York: Oxford University Press, 2004). On the impact of the March First movement, see Chong-sik Lee, *The Politics of Korean Nationalism* (Berkeley: University of California Press, 1963).

12. William R. Keylor, "Versailles and International Diplomacy," in Manfred F. Boemeke et al., eds., *The Treaty of Versailles*, 476–478.

13. On this see, for example, Ronald Robinson, "Non-European Foundations of European Imperialism: Sketch for a Theory of Collaboration," in *Studies in the Theory of Imperialism*, ed. Roger Owen and Bob Sutcliffe (London: Longman, 1972), 117–142.

14. Henri Grimal, *Decolonization: The British, French, Dutch and Belgian Empires, 1919–1963* (Boulder, Colo.: Westview, 1978), 17–18. Also see John Gallagher, "Nationalisms and the Crisis of Empire, 1919–1922," *Modern Asian Studies* 15:3 (1981), 355–368.

15. James Mayall, *Nationalism and International Society* (Cambridge: Cambridge University Press, 1990), 44–45.

16. Michael Adas, "Contested Hegemony: The Great War and the Afro-Asian Assault on the Civilizing Mission Ideology," *Journal of World History* 15:1 (2004): 31–63.

17. Judith M. Brown, "War and the Colonial Relationship: Britain, India, and the War of 1914–18," in DeWitt C. Ellinwood and S. D. Pradhan, eds., *India and World War I* (New Delhi: South Asia Books, 1978); Xu Guoqi, *China and the Great War: China's Pursuit of a New National Identity and Internationalization* (Cambridge: Cambridge University Press, 2005), chap. 4.

18. This theme is developed further in Erez Manela, "Imagining Woodrow Wilson in Asia: Dreams of East-West Harmony and the Revolt against Empire in 1919," *American Historical Review* 111:5 (2006), 1327–1351.

19. Both international and transnational approaches to history are increasingly popular and important, but there is yet no consensus as to the precise definition of each term and the distinctions between them. The usages suggested here, while common and commonsensical, are not canonical. For the efforts to define these terms and the perspectives and practices they entail, see "*AHR* Conversation: On Transnational History," *American Historical Review* 111:5 (2006), 1441–1464; Akira Iriye, "Transnational History," *Contemporary European History* 13:2 (2004), 211–222.

PART I

1. Press Conference, 3 Aug. 1914, in Arthur Link et al., eds., *The Papers of Woodrow Wilson* [*PWW*], 69 vols. (Princeton, N.J.: Princeton University Press, 1966–1994), 30:332; Public Statement, 18 Aug. 1914, *PWW*, 30:394.

2. Arthur Walworth, *Woodrow Wilson*, 3d ed. (New York: Norton, 1978), 2:208.

CHAPTER 1

1. Charles T. Thompson, *The Peace Conference Day by Day: A Presidential Pilgrimage Leading to the Discovery of Europe* (New York: Brentano's, 1920), 1–15; "Two Million Cheer Wilson," *New York Times*, 15 Dec. 1918, 1; Thomas J. Knock, *To End All Wars: Woodrow Wilson and the Quest for a New World Order* (Princeton, N.J.: Princeton University Press, 1995), 194.

2. Thompson, *The Peace Conference Day by Day*, 55–56, 67–68. The ecstatic receptions Wilson received upon his arrival in Europe have been extensively documented; see, e.g., Arthur Walworth, *Woodrow Wilson*, 3d ed. (New York: Norton, 1978), 2:221–234.

3. Cited in Stephen Bonsal, *Suitors and Suppliants: The Little Nations at Versailles* (New York: Prentice-Hall, 1946), 262.

4. On the Congress of Vienna, see Paul W. Schroeder, *The Transformation of European Politics, 1763–1848* (New York: Oxford University Press, 1994), chap. 12. On U.S. diplomacy in the Second World War, see Warren F. Kimball, *The Juggler: Franklin Roosevelt as Wartime Statesman* (Princeton, N.J.: Princeton University Press, 1991).

5. John Milton Cooper, Jr., *The Warrior and the Priest: Woodrow Wilson and Theodore Roosevelt* (Cambridge, Mass.: Harvard University Press, 1983), chaps. 17–19.

6. James R. Mock and Cedric Larson, *Words That Won the War: The Story of the Committee on Public Information, 1917–1919* (Princeton, N.J.: Princeton University Press, 1939), 235–236.

7. The American pursuit of a revised Wilsonian program in the wake of World War II was much more circumspect, and could not replicate the sense of wide open possibility of 1918–1919. But see Elizabeth Borgwardt, *A New Deal for the World: America's Vision for Human Rights* (Cambridge, Mass.: Harvard University Press, 2005), 61–86, 141–193.

8. There is an extensive scholarly debate, which is beyond the scope of the present study, on how Wilson came to shape his postwar plans generally, with scholarly opinion dividing broadly among three different views of Wilson's motivation: idealism, realism, and opportunism. Knock, *To End All Wars*, is one of the most recent and comprehensive statements of the idealist position. For Wilson as a strategic realist see, e.g., Frank Ninkovich, *Modernity and Power: A History of the Domino Theory in the Twentieth Century* (Chicago: University of Chicago Press, 1994), 44–68; and Ross A. Kennedy, "Woodrow Wilson, World War I, and an American Conception of National Security," *Diplomatic History* 25:1 (Winter 2001), 1–31. For an interpretation that emphasizes the tactical and opportunistic nature of Wilson's postwar plans, see John A. Thompson, "More Tactics Than Strategy: Woodrow Wilson and World War I, 1914–1919," in *Artists of Power: Theodore Roosevelt, Woodrow Wilson, and Their Enduring Impact on U.S. Foreign Policy*, ed. William N. Tilchin and Charles E. Neu (Westport, Conn.: Praeger Security International, 2006), 95–115.

9. The discussion that follows traces the evolution of Wilson's public rhetoric in the course of the war as it might have appeared from the perspectives of his audiences, both intended and unintended. It does not detail the broader political or philosophical genealogies of Wilson's ideas, nor offer a sustained critique of his

motives for adopting them or of their coherence and practicality, though these issues are occasionally broached. For discussion of Wilson's ideas on international order, and on self-determination in particular, see Michla Pomerance, "The United States and Self-Determination: Perspectives on the Wilsonian Conception," *American Journal of International Law* 70:1 (Jan. 1976), 1–27; Allen Lynch, "Woodrow Wilson and the Principle of 'National Self-Determination': A Reconsideration," *Review of International Studies* 28 (2002), 419–436.

10. On U.S. neutrality policy prior to April 1917, see John Milton Cooper, Jr., *The Vanity of Power: American Isolationism and the First World War, 1914–1917* (Westport, Conn.: Greenwood, 1969); Ernest R. May, *The World War and American Isolation, 1914–1917* (Cambridge, Mass.: Harvard University Press, 1959); Charles Seymour, *American Neutrality, 1914–1917: Essays on the Causes of American Intervention in the World War* (New Haven, Conn.: Yale University Press, 1935). An insightful analysis of the domestic sources of Wilson's policy toward the war is John A. Thompson, "Woodrow Wilson and World War I: A Reappraisal," *Journal of American Studies* 19 (1985), 325–348.

11. An Address in Washington to the League to Enforce Peace, 27 May 1916, *PWW*, 37:113–117. The liberal *New Republic* immediately dubbed this speech as a great utterance that "engineered a decisive turning point in the history of the modern world." See Knock, *To End All Wars*, 77–78.

12. A Draft of the National Democratic Platform of 1916, c. 10 June 1916, *PWW*, 37:195.

13. An Address to the Senate, 22 Jan. 1917, *PWW*, 40:533–537.

14. Ibid., 40:536.

15. On the relationship between the domestic reform movement and the aspirations of wartime liberal internationalism to reform international society, see Alan Dawley, *Changing the World: American Progressives in War and Revolution* (Princeton, N.J.: Princeton University Press, 2003).

16. An Address to the Senate, 22 Jan. 1917, *PWW*, 40:537–539.

17. Ibid., 40:536–539. See also Lloyd E. Ambrosius, *Wilsonianism: Woodrow Wilson and His Legacy in American Foreign Relations* (New York: Palgrave Macmillan, 2002), 129.

18. Knock, *To End All Wars*, 114; Arthur S. Link, *The Higher Realism of Woodrow Wilson and Other Essays* (Nashville, Tenn.: Vanderbilt University Press, 1971), 106.

19. Knock, *To End All Wars*, 115.

20. Robert Lansing, *The Peace Negotiations: A Personal Narrative* (Boston: Houghton Mifflin, 1921), 97, 101–102. Also see Lawrence E. Gelfand, *The Inquiry: American Preparations for Peace, 1917–1919* (New Haven, Conn.: Yale University Press, 1963), 229–230.

21. Robert D. Schulzinger, *Time for War: The United States and Vietnam, 1941–1975* (New York: Oxford University Press, 1997), 9.

22. N. Gordon Levin, *Woodrow Wilson and World Politics: America's Response to War and Revolution* (New York: Oxford University Press, 1968), 237, 247–248. A similar conclusion is reached in Pomerance, "The United States and Self-Determination," 25. Both Levin and Pomerance, however, devote no more than a paragraph to the question of Wilson's view on the applicability of self-determination to colonial peoples.

23. Arthur Walworth, *Wilson and His Peacemakers: American Diplomacy at the Paris Peace Conference, 1919* (New York: Norton, 1986), 72–81; Gelfand, *The Inquiry*, 231–327. For a broader history of the mandate system as it operated in Africa, see Michael D. Callahan, *Mandates and Empire: The League of Nations and Africa, 1914–1931* (Brighton, England: Sussex Academic Press, 1999).

24. This is evident in the protocols of the Paris negotiations and in Wilson's papers from the period. See *PWW*, vols. 53–57; Paul Mantoux, *The Deliberations of the Council of Four (March 24–June 28, 1919): Notes of the Official Interpreter*, 2 vols., trans. and ed. Arthur S. Link with Manfred F. Boemeke (Princeton, N.J.: Princeton University Press, 1992); Walworth, *Wilson and His Peacemakers*, parts 2–4.

25. *PWW*, 15:462 n. 2, 15:32. The first black student to receive an undergraduate degree from Princeton graduated in 1947.

26. For example, see A News Report of a Campaign Speech in Phillipsburg, New Jersey, 22 Oct. 1910, *PWW* 21:390–391.

27. Link, *Higher Realism*, 261.

28. Studies on the segregation policy of the Wilson administration agree that, while there is no evidence that Wilson initiated the moves toward segregation in the federal bureaucracy, he was clearly aware of these policies and did nothing to discourage them. See Earl W. Crosby, "Progressive Segregation in the Wilson Administration," *Potomac Review* 6:2 (1973), 41–57; Henry Blumenthal, "Woodrow Wilson and the Race Question," *Journal of Negro History* 48:1 (1963), 1–21; Kathleen L. Wolgemuth, "Woodrow Wilson and Federal Segregation," *Journal of Negro History* 44:2 (1959), 158–173. McAdoo married Wilson's youngest daughter, Eleanor, at the White House in May 1914.

29. Dixon to Wilson, 27 July 1913, *PWW*, 28:88–89; Wilson to Dixon, 29 July 1913, *PWW*, 28:94.

30. On the relationship between religious faith and universalism in Wilson's thought, see Lloyd E. Ambrosius, *Wilsonian Statecraft: Theory and Practice of Liberal Internationalism during World War I* (Wilmington, Del.: Scholarly Resources, 1991), 10–13.

31. Remarks by Wilson and a Dialogue, 12 Nov. 1914, *PWW*, 31:303. For the full transcript of the meeting, with annotations, see Christine A. Lunardini, "Standing Firm: William Monroe Trotter's Meetings with Woodrow Wilson, 1913–1914," *Journal of Negro History* 64:3 (1979), 244–264. Also see Cooper, *The Warrior and the Priest*, 273–274.

32. Kendrick A. Clements, *Woodrow Wilson: World Statesman* (1987; rpt., Chicago: Dee, 1999), 97–101; Cooper, *The Warrior and the Priest*, 210–211. One of the episodes most often cited as indicating Wilson's virulent racism is the February 1915 White House showing of D. W. Griffith's film *The Birth of a Nation*, which was based on Thomas Dixon's white supremacist novel and play *The Clansman*. Some Wilson biographers, however, have cast doubt on this interpretation of the event. Arthur Link has pointed out that Dixon, who had engineered the showing, admitted that he did not tell Wilson beforehand what the movie was about; and that an eyewitness account suggested that Wilson did not show much interest in the movie. See *PWW*, 32:142 n. 1, 32:267 n. 1. On the film itself, see John Hope Franklin, "'Birth of a Nation': Propaganda as History," *Massachusetts Review* 20:3 (1979), 417–434.

33. A News Report of a Lecture on Constitutional Government, 2 Nov. 1898, *PWW*, 11:66; A News Report of an Alumni Affair, 14 Jan. 1899, *PWW*, 11:94; A Report of a Speech on Patriotism in Waterbury, Connecticut, 14 Dec. 1899, *PWW*, 11:298–299. See also Lynch, "Woodrow Wilson and the Principle of 'National Self-Determination,'" 423; Niels Aage Thorsen, *The Political Thought of Woodrow Wilson, 1875–1910* (Princeton, N.J.: Princeton University Press, 1988), 164–166, 174–180.

34. A Report of a Speech on Patriotism in Waterbury, Connecticut, 14 Dec. 1899, *PWW*, 11:298–299.

35. A Newspaper Report of a Public Address and an Alumni Meeting in Harrisburg, Pennsylvania, 24 Feb. 1900, *PWW*, 11:440.

36. An Address to the Lotos Club of New York, 3 Feb. 1906, *PWW*, 16:297–298.

37. Filipinos, he said on one occasion, "can have liberty no cheaper than we got it. They must first take the discipline of law, must first love order and instinctively yield to it. . . . We are old in this learning and must be their tutors." An address entitled "The Ideals of America" given in Trenton, N.J., 26 Dec. 1901, *PWW*, 12:217–218, 222. For more on Wilson's view of the relationship between progress and order and on the gradual and "organic" nature of political progress, see Ambrosius, *Wilsonian Statecraft*, 8–9.

38. In an article entitled "Democracy and Efficiency," published in the *Atlantic Monthly*, Mar. 1901, *PWW*, 12:17–18.

39. A Newspaper Report of an Address on Americanism in Wilmington, Delaware, 7 Dec. 1900, *PWW*, 12:44; A Newspaper Report of a Lecture in Waterbury, Connecticut, 13 Dec. 1900, *PWW*, 12:47–48.

40. Wilson to Allen Wickham Corwin, 10 Sept. 1900, *PWW*, 11:573.

41. On this, see Matthew Frye Jacobson, *Barbarian Virtues: The United States Encounters Foreign Peoples at Home and Abroad, 1876–1917* (New York: Hill and Wang, 2000), 164, 180–181, 222–223, 234–246. For the role of racist views among American anti-imperialists at the time, see Robert L. Beisner, *Twelve against Empire: The Anti-Imperialists, 1898–1900* (New York: McGraw-Hill, 1968).

42. Clements, *Woodrow Wilson*, 139. Harrison was recommended to Wilson by his secretary of state, William Jennings Bryan, a long-time pacifist and anti-imperialist.

43. An Annual Message to Congress, 2 Dec. 1913, *PWW*, 29:8–9.

44. On this point, see also Ambrosius, *Woodrow Wilson and the American Diplomatic Tradition*, 10–11. Ambrosius recognizes the ambivalence inherent in Wilson's views on Filipino self-government at the turn of the century, but does not remark on the evolution apparent in his later views.

45. An Annual Message to Congress, 2 Dec. 1913, *PWW*, 29:8–9. In his last Annual Message to Congress, in December 1920, Wilson again reminded Congress that "the Philippine Islands have succeeded in maintaining a stable government since the last action of the Congress on their behalf," and thus "it is now our liberty and our duty to keep our promise to the people of those Islands by granting them the independence which they so honorably covet." An Annual Message on the State of the Union, 7 Dec. 1920, *PWW*, 66:490.

46. Walworth, *Woodrow Wilson*, book 2, chap. 21; Paul V. N. Henderson, "Woodrow Wilson, Victoriano Huerta, and the Recognition Issue in Mexico," *Americas: A Quarterly Review of Inter-American Cultural History* 41:2 (1984), 151–176;

Clifford W. Trow, "Woodrow Wilson and the Mexican Interventionist Movement of 1919," *Journal of American History* 58:1 (1971), 46–72. Also see on this period John Milton Cooper, " 'An Irony of Fate': Woodrow Wilson's Pre–World War I Diplomacy," *Diplomatic History* 3:4 (1979), 425–437.

47. An Address on Preparedness in Topeka, Kansas, 2 Feb. 1916, *PWW*, 36:94–95.

48. A Statement to the American People, 26 July 1918, *PWW*, 49:97–98. See also "President Demands that Lynchings End," *New York Times*, 27 July 1918, 7; "Mr. Wilson on the Mob Spirit," *New York Times*, 27 July 1918, 8. The latter piece echoed the president's perspective on the relationship between domestic atrocities and foreign affairs, concluding: "We are fighting arbitrary, cruel, law-scorning, and violent Powers. Let our hands be clean from any tincture of their iniquity."

49. An Address to the Senate, 30 Sept. 1918, *PWW*, 51:158–161. Wilson repeated the call for ratification of the amendment in his annual address to Congress on 2 Dec. 1918, *PWW*, 53:277. For Wilson's attitudes toward the female suffrage movement, see Sally Hunter Graham, "Woodrow Wilson, Alice Paul, and the Woman Suffrage Movement," *Political Science Quarterly* 98 (1983–1984), 665–679; Christine A. Lunardini and Thomas J. Knock, "Woodrow Wilson and Woman Suffrage: A New Look," *Political Science Quarterly* 95 (1980–1981), 655–671.

50. Jonathan Rosenberg, "For Democracy, Not Hypocrisy: World War and Race Relations in the United States, 1914–1919," *International History Review* 21:3 (Sept. 1999), 592–593.

CHAPTER 2

1. The Second Inaugural Address, *PWW*, 41:332–335.

2. For a broad perspective on this transformation, see Daniel Philpott, *Revolutions in Sovereignty: How Ideas Shaped Modern International Relations* (Princeton, N.J.: Princeton University Press, 2001).

3. The U.S. position evolved, for example, from a desire to preserve the Austro-Hungarian state in some form with autonomy for its constituent peoples to support for its complete dissolution. For explanation of the circumstances that led to that shift, see Lansing to the Swedish minister, 18 Oct. 1918, in Albert Shaw, ed., *The Messages and Papers of Woodrow Wilson*, 2 vols. (New York: Review of Reviews Corporation, 1924), 1:540–541; Michla Pomerance, "The United States and Self-Determination: Perspectives on the Wilsonian Conception," *American Journal of International Law* 70 (1976), 18–19.

4. An Address to a Joint Session of Congress, 2 Apr. 1917, *PWW*, 41:523–527.

5. Ibid., 41:524.

6. Message delivered to the provisional government on 26 May 1917 and made public on 9 June. *PWW*, 42:365–367.

7. Laurence W. Martin, *Peace without Victory: Woodrow Wilson and the British Liberals* (New Haven, Conn.: Yale University Press, 1958), 57–58. On the UDC war aims proposals, see also Thomas J. Knock, *To End All Wars: Woodrow Wilson and the Quest for a New World Order* (Princeton, N.J.: Princeton University Press, 1995), 36–38. For the UDC and its wartime impact in Britain more generally, see Sally Harris, *Out of*

Control: British Foreign Policy and the Union of Democratic Control, 1914–1918 (Hull, England: University of Hull Press, 1996).

8. George W. Egerton, *Great Britain and the Creation of the League of Nations* (Chapel Hill: University of North Carolina Press, 1978), 49–54.

9. Arno J. Mayer, *Wilson vs. Lenin: Political Origins of the New Diplomacy, 1917–1918* (Cleveland, Ohio: World, 1964), 74–76.

10. V. I. Lenin, *Imperialism, the Highest Stage of Capitalism* (Moscow: Foreign Languages Publishing House, 1920), first published in early 1917; Lenin, "The Socialist Revolution and the Right of Nations to Self-Determination," in his *Collected Works*, 45 vols. (Moscow: Progress, 1960–1970), 22:143–156 (first published in Oct. 1916).

11. For a detailed analysis of the early socialist and Bolshevik debates on the national question, see Jeremy Smith, *The Bolsheviks and the National Question, 1917–1923* (London: Macmillan, 1999), 8–20.

12. Mayer, *Wilson vs. Lenin*, 248, 298–303.

13. Address from the Bolsheviks "To Peoples and Governments of Allied Countries," 31 Dec. 1917, included in David Rowland Francis to Robert Lansing, *PWW*, 45:412–413. For more on the Bolshevik impact on the postwar settlement, see John M. Thompson, *Russia, Bolshevism, and the Versailles Peace* (Princeton, N.J.: Princeton University Press, 1966).

14. Wilson to House, 21 July 1917, *PWW*, 43:238. Also see Lloyd George, *Memoirs of the Peace Conference*, 2 vols. (New Haven, Conn.: Yale University Press, 1939), 2:497; Egerton, *Great Britain*, 44–45; Martin, *Peace without Victory*, 40–41. For analyses of the British views of Wilson and his wartime power over them, see A. P. Thornton, *The Imperial Idea and Its Enemies*, 2d ed. (London: Macmillan, 1985), 150–151; G. R. Conyne, *Woodrow Wilson: British Perspectives, 1912–1921* (London: Macmillan, 1992), 104–120. For the French attitude to Wilson, see David Stevenson, "French War Aims and the American Challenge, 1914–1918," *Historical Journal* 22:4 (1979), 883–884; Derek Benjamin Heater, *National Self-Determination: Woodrow Wilson and His Legacy* (New York: St. Martin's, 1994), 29–30; Knock, *To End All Wars*, 114–115, 145.

15. Seth P. Tillman, *Anglo-American Relations at the Paris Peace Conference of 1919* (Princeton, N.J.: Princeton University Press, 1961), 26; Paul Kennedy, *The Realities behind Diplomacy: Background Influences on British External Policy, 1865–1980* (London: Allen & Unwin, 1981), 161–165.

16. Knock, *To End All Wars*, 142–143. One of the best expressions of the postwar vision of the British Left is presented in Charles A. McCurdy, *A Clean Peace: The War Aims of British Labour: Complete Text of the Official War Aims Memorandum of the Inter-Allied Labour and Socialist Conference, Held in London, February 23, 1918* (New York: Doran, 1918).

17. Egerton, *Great Britain*, 57–59. On the Wilson-Smuts relationship, see George Curry, "Woodrow Wilson, Jan Smuts and the Versailles Settlement," *American Historical Review* 66 (1961), 968–986.

18. For more on the events leading to the 5 January speech, see Mayer, *Wilson vs. Lenin*, 313–328; David R. Woodward, "The Origins and Intent of David Lloyd George's January 5 War Aims Speech," *Historian* 34 (Nov. 1971), 22–39; and Sterling J. Kernek, *Distractions of Peace during War: The Lloyd George Government's Reactions to*

Woodrow Wilson, December 1916–November 1918 (Philadelphia: American Philosophical Society, 1975), 72–73.

19. Knock, *To End All Wars*, 143. This address has been published as David Lloyd George, *British War Aims: Statement by the Prime Minister, the Right Honourable David Lloyd George, on January 5, 1918* (London: Hazell, Watson & Viney, 1918).

20. David Lloyd George, *Memoirs of the Peace Conference*, 2 vols. (New Haven, Conn.: Yale University Press, 1939), 2:495–496; Egerton, *Great Britain*, 59–61.

21. Address to a Joint Session of Congress, 8 Jan. 1918, *PWW*, 45:534–539.

22. The memorandum, entitled "The Present Situation: The War Aims and Peace Terms It Suggests," is reproduced in *PWW*, 45:459–475. Its authors were Sidney Mezes, president of the College of the City of New York and head of the Inquiry; David Hunter Miller, an expert on international law; and the young progressive journalist Walter Lippmann.

23. *PWW*, 45:552. On House's relationship with Wilson and his role during the war and the peace conference, see Alexander L. George and Juliette L. George, *Woodrow Wilson and Colonel House: A Personality Study* (New York: Dover, 1964); Inga Floto, *Colonel House in Paris: A Study of American Policy at the Paris Peace Conference, 1919* (Princeton, N.J.: Princeton University Press, 1973); and Joyce G. Williams, *Colonel House and Sir Edward Grey: A Study in Anglo-American Diplomacy* (Lanham, Md.: University Press of America, 1984).

24. See Mayer, *Wilson vs. Lenin*, esp. 329–367. The text of the Bolshevik peace initiative of December 1917 can be found in *PWW*, 45:411–414. For more on Wilson's policy toward revolutionary Russia, see Thompson, *Russia, Bolshevism, and the Versailles Peace*; Betty Miller Unterberger, *The United States, Revolutionary Russia, and the Rise of Czechoslovakia* (Chapel Hill: University of North Carolina Press, 1989); David S. Foglesong, *America's Secret War against Bolshevism: U.S. Intervention in the Russian Civil War, 1917–1920* (Chapel Hill: University of North Carolina Press, 1995); Georg Schild, *Between Ideology and Realpolitik: Woodrow Wilson and the Russian Revolution, 1917–1921* (Westport, Conn.: Greenwood, 1995).

25. See Knock, *To End All Wars*, 144–145; and Betty Miller Unterberger, "The United States and National Self-Determination: A Wilsonian Perspective," *Presidential Studies Quarterly* 26 (1996), 929–931. Knock has argued that it was Lenin's proclamations in the spring of 1917 that echoed Wilson's "Peace without Victory" address in January of that year. Knock, *To End All Wars*, 138.

26. Address to Congress, 11 Feb. 1918, *PWW*, 46:321.

27. Robert Lansing, *The Peace Negotiations: A Personal Narrative* (Boston: Houghton Mifflin, 1921), 96, 104.

28. This distinction between Wilson's understanding of the meaning of self-determination and the ethno-national interpretation of the term is developed in detail in Trygve Throntveit, "The Fable of the Fourteen Points," paper delivered at the Princeton Institute for International and Regional Studies, Princeton University, 8 Apr. 2006, cited with permission. Also see Lloyd E. Ambrosius, "Dilemmas of National Self-Determination: Woodrow Wilson's Legacy," in his *Wilsonianism: Woodrow Wilson and His Legacy in American Foreign Relations* (New York: Palgrave Macmillan, 2002), 125–143; William R. Keylor, "Versailles and International Diplomacy," in Manfred

F. Boemeke, Gerald D. Feldman, and Elisabeth Glaser, eds., *The Treaty of Versailles: A Reassessment after 75 Years* (Cambridge: Cambridge University Press, 1998), 475 and n. 12 there. For Wilson's keen awareness of the multiethnic character of U.S. society, see, e.g., his interview with Frank Worthington, the British Deputy Chief Censor, on 28 Dec. 1918, in which he said that the term Anglo-Saxon could "no longer be rightly applied to the people of the United States." *PWW*, 53:573–576.

29. See N. Gordon Levin, *Woodrow Wilson and World Politics: America's Response to War and Revolution* (New York: Oxford University Press, 1968), 247–251.

30. Address at Mount Vernon, 4 July 1918, *PWW*, 48:515–516.

31. Ibid., 48:516–517.

32. Address Opening the New York Campaign for the Fourth Liberty Loan, 27 Sept. 1918, *PWW*, 51:127–133.

33. Address at the Sorbonne, 21 Dec. 1918; remarks at Buckingham Palace, 27 Dec. 1918; address at the London Guildhall, 28 Dec. 1918; address at Free Trade Hall in Manchester, 30 Dec. 1918; address to the Italian Parliament, 3 Jan. 1919; remarks in Genoa, 5 Jan. 1919; remarks at Milan train station, 5 Jan. 1919; remarks at Turin, 6 Jan. 1919. All in *PWW*, 53:461–463, 522–524, 531–533, 549–552, 597–599, 614–616, 622–624.

34. John Maynard Keynes, *The Economic Consequences of the Peace* (London: Macmillan, 1919), 34–35. Keynes's book was one of the earliest and most influential critiques of Wilson's performance at Paris. For more on him, see Robert Skidelsky, *John Maynard Keynes: A Biography* (London: Macmillan, 1983).

35. Daniel R. Headrick, *The Invisible Weapon: Telecommunications and International Politics, 1851–1945* (New York: Oxford University Press, 1991), 20–24, 40, 56–62, 130–133. On the impact of the telegraph on diplomacy, see David Paull Nickles, *Under the Wire: How the Telegraph Changed Diplomacy* (Cambridge, Mass.: Harvard University Press, 2003).

36. Donald Read, *The Power of News: The History of Reuters*, 2d ed. (New York: Oxford University Press, 1999), 36.

37. Ibid., 49, 72.

38. Ibid., 57–59.

39. The term "propaganda" is used here as a neutral term, as it was at the time, without the negative overtones that it subsequently acquired.

40. Peter Buitenhuis, "Selling the Great War," *Canadian Review of American Studies* 7:2 (Fall 1976), 139. George Creel, who headed the Committee on Public Information during the war, titled his book describing its activities *How We Advertised America* (New York: Harper, 1920).

41. H. G. Wells, *The War That Will End War* (London: Palmer, 1914), 91.

42. Wilson to Bryan, 10 May 1915, *PWW*, 33:139. Also see James D. Startt, "American Propaganda in Britain during World War I," *Prologue* 28:1 (Spring 1996), 20–21.

43. James R. Mock and Cedric Larson, *Words That Won the War: The Story of the Committee on Public Information, 1917–1919* (Princeton, N.J.: Princeton University Press, 1939), 59. On Creel's work for Wilson and the latter's handling of domestic public opinion, see Robert C. Hilderbrand, *Power and the People: Executive Management of Public Opinion in Foreign Affairs, 1897–1921* (Chapel Hill: University of North Carolina Press, 1981), chaps. 5–7. For an interesting study of the attitudes and work of progressive

U.S. journalists, including Creel, during the war, see John A. Thompson, *Reformers and War: American Progressive Publicists and the First World War* (Cambridge: Cambridge University Press, 1987).

44. George Creel, *Complete Report of the Chairman of the Committee on Public Information* (Washington, D.C.: U.S. Government Printing Office, 1920), 1.

45. Mock and Larson, *Words That Won the War*, 48–66. Given its importance in the U.S. war effort, the CPI, and especially its operations abroad, has been surprisingly little studied. Stephen Vaughn, *Holding Fast the Inner Lines: Democracy, Nationalism, and the Committee on Public Information* (Chapel Hill: University of North Carolina Press, 1980), deals exclusively with the CPI's domestic operations. A useful but very brief discussion of the CPI foreign efforts within the general context of wartime American society is found in David M. Kennedy, *Over Here: The First World War and American Society* (New York: Oxford University Press, 1980), 352–354. For a somewhat more detailed discussion of the CPI's foreign operations, one has to go back to Mock and Larson, *Words That Won the War*, and to George Creel's own writings, including the *Complete Report of the Chairman of the Committee on Public Information* (1920) and *How We Advertised America* (1920). Also useful for the CPI's foreign operations in a few selected locations is Gregg Wolper, "The Origins of Public Diplomacy: Woodrow Wilson, George Creel, and the Committee on Public Information" (Ph.D. diss., University of Chicago, 1991).

46. Creel, *Complete Report*, 2.

47. Ibid., 4. Domestic critics often accused the CPI of press censorship, and soon after the war the organization was quickly disbanded amid a storm of congressional criticism.

48. Ibid., 3–4.

49. Mock and Larson, *Words That Won the War*, 235, 237–238.

50. Ibid., 247.

51. Poole recounted his role at the CPI in his autobiography, Ernest Poole, *The Bridge: My Own Story* (New York: Macmillan, 1940).

52. Mock and Larson, *Words That Won the War*, 241–242; Creel, *Complete Report*, 6. The dissemination of Wilsonian propaganda in Asia will be discussed in more detail in the following chapters.

53. Walworth, *Wilson and His Peacemakers*, 23–24 and nn. 3 and 4 there.

54. Creel, *Complete Report*, 5. On the rapid spread and impact of wireless communication technology during World War I, see Daniel R. Headrick, *The Tentacles of Progress: Technology Transfer in the Age of Imperialism, 1850–1940* (New York: Oxford University Press, 1988), 97–144.

55. Mock and Larson, *Words That Won the War*, 240–241.

56. Creel, *Complete Report*, 112.

57. Ibid., 5, 113–114, 124–125.

58. Ibid., 5–6.

59. Hans Schmidt, "Democracy for China: American Propaganda and the May Fourth Movement," *Diplomatic History* 22:1 (1998), 23 n. 43.

60. Mock and Larson, *Words That Won the War*, 235–236.

61. See, e.g., the Calcutta daily *Amrita Bazar Patrika* [*ABP*], 6 July 1918, 3, where a laudatory report of Wilson's July Fourth address sat next to headlines announcing "Further Bolshevik Submission to Germany" and reporting on the march of White forces on Moscow. *ABP*, 16 Jan. 1919, in the "Reuters Telegrams" section, reported on "Bolshevik Destruction" in Poland and losses in Estonia; a separate item associated the spread of Bolshevism in Germany with riots and criminality. The Madras daily *New India*, 15 Jan. 1919, also reported on the "Bolshevist Peril" in numerous items on p. 9. Also see "Eguo geming xiaoxi" [News of the Russian Revolution], in the Shanghai daily *Shibao*, 8 Jan. 1918, 2; and 15 Jan. 1918, 2; and items on the Russian Bolsheviks in *Shibao*, 17 Dec. 1918, 1; 30 Dec. 1918, 1; and 7 Jan. 1919, 2. *Shenbao*, also a Shanghai daily, reported on 13 Jan. 1919 on the "miserable conditions" of Chinese laborers in Russia who were being conscripted into the Red Army. Also see *Peking Leader*, 12 July 1918, 3, "Full Story of How China Is Menaced by the Bolsheviki: Horrors in Russian Turkistan." On Lenin as a mysterious figure, see Sudhindra Bose, "The Russian Situation," in the Calcutta magazine *Modern Review* 25 (1919), 131; also "Lenin," in the Poona (Pune) weekly *Mahratta*, 2 Feb. 1918.

62. Michael Weiner, "Comintern in East Asia, 1919–39," in *The Comintern: A History of International Communism from Lenin to Stalin*, ed. Kevin McDermott and Jeremy Agnew (London: Macmillan, 1996), 158–163. Weiner notes that at the First Comintern Congress in March 1919 "very little time or discussion was devoted to the 'colonial' question" and that Asian representation there was insignificant. By the Second Comintern Congress in the summer of 1920, though, the failure of the European revolutions, on the one hand, and the eruption of mass anticolonial protests in Asia, on the other, gave Asian communists a more substantial role.

PART II

1. "Wilson Visits Grandfather's Church; Cheered in Carlisle and Manchester," *New York Times*, 30 Dec. 1918, 1; Thompson, *The Peace Conference*, 54–74.

2. Cooper, *The Warrior and the Priest*, 338–342; Knock, *To End All Wars*, 205–206.

3. Walworth, *Wilson and His Peacemakers*, 23–39; Clarence G. Contee, "Dubois, the NAACP, and the Pan-African Congress of 1919," *Journal of Negro History* 57:1 (1972), 13–28.

4. Petitions found in the files of the Chinese delegation to the conference, WJB, RG 03–37, box 27, vol. 2.

5. MacMillan, *Paris 1919*, 410–426. Also see Wilson to Wise, 31 Aug. 1918, NAUK, FO 371/4354/351.

6. Irish and Catalan petitions are in SHAT, fonds Clemenceau, 6 N 74 and 75.

7. *Claims of Persia before the Conference of the Preliminaries of the Peace at Paris*, USNA, RG 256, 891.00/16; *Memorandum on Persia's Wishes and Her Aspirations*, Apr. 1919, RG 256, 891.00/27.

8. Numerous Armenian memoranda and petitions are found in USNA, RG 256, 867B.00/14–118. See also Assyrian Claims, RG 256, 867S.00/37; Arslan to Wilson, 29 Jan.

1919, RG 256, 890B.00/12; Polk to Paris, 7 Jan. 1919, RG 256, 867S.01/1; Harry Hansen, *The Adventures of the Fourteen Points* (New York: Century, 1919), 115–116.

9. Imam of Yemen to Wilson, 22 Dec. 1918, USNA, RG 256, 890B.00/7; memorandum from the Tunisian nation to President Wilson and the peace conference, WJB, RG 03–37, box 28, vol. 1; Cuongde to delegates attending the peace conference, 1 Feb. 1919, MAE, A-Paix, vol. 322.

10. David Hunter Miller, *The Drafting of the Covenant* (New York: Putnam's, 1928), 2:99.

11. Ibid., 2:94, 1:53.

12. From the Diary of Edith Benham, 2 Feb. 1919, *PWW*, 54:432–433.

13. Miller, *The Drafting of the Covenant*, 2:727. See also Erez Manela, "A Man Ahead of His Time? Wilsonian Globalism and the Doctrine of Preemption," *International Journal* 60:4 (2005), 1115–1124.

14. An Address to the Third Plenary Session of the Peace Conference, 14 Feb. 1919, *PWW*, 55:164–178. On the drafting process, see Knock, *To End All Wars*, 210–226.

15. Recent research, however, has begun to show that the league's mandate commission was not quite as useless as we often imagine. See Susan Pedersen, "Settler Colonialism at the Bar of the League of Nations," in Caroline Elkins and Susan Pedersen, eds., *Settler Colonialism in the Twentieth Century: Projects, Practices, Legacies* (New York: Routledge, 2005), 113–134.

CHAPTER 3

1. Muhammad Husayn Haykal, *Mudhakkirat fi al-Siyasa al-Misriyya* [Memoirs of Egyptian Politics] (Cairo: Dar al-Ma'arif, 1977), 1:67. On Haykal and his role in Egyptian intellectual and cultural life in this era, see Charles D. Smith, *Islam and the Search for Social Order in Modern Egypt: A Biography of Muhammad Husayn Haykal* (Albany: State University of New York Press, 1983). The friend, according to Haykal, was 'Abd al-Rahman al-Rafi'i, later one of Egypt's leading intellectuals and historians.

2. "Al-duktur Wilsun yatlubu min al-majlis i'lan al-harb 'ala Almania" [Dr. Wilson Asks Congress to Declare War on Germany], *Al-Ahram*, 4 Apr. 1917; "Amrika wa-Almania fi harb" [The U.S. and Germany at War], and "Khitab al-ra'is Wilsun" [President Wilson's Address], *Al-Ahram*, 5 Apr. 1917; "Majlis al-Shuyukh al-Amriki yuqarriru i'lan al-harb" [The U.S. Senate Declares War], *Al-Ahram*, 6 Apr. 1917; "Bad' al-harb bayna Amrika wa-Almania" [The War between the United States and Germany Begins], *Al-Ahram*, 8 Apr. 1917; "Amrika tujannidu thalathat malayin muqatil" [The United States Drafting Three Million Soldiers], *Al-Ahram*, 9 Apr. 1917.

3. "Majhud Amrika" [The U.S. Effort], *Al-Ahram*, 6 Jan. 1918; "Khutba lil-duktur Wilsun" [A Speech by Dr. Wilson], *Al-Ahram*, 10 Jan. 1918; "Khutbat al-ra'is Wilson" [President Wilson's Speech], *Al-Ahram*, 11 Jan. 1918.

4. On the CPI's propaganda effort in Britain, which influenced the information that reached Egypt through British conduits, see Startt, "American Propaganda in Britain," 17–33; Buitenhuis, "Selling the Great War," 139–150.

5. P. J. Vatikiotis, *The History of Modern Egypt*, 4th ed. (Baltimore, Md.: Johns Hopkins University Press, 1991), 179–188; Ami Ayalon, *The Press in the Arab Middle East: A History* (New York: Oxford University Press, 1995), 51–62.

6. *Al-Ahram*, 8 Apr. 1917 and 6 Jan. 1918, as cited in notes 2 and 3 above.

7. "4 yuniu 1776, 'id istiqlal Amrika" [Fourth of July 1776, America's Independence Day], *Al-Ahram*, 5 July 1918; "Al-'id al-watani al-Amriki: Khitab al-ra'is Wilsun" [America's National Holiday: President Wilson's Address], *Al-Ahram*, 6 July 1918.

8. 'Abd al-Rahman Rafi'i, *Thawrat Sanat 1919: Tarikh Misr al-Qawmi min Sanat 1914 ila Sanat 1921* [The 1919 Revolution: The National History of Egypt, 1914–1921] (Cairo: Maktabat al-Nahda al-Misriyya, 1955), 57; 'Abd al-Khaliq Lashin, *Sa'd Zaghlul wa-Dawruhu fi al-Siyasa al-Misriyya* [Sa'd Zaghlul and His Role in the Politics of Egypt] (Cairo: Maktabat Madbuli, 1975), 126–127.

9. "Résumé of the political situation in Egypt," Gary to secretary of state, 15 Feb. 1919, USNA, RG 256, 883.00/28, pp. 1–3. Also see Janice J. Terry, *The Wafd, 1919–1952* (London: Third World Centre for Research and Publishing, 1982), 71–73; M. W. Daly, *The Sirdar: Sir Reginald Wingate and the British Empire in the Middle East* (Philadelphia: American Philosophical Society, 1997), 276–282.

10. Tusun's and others' accounts on the initial formation of the Wafd are elaborated in *Khamsin 'Ama 'ala Thawrat 1919* [The 1919 Revolution after Fifty Years] (Cairo: Mu'assasa al-Ahram, Markaz al-Watha'iq wal-Buhuth al-Ta'rikhiyya li-Misr al-Mu'asira, 1970), 121–131. Also see Elie Kedourie, "Sa'd Zaghlul and the British," in his *The Chatham House Version and Other Middle-Eastern Studies* (New York: Praeger, 1970), 90, 93–94; Janice J. Terry, "Official British Reaction to Egyptian Nationalism after World War I," *Al-Abhath* 21:2–4 (1968), 15–18. On Wingate's term in Egypt see Donald C. Coventry, "The Public Career of Sir Francis Reginald Wingate, High Commissioner for Egypt: 1917–1919." Ph.D. diss., American University, 1989.

11. Gary to Lansing, 11 Nov. 1918, USNA, RG 256, 883.00/2. On Egyptian expectations for Wilson's support, see also Gary's report to DOS, 29 Jan. 1919, RG 256, 883.00/12.

12. On the impact of the American Civil War on the Egyptian economy, see Sven Beckert, "Emancipation and Empire: Reconstructing the Worldwide Web of Cotton Production in the Age of the American Civil War," *American Historical Review* 109:5 (Dec. 2004), 1405–1438.

13. Donald Malcolm Reid, "The 'Urabi Revolution and the British Conquest," in *The Cambridge History of Egypt*, ed. M. W. Daly (Cambridge: Cambridge University Press, 1998), 2:217–238; Arthur Goldschmidt, Jr., *Modern Egypt: The Formation of a Nation-State* (Boulder, Colo.: Westview, 1988), 33–37. For an exposition of the sociocultural aspects of the uprising, see Juan R. I. Cole, *Colonialism and Revolution in the Middle East: Social and Cultural Origins of Egypt's 'Urabi Movement* (Princeton, N.J.: Princeton University Press, 1993).

14. On the responses of Kamil and other non-European thinkers to the rise of Japan see Cemil Aydin, "A Global Anti-Western Moment? The Russo-Japanese War, Decolonization, and Asian Modernity," in Sebastian Conrad and Dominic Sachsenmaier, eds., *Conceptions of World Order: Global Historical Approaches* (New York: Palgrave Macmillan, 2007), 213–236. For more on this period in general see M. W. Daly, "The British Occupation, 1882–1922," in Daly, *The Cambridge History*, 239–245. See also P. J. Vatikiotis,

The History of Modern Egypt, 4th ed. (Baltimore, Md.: Johns Hopkins University Press, 1991), 169–245; Albert Hourani, *Arabic Thought in the Liberal Age, 1798–1939* (Cambridge: Cambridge University Press, 1962), chap. 8; Israel Gershoni and James Jankowski, *Egypt, Islam and the Arabs: The Search for Egyptian Nationhood, 1900–1930* (New York: Oxford University Press, 1986), 3–54; and Dennis Walker, "Pan-Islamism as a Modern Ideology in the Egyptian Independence Movement of Mustafa Kamil," *Hamdard Islamicus* 17:1 (1994), 57–109.

15. Vatikiotis, *Modern Egypt*, 253–257; Daly, "The British Occupation," 245–247. See also Keith Jeffery, *The British Army and the Crisis of Empire, 1918–22* (Manchester, England: Manchester University Press, 1984), 110–113; and, for a class-analysis perspective on this period, Marius Deeb, *Party Politics in Egypt: The Wafd and Its Rivals, 1919–1939* (London: Ithaca, 1979), 22–38.

16. After 1867 the Egyptian monarch was known by the title "khedive," an Ottoman term roughly translated as "viceroy." In 1914, when the British formally severed Egypt from the Ottoman empire, they made its ruler a sultan to suggest that he was no longer under the sultan in Istanbul. In 1922, when Great Britain granted Egypt nominal independence, the monarch's title changed again to king.

17. Wingate to Balfour, 17 Nov. 1918, *British Documents on Foreign Affairs: Reports and Papers from the Foreign Office Confidential Print* [*BDFA*], series G, part II: *Africa, 1914–1939*, 1:86. Also see Kedourie, "Sa'd Zaghlul"; Hourani, *Arabic Thought in the Liberal Age*, 209–221.

18. Wingate to Balfour, 17 Nov. 1918, *BDFA*, series G, part II, 1:86.

19. Kedourie, "Sa'd Zaghlul," 96–97. Also see John Darwin, *Britain, Egypt and the Middle East: Imperial Policy in the Aftermath of War, 1918–1922* (London: Macmillan, 1981), 66–79.

20. Symes to Zaghlul, 1 Dec. 1918; Zaghlul to Wingate, 3 Dec. 1918; and Zaghlul to Lloyd George, 4 Dec. and 12 Jan. 1918, in USNA, RG 256, 883.00/147, pp. 28–31. On the Arab delegation in Paris, see MacMillan, *Paris 1919*, 387–395; Fromkin, *Peace to End All Peace*, 394–397.

21. Terry, "Official British Reaction," 19–20; Terry, *Wafd*, 84–100. Also see Gershoni and Jankowski, *Egypt, Islam and the Arabs*, 44; Kedourie, "Sa'd Zaghlul," 97–98.

22. "Dr. Wilson in Europe," *Al-Ahram*, 15 Dec. 1918, large headline on front page.

23. Reported in *Al-Ahram*, 16, 17, 23, 24, and 30 Dec. 1918.

24. A petition from Leon S. Farhj, an official at the Egyptian Ministry of Agriculture, 11 Dec. 1918, and a petition from members of the "Egyptian National Delegation," 12 Dec. 1918, enclosed in Gary to secretary of state, 30 Dec. 1918, USNA, RG 256, 883.00/4; and FW 883.00/30.

25. See, for example, the list of signatories in a petition from residents of the Nile delta town of Mansura, enclosed in Gary to secretary of state, 30 Dec. 1918, USNA, RG 256, 883.00/4.

26. Gary to DOS, 19 Dec. 1918, USNA, RG 256, 883.00/3.

27. Gary to DOS, 30 Jan. 1919, USNA, RG 256, 883.00/13.

28. A petition from Zaghlul to Gary and other foreign representatives in Egypt, 6 Dec. 1918, in Gary to secretary of state, 16 Dec. 1918, USNA, RG 256, 883.00/5. The

petition included two documents, in both French and English: "Appeal to Representatives of Nations Accredited to Egypt" and "A Brief Summary of the Views of the Egyptian People regarding Their Destiny." The call for Egyptian independence under "the guidance of the League of Nations" was repeated in a petition from the Egyptian Association in Paris, in USNA, RG 256, 883.00/49.

29. Zaghlul to Wilson, 14 Dec. 1918, in Egyptian Delegation to the Peace Conference, *Collection of Official Correspondence from November 11, 1918 to July 14, 1919* (Paris: Published by the Delegation, 1919), 47.

30. Zaghlul to Wilson, 27 Dec. 1918, in Egyptian Delegation, *Official Correspondence*, 50. See also Zaghlul to Wilson, 3 Jan. 1919, in ibid., 51; and Zaghlul's declaration of Egyptian independence, enclosed in Gary to secretary of state, 16 Dec. 1918, USNA, RG 256, 883.00/5.

31. Zaghlul to Wilson, 13 Jan. 1919, in Egyptian Delegation, *Official Correspondence*, 52; Sa'd Zaghlul, *Mudhakkirat Sa'd Zaghlul* [The Diaries of Sa'd Zaghlul], ed. 'Abd al-'Azim Ramadan, 9 vols. (Cairo: Al-Hay'a al-Misriyya al-'Amma lil-Kitab, 1987–1998), 9:22.

32. "Résumé of the political situation in Egypt," Gary to secretary of state, 15 Feb. 1919, USNA, RG 256, 883.00/28, pp. 3–4; Egyptian National Mission to the Delegates to the Peace Conference, 28 Jan. 1919, NAUK, FO 608/212, fol. 205–208.

33. Zaghlul to Gary, 4 Mar. 1919, RG 256, FW 883.00/36.

34. Terry, "Official British Reaction," 21–22. Rushdi's letter of resignation of 23 Dec. 1919 is found in USNA, RG 256, 883.00/147, pp. 31–32.

35. Daly, *Sirdar*, 289–299.

36. Gary to DOS, 29 Jan. 1919, USNA, RG 256, 883.00/12.

37. Enclosed in Gary to secretary of state, 4 Feb. 1919, USNA, RG 256, 883.00/19; and in Gary to secretary of state, 17 Feb. 1919, RG 256, 883.00/29.

38. Enclosed in Gary to secretary of state, 3 Feb. 1919, USNA, RG 256, 883.00/16. The fifteen additional signatories were listed as follows: Ali Sha'rawi, member of the Legislative Assembly; 'Abd al-Aziz Fahmi, member of the Legislative Assembly and head of the Lawyer's Association; Muhammad 'Ali 'Alluba, member of the Legislative Assembly; 'Abd al-Latif Makabbati, member of the Legislative Assembly; Muhammad Mahmud, former prefect; Ahmad Lutfi al-Sayyid, former director of the National Library; Isma'il Sidqi, former government minister; Sinut Hanna, member of the Legislative Assembly and leading Copt; Hamad al-Basil, member of the Legislative Assembly; Mahmud Abu al-Nasr, former head of the Lawyer's Association; George Khayyat, leading Copt; Dr. Hafiz Afifi, a Cairo physician; Husayn Wasif, member of the Legislative Assembly; Michel Lutfallah, member of the Legislative Assembly; 'Abd al-Khalik Madhkur, head of Cairo merchants.

39. Zaghlul to Gary, 4 Mar. 1919, RG 256, 883.00/36.

40. Isma'il Labib to Muhammad Farid, 24 Dec. 1918, in Muhammad Farid, *Awraq Muhammad Farid* [The Papers of Muhammad Farid], vol. 2, part 1: *Correspondence*, ed. Mustafa al-Nahhas Jabr (Cairo: Al-Hay'a al-Misriyya al-'Amma lil-Kitab, 1986); Isma'il Sidqi, *Mudhakkirati* [My Memoirs], ed. Sami Abu al-Nur (Cairo: Madbuli, 1991), 43–44.

41. Enclosed in Kent to Wilson, 10 Dec. 1918, LOC, WWP, series 5b, reel 385.

42. Farid to Wilson, 5 Feb. 1919, RG 256, 883.00/20; see also National party declaration in RG 256, 883.00/79. The efforts of the National party to petition Wilson are recounted in Muhammad Farid's memoir, *Awraq Muhammad Farid*, vol. 1: *Mudhakkirati Ba'd al-Hijra, 1904–1919* [The Papers of Muhammad Farid, vol. 1: My Memoirs in Exile, 1904–1919] (Cairo: Al-Hay'a al-Misriyya al-'Amma lil-Kitab, 1978), 421, 425–427.

43. See, for example, the Egyptian Association of Paris to the President of the Delegation of the United States of America, 8 Feb. 1919, USNA, RG 256, 883.00/22. As the other chapters indicate, Egyptian nationalists were hardly alone in this.

44. Petition from the Egyptian Committee in Geneva, 31 Jan. 1919, enclosed in USNA, RG 256, 883.00/14. The petition was signed by Muhammad Fahmi, president of the Young Egyptian Committee in Europe; 'Ali Shamsi, deputy of the Egyptian Legislative Assembly; Isma'il Labib, committee member of the Egyptian National party; and Yihya Dardiri, vice president of the Sphinx Society. The pamphlet included the following sections: "Egypt and the Wilsonian Principle"; "Egyptian Autonomy Previous to the English Occupation"; "English Rule in Egypt"; "Is Egypt Capable of Governing Herself?"; "The 'Prosperity' of Egypt"; and "Do Egyptians Admit the English Domination?" On these efforts, see also Farid, *Mudhakkirati Ba'd al-Hijra*, 425–426.

45. Balfour to Curzon, 20 Feb. 1919, NAUK, FO 608/212, fol. 245; Hankey to Dutasta, 28 Feb. 1919, FO 608/213, fol. 9.

46. Grew to Close, 8 Feb. 1919, USNA, RG 256, 883.00/17.

47. Lansing, *Peace Negotiations*, 196. Lansing's position was also supported by the Inquiry experts. See Gelfand, *The Inquiry*, 238, 255.

48. Dulles to Beer, 7 Feb. 1919, and Beer to Dulles, 8 Feb. 1919, USNA, RG 256, 883.00/21; Close to Grew, 4 Feb. 1919, USNA, RG 256, 883.00/17.

49. Gary to Zaghlul, 6 Dec. 1918, USNA, RG 256, 883.00/5.

50. Gary to secretary of state, 16 Dec. 1918, USNA, RG 256, 883.00/5 and FW 883.00/24; Gary to DOS, 19 Dec. 1918, RG 256, 883.00/3; Gary to secretary of state, 30 Dec. 1918, RG 256, 883.00/4. Following instructions from the DOS, Gary forwarded all the Egyptian petitions he received both to Washington and to Paris, but also continued to advise that the United States recognize the protectorate; see Gary to secretary of state, 3 Feb. 1919, RG 256, 883.00/16; Gary to secretary of state, 15 Feb. 1919, RG 256, 883.00/28, pp. 3–4, 6–7.

51. Petition from the Egyptian Committee in Geneva, 31 Jan. 1919, USNA, RG 256, 883.00/14.

CHAPTER 4

1. From Sastri's foreword to a collection entitled *Woodrow Wilson's Message for Eastern Nations, Selected by Himself from His Public Addresses* (Calcutta: Association Press, 1925), iv–v.

2. An Address to a Joint Session of Congress, 2 Apr. 1917, *PWW*, 41:526.

3. "America Asks for War," *ABP*, Calcutta, 5 Apr. 1917.

4. On Besant's multifaceted career see Anne Taylor, *Annie Besant: A Biography* (Oxford: Oxford University Press, 1992), and Jyoti Chandra, *Annie Besant: From Theosophy to Nationalism* (Delhi: K.K. Publications, 2001).

5. Subramanya Aiyar to Woodrow Wilson, 24 June 1917, in the National Archives of India, New Delhi [NAI], Home Department/Political Branch, Deposit File, Feb. 1918, file no. 36, entitled: "Action taken in regard to a letter sent by Sir Subramanya Aiyar to the President of the United States of America invoking his aid in obtaining Home Rule for India," pp. 3–6.

6. Lansing to Tumulty, 4 Oct. 1917, USNA, RG 59, 845.00/212.

7. As reported in "Message to President Wilson," *Young India* 1:1 (Jan. 1918), 5. As noted later in this chapter, *Young India* was a monthly published in the United States by the exiled Indian nationalist Lala Lajpat Rai.

8. See also reports on the Aiyar controversy in *New Times*, 19 June 1918; *Mahratta*, 30 June 1918, in "Bombay Press Abstract 1918," India Office Records, British Library, London [IOR], L/R/5/174, p. 10; and *New India*, 13 June 1918, in "Madras Press Abstract 1918," IOR, L/R/5/125, p. 892. Also see Sudhindra Bose of the State University of Iowa, Iowa City, to the editor of *India*, the organ of the Indian National Congress in Great Britain, 22 Oct. 1917, enclosed in USNA, RG 59, 845.00/217; and the exchanges and reports on the matter between British officials in India and London in Department of Criminal Investigations Notes, 7 Jan. 1918, NAI, Home/Political, Deposit File, Feb. 1918, no. 36, p. 13; Hiquell to Davidson, Chief Secretary to Government of Madras, 22 Jan. 1918, ibid., p. 18; India Office to Sir J. H. Du Boulay, Secretary to the Government of India, Home Dept., 1 Nov. 1917, NAI, Home/Political, Deposit File, Feb. 1918, no. 36, pp. 1–6.

9. Extract from the *Indian Social Reformer* of Bombay, 31 Mar. 1918, in NAI, Home/Political, Deposit File, Apr. 1918, no. 25, describes the "stormy interview" between Aiyar and the viceroy. For Montagu's visit to India, see his *An Indian Diary* (London: Heinemann, 1930); and Shane Ryland, "Edwin Montagu in India, 1917–1918: Politics of the Montagu-Chelmsford Report," *South Asia* 3 (1973), 79–92.

10. Montagu to Chelmsford, 16 May 1918, and Chelmsford to Montagu, 13 June 1918, NMML, Chelmsford Papers (microfilm), roll 2 (Correspondence with the Secretary of State for India, 1918); Montagu to Chelmsford, 15 June 1918, NAI, Montagu Papers, microfilm no. 1930, roll 1.

11. Sumit Sarkar, *Modern India, 1885–1947*, 2d ed. (London: Macmillan, 1989), 88–89; Bipan Chandra et al., *India's Struggle for Independence, 1857–1947* (New Delhi: Viking, 1988), 61–70.

12. Presidential Address of Dadabhai Naoroji, Twenty-second Session of the Indian National Congress, Calcutta, Dec. 1906, in *Congress Presidential Addresses*, ed. A. M. Zaidi (New Delhi: Indian Institute of Applied Political Research, 1986), 2:294–297.

13. *Speeches and Writings of Gopal Krishna Gokhale*, ed. D. G. Karve and D. V. Ambekar (Bombay: Asia Publishing House, 1966), 2:201. Gokhale (1866–1915) was a major figure in the early Indian national movement until his death in 1915. Mahatma Gandhi, despite his far more radical brand of politics, often referred to Gokhale as his "political guru." See M. K. Gandhi, *Gokhale: My Political Guru* (Ahmedabad: Navajivan, 1955).

14. On Tilak, who will figure prominently in chap. 8 below, see Richard I. Cashman, *The Myth of the Lokamanya: Tilak and Mass Politics in Maharashtra* (Berkeley: University of California Press, 1975).

15. On the Swadeshi movement, see Leonard A. Gordon, *Bengal: The Nationalist Movement, 1876–1940* (New York: Columbia University Press, 1974), 77–100; and Sumit Sarkar, *The Swadeshi Movement in Bengal, 1903–1908* (New Delhi: People's, 1973).

16. Jawaharlal Nehru, *Jawaharlal Nehru: An Autobiography* (London: Lane, 1936), 27.

17. Chandra et al., *India's Struggle*, 146–158. On Indian revolutionary activities in the United States, see the detailed study by L. P. Mathur, *Indian Revolutionary Movement in the United States of America* (New Delhi: Chand, 1970).

18. Percival Spear, *The Oxford History of Modern India, 1740–1975*, 2d ed. (Oxford: Oxford University Press, 1978), 334.

19. S. R. Bakshi, *Home Rule Movement* (New Delhi: Capital, 1984), 9, citing the Report of the Indian National Congress, Madras, 1914.

20. Spear, *Oxford History*, 335.

21. Poona District Congress Committee Papers, file no. 5, "Resolutions of the Bombay Provincial Congresses, 1916–1920," p. 99, held at the Manuscript Division of the Nehru Memorial Museum and Library, New Delhi [NMML].

22. Sarkar, *Modern India*, 147–149; see also A. C. Bose, "Indian Revolutionaries during the First World War: A Study of Their Aims and Weaknesses," in *India and World War I*, ed. DeWitt C. Ellinwood and S. D. Pradhan (New Delhi: South Asia Books, 1978), 109–125.

23. For a detailed analysis of the impact of the war on the Indian economy, see Krishnan G. Saini, "The Economic Aspects of India's Participation in the First World War," in Ellinwood and Pradhan, *India and World War I*, 141–176.

24. Speech by Surendranath Banerjee at the 1916 Congress, quoted in M. R. Jayakar, *The Story of My Life* (Bombay: Asia Publishing House, 1958), 1:156.

25. Speech by Madan Mohan Malaviya in the Imperial Legislative Council, 23 Mar. 1917, cited in Judith M. Brown, *Modern India: The Origins of an Asian Democracy*, 2d ed. (Oxford: Oxford University Press, 1994), 198.

26. "Rules of the All-India Home Rule League," NMML, Jawaharlal Nehru Papers, part II, Subject Files, file no. 116, "Proceedings of All-India Home Rule League Conference, 31 Dec. 1918," p. 49; Bakshi, *Home Rule Movement*, 32. For more on the home rule movement, see Chandra et al., *India's Struggle*, 159–169.

27. *Selected Documents on the Constitutional History of the British Empire and Commonwealth*, vol. 6: *The Dominions and India since 1900*, ed. Frederick Madden and John Darwin (Westport, Conn.: Greenwood, 1993), 678–679. Also see Judith M. Brown, "War and the Colonial Relationship: Britain, India, and the War of 1914–18," in Ellinwood and Pradhan, *India and World War I*, 19–43.

28. Brown, *Modern India*, 139. See also S. Natarajan, *A History of the Press in India* (Bombay: Asia Publishing House, 1962), 147–225; Nadig Krishna Murthy, *Indian Journalism: Origin, Growth and Development of Indian Journalism, from Asoka to Nehru* (Mysore, India: University of Mysore, 1966), chap. 8.

29. For a full-scale study of the control and censorship of the press in British India, see N. Gerald Barrier, *Banned: Controversial Literature and Political Control in British India, 1907–1947* (Columbia: University of Missouri Press, 1974).

30. Natarajan, *Press in India*, 183.

31. "India and the World War," *Young India* 1:2 (Feb. 1918), 2.

32. Sudhindra Bose to the editor of *India*, 22 Oct. 1917, enclosed in memorandum from British ambassador Cecil Arthur Spring Rice to the Department of State, 2 Jan. 1918, USNA, RG 59, 845.00/217.

33. Diwakar Prasad Singh, *American Attitude towards the Indian Nationalist Movement* (New Delhi: Munshiram Manoharlal, 1974), 208–209.

34. Secretary of state to consul general in Calcutta, 18 Apr. 1918, USNA, RG 59, 845.00/219a.

35. Ram Chandra to Wilson, n.d., but received at State Department on 23 June 1917, USNA, RG 59, 845.00/210. Chandra continued to appeal publicly to Wilson to liberate India and other British possessions. See, e.g., "More War Urged by Hindu Editor," *Los Angeles Times*, 27 Feb. 1918, 11.

36. See "Two Killed in Hindus' Feud," *Los Angeles Times*, 24 Apr. 1918, 14; "Hindu Spies Sent to Jail," *Los Angeles Times*, 1 May 1918, 12. On the trial more generally, see Don Dignan, "The Hindu Conspiracy in Anglo-American Relations during World War I," *Pacific Historical Review* 40:1 (1971), 57–76.

37. Lala Lajpat Rai, *Autobiographical Writings*, ed. Vijaya Chandra Joshi (Delhi and Jullundur: University Publishers, 1965), 11–34, 197–220.

38. Lala Lajpat Rai, "On Education," Apr. 1919, in Lajpat Rai, *Selected Documents of Lala Lajpat Rai, 1906–1928*, ed. Ravindra Kumar (New Delhi: Anmol, 1992), 2:104–127.

39. Lajpat Rai, "Farewell to America," in Lala Lajpat Rai, *Writings and Speeches*, 2 vols., ed. Vijaya Chandra Joshi (Delhi and Jullundur: University Publishers, 1966), 1:390–391. The emphasis on "national efficiency" was a common theme in progressive and nationalist political thought and practice at the time. See Geoffrey Searle, *The Quest for National Efficiency: A Study in British Politics and Political Thought, 1899–1914* (Oxford: Blackwell, 1971).

40. Lajpat Rai, *The United States of America: A Hindu's Impressions and a Study* (Calcutta: Chatterjee, 1916). The *New York Times* review was published on 21 Jan. 1917, BR2. On the close trans-Atlantic connections among the progressive intellectuals and activists that Lajpat Rai met both in Britain and the United States, see Daniel T. Rodgers, *Atlantic Crossings: Social Politics in a Progressive Age* (Cambridge, Mass.: Belknap, 1998).

41. Lajpat Rai, *The United States of America*, iii–vi, 63.

42. Ibid., 107–126.

43. Ibid., 298.

44. Ibid., 300–323. Around the same time, Lajpat Rai published in New York City another book, *Young India: An Interpretation and a History of the Nationalist Movement from Within* (New York: Huebsch, 1916), which was indeed banned from India by the British censors. The censorship, however, was at best only partially successful, and while it may have limited the circulation of this and other banned books in India, it largely failed in limiting the circulation of the ideas of their authors. See Lajpat Rai, *Selected Documents*, 2:46–67, 2:99–104.

45. Lajpat Rai, *Autobiographical Writings*, 199, 218–220.

46. Lajpat Rai, *Young India*, 222–223. For more, see Lajpat Rai, "Recollections of His Life and Work for an Independent India while Living in the United States and Japan, 1914–1917," NAI, Lajpat Rai Collection; Alan Raucher, "American Anti-Imperialists and the Pro-India Movement, 1900–1932," *Pacific Historical Review* 43:1 (1974), 94–100; Naeem Gul Rathore, "Indian Nationalist Agitation in the United States: A Study of Lala Lajpat Rai and the India Home Rule League of America, 1914–1920" (Ph.D. diss., Columbia University, 1965).

47. *Hindi Brahman Samachar* (Jagadhri), 18 Mar. 1918, in "Punjab Press Abstract 1918," IOR, L/R/5/200, p. 181.

48. See Lajpat Rai's correspondence with Lippmann in *Perspectives on Indian National Movement: Selected Correspondence of Lala Lajpat Rai*, ed. Joginder Singh Dhanki (New Delhi: National Book Organisation, 1998), 79, 80, 83, 93.

49. J. S. Dhanki, *Lala Lajpat Rai and Indian Nationalism* (Jalandhar, India: ABS, 1990), 176–178.

50. See "An Indian View of the Great European War," *New York Times*, 21 Feb. 1915, SM9; and 18 June 1916. Also see "What India Wants," *New York Times*, 31 May 1916, 12; How India Wears Her British Head," *New York Times*, 13 June 1916, 10; "Who Holds the Reins in India," *New York Times*, 2 July 1916, E2.

51. Lajpat Rai to Huebsch, 3 Jan. 1918, in *Selected Correspondence of Lala Lajpat Rai*, 107; Dhanki, *Lajpat Rai*, 187–188.

52. Lajpat Rai, "Farewell to America," in *Writings and Speeches*, 1:393; *Nation*, 14 Mar. 1918, 286, and 1 Feb. 1919, 163.

53. *Young India* 1:2 (Feb. 1918), 11.

54. "Editorials," *Young India* 1:3 (Mar. 1918), 1–3.

55. "India and the World War," *Young India* 1:2 (Feb. 1918), 2–3.

56. M. N. Roy, *Selected Works of M. N. Roy*, 4 vols., ed. Sibnarayan Ray (New Delhi: Oxford University Press, 1987), 1:11–19. After the war, Roy would become one of the founders of Indian communism and a leading figure in the Third Communist International, and still later, in the 1940s, he would abandon communism to advocate a philosophy of "radical humanism," a mixture of socialist and liberal ideas.

57. Open letter to Wilson, written in late 1917, in Roy, *Selected Works*, 1:67–83.

58. Vasant D. Rao, "Tilak's Attitude towards the Montagu-Chelmsford Reforms," *Journal of Indian History* 56 (1978), 172–173; *Observer* (Lahore), 11 May 1918, IOR, L/R/5/200, p. 277.

59. Pamphlet by M. M. Malaviya on the Montagu-Chelmsford report, dated Allahabad, 1 Aug. 1918, NMML, Malaviya Papers (microfilm), roll 1.

60. Tagore to Rothenstein, 14 Feb. 1913, cited in Stephen N. Hay, "Rabindranath Tagore in America," *American Quarterly* 14:3 (Autumn 1962), 443.

61. Hay, "Tagore in America," 447, 449.

62. Woodrow Wilson to Macmillan and Company, 9 Apr. 1917, *PWW*, 42:21; Hay, "Tagore in America," 451–452.

63. Hay, "Tagore in America," 458; Lajpat Rai, *The United States of America*, 107–126.

64. E.g., *Mahratta*, 11 June 1916; *ABP*, 22 Feb. 1919; Lajpat Rai, *The United States*, 296–325; *Mahratta*, 17 Dec. 1916.

65. "Editorial Notes and News," *Young India* 2:1 (Jan. 1919), 3. Also see the same theme in the leading article in the *Tribune* (Lahore), 13 Mar. 1917, in "Punjab Press Abstract, 1917," IOR, L/R/5/199. Citing U.S. rule in the Philippines as a positive model for colonial rule compared to the practices of other colonial powers was a common practice among anticolonial nationalists at the time, not only in India. See, e.g., this theme in a petition to the peace conference from Prince Cuong De, a descendant of the Vietnamese royal house who opposed French rule and resided in exile in Japan, 1 Feb. 1919, MAE, A-Paix, vol. 322.

66. "Editorial Notes and News," *Young India* 1:12 (Dec. 1918), 5.

67. "Editorial Notes and News," *Young India* 2:1 (Jan. 1919), 3.

68. *New India*, 6 and 11 Jan. 1919; *ABP*, 18 Feb. 1919. *New India* was published daily in Madras (Chennai) and associated with Annie Besant's India Home Rule League.

69. *Mahratta*, 2 Feb. 1919.

70. *Young India* 2:1 (Jan. 1919), 2.

71. *Mahratta*, 6 Oct. 1918, in "Bombay Press Abstract, 1918," IOR, L/R/5/174, p. 19; *Tribune* (Lahore), 20 Dec. 1918, in "Punjab Press Abstract, 1919," IOR, L/R/5/201, p. 3. The *New York Times* boasted at the time: "Extracts from President Wilson's speeches are being quoted by villagers in the remotest part of India," and his words "have gripped their hearts as nothing else has done since the war began." See "Wilson's Words in India," *New York Times*, 5 Oct. 1918, 12, col. 7.

72. The Urdu *Bulletin* (Lahore), 31 Oct. 1918, IOR, L/R/5/200, p. 553. Very similar sentiments were expressed in the *Hindustan* (Lahore), 1 Nov. 1918, ibid., p. 554.

73. *Hindi Brahmin Samachar*, 25 Nov. 1918; *Kesari* (Poona), n.d., IOR, L/R/5/200, p. 596.

74. Thirty-third INC session, Delhi, Dec. 1918, NMML, All-India Congress Committee [AICC], file 1, part II, p. 347. Also see Patel to Khaparde, 21 Jan. 1919, in *Selected Documents of Lokamanya Bal Gangadhar Tilak, 1880–1920*, 4 vols., ed. Ravindra Kumar (New Delhi: Anmol, 1992), 3:168.

75. Proceedings of All-India Home Rule League Conference, Delhi, 31 Dec. 1918, Jawaharlal Nehru Papers, part II, Subject Files, file no. 116, p. 11.

76. Resolutions of All-India Muslim League, 31 Dec. 1918, IOR, L/PJ/6/1573.

77. This concern among Indian Muslims developed by mid-1919 into the Khilafat movement—whose name derived from the Ottoman sultan's role as the caliph, or khalif, of the Islamic world—to protest rumored Allied plans to depose him. It won the endorsement of Gandhi, who was eager to bring the Muslims into his noncooperation movement. The Khilafat issue, an important stage in the emergence of a separate Muslim polity in South Asia, has been well studied, and in current scholarship it often appears as the only issue related to the Paris Peace Conference that occupied Indian nationalists. See Gail Minault, *The Khilafat Movement: Religious Symbolism and Political Mobilization in India* (New York: Columbia University Press, 1982); M. Naeem Qureshi, *Pan-Islam in British Indian Politics: A Study of the Khilafat Movement, 1918–1924* (Leiden, Netherlands: Brill, 1999).

78. Montagu to Chelmsford, 22 Oct. 1918, NAI, Montagu Papers, roll 1.

79. Montagu to Chelmsford, 11 Jan. 1919, NMML, Chelmsford Papers, roll 4; Montagu to Chelmsford, 28 Nov. 1918, NAI, Montagu Papers, roll 1.

80. Chelmsford to Montagu, 14 Jan. 1919; and Chelmsford to Montagu, 22 Jan. 1919, NMML, Chelmsford Papers, roll 4.

CHAPTER 5

1. Hollington K. Tong, "What Can President Wilson Do for China?" *Millard's Review*, 16 Nov. 1918, 431–434. This article was printed in Chinese translation in the popular Shanghai daily *Shibao*, 18 Dec. 1918, 1, under the title "Zhongguo yu heping huiyi" [China and the Peace Conference].

2. "Mei zongtong zhi yihe tiaojian" [U.S. President's Conditions for Peace Talks], *Shibao*, 11 Jan. 1918, 2. Also "Mei zongtong yanshuo heping tiaojian" [U.S. President Announces Peace Conditions], *Dagongbao*, 11 Jan. 1918, 3. *Shibao* was a major Shanghai daily with a liberal reputation; on its emergence and impact, see Joan Judge, *Print and Politics: "Shibao" and the Culture of Reform in Late Qing China* (Stanford, Calif.: Stanford University Press, 1996). *Dagongbao* was a major daily published in Tianjin.

3. "Cejin yongjiu hepinghui xuanyan shu" [On the Plan for a Conference for Permanent Peace], *Shibao*, 16 Dec. 1918.

4. At the time, only U.S. envoys to the capitals of the great powers received the rank of ambassador, while diplomatic representatives to states considered "small powers," like China, carried the rank of minister.

5. Creel, *How We Advertised America*, 358–361; Hans Schmidt, "Democracy for China: American Propaganda and the May Fourth Movement," *Diplomatic History* 22:1 (1998), 3.

6. The plan for CPI operations was prepared by journalist John B. Powell (1888–1947), who was then at the initial phase of a long journalistic career in China. On him, see John B. Powell, *My Twenty-Five Years in China* (New York: Macmillan, 1945).

7. Carl Crow, "The Great War on the China Front," unpublished typescript, Carl Crow Papers, Western Historical Manuscript Collection, University of Missouri, Columbia, pp. 11–12. Also see Schmidt, "Democracy for China," 4. Crow, like Creel himself, was a product of the "Missouri school" of American journalism in the Progressive Era. For his post-1920 career in China and a comparison with a later China journalist from the Missouri school, Edgar Snow, see Jerry Israel, "Carl Crow, Edgar Snow, and Shifting American Journalistic Perceptions of China," in *America Views China: American Images of China Then and Now* (Bethlehem, Pa.: Lehigh University Press, 1991), 148–168.

8. Crow, "Great War," 13.

9. Ibid., 14–15; also see Kazuyuki Matsuo, "American Propaganda in China: The U.S. Committee on Public Information, 1918–1919," *Journal of American and Canadian Studies* [Japan] 14 (1996), 28.

10. Schmidt, "Democracy for China," 4–5. Chow Tse-tsung estimated that some 700 new periodicals were founded between 1915 and 1923, and he lists 587 of them by

name. See Chow Tse-tsung, *Research Guide to the May Fourth Movement* (Cambridge, Mass.: Harvard University Press, 1963), 1.

11. Schmidt, "Democracy for China," 11–12.

12. Creel, *How We Advertised America*, 362–363; Jerry Israel, *Progressivism and the Open Door: America and China, 1905–1921* (Pittsburgh, Pa.: University of Pittsburgh Press, 1971), 157–160.

13. Creel, *How We Advertised America*, 279. *Millard's Review*, 30 Nov. 1918, 535, published an ad for the "first release in China" of *Pershing's Crusaders* at the Olympic Theatre in Shanghai.

14. Crow, "Great War," 17–18; Creel, *How We Advertised America*, 362; Schmidt, "Democracy for China," 3.

15. "Meiguo zongtong Wei-er-xun canzhan yanshuo chuban" [U.S. President Wilson's Wartime Addresses Published], *Shibao*, 16 Nov. 1918; the ad appeared several more times in this newspaper over the next weeks. Also in *Shenbao*, 21 Nov. 1918, 1; *Millard's Review*, 23 Nov. 1918. *Shenbao* was a major daily published in Shanghai but read across China. On its reach into the countryside during this period, see Henrietta Harrison, "Newspapers and Nationalism in Rural China 1890–1929," *Past & Present* 166 (2000).

16. *Millard's Review*, 23 Nov. 1918. The following issue, on 30 Nov. 1918, carried on p. 542 an advertisement for the volumes. The price was 25 cents for the Chinese edition and 50 cents for the bilingual edition. The translator, Jiang Menglin, was a leading liberal intellectual who had studied in the United States from 1908 to 1917 and received his Ph.D. under John Dewey from Columbia University.

17. Crow, "Great War," 18–21. Also see Carl Crow, *China Takes Her Place* (New York: Harper, 1944), 113–115; and Carl Crow, *I Speak for the Chinese* (New York: Harper, 1937), 27–29. On Feng and his role throughout the nationalist period, see James E. Sheridan, *Chinese Warlord: The Career of Feng Yü-hsiang* (Stanford, Calif.: Stanford University Press, 1966).

18. Creel, *How We Advertised America*, 362; Matsuo, "American Propaganda in China," 29; Xu Guoqi, *China and the Great War: China's Pursuit of a New National Identity and Internationalization* (Cambridge: Cambridge University Press, 2005), 245.

19. Letter from Carl Crow to the New York office of CPI, 23 Nov. 1918, cited in Matsuo, "American Propaganda in China," 30.

20. Demetrio Boersner, *The Bolsheviks and the National and Colonial Question (1917–1928)* (Geneva: Droz, 1957), 64–82. See also Arif Dirlik, *The Origins of Chinese Communism* (Oxford: Oxford University Press, 1989), 24.

21. Tao Wenzhao, *Zhong-Mei guanxi shi, 1911–1950* [Sino-American Relations, 1911–1950] (Chongqing: Chongqing Press, 1993), 47.

22. *Shibao*, 24 and 27–29 Dec. 1918. "Yingwang yu Mei zongtong zhi yanshuo" [The Speeches of the King of England and the U.S. President], *Shenbao*, 30 Dec. 1918. *Shibao*, 24 Dec. 1918, 1, noted that Wilson received an honorary doctoral degree from Sorbonne University; *Shibao*, 29 Dec. 1918, 1, reported that "two million Londoners lined the streets to welcome Wilson."

23. Letter by "X," *North China Herald* (Shanghai), 21 Dec. 1918, cited in Schmidt, "Democracy for China," 16.

24. Cited in Schmidt, "Democracy for China," 11.

25. Jordan to Balfour, 23 Dec. 1918, cited in Madeleine Chi, "China and Unequal Treaties at the Paris Peace Conference of 1919," *Asian Profile* 1:1 (Aug. 1973), 51.

26. See James Townsend, "Chinese Nationalism," *Australian Journal of Chinese Affairs* 27 (Jan. 1992), 97–130, for a survey of the literature on Chinese nationalism. As Townsend points out, one of the most influential accounts of the emergence of Chinese nationalism to replace Confucian "culturalism" around the turn of the twentieth century is Joseph Levenson, *Confucian China and Its Modern Fate: A Trilogy* (Berkeley: University of California Press, 1968), esp. 1:95–108. For a narrative account of the rise of Chinese nationalism as a political and cultural force around 1900, see Jonathan D. Spence, *The Search for Modern China*, 2d ed. (New York: Norton, 1999), chaps. 7–10.

27. The events surrounding the submission of the 1895 memorial are described in Jonathan D. Spence, *The Gate of Heavenly Peace: The Chinese and Their Revolution, 1895–1980* (New York: Viking, 1981), 6–14. Kang Youwei would remain one of the most prominent intellectuals and reformers in China into the 1920s; on him, see Hsiao Kung-chuan, *A Modern China and a New World: Kang Yu-wei, Reformer and Utopian, 1858–1927* (Seattle: University of Washington Press, 1975); Hao Chang, *Chinese Intellectuals in Crisis: Search for Order and Meaning, 1890–1911* (Berkeley: University of California Press, 1987), chap. 2.

28. Andrew J. Nathan, *Chinese Democracy* (New York: Knopf, 1985), x.

29. For a detailed analysis of the emergence of a popular press and a mass audience in China, see Leo Lee and Andrew J. Nathan, "The Beginnings of Mass Culture," in *Popular Culture in Late Imperial China*, eds. David Johnson, Andrew J. Nathan, and Evelyn S. Rawski (Berkeley: University of California Press, 1985), 368–378; and Joan Judge, *Print and Politics: "Shibao" and the Culture of Reform in Late Qing China* (Stanford, Calif.: Stanford University Press, 1996).

30. This group constituted what Ernest May has dubbed a "foreign policy public." See Ernest R. May, *American Imperialism: A Speculative Essay* (New York: Atheneum, 1968). The role of "print capitalism" in the formation of national identity was, of course, a major theme in Benedict Anderson, *Imagined Communities: Reflections on the Origin and Spread of Nationalism*, rev. ed. (London: Verso, 1991).

31. Tan Sitong, another prominent leader of the reforms, chose to offer himself for martyrdom and was executed by the Qing authorities, becoming a hero to young anti-Manchu revolutionaries. See Immanuel C. Y. Hsü, *The Rise of Modern China*, 6th ed. (New York: Oxford University Press, 2000), 355–386.

32. One of the best known statements of anti-Qing sentiments was Zou Rong's *The Revolutionary Army*, published in 1903. It called upon the Chinese people to "cleanse" themselves of the rule of the "furry and horned" Manchus so that China could become "a great country in the world" and "the descendants of the Yellow Emperor" would "all become Washingtons." Zou Rong, *The Revolutionary Army*, John Lust, trans. (The Hague: Mouton, 1968), 1; see also Spence, *Gate of Heavenly Peace*, 47–50.

33. C. Martin Wilbur, *Sun Yat-sen: Frustrated Patriot* (New York: Columbia University Press, 1976), esp. chap. 3.

34. Sun Yat-sen declared in 1912: "The revolution has finally succeeded today… due to the power of the press. The press enjoys this power because it is able to instill ideas in people's minds." Sun's speech in Shanghai entitled "The Popular Mind Depends on the Power of the Press," 16 Apr. 1912, is reproduced in Julie Lee Wei, Ramon H. Myers, and Donald G. Gillin, eds., *Prescriptions for Saving China: Selected Writings of Sun Yat-sen* (Stanford, Calif.: Hoover Institution Press, 1994), 70–71. For a historiographical survey of the literature on the development of the press in China post-1911, see Stephen R. MacKinnon, "Toward a History of the Chinese Press in the Republican Period," *Modern China* 23:1 (Jan. 1997), 4.

35. For a detailed analysis of this process, see Zhang Yongjin, *China in the International System, 1918–1920: The Middle Kingdom at the Periphery* (Oxford: St. Anthony's/Macmillan, 1991), 15–38.

36. Kang Youwei, "Jiu wang lun" [Saving the Nation from Extinction], originally written in 1911, can be found in *Kang Youwei zhenglun ji* [The Political Writings of Kang Youwei], ed. Yang Zhijun (Beijing: Zhonghua shuju, 1981), 2:653. On Chinese views on U.S. rule in the Philippines, see Rebecca E. Karl, *Staging the World: Chinese Nationalism at the Turn of the Twentieth Century* (Durham, N.C.: Duke University Press, 2002), chap. 4; Michael H. Hunt, *The Genesis of Chinese Communist Foreign Policy* (New York: Columbia University Press, 1996), 90.

37. Zhi Fei, "Zhimin de wenti" [The Colonial Question], *Guomin Gongbao*, 6 Dec. 1918, 5, which is part of a series of articles entitled "Lun Ouzhanhou zhi heping huiyi" [On the Postwar Peace Conference]. *Guomin Gongbao* was a major Beijing daily and considered a venue for "liberal opinion." On this paper, see Hu Suh [Hu Shi], "Intellectual China in 1919," *Chinese Social and Political Science Review* 4:4 (Dec. 1919), 345–355.

38. F. Gilbert Chan, "The American Revolution and the Rise of Afro-Asian Nationalism, with Special Reference to Sun Yat-Sen and the Chinese Experience," *Asian Profile* 10:3 (1982), 209–219; Michael H. Hunt, *The Making of a Special Relationship: The United States and China to 1914* (New York: Columbia University Press, 1983), 258–266.

39. A Statement on the Pending Chinese Loan, 18 Mar. 1913, *PWW*, 27:193. The report on the cabinet meeting on 18 Apr. 1913, in which Yuan's call was discussed, is found in *PWW*, 27:328–333.

40. For a detailed examination of China's motivations for entering the war on the Allied side, see Stephen G. Craft, "Angling for an Invitation to Paris: China's Entry into the First World War," *International History Review* 16:1 (1994), 1–24. Also see Xu, *China and the Great War*, esp. chap. 5.

41. Schmidt, "Democracy for China," 10; *Peking Leader*, 26 Nov. 1918, enclosed in USNA, RG 256, 893.00/11. Also see similar sentiments in *Peking Leader*, 3–5 Nov. 1919, in RG 256, 893.00/5; and Foreign Minister of Canton Government to Lansing, 23 Jan. 1919, RG 256, 893.00/18.

42. Tang Zhenchang, *Cai Yuanpei Zhuan* [The Biography of Cai Yuanpei] (Shanghai: Shanghai renmin chubanshe, 1985), 159. On Cai, also see William J. Duiker, *Ts'ai Yuan-pei: Educator of Modern China* (University Park: Pennsylvania State University Press, 1977).

43. Editorial in *Meizhou Pinglun* [Weekly Review], 22 Dec. 1918, reproduced in *Duxiu wencun* [The Surviving Writings of Chen Duxiu] (Hefei: Anhui renmin chubanshe, 1987), 388. On Chen, see Lee Feigon, *Chen Duxiu, Founder of the Chinese Communist Party* (Princeton, N.J.: Princeton University Press, 1983).

44. *Dongfang Zazhi* [Eastern Magazine] 16:2 (Feb. 1919), cited in Xu, *China and the Great War*, 246. Liang has been one of the most studied Chinese intellectuals in modern times. See, for example, Joseph Levenson, *Liang Chi-chao and the Mind of Modern China* (Cambridge, Mass.: Harvard University Press, 1953); Philip Huang, *Liang Ch'i-ch'ao and Modern Chinese Liberalism* (Seattle: University of Washington Press, 1972); Tang Xiaobing, *Global Space and the Nationalist Discourse of Modernity: The Historical Thinking of Liang Qichao* (Stanford, Calif.: Stanford University Press, 1996).

45. "Wei-er-xun" [Wilson] and "Jielu Wei-er-xun 'xunci'" [An Excerpt from Wilson's "Admonition"], in *Hu Shi liuxue riji* [Hu Shi's Diary while Studying Abroad] (Changsha: Yuelu shu she, 2000), 208, 334. Jerome Grieder notes that it seems likely that Hu's image of Wilson "remained with him in later years, providing an example of the kind of political behavior, very Confucian in his description of it, that he strove to emulate." Jerome B. Grieder, *Hu Shih and the Chinese Renaissance: Liberalism in the Chinese Revolution, 1917–37* (Cambridge, Mass.: Harvard University Press, 1970), 52.

46. Xu, *China and the Great War*, 206–207.

47. E.g., Yang Chao to Liang Qichao, 18 Feb. 1919, refers to the league as "wanguo datong meng," literally, the "all-nations league of great unity." Waijiaobu (Chinese Foreign Ministry) Archives, Institute of Modern History, Academia Sinica, Taipei, Taiwan [WJB], RG 03–37, box 26, folder 2. The term "league of nations" was also often rendered as "guoji datong meng," literally, "league of international unity." Like other terms in Confucian philosophy, *datong* is difficult to translate into English. Laurence G. Thompson, who translated Kang's book, rendered it as "one world," but noted more than a dozen other possibilities. Jonathan D. Spence has translated it as "great community," and Kang Youwei himself rendered the term into English literally as "great concord." See *Ta t'ung shu: The One-World Philosophy of K'ang Yu-wei*, trans. Laurence G. Thompson (London: Allen & Unwin, 1958), esp. 29–30; Jonathan D. Spence, *The Gate of Heavenly Peace: The Chinese and Their Revolution* (New York: Viking, 1981), 64–73; Chow Tse-tsung, *The May Fourth Movement: Intellectual Revolution in Modern China* (Cambridge, Mass.: Harvard University Press, 1960), 97–98 and note n there. For more on Kang and his ideas, see Prasenjit Duara, "Transnationalism and the Predicament of Sovereignty: China, 1900–1945," *American Historical Review* 102:4 (1997): 1034–1035; Kung-chuan Hsiao, *A Modern China and a New World: Kang Yu-wei, Reformer and Utopian, 1858–1927* (Seattle: University of Washington Press, 1975), esp. part 4; Jung-pang Lo, ed., *K'ang Yu-wei: A Biography and a Symposium* (Tucson: University of Arizona Press, 1967), esp. 341–354.

48. "Cu Nan Bei su yihe yi ying Ouzhou heju dian" [A Call to North and South to Make Peace Quickly in View of the European Peace Conference], *Shibao*, 30 Dec. 1918, reproduced in *Kang Youwei zhenglun ji* [The Political Writings of Kang Youwei], ed. Yang Zhijun (Beijing: Zhonghua shuju, 1981), 2:1061–1063; Hollington Tong, "Kang

Yu-wei as Chinese Advocate of League of Nations," *Millard's Review*, 8 Feb. 1919, 342–345.

49. Kun to Wilson, 23 Dec. 1918, WWP, series 5d, reel 421.

50. Li Dazhao, "Wei-er-xun yu pinghe" [Wilson and Peace], 11 Feb. 1917, in *Li Dazhao wenji* [Writings of Li Dazhao] (Beijing: Renmin chubanshe, 1999), 1:271. Li's biographer, Maurice Meisner, has suggested that Li's writings praising Wilson were "probably something less than truly reflective of Li's feelings," since Li "had never shared the new intelligentsia's faith in the West, and the betrayal of Chinese interests at Versailles must have come to him as less a disillusionment than a confirmation of [his] deep-seated suspicions [of] the Western world." This interpretation is plausible, but Li's uniqueness in this regard among the "new intelligentsia" only serves to underscore the faith that most Chinese intellectuals had in the possibilities that the Wilsonian moment held for China. See Maurice Meisner, *Li Ta-chao and the Origins of Chinese Marxism* (Cambridge, Mass.: Harvard University Press, 1967), 96–97.

51. Li Dazhao, "Bolshevism de shengli" [The Victory of Bolshevism], *Xin Qingnian* [New Youth] 5:5, dated 15 Oct. 1918 but, given the references to the victory celebrations, clearly published in November. The word "Bolshevism" was rendered in English in the title of the piece. Liebknecht was a leader of the German radical socialist Spartacus League; Scheidemann was the German Social Democratic politician who announced the establishment of a German republic on 9 Nov. 1918. References in Li's article suggest that he gleaned news about the Bolsheviks mainly from British papers he read in Beijing; he also cited Trotsky's book *The Bolsheviki and World Peace*, published in New York in 1918. However, the article also shows that Li still had at best a fragmentary grasp of Bolshevik ideas and politics, since he listed Scheidemann, whom Lenin considered a contemptible "social chauvinist," together with Lenin and Trotsky as part of the revolutionary vanguard. For Lenin's dim opinion of Scheidemann, see, e.g., V. I. Lenin, *The State and Revolution* (London: British Socialist Party, 1919), preface. On Li's role as a pioneering Chinese Marxist, see Maurice Meisner, *Li Ta-chao and the Origins of Chinese Marxism* (Cambridge, Mass.: Harvard University Press, 1967); Li Danyang, "Makesi xueshuo yanjiuhui yu Zhongguo gongchanzhuyi zuzhi de qiyuan" [The Society for the Study of Marxism and the Origins of Communist Organization in China], *Shixue yuekan* [Journal of Historical Science] 6 (2004), 51–59.

52. See *Xin Qingnian* 6:4 (15 Apr. 1919) and 6:5 (15 May 1919).

53. Based on a survey of *Shibao* and *Dagongbao* from Nov. 1918 to Feb. 1919.

54. An Address to the Senate, 22 Jan. 1917, *PWW*, 40:536; Wilson's Address to a Joint Session of Congress, 8 Jan. 1918, *PWW*, 45:539.

55. Noel H. Pugach, *Paul S. Reinsch: Open Door Diplomat in Action* (Millwood, N.Y.: KTO, 1979).

56. Reinsch interviews on 5 and 12 Oct. 1918, cited in Pugach, *Paul S. Reinsch*, 252.

57. Reinsch to Wilson, 10 Jan. 1919, *PWW*, 54:77–82.

58. Reinsch to Polk, 6 Jan. 1919, communicated to Wilson's private secretary, Gilbert Close, on 15 Jan. 1919, *PWW*, 54:77–82. Also see Reinsch to Lansing, 8 Nov. 1918, USNA, RG 256, 893.01/1.

59. Exchange between Wu in Beijing and Koo in Washington, 29 Mar. [1918], WJB, RG 03–12 (Archives of Chinese Legation in Washington), box 8, folder 2, pp. 482–487.

60. Koo to Lansing, 25 Nov. 1918, in WJB, RG 03–12, box 8, folder 2, p. 477. For full details, see *Canyu Ouzhou heping dahui fenlei baogao* [Report on Participation in the European Peace Conference] (Washington, D.C.: Chinese Legation, n.d.), 866–907; "Strategies for the Paris Peace Conference," 27 Feb. 1919, WJB, 03–37, 7:3. On legal extraterritoriality in China and especially its implications for the United States, see Eileen P. Scully, *Bargaining with the State from Afar: American Citizenship in Treaty Port China, 1844–1942* (New York: Columbia University Press, 2001).

61. Russell H. Fifield, *Woodrow Wilson and the Far East: The Diplomacy of the Shantung Question* (Hamden, Conn.: Archon, 1965), 183. Lu's name often appears in the literature in the French transcription, Lou Tseng-tsiang.

62. Hornbeck Papers, box 328, folder "Paris Peace Conference: China, Peace Commissioners."

63. After his wife's death in 1926, Lu entered the Benedictine Abbey of St. Andrew in Bruges, Belgium, where he remained as a monk until his death in 1949. For more on Lu's life, see Nicholas M. Keegan, "From Chancery to Cloister: The Chinese Diplomat Who Became a Benedictine Monk," *Diplomacy & Statecraft* 10:1 (1999), 172–185.

64. Chengting Thomas Wang, "Looking Back and Looking Forward" (unpublished autobiography), Archives and Manuscripts, Yale University, New Haven, Conn., 102. A second southern representative, C. C. Wu, was added to the delegation in February, replacing Wei.

65. WJB, RG 03–37, box 8, folder 1; Hornbeck Papers, box 328, folder "Paris Peace Conference: China, Peace Commissioners"; V. K. Wellington Koo, *The Wellington Koo Memoir*, 7 vols. (New York: Columbia University, East Asian Institute, 1976), 2:168. Koo went on to have a distinguished diplomatic career, leading the Chinese delegation to the 1945 San Francisco conference that established the United Nations. After his retirement from the foreign service, he was appointed a judge on the International Court of Justice in the Hague, where he served from 1957 to 1967. He died in 1985, at the age of ninety-eight. On his career see Pao-chin Chu, *V. K. Wellington Koo: A Case Study of China's Diplomat and Diplomacy of Nationalism, 1912–1966* (Hong Kong: Chinese University Press, 1981).

66. V. K. Wellington Koo, "China and the League of Nations," in V. K. Wellington Koo and Cheng-ting T. Wang, *China and the League of Nations* (London: Allen & Unwin, 1919), 2.

67. *Canyu Ouzhou heping*, 762–766; Wang, "Looking Back," 102.

68. Fifield, *Woodrow Wilson and the Far East*, 179–181; Zhang, *China in the International System*, 51–52.

69. "Oriental Press Comment, No. 11," 12 Feb. 1919, in E. T. Williams, "Recollections" (unpublished typescript), E. T. Williams Papers, Bancroft Library, University of California, Berkeley, 281.

70. On the Shanghai peace conference of 1919, see Allen Yuk-Lun Fung, "The Struggle over the Constitution: Chinese Politics, 1917–1919" (Ph.D. diss., Harvard University, 1996), 186–238; Andrew J. Nathan, *Peking Politics, 1918–1923* (Berkeley: University of California Press, 1976), esp. 138–144.

71. Fifield, *Woodrow Wilson and the Far East*, 187–188; Madeleine Chi, "China and Unequal Treaties at the Paris Peace Conference of 1919," *Asian Profile* 1:1 (1973), 52.

72. E.g., Ding Bianlin and Yang Chao of the Central Union of Chinese Students in Great Britain and Ireland to the Chinese Delegation to the PPC, 8 Mar. 1919, WJB, 03–37, 27:2.

73. *Telegrams Received by the Chinese Delegation in Support of Their Stand on the Shantung Question* (Paris: [Chinese Delegation, 1919]). The telegrams printed in the pamphlet carry dates between February and April 1919.

74. Enclosed in Jordan to Curzon, 7 May 1919, NAUK, FO 608/210, fol. 443–444.

75. No date on petition, but the accompanying telegram is dated 21 Jan. 1919. NAUK, FO 608/209, fol. 287.

76. Liang to Wilson, 30 Jan. 1919, WWP, series 5d, reel 429.

77. Yang Chao, Secretary of the Central Union of Chinese Students in Great Britain and Ireland to Liang Qichao, 18 Feb. 1919, WJB, 03–37, 26:2. Liang recorded his impressions of the conference in "Bali hehui niaokan" [A Survey of the Paris Peace Conference], in *Liang Qichao quanji* [The Complete Works of Liang Qichao] (Beijing: Beijing chubanshe, 1999), 5:3000–3010.

CHAPTER 6

1. Michael Edson Robinson, *Cultural Nationalism in Colonial Korea, 1920–1925* (Seattle: University of Washington Press, 1988), 3–4; Chong-sik Lee, *The Politics of Korean Nationalism* (Berkeley: University of California Press, 1963), 113–118; Carter J. Eckert, Ki-Baik Lee, Young Ick Lew, Michael Robinson, and Edward W. Wagner, *Korea Old and New: A History* (Cambridge, Mass.: Harvard University Press, 1990), 278. Frank Baldwin's 1969 Ph.D. dissertation, "The March First Movement: Korean Challenge and Japanese Response" (Columbia University), though never published, is still the most thorough study of the movement in the English language. Also see Timothy S. Lee, "A Political Factor in the Rise of Protestantism in Korea: Protestantism and the 1919 March First Movement," *Church History* 69:1 (Mar. 2000), 131 n. 36.

2. For more on premodern China's foreign relations and the tribute system, see John K. Fairbank, ed., *The Chinese World Order: Traditional China's Foreign Relations* (Cambridge, Mass.: Harvard University Press, 1968).

3. Eckert et al., *Korea Old and New*, 192–198. For more on the 1871 war, see Gordon H. Chang, "Whose 'Barbarism'? Whose 'Treachery'? Race and Civilization in the Unknown United States–Korea War of 1871," *Journal of American History* 89:4 (Mar. 2003), 1331–1365.

4. Eckert et al., *Korea Old and New*, 200–201. On the unequal treaties with Japan and the responses of Japanese diplomacy, see Michael R. Auslin, *Negotiating with Imperialism: The Unequal Treaties and the Culture of Japanese Diplomacy* (Cambridge, Mass.: Harvard University Press, 2004).

5. The reference to the 1882 treaty would be made in almost every Korean petition for U.S. assistance against Japan. See, e.g., the petition from the New Korea Association to Robert Lansing, 2 Dec. 1918, USNA, RG 256, 895.00/1.

6. Lee, *Korean Nationalism*, 97.

7. Eckert et al., *Korea Old and New*, 232–236.

8. For a detailed analysis of the Independence Club and its significance, see Se-ŭng O, *Dr. Philip Jaisohn's Reform Movement, 1896–1898: A Critical Appraisal of the Independence Club* (Lanham, Md.: University Press of America, 1995); and Vipan Chandra, *Imperialism, Resistance, and Reform in Late Nineteenth-Century Korea: Enlightenment and the Independence Club* (Berkeley: Center for Korean Studies, Institute of East Asian Studies, University of California, 1988).

9. Cemil Aydin, "A Global Anti-Western Moment? The Russo-Japanese War, Decolonization, and Asian Modernity," in Conrad and Sachsenmaier, eds., *Conceptions of World Order.*

10. Bong-youn Choy, *Koreans in America* (Chicago: Nelson-Hall, 1979), 142–143; Warren Y. Kim, *Koreans in America* (Seoul: Po Chin Chai, 1971), 73–74; Robert T. Oliver, *Syngman Rhee: The Man behind the Myth* (New York: Dodd Mead, 1954), 84–90. The text of the Korean petition to Roosevelt is printed in F. A. McKenzie, *The Tragedy of Korea* (London: Hodder and Stoughton, 1908), 311–312.

11. See, for example, Homer B. Hulbert, "American Policy in the Cases of Korea and Belgium," *New York Times*, 5 Mar. 1916, 20; "Roosevelt the Practical," *Milwaukee Journal*, 25 Feb. 1916, in USNA, RG 59, 895.00/569–1/2.

12. For more on this debate, see John Edward Wilz, "Did the United States Betray Korea in 1905?" *Pacific Historical Review* 16 (1985), 243–270.

13. Eckert et al., *Korea Old and New*, 244–253.

14. In 1897, Kojong had declared himself emperor to emphasize Korea's newly sovereign status and its emergence from under Chinese suzerainty. Previously, Korean rulers of the Yi dynasty had been styled "kings" to indicate their subservience to the Chinese emperor.

15. Lee, *Korean Nationalism*, 77–79; Choy, *Koreans in America*, 144–145.

16. Eckert et al., *Korea Old and New*, 260.

17. Lee, *Korean Nationalism*, 98–99, 102–103.

18. Ibid., 129; Kenneth M. Wells, "Background to the March First Movement: Koreans in Japan, 1905–1919," *Korean Studies* 13 (1989), 8.

19. Choy, *Koreans in America*, 152; Lee, *Korean Nationalism*, 102–103. An oral history interview with Chung, who was also known as Henry Deyoung, appeared in Sonia Shinn Sunoo, *Korea Kaleidoscope: Oral Histories* (Davis, Calif.: Korean Oral History Project, 1982). I thank Philip Cuddy for bringing that source to my attention.

20. Rhee et al. to Wilson, 25 Nov. and 22 Dec. 1918, WWP, series 5b, reel 387; and Rhee et al. to Wilson, 30 Dec. 1918, WWP, series 5d, reel 424. The Korean delegates also petitioned the Senate Foreign Relations Committee, urging it to have the president champion the Korean cause at the peace conference. Chung to Committee, 20 Jan. 1919, Hornbeck Papers, box 270, folder "Korean Petitions."

21. Baldwin, "The March First Movement," 16.

22. Pyong-choon Hahm, "The Korean Perception of the United States," in *Korea and the United States: A Century of Cooperation*, ed. Youngnok Koo and Dae-sook Suh (Honolulu: University of Hawaii Press, 1984), 23–52.

23. Ray Stannard Baker, *Woodrow Wilson and World Settlement*, 3 vols. (Garden City, N.Y.: Doubleday, Page, 1922), 1:6.

24. New Korea Association to the secretary of state, 2 Dec. 1918, USNA, RG 256, 895.00/1.

25. Baldwin, "The March First Movement," 32–33.

26. Both Chang and Yŏ would later become important leaders of the nationalist movement; see Wells, "Background to the March First Movement," 12. Baldwin, "The March First Movement," 35, writes that the New Korea Youth Association/party was only formed, on an ad hoc basis, in November, but Lee, *Korean Nationalism*, 103, agrees with Wells that the organization had been founded that summer.

27. In his autobiography, Yŏ claimed that Crane personally promised help on Korean independence. Another account on the contacts between Koreans in Shanghai and Crane, however, does not mention such a specific promise. Baldwin finds the latter account more plausible. See Baldwin, "The March First Movement," 244–245 n. 11. Crane, secretive and circumspect, still awaits a proper biography. For now, see the somewhat hagiographic David Hapgood, *Charles R. Crane: The Man Who Bet on People* ([Hanover, N.H.:] Institute of Current World Affairs, 2000).

28. Thomas F. Millard, *Democracy and the Eastern Question: The Problem of the Far East as Demonstrated by the Great War, and Its Relation to the United States of America* (New York: Century, 1919), 37–40. Although Millard was sympathetic to the Korean cause and conceded that in principle Koreans were as entitled to self-determination as anyone, he thought there was little chance that the Korean case would actually come before the conference. Baldwin, "The March First Movement," 35–36. Also see Lee, *Korean Nationalism*, 103–104.

29. Lee, *Korean Nationalism*, 104. After 1919, Kim was involved in nationalist activities in China and Manchuria, and he returned to Korea in 1945. See Baldwin, "The March First Movement," 246; Lee, "A Political Factor in the Rise of Protestantism in Korea," 132.

30. Baldwin, "The March First Movement," 36 and 246 n. 17.

31. Wells, "Background to the March First Movement," 13. Yi Kwangsu, considered the first modern Korean novelist, fled to Shanghai in the aftermath of the February 8 movement, but returned to Korea in 1921 and adopted a gradualist approach to building modern Korean national identity and culture. Baldwin, "The March First Movement," 249.

32. Wells, "Background to the March First Movement," 12. Also see "Independence Movement in Japan," *Young Korea* 1:3 (May 1919), 83–85; Lee, *Korean Nationalism*, 104–106.

33. Louise Yim, *My Forty Year Fight for Korea* (New York: Wyn, 1951), 101.

34. Dae-yeol Ku, *Korea under Colonialism: The March First Movement and Anglo-Japanese Relations* (Seoul: Seoul Computer Press, 1985), 45; Lee, *Korean Nationalism*, 107.

35. Consulate General, Seoul, to State Department, 10 Jan. 1919, cited in Baldwin, "The March First Movement," 252–253.

36. Eckert et al., *Korea Old and New*, 277; Lee, *Korean Nationalism*, 106–107.

37. Lee, "A Political Factor in the Rise of Protestantism in Korea," 132.

38. Yim, *My Forty Year Fight*, 102–103; Lee, *Korean Nationalism*, 107–109. For a detailed analysis of the planning stage of the movement, see Baldwin, "The March First Movement," chap. 4.

39. Sixteen of the signatories were Christian leaders, fifteen belonged to the Ch'ongdogyo, and two were Buddhists.

40. Cited in Baldwin, "The March First Movement," appendix, 224–227. A slightly different translation, which does not alter the meaning of the passage, is offered in Han-Kyo Kim, "The Declaration of Independence, March 1, 1919: A New Translation," *Korean Studies* 13 (1989), 1–4.

41. On this, see Baldwin, "The March First Movement," 78 and n. 1 there.

42. Lee, *Korean Nationalism*, 111–112.

43. Cited in Baldwin, "The March First Movement," 80. On the day's events, see also the British missionary eyewitness report in NAUK, FO 262/1406, fol. 33–35. Also see Hildi Kang, comp., *Under the Black Umbrella: Voices from Colonial Korea, 1910–1945* (Ithaca, N.Y.: Cornell University Press, 2001), 17–23.

44. Baldwin, "The March First Movement," 82–83, 277 n. 15. Thirty years old at the time, Schofield was a veterinarian and a Presbyterian missionary. He had arrived in Korea in 1916 and was deported by the Japanese authorities in 1920 for his involvement with the independence movement. He returned in 1958, however, and remained in Korea until his death in 1970.

45. See reports from British Consulate-General in Seoul on 4, 13, and 17 Mar. 1919, in NAUK, FO 262/1406, fol. 23–24, 30–37, 50–51; Annual Report, 1919, Korea, in FO 410/69, pp. 38–41; Lee, *Korean Nationalism*, 112–118.

46. Lee, *Korean Nationalism*, 122, citing the Japanese Gendarmerie Report. The rumor was also noted in Smith to Gulick, 16 Oct. 1919, PHS, RG 140, 16:14.

47. DOS to Morris, 31 Mar. 1919, USNA, RG 59, 895.00/582a, and Morris to DOS, 4 Apr. 1919, RG 59, 895.00/583. The U.S. minister in Tokyo confirmed that he had heard that story repeated from several sources, but reported that he had not seen it in print anywhere.

48. Reiner to Reinsch, 10 Mar. 1919, USNA, RG 256, 895.00/5.

PART III

1. Knock, *To End All Wars*, 227–245.
2. Thompson, *The Peace Conference*, 242.
3. MacMillan, *Paris 1919*, chaps. 20, 22.
4. Ibid., 459–478.

CHAPTER 7

1. Zaghlul, *Mudhakkirat*, 9:35–43; Sidqi, *Mudhakkirati*, 46–49; Gary to the secretary of state, 10 Mar. 1919, USNA, RG 256, 883.00/37. See also Kedourie, "Sa'd Zaghlul," 98–99.

2. Lashin, *Sa'd Zaghlul*, 128. In his memoirs, Zaghlul himself only mentions that the searchers found "several documents" that were "not important" (Zaghlul, *Mudhakkirat*, 9:36). It is hard to verify Lashin's version beyond doubt, but even if it is apocryphal, it reflects the close connection made in subsequent Egyptian interpretations of the 1919 Revolution between Zaghlul's political activities and Wilson's rhetoric.

3. "Arrest of Sa'd Basha," *Al-Ahram*, 10 Mar. 1919; "Student Demonstration," *Al-Ahram*, 11 Mar. 1919, and on days thereafter. On the revolt of the peasants, see Ellis Goldberg, "Peasants in Revolt, Egypt 1919," *International Journal of Middle East Studies* 24:2 (1992), 261–280.

4. See Political Intelligence Department [PID] reports in NAUK, FO 371/4373, pp. 35, 51. Also Gary to the secretary of state, 10, 11, and 16 Mar. 1919, USNA, RG 256, 883.00/37, pp. 41 and 53. The most detailed account of the protests and clashes of the 1919 Revolution can be found in the documentary collection *Khamsin 'Ama*, 188–224.

5. Rafi'i, *Thawrat Sanat 1919*, 5. These events were reported in the United States by the *Nation*, 2 Aug. 1919, 135. See also Vatikiotis, *Modern Egypt*, 266–267.

6. Zaghlul cited in Yunan Labib Rizk, "The Cataclysm," *Al-Ahram Weekly*, No. 454 (4–10 Nov. 1999); 'Abd al-'Azim Ramadan, *Thawrat 1919 fi Daw' Mudhakkirat Sa'd Zaghlul* [The 1919 Revolution in Light of Sa'd Zaghlul's Memoirs] (Cairo: Al-Hay'ah al-Misriyya al-'Amma lil-Kitab, 2002), 5.

7. Gary to the secretary of state, 12 Mar. 1919, USNA, RG 256, 883.00/41–1/2.

8. Farid et al. to Wilson, 15 Mar. 1919, LOC, WWP, series 5b, reel 395; petition signed by twenty-one Egyptian notables, enclosed in Gary to secretary of state, USNA, RG 256, 883.00/47; petition of 7 Apr. 1919, enclosed in USNA, RG 256, 883.00/98.

9. See petition signed by some one hundred residents of the town of Tanta, enclosed in Gary to secretary of state, 10 Mar. 1919, USNA, RG 256, FW 883.00/38; and several protest telegrams, dated 12–13 Mar. 1919, from the residents of various villages in Upper Egypt, in Gary to secretary of state, 14 Mar. 1919, RG 256, 883.00/46. Similar messages came from Egyptians abroad, e.g., Kadi, in the name of the "Egyptians of Manchester," to Wilson, 13 Mar. 1919, in Grew to Close, 14 Mar. 1919, USNA, RG 256, 883.00/42; Close to Kadi, 20 Mar. 1919, *PWW*, 56:122; petition from the Egyptian Association in Paris, in RG 256, 883.00/49.

10. Zaghlul, *Mudhakkirat*, 9:155, editor's note.

11. Enclosed in Gary to the secretary of state, 20 Apr. 1919, USNA, RG 59, 883.00/166. Also see Gary to the secretary of state, 24 Mar. 1919, RG 59, 883.00/128.

12. Enclosed in Gary to the secretary of state, 26 Mar. 1919, USNA, RG 59, 883.00/135. Also see "Voice of Egyptian Women," *Al-Ahram*, 16 Apr. 1919; "The Egyptian Woman, Yesterday and Today," *Al-Ahram*, 20 Apr. 1919.

13. Ramadan, *Thawrat 1919*, 5–6. For the relationship between nationalist and feminist commitments among Egyptian women, see Huda Sha'rawi, *Harem Years: The Memoirs of an Egyptian Feminist, 1879–1924*, ed. Margot Badran (New York: Feminist Press, 1987); and Margot Badran, *Feminists, Islam and Nation: Gender and the Making of Modern Egypt* (Princeton, N.J.: Princeton University Press, 1995).

14. Curzon to Balfour, 16 Mar. 1919, NAUK, FO 608/213, fol. 118–126.

15. Allenby to Balfour, 4 and 6 Apr. 1919, NAUK, FO 608/213, fol. 176–177, 179; Gary to the secretary of state, 7 Apr. 1919, USNA, RG 256, 883.00/91. Also see Terry, *Wafd*, 106–113.

16. Gary to the secretary of state, 10 Apr. 1919, USNA, RG 256, 883.00/93. British military intelligence kept close watch on the Egyptian delegation and its activities in Europe; see G.H.Q. to D.M.I., 13 Apr. 1919, NAUK, FO 608/213, fol. 198–199.

17. Zaghlul, *Mudhakkirat*, 9:68.

18. Ibid., 9:86.

19. Ibid., 9:92–93.

20. Allenby to Balfour, 15, 19, and 20 Apr. 1919, NAUK, FO 608/213, fol. 191, 197, 209.

21. Balfour to Wiseman, 17 Apr. 1919, William Wiseman Papers, Yale University Library, series I, box 9, fol. 204.

22. PID report, 17 Apr. 1919, NAUK, FO 371/4373, fol. 53. A Socialist party was formed in Egypt only in 1920, and though it joined the Communist International in 1922, until World War II it never had more than a few hundred members, the large majority of them foreign residents in Egypt. See Walter Z. Laqueur, *Communism and Nationalism in the Middle East*, 3d ed. (London: Routledge & Kegan Paul, 1961), 31–39.

23. Wiseman to House, 18 Apr. 1919, Edward Mandell House Papers, Yale University Library, series I, box 123, folder 4331. Allenby, too, was anxious to obtain U.S. recognition of the protectorate. See Allenby to Balfour, 4 Apr. 1919, NAUK, FO 608/213, fol. 176–177.

24. Gelfand, *The Inquiry*, 238, 255.

25. Charles R. Watson, Honorary Secretary of the Board of Foreign Missions of the United Presbyterian Church of North America, to the American Commission to Negotiate Peace, 18 Apr. 1919, USNA, RG 256, 883.00/105.

26. Gary to the secretary of state, 16 Mar. 1919, USNA, RG 256, 883.00/53; 20 Mar. 1919, RG 256, 883.00/63; 27 Mar. 1919, RG 256, 883.00/74; 10 Apr. 1919, RG 256, 883.00/94.

27. Gary to the secretary of state, 18 Mar. 1919, USNA, RG 256, 883.00/55; Lansing to Wilson, 21 Mar. 1919, *PWW*, 56:154–155.

28. Gary to secretary of state, 15 Apr. 1919, USNA, RG 256, 883.00/102; 16 Apr. 1919, RG 256, 883.00/103.

29. House diary, 18 Apr. 1919, *PWW*, 57:466; House to Balfour, 19 Apr. 1919, *PWW*, 57:499. On the crisis atmosphere at the peace conference in April 1919, see Walworth, *Wilson and His Peacemakers*, 277–301.

30. Deliberations of the Senate Committee on Foreign Relations, 12 Sept. 1919, cited in George E. Noble, "The Voice of Egypt," *Nation*, 3 Jan. 1920, 864.

31. The text of this instruction was signed by Wilson himself. See Wilson to Lansing, 21 Apr. 1919, and Lansing to Balfour, 21 Apr. 1919, USNA, RG 256, 883.00/107.

32. Balfour to Lansing, 23 Apr. 1919, USNA, RG 256, 883.00/111; Gary to secretary of state, 22 Apr. 1919, RG 256, 883.00/110.

33. Curzon to Balfour, 23 Apr. 1919, NAUK, FO 608/213, fol. 229–230.

34. George Ambrose Lloyd, *Egypt since Cromer* (London: Macmillan, 1933), 1:342.

35. Davis to secretary of state, 25 Apr. 1919, USNA, RG 256, 883.00/113; "President Wilson and Egypt," *Al-Watan*, Apr. 1919; "A Similarity of Ideals," *Egyptian Mail*, 24 Apr. 1919; and "The Recognition of the Protectorate," *La Bourse Egyptienne*, 24 Apr. 1919, enclosed in Gary to the secretary of state, 26 Apr. 1919, USNA, RG 256, FW 883.00/115.

36. Gary to the secretary of state, 26 Apr. 1919, USNA, RG 256, FW 883.00/115, and RG 59, 883.00/162. See also *Khamsin 'Ama*, 407–408; Vatikiotis, *Modern Egypt*, 268.

37. NAUK, FO 608/213, fol. 195; USNA, RG 256, 883.00/147, p. 38.

38. Muhammad 'Ali 'Alluba, *Dhikriyyat Ijtima'iyya wa-Siyasiyya* [Social and Political Memoirs] (Cairo: Al-Hay'a al-Misriyya al-'Amma lil-Kitab, 1988), 118; Ahmad

Lutfi Al-Sayyid, *Qissat Hayati* [The Story of My Life] (Cairo: Dar al-Hilal, 1962), 180–181; Lashin, *Sa'd Zaghlul*, 236. See also Ramadan, *Thawrat 1919*, 63; 'Abbas Mahmud 'Aqqad, *Sa'd Zaghlul: Sirah wa-Tahiyya* [Sa'd Zaghlul: A Biography and Salute] (Cairo: Dar al-Shuruq, 1975), 268–271; Husayn Fawzi Najjar, *Sa'd Zaghlul: al-Za'im wal-Za'ama* [Sa'd Zaghlul: The Leader and His Leadership] (Cairo: Maktabat Madbūlī, 1986), 66–67; Balfour to Curzon, 5 May 1919, NAUK, FO 608/213, fol. 277. Zaghlul stopped writing in his diary between 13 Apr. and 20 Sept. 1919, so his immediate reaction to the news of the U.S. recognition of the protectorate was not recorded there.

39. Haykal, *Mudhakkirat*, 1:81.

40. 'Abd al-Rahman Fahmi, *Mudhakkirat 'Abd al-Rahman Fahmi: Yawmiyyat Misr al-Siyasiyya* [The Memoirs of 'Abd al-Rahman Fahmi: A Diary of Egyptian Politics], 2 vols., ed. Yunan Labib Rizq (Cairo: Al-Hay'a al-Misriyya lil-Kitab, 1988–1993), 1:273.

41. Farid, *Mudhakkirati*, 432–433.

42. Ramadan, *Thawrat 1919*, 64.

43. See, e.g., Zaghlul's interview in *l'Humanité*, 26 Apr. 1919, summarized in NAUK, FO 608/213, fol. 238–239; extract from the *New York Herald*, 4 May 1919, in FO 608/213, fol. 273; Derby to high commissioner, 3 May 1919, FO 608/213, fol. 270; Derby to Curzon, 8 May 1919, FO 608/213, fol. 309–310. Also see 'Alluba, *Dhikriyyat*, 119–120.

44. Sidqi, *Mudhakkirati*, 50–51.

45. Egyptian Association in Great Britain to U.S. ambassador in Paris, 25 Apr. 1919, USNA, RG 256, 883.00/114. Also see their petition in RG 256, 883.00/121; and Egyptian Association in Paris to American Mission, 30 June 1919, RG 256, 883.00/129. Egyptian petitions were circulated to all the delegations present at the peace conference and are found, for example, in the records of the Chinese delegation (WJB, RG 03–37, box 27, folder 2).

46. Enclosed in vice consul in charge to the secretary of state, 29 Apr. 1919, USNA, RG 59 883.00/179.

47. Enclosed in Gary to the secretary of state, 5 May 1919, USNA, RG 59, 883.00/181.

48. Allenby telegram, 29 Apr. 1919, NAUK, FO 608/213, fol. 256–257; Gary to the secretary of state, 26 Apr. 1919, USNA, RG 59, 883.00/162; and 26 Apr. 1919, RG 256, FW 883.00/115. This assessment was shared by the British Foreign Office. See PID report, 24 Apr. 1919, NAUK, FO 371/4373, fol. 56.

49. Tuck to the secretary of state, 28 Apr. 1919, USNA, RG 59, 883.00/151.

50. Zaghlul to Lloyd George, 12 May 1919, NAUK, FO 608/213, fol. 353.

51. Close to Zaghlul, 24 Apr. and 9 June 1919, in Egyptian Delegation to the Peace Conference, *Collection of Official Correspondence from November 11, 1918 to July 14, 1919* (Paris: Published by the Delegation, 1919), 55, 61.

52. Zaghlul to Wilson, 18 June 1919, *PWW*, 61:8.

53. This publication, titled *Collection of Official Correspondence from November 11, 1918 to July 14, 1919*, was widely distributed to universities, media outlets, and public figures in the English-speaking world.

54. Letter to British House of Commons, 14 July 1919, in USNA, RG 256, 883.00/147. Part IV, Section VI of the Versailles Treaty (Articles 147–154) established the status of Egypt as a British protectorate.

55. *Egyptian Gazette*, n.d., enclosed in USNA, RG 256, 883.00/142.

56. "Egypt and America," *Wadi al-Nil*, 13 Sept. 1919, in USNA, RG 256, 883.00/157; *Egyptian Gazette*, 10 Oct. 1919, in RG 256, 883.00/142; Gary to the secretary of state, 24 Nov. 1919, *Foreign Relations of the United States* [*FRUS*], 1919, 2:206. For the British perspective on this incident, see *BDFA*, series G, part II, 1:321–322; also see Lashin, *Sa'd Zaghlul*, 238. Article 147 of the Treaty of Versailles affirmed German recognition of the British protectorate over Egypt, and thus the issue was part of the Senate deliberations regarding the treaty.

57. "Egypt and the American Senate," *Misr*, 13 Sept. 1919, *Al-Ahali*, 10 Sept. 1919, enclosed in Gary to the secretary of state, 24 Nov. 1919, USNA, RG 256, 883.00/157.

58. On the "standard of civilization" see Gerrit W. Gong, *The Standard of 'Civilization' in International Society* (Oxford: Clarendon, 1984).

59. "Egypt and the American Senate," *Misr*, 13 Sept. 1919, enclosed in Gary to the secretary of state, 24 Nov. 1919, USNA, RG 256, 883.00/157.

60. On Folk see Steven L. Piott, *Holy Joe: Joseph W. Folk and the Missouri Idea* (Columbia: University of Missouri Press, 1998).

61. *Treaty of Peace with Germany: Hearings before the Committee on Foreign Relations, United States Senate* (Washington, D.C.: U.S. Government Printing Office, 1919), hearing on 23 Aug. 1919, 655 and 671.

62. Zaghlul, *Mudhakkirat*, 9:124; *BDFA*, series G, part II, 1:321. Also on the Senate hearings, see Ambrosius, *Woodrow Wilson and the American Diplomatic Tradition: The Treaty Fight in Perspective* (Cambridge: Cambridge University Press, 1987), 169–171. Folk, it should be noted, did not do this work free of charge. In 1926, three years after his death, his widow would arrive in Egypt to sue the Wafd for more than $600,000 "for the services rendered by her husband on behalf of the Egyptian cause." Following a spirited courtroom debate in which the defense argued that, since the United States' government never intervened effectively in Egypt's favor the Wafd owed Folk nothing, the court noted that Folk nevertheless rendered a service to the Egyptian delegation and required the Wafd to pay his widow $55,000. The decision was upheld on appeal, but with the party's coffers empty, it is doubtful that the money was ever paid. See Yunan Labib Rizk, "Mrs Faulk [*sic*] Comes to Cairo," *Al-Ahram Weekly*, No. 550 (6–12 Sept. 2001).

63. Zaghlul, *Mudhakkirat*, 9:104.

64. Ibid., 9:105–111.

65. Zaghlul to Polk, 11 Sept. 1919, USNA, RG 256, 883.00/137; Davis to the secretary of state, 26 Nov. 1919, RG 59, 883.00/213.

66. Mahmoud [Mahmud] to the secretary of state, 26 Nov. 1919, USNA, RG 59, 883.00/214; Haykal, *Mudhakkirat*, 1:83.

67. See Noble, "The Voice of Egypt," 861–864, and further articles in the *Nation* on 3 May 1919, 715; 2 Aug. 1919, 135; 6 Dec. 1919, 705; and 3 Jan. 1920, 846; statement by Frank Walsh, chairman of the American Committee on Irish Independence, *PWW*, 62:324–326.

68. *PWW*, 64:49; Zaghlul, *Mudhakkirat*, 9:153–154; Owen to Lansing, *FRUS*, 1919, 2:207–209; also see Lindsay to Curzon, 21 Aug. 1919, *BDFA*, series G, part II, 1:320–321,

where mention is made of a speech by the prominent progressive Senator William Borah, who criticized British conduct in Egypt.

69. Cablegram from Zaghlul to Wilson, 23 Nov. 1919, USNA, RG 59, 883.00/212. This communication was reported in the *New York Times*, 26 Nov. 1919, 13.

70. Zaghlul, *Mudhakkirat*, 9:148–149.

71. Gary reported on the strikes and protests that preceded Milner's arrival in Gary to secretary of state, 22 Oct. 1919, USNA, RG 256, 883.00/145. He received numerous telegrams from Egyptians protesting against the Milner commission and emphasizing that Egypt demanded complete independence. See Gary to secretary of state, 10 and 14 Oct. 1919, RG 256, 883.00/141–142. Also see John D. McIntyre, Jr., *The Boycott of the Milner Mission: A Study in Egyptian Nationalism* (New York: Lang, 1985), 200–201; Daly, "The British Occupation," 249–250.

72. Quoted in *Egyptian Gazette*, 10 Oct. 1919, enclosed in USNA, RG 256, 883.00/142.

73. Zaghlul to Curzon, 9 Dec. 1919, *BDFA*, series G, part II, 1:359–363.

Chapter 8

1. MacMillan, *Paris 1919*, 403.

2. See, for example, *Andhrapatrika*, 20 Nov. 1918; *Manorama*, 22 Nov. 1918; *Kistnapatrika*, 23 Nov. 1918; all in "Madras Press Abstract, 1918," IOR, L/R/5/125, pp. 1710–1711.

3. *Andhrapatrika*, 2 Dec. 1918, in "Madras Press Abstract, 1918," IOR, L/R/5/125, p. 1729.

4. Chelmsford to Montagu, 25 Feb. 1919, NMML, Chelmsford Papers, roll 4.

5. Montagu to Chelmsford, 27 Feb. 1919, NMML, Chelmsford Papers, roll 4.

6. Montagu to Chelmsford, 18 Feb. 1919, NAI, Montagu Papers, roll 1.

7. Montagu to Chelmsford, 22 Jan. 1919, NAI, Montagu Papers, roll 1.

8. Montagu to Chelmsford, 1 May 1919, NAI, Montagu Papers, roll 1. On the evolution of the rules and norms of external and internal self-determination and the distinctions between them, see Antonio Cassese, *Self-Determination of Peoples: A Legal Reappraisal* (Cambridge: Cambridge University Press, 1995), esp. 67–140.

9. *Letters of Lokamanya Tilak*, ed. M. D. Vidwans (Poona: Kesari Prakashan, 1966), 189–196. The book in question was Valentine Chirol, *Indian Unrest* (London: Macmillan, 1910). Tilak's attempts to obtain a visa are reflected in Tilak to Viceroy's Office, 4 and 5 Apr. 1918; Montagu to Chelmsford, 11 Apr. 1918; Tilak to Private Secretary to His Excellency the Viceroy, 12 Apr. 1918, all in NAI, Home/Political, A Files, June 1918, nos. 194–212.

10. Rao, "Tilak's Attitude"; see also T. V. Parvate, *Bal Gangadhar Tilak: A Narrative and Interpretive Review of His Life, Career and Contemporary Events* (Ahmedabad, India: Navajivan, 1958), 447.

11. By the time that the full Indian deputation was allowed to come to London, in April 1919, the possibility for effective action vis-à-vis the peace conference had passed.

12. Memorandum, dated London, 11 Dec. 1918, enclosed in Tilak's letter to Khaparde, 18 Dec. 1918, NAI, G. S. Khaparde Papers [KP], file 1, pp. 1–2.

13. Lajpat Rai, "A Hindu Under-Secretary for India," *Nation*, 1 Feb. 1919, 163.

14. Tilak to Khaparde, London, 16 Jan. 1919, NAI, KP, file 2, p. 110.

15. Tilak to Lloyd George, 2 Jan. 1919, LOC, WWP, series 5f, reel 446.

16. Manisha Dikholkar, *The History of India's Freedom Struggle in Britain: British Reaction and Responses (1885–1920)* (Bombay: Himalaya, 1996), 192–194; G. P. Pradhan and A. K. Bhagwat, *Lokamanya Tilak: A Biography* (Bombay: Jaico, 1959), 327; Singh, *American Attitude*, 224.

17. Tilak to Wilson, 2 Jan. 1919, LOC, WWP, series 5f, reel 446.

18. *Self-Determination for India* (London: India Home Rule League, 1918).

19. See Lajpat Rai to Hardikar, 21 Feb. 1919, where the former reports selling some copies of the pamphlet in Boston. Lajpat Rai, *Selected Correspondence*, 122.

20. *Self-Determination for India*, 5–7.

21. Ibid., 6–8.

22. Ibid., 8–11.

23. Ibid., 11–14.

24. Close to Tilak, 14 Jan. 1919, quoted in *Mahratta*, 19 Oct. 1919.

25. Wilson to Tumulty, 27 June 1919, *PWW*, 61:291.

26. Foreign Office memo, 12 Feb. 1919, NAUK, FO 608/211, fol. 124–125. See also Pradhan and Bhagwat, *Lokamanya Tilak*, 323, on Tilak's attempts to travel to Paris; and Rao, "Tilak's Attitude," 174–175.

27. See discussion in *Mahratta*, 19 Oct. and 9 Nov. 1919.

28. Tilak to D. W. Gokhale, dated London, 23 Jan. 1919, NAI, KP, file 1, pp. 4–7. Emphasis in the original.

29. Burma Provincial Congress Committee [PCC] to secretary of AICC, 15 Jan. 1919, NMML, AICC Papers, file 7, pp. 3–5; Secretary of Bihar and Orissa PCC to secretary of AICC, 1 Feb. 1919, ibid., file no. 6, p. 171; Secretary of Bengal PCC to secretary of AICC, 7 Feb. 1919, ibid., file no. 6, p. 183; Secretary of Madras PCC to AICC, 13 Feb. 1919, ibid., file no. 6, p. 193.

30. Tilak to D. W. Gokhale, dated London, 23 Jan. 1919, NAI, KP, file 1, pp. 4–7. Also see Pradhan and Bhagwat, *Lokamanya Tilak*, 324; Rao, "Tilak's Attitude," 175.

31. Tilak to D. W. Gokhale, dated London, 6 Feb. 1919, NAI, KP, file 1, p. 10; unsigned memorandum entitled "How We Get On II," enclosed in Tilak's letter from London, 20 Mar. 1919, ibid., pp. 13–14; memorandum entitled "How We Are Getting On" by B. S. Moonje, with the words "with BG Tilak's compliments" added in the margin, dated London, 18 Sept. 1919, ibid., pp. 45–47.

32. Tilak to D. W. Gokhale, dated London, 23 Jan. 1919, NAI, KP, file 1, pp. 4–7; unsigned memorandum entitled "How We Get On II," enclosed in Tilak's letter from London, 20 Mar. 1919, ibid., pp. 13–14.

33. Tilak to D. W. Gokhale, dated London, 6 Feb. 1919, NAI, KP, file 1, pp. 8–10.

34. Dutasta to Sir Maurice Hankey, Secretary of the British Delegation, 22 Feb. 1919; and Hankey to Dutasta, 28 Feb. 1919, NAUK, FO 608/211, fol. 128–137.

35. Tilak to D. W. Gokhale, 3 Apr. 1919, in *Selected Documents of Lokamanya Tilak*, 3:179.

36. Judith M. Brown, *Gandhi's Rise to Power: Indian Politics, 1915–1922* (Cambridge: Cambridge University Press, 1972), 160.

37. Based on a survey of the dailies *Amrita Bazar Patrika* (Calcutta), *New India* (Madras), and *Tribune* (Lahore).

38. Brown, *Gandhi's Rise*, 160; Gandhi to Chelmsford, 24 Feb. and 11 Mar. 1919, NMML, Chelmsford Papers, roll 10. Also see R. Kumar, ed., *Essays on Gandhian Politics: The Rowlatt Satyagraha of 1919* (Oxford: Clarendon, 1971). *Satyagraha* is a Hindi term that literally connotes the devotion to or pursuit of truth, and was the name that Gandhi gave to his philosophy and method of nonviolent resistance. For a detailed treatment see Joan V. Bondurant, *Conquest of Violence: The Gandhian Philosophy of Conflict*. New rev. ed. (Princeton, N.J.: Princeton University Press, 1988).

39. See K. L. Tuteja, "Jallianwala Bagh: A Critical Juncture in the Indian National Movement," *Social Scientist* 25 (1997), 25–61. Twenty-one years later, on 13 Mar. 1940, an Indian revolutionary named Udham Singh shot and killed Sir Michael O'Dwyer, who had been the lieutenant governor of Punjab at the time of the massacre, in Caxton Hall, London. Singh was convicted for murder and hanged that summer.

40. Malaviya to Lloyd George, Lord Sinha, and the Maharaja of Bikanir, Resolutions of the Bombay session of AICC, Apr. 1919, NMML, AICC Papers, file no. 5, pp. 97–99; IOR, V/26/262/9 (Hunter Committee Report), 7:3; *Report of the Committee Appointed by the Government of India to Investigate the Disturbances in the Punjab, etc.* (London: His Majesty's Stationery Office, 1920), 57.

41. M. K. Gandhi, *Hind Swaraj*, 5th English ed. (1908; 5th ed., Madras: Ganesh, 1922), 6, 119.

42. V. S. Srinivasa Sastri to S. G. Vaze, 28 Nov. 1918, NAI, Sastri Papers, serial no. 278. For more on Sastri, see Ray T. Smith, "V. S. Srinivasa Sastri and the Moderate Style in Indian Politics," *South Asia* 2 (1972), 81–100. On Andrews (1871–1940), see Hugh Tinker, *The Ordeal of Love: C. F. Andrews and India* (New Delhi: Oxford University Press, 1979). On his relationship with Gandhi, see David M. Gracie, ed., *Gandhi and Charlie: The Story of a Friendship, as Told through the Letters and Writings of Mohandas K. Gandhi and Rev'd Charles Freer Andrews* (Cambridge, Mass.: Cowley, 1989).

43. M. K. Gandhi to C. F. Andrews, 25 Feb. 1919, in *The Collected Works of Mahatma Gandhi* (Delhi: Publications Division, Ministry of Information and Broadcasting, Government of India, 1958–), 15:104–105.

44. Speech on Satyagraha, Madras, 20 Mar. 1919, in Gandhi, *Collected Works*, 15:142; An Address to the Third Plenary Session of the Peace Conference, 14 Feb. 1919, *PWW*, 55:175.

45. An Address in the City Auditorium at Pueblo, Colorado, 25 Sept. 1919, *PWW*, 63:505.

46. See Taraknath Das to Bainbridge Colby, 6 Sept. 1920, USNA, RG 59, 845.00/250. On Lajpat Rai's relationship with Du Bois, see Dhanki, *Lajpat Rai*, 200. Smedley would later would travel to China and spend much time with Mao Zedong and the Chinese Communists, on whom she reported in the Western press and wrote several sympathetic books. On her fascinating life, see Ruth Price, *The Lives of Agnes Smedley* (New York: Oxford University Press, 2005). Chap. 3 deals with her involvement with Indian nationalists in New York City.

47. Alan Raucher, "American Anti-Imperialists and the Pro-India Movement, 1900–1932," *Pacific Historical Review* 18:1 (1974), 84–85.

48. Dhanki, *Lajpat Rai*, 189–190; *New York Times*, 22 June 1919, 12, reports on De Valera's visit in New York City.

49. Materials enclosed in letter from the U.S. correspondent of the *Daily Telegraph* to Louis Tracy, head of the British Bureau of Information in New York. This letter was forwarded in May 1919 to the Foreign Office in London and from there to the India Office. IOR, L/PJ/6/1568. Also see Dhanki, *Lajpat Rai*, 179–183, 201–203.

50. 29 Jan. 1920, L/PJ/6/1641. The same number also includes further dispatches from R. C. Lindsay to Lord Curzon on Indian propaganda efforts in the United States, which were supported by Hearst papers and those owned by Sinn Fein, and on ways to counteract them with British information.

51. Malone was a colorful character. In the 1920s, he would become a well-known international divorce lawyer and continue to champion liberal causes; his best-known court appearance would be as Clarence Darrow's partner on the defense team in the 1925 Scopes Trial, where he delivered a memorable oration. He later became an entertainment lawyer and an actor and played the role of Winston Churchill in the 1943 Hollywood propaganda film *A Mission to Moscow*. See Malone's obituary in *New York Times*, 6 Oct. 1950, 25.

52. "Statement of Mr. Dudley Field Malone," in *Treaty of Peace with Germany*, 750–756.

53. Tilak to Vidwans, 18 Sept. 1919, in Vidwans, *Letters of Lokamanya Tilak*, 280.

54. Memorandum by B. S. Moonje, London, 18 Sept. 1919, NAI, KP, file 1, pp. 45–47; *New York Times*, 19 Aug. 1919, 13; and 30 Aug. 1919, 2.

55. *Mahratta*, 14 Dec. 1919, cited in Parvate, *Tilak*, 463–464; also see 489–490.

56. Stanley A. Wolpert, *Tilak and Gokhale: Revolution and Reform in the Making of Modern India* (Berkeley: University of California Press, 1962), 293–294; Dhananjay Keer, *Lokamanya Tilak: Father of the Indian Freedom Struggle*. 2d ed. (Bombay: Popular Prakashan, 1969), 442–443.

57. Lajpat Rai, "Farewell to America," in *Writings and Speeches*, 1:393–394.

58. Appeal dated 25 July 1919 and published in the *Tribune*, 4 Sept. 1919, in Lajpat Rai, *Writings and Speeches*, 1:317–323.

59. Published Dec. 1919; see Lajpat Rai, *Writings and Speeches*, 1:345–347.

60. Dhanki, *Lajpat Rai*, 203–207.

61. "Long Live Lalaji," *Young India* (Ahmedabad, 22 Nov. 1928), 388.

62. Ainslie T. Embree, "The Function of Gandhi in Indian Nationalism," in *The Meanings of Gandhi*, ed. Paul F. Power (Manoa: University of Hawaii Press, 1971), 67.

63. Peter Heehs, *India's Freedom Struggle, 1857–1947: A Short History* (New Delhi: Oxford University Press, 1988), 90–94.

64. For one perspective on this process, see Ravinder Kumar, "From Swaraj to Purna Swaraj: Nationalist Politics in the City of Bombay, 1920–32," in *Congress and the Raj: Facets of the Indian Struggle, 1917–1947*, ed. D. A. Low (London: Heinemann, 1977).

CHAPTER 9

1. Memorandum of a Conversation at an Audience with the President of the United States, Woodrow Wilson, at the White House, 26 Nov. 1918, *PWW*, 57:632–634;

Koo, *Memoir*, 2:173–175. For a detailed study of Koo's diplomacy see Stephen G. Craft, *V. K. Wellington Koo and the Emergence of Modern China* (Lexington: University Press of Kentucky, 2004).

2. Bruce A. Elleman, "Did Woodrow Wilson Really Betray the Republic of China at Versailles?" *American Asian Review* 13:1 (1995), 2–10; Koo, *Memoir*, 2:162–163, 177; Clemenceau to Lu, 14 May 1919, WJB, RG 03–37, box 14, folder 3.

3. Wang, "Looking Back," 104.

4. On the origin and nature of the German rights in Shandong Province, see John E. Schrecker, *Imperialism and Chinese Nationalism: Germany in Shantung* (Cambridge, Mass.: Harvard University Press, 1971).

5. The other Japanese demands in the Twenty-One Demands included a special role for it in Manchuria and Inner Mongolia; joint operation of China's coal and steel industry; nonalienation of coastal areas to third powers; and the admission of Japanese advisers to various Chinese government offices. Hsü, *The Rise of Modern China*, 580, 597–598; Roy Watson Curry, *Woodrow Wilson and Far Eastern Policy, 1913–1921* (New York: Bookman, 1957), 264.

6. *Papers Relating to the Foreign Relations of the United States: The Paris Peace Conference, 1919* (Washington, D.C.: U.S. Government Printing Office, 1943), 3:754–757; *Canyu Ouzhou heping*, 768–769; E. T. Williams, "Recollections" (unpublished typescript), E. T. Williams Papers, Bancroft Library, University of California, Berkeley, 223–225.

7. Williams to Long, 21 Feb. 1919, Williams Papers, box 1, folder "Outgoing Correspondence."

8. "Bali huiyi zhi zhongguo wenti" [The Chinese Question at the Paris Conference], *Shenbao*, 4 Feb. 1919.

9. Wunsz King, *China at the Peace Conference in 1919* (Jamaica, N.Y.: St. John's University Press, 1961), 3. King was a secretary to the Chinese delegation at the peace conference.

10. See Koo's interview with Williams, 21 Apr. 1919, in the Papers of V. K. Wellington Koo, Rare Book and Manuscript Library, Columbia University, box 1; Chi, "China and Unequal Treaties," 52.

11. Williams memo dated 9 Apr. 1919, in "Recollections," 284–285.

12. MacMillan, *Paris 1919*, 331.

13. Dom Pierre-Célestin Lou Tseng-tsiang, *Souvenirs et pensées: Lettre à mes amis de Grande-Bretagne et d'Amérique* (1948; rpt., Paris: Dominique Martin Morin, 1993), 60; Ray Stannard Baker, *What Wilson Did at Paris* (Garden City, N.Y., 1922), 97.

14. Chinese Delegation to the Paris Peace Conference, *The Claim of China: Submitting for Abrogation by the Peace Conference the Treaties and Notes Made and Exchanged by and between China and Japan on May 25, 1915, as a Transaction Arising out of and Connected with the War between the Allied and Associated States and the Central Powers* (Paris: Impr. de Vaugirard, 1919).

15. Wilson to Lansing, 7 Feb. 1919, *PWW*, 54:548; Lansing to Polk, 11 Feb. 1919, Long Papers, box 186. An account of the Japanese machinations in Beijing, often referred to as the "Obata incident" after the Japanese minister in Beijing, is provided in Fifield, *Woodrow Wilson and the Far East*, 145–148. For a Chinese nationalist

perspective on the same events, see Min-ch'ien T. Z. Tyau, *China Awakened* (New York: Macmillan, 1922), 318–321.

16. See the comments by Lloyd George and Clemenceau during the discussions of the Shandong question in the Supreme Council on 22 April, in Paul Mantoux, *The Deliberations of the Council of Four (March 24–June 28, 1919): Notes of the Official Interpreter*, 2 vols., trans. and ed. Arthur S. Link with Manfred F. Boemeke (Princeton, N.J.: Princeton University Press, 1992), 1:319–322. By that point, with Orlando's departure, the Council of Four had been reduced to three.

17. *Canyu Ouzhou heping*, 771.

18. See "Ishii's Plea Stirs Western Senators: They Quickly Reject the Proposal of No Racial Discrimination as a League Rule," *New York Times*, 16 Mar. 1919, 3; "Council Opposes Racial Equality: Anti-Japanese Resolution May Be Cabled to Peace Conference," *Los Angeles Times*, 11 Apr. 1919, 12.

19. The definitive work on this episode is Naoko Shimazu, *Japan, Race and Equality: The Racial Equality Proposal of 1919* (London: Routledge, 1998). See also Paul Gordon Lauren, "Human Rights in History: Diplomacy and Racial Equality at the Paris Peace Conference," *Diplomatic History* 3 (1978), 257–278.

20. A Memorandum by Ray Stannard Baker, 29 Apr. 1919, *PWW*, 58:230–231; Walworth, *Wilson and His Peacemakers*, 277–301.

21. Mantoux, *Deliberations of the Council of Four*, 1:329–336.

22. Williams, "Recollections," 255–257; Lansing-Chinda memorandum of conversation, 26 Apr. 1919, in Baker Papers (Princeton), box 9, folder "April 26, 1919."

23. The experts' report, dated 24 Apr. 1919, is found in WWP, series 5b, reel 402.

24. *Canyu Ouzhou heping*, 774–777; Wang, "Looking Back," 107.

25. Williams to Long, 28 Apr. 1919, Breckenridge Long Papers, Library of Congress, box 186.

26. House to Wilson, 29 Apr. 1919, *PWW*, 58:228–229.

27. See the final discussions of the question in the Supreme Council, 28–30 April, in Mantoux, *Deliberations of the Council of Four*, 1:399–408, 425–427.

28. Williams, "Recollections," 289; Hornbeck to Williams, 19 Dec. 1941, Hornbeck Papers, box 443, folder "Williams, E. T."

29. Koo to John Bassett Moore, 21 May 1919, cited in Stephen G. Craft, "John Bassett Moore, Robert Lansing, and the Shandong Question," *Pacific Historical Review* 66:2 (1997), 239.

30. E. T. Williams to Breckinridge Long, 5 May 1919, LOC, Long Papers, box 186; Williams, "Recollections," 289–290.

31. Lu to Council of Three, 4 May 1919, NAUK, FO 608/210, fol. 347–348; Hornbeck Papers, box 328, folder "Paris Peace Conference: Chinese Delegation Protest, May 4."

32. Hornbeck Papers, box 328, folder "PPC: China's Statement to the Press, May 6, 1919."

33. Williams, a keen observer, described the dynamics of the American commission: The president was "overworked"; House "seems to flock by himself"; and the other three peace commissioners met every day, but "their advice was usually ignored." Williams to Long, 5 May 1919, Long Papers, box 186.

34. Enclosed in Bliss to Williams, 1 May 1919, Williams Papers, box 1, folder "Bliss, Tasker."

35. Lansing, *Peace Negotiations*, 257–263. See also Curry, *Woodrow Wilson and Far Eastern Policy*, 277; and Fifield, *Woodrow Wilson and the Far East*, 298–301.

36. Hornbeck to House, 5 May 1919, Hornbeck Papers, box 207, folder "House, Colonel E. M."

37. Williams to Long, 5 May 1919, LOC, Long Papers, box 186.

38. Ibid., 3 July 1919, LOC, Long Papers, box 62.

39. Reinsch to DOS, 2 May 1919, in Williams, "Recollections," 276–277.

40. Reinsch to DOS, 3 May 1919, in ibid., 277.

41. Paul Reinsch, *An American Diplomat in China* (Garden City, N.Y.: Doubleday, 1922), 361, 364–367.

42. An interview with an alumnus of the National University of Beijing is in Tsi C. Wang, *The Youth Movement in China* (New York: New Republic, 1927), 161–162.

43. Wang, *The Youth Movement*, 163–164. On the role of Tiananmen as a central locus of protest in modern Chinese history, see Jonathan D. Spence, "Tiananmen," in his *Chinese Roundabout: Essays in History and Culture* (New York: Norton, 1992), 293–303.

44. Vera Schwarcz, *The Chinese Enlightenment: Intellectual Trends and the Legacy of the May Fourth Movement of 1919* (Berkeley: University of California Press, 1986), 14–15.

45. Chow, *The May Fourth Movement*, 99–115.

46. "Beijing xuejie zhi da judong" [A Great Movement among Beijing Students], *Dagongbao*, 5 May 1919, 42.

47. Report of U.S. military attaché in Beijing, 5 May 1919, in Williams, "Recollections," 283. For a full, detailed account of the events, see Chow, *The May Fourth Movement*, chaps. 5–6.

48. From "The Students' Strike: An Explanation," a leaflet published by the Shanghai Student Union in English in 1919, preserved in the Missions Library of Union Theological Seminary, New York, as quoted in Kiang Wen-han, *The Chinese Student Movement* (New York: King's Crown, 1948), 36. This publication was also used in the campaigns of Chinese students abroad; e.g., it was reproduced in a pamphlet published by the Publicity Bureau of the Chinese Students in the University of Illinois, entitled *Is Japan a Burning Menace to the World's Peace?* (7 Aug. 1919).

49. Hu Suh [Hu Shi], "Intellectual China in 1919," *Chinese Social and Political Science Review* 4:4 (Dec. 1919), 346–347.

50. There is a large body of scholarship on the May Fourth movement and its importance in the history of modern China. Chow Tse-tsung, *The May Fourth Movement: Intellectual Revolution in Modern China* (Cambridge, Mass.: Harvard University Press, 1960) is still the most detailed account of the events and context of the movement. A more recent account, Rana Mitter, *A Bitter Revolution: China's Struggle with the Modern World* (New York: Oxford University Press, 2004), places the movement at the center of China's struggle with modernity. Much of the literature uses the term "May Fourth movement" to mean a broad range of cultural, intellectual, and literary movements in China from 1915 to 1923, including literary reform, feminism, interest in science

and democracy, and ideologies such as anarchism, liberalism, and communism. See, e.g., Benjamin I. Schwartz, ed., *Reflections on the May Fourth Movement: A Symposium* (Cambridge, Mass.: Harvard University Press, 1972); Schwarcz, *The Chinese Enlightenment*; Charlotte Furth, "Intellectual Change: From the Reform Movement to the May Fourth Movement, 1895–1920," in *The Cambridge History of China*, vol. 12, *Republican China 1912–1949, Part I*, ed. John K. Fairbank (Cambridge: Cambridge University Press, 1983). Joseph T. Chen, however, has argued for distinguishing the largely political character of the movement itself from the cultural and intellectual trends of the broader "new culture movement." See his "The May Fourth Movement Redefined," *Modern Asian Studies* 4:1 (1970), 63–81.

51. Bonsal, *Suitors and Suppliants*, 242–243.

52. "The Chinese in Tokyo" to M. Edmond Bapst, French ambassador in Tokyo, 7 May 1919. The petition is attached to Bapst to Pichon, 8 May 1919, Archives du Ministère des Affaires Etrangères, Quai d'Orsay, Paris [MAE], Correspondance Politique et Commerciale, 1914–1940, A Paix, vol. 322 (Japon—conditions politiques de la Paix), fol. 29–36.

53. The Guomindang attempted to reunify the country in the "northern expedition" of 1926–1927, but failed to stamp out the power of regional warlords, and China was not effectively unified until after the communist victory in 1949.

54. Fung, "Struggle over the Constitution," 239ff., 265–268.

55. Liang Chi-chao, "China & the Shantung Settlement, A Tragic Disappointment," *Manchester Guardian*, 16 June 1919, Hornbeck Papers, box 382, folder "Shantung: Misc."

56. Hornbeck memo, Hornbeck Papers, box 328, folder "PPC: Chinese Petitions."

57. On Loy Chang, see "Large Audience at 'Chinese Night,' " in the MIT student paper, the *Tech* 33:80 (1 Dec. 1913). Chang "spoke very eloquently on the cosmopolitan ideal" and said that "no nation today could live by itself, since the nations of the world are physically bound together by modern means of rapid transportation and communication."

58. Chinese Patriotic Committee in New York City, *Might or Right? The Fourteen Points and the Disposition of Kiao-Chau* (May 1919). Other pamphlets produced by the Chinese Patriotic Committee (the secretary of the committee was listed as K. P. Wang) included *China versus Japan* by Ge-Zay Wood in February 1919 and *China's Claims at the Peace Table* in March.

59. Chinese Patriotic Committee, *Might or Right?* 4, 6.

60. Ibid., 7–8.

61. E.g., petition from Chang'an Lawyers' Association in Qingdao, calling on the peace delegates to "fight strongly" and reject the powers' decision on Shandong, 25 June 1919, WJB, RG 03–37, box 9, folder 1; and Chinese Returned Students from Europe and America in Canton to French consul in Shameen, n.d., MAE, A Paix, vol. 322, fol. 48–51. The People of Xiangyin County vowed to risk all to fight Japanese "bullying" on Qingdao; People of Xiangyin County, Hunan Province, to MFA, 13 June 1919, WJB, RG 03–37, box 9, folder 1. The governor of Yunnan Province, Tang Jiyao, also protested the decision to French premier Clemenceau and expressed his hope for justice. Tang to Clemenceau, 19 May 1919, Fond Clemenceau, 6 N 75, dossier "Chine," in Service Historique de l'Armée de Terre [SHAT], Vincennes.

62. Gu Weijun to MFA, 12 Sept. 1919, WJB, 03–12, 8:3.

63. Hornbeck to Wilson, 5 June 1919; Hornbeck to Lansing, 6 June 1919; Wilson to Lansing, 12 June 1919; Lansing to Wilson, 16 June 1919; Wilson to Lansing, 20 June 1919, all in Hornbeck Papers, box 382, folder "Shantung: Decision at the Peace Conference."

64. Koo conversation with House, Hôtel Crillon, 22 May 1919, Koo Papers, box 1; *Canyu Ouzhou heping*, 780–784. See also memorandum by William Dennis Cullen, legal adviser to the Chinese government, advising not to sign unless reservations are entered; 28 May 1919, WJB, 03–37, box 13, folder 2.

65. *Canyu Ouzhou heping*, 786–790; Wang, "Looking Back," 107–108; Mantoux, *Deliberations of the Council of Four*, 2:551–552.

66. Koo to Lansing, 25 June 1919, and Koo to Wilson, 27 June 1919, WJB, RG 03–37, box 22, folder 4; Chinese Delegations Press Statement, 28 June 1919, Baker Papers (Princeton), box 10, folder "June 28, 1919."

67. Wang, "Looking Back," 108.

68. See, for example, Consul General in Canada to Foreign Ministry, 16 Aug. 1919, WJB, RG 03–37, box 10, folder 1; Consul General in San Francisco to Foreign Ministry, 6 Nov. 1919, WJB, RG 03–37, box 10, folder 2.

69. Fung, "Struggle over the Constitution," 256–259; Zhang, *China in the International System*, 93.

70. Lu and Wang to Wilson, 28 June 1919, WWP, series 5b, reel 413; Lu and Wang to Clemenceau, 28 June 1919, WWP, series 6j, reel 464.

71. Wang, "Looking Back," 108–109; Zhang, *China in the International System*, 94–95; Chow, *The May Fourth Movement*, 165–166.

72. *Congressional Record* (Washington, D.C.: U.S. Government Printing Office, 1873–), 66:1, 15 July 1919, 2592–2616.

73. John Milton Cooper, Jr., *Breaking the Heart of the World: Woodrow Wilson and the Fight for the League of Nations* (Cambridge: Cambridge University Press, 2001), 88–89, 110, 140–141.

74. The Shandong Amendment was passed by the Foreign Relations Committee on 23 Aug. 1919, and, with somewhat "softened language," by the full Senate in March 1920. *Congressional Record* 66:2, 2 Mar. 1920, 3848–3864; Cooper, *Breaking the Heart*, 147, 152, 343.

75. See, e.g., report on a big public rally in Jiangsu Province against the treaty, 5 July 1919, WJB, box 9 folder 2; report on a strike protesting the treaty by the merchants' association in Xiangtan County, Hunan Province, 10 July 1919, WJB, box 9, folder 2; report on boycotts and demonstrations across the country, MFA memo, 5 Sept. 1919, WJB, 03–12, 8:3.

76. Mao Zedong, "Afghanistan Picks Up the Sword" and "So Much for National Self-Determination!" in *Xiang River Review*, 14 July 1919. Reproduced in Schram, *Mao's Road to Power*, 1:335, 337.

77. Michael H. Hunt, *The Genesis of Chinese Communist Foreign Policy* (New York: Columbia University Press, 1996), 77–78.

78. Mao Zedong, "Poor Wilson," *Xiang River Review*, 14 July 1919, in Schram, *Mao's Road to Power*, 1:338.

79. The term "extremist" (*guoji* in Chinese) was commonly used at the time for the Bolsheviks. Mao Zedong, "Study of the Extremist Party," *Xiang River Review*, 14 July 1919, in Schram, *Mao's Road to Power*, 1:332 and n. 1.

80. Chen, "The May Fourth Movement Redefined," 80.

81. For a detailed analysis of earlier influences of Russian revolutionism on Chinese public opinion, see Don C. Price, *Russia and the Roots of the Chinese Revolution, 1896–1911* (Cambridge, Mass.: Harvard University Press, 1974).

82. Dirlik, *The Origins of Chinese Communism*, 41.

CHAPTER 10

1. Report from British Consulate-General in Seoul, 13 May 1919, NAUK, FO 262/1406, fol. 158–160. Data on Korean casualties during the March First movement vary significantly. Baldwin, relying on Korean sources, estimates more than 7,000 killed and more than 45,000 wounded, though the official Japanese statistics were far lower. The Japanese forces suffered 8 dead and 158 wounded. Baldwin, "The March First Movement," 232–235.

2. Hundreds of testimonials from victims of the colonial police were prepared by Korean nationalists and missionaries. American missionaries in Korea interviewed dozens of released detainees, apparently with special emphasis on women, and sometimes produced verbatim transcripts of the interviews ("Story of Released Girl Prisoner," numbered 1, 2, 3, etc.). See Presbyterian Historical Society (Philadelphia, Pa.) [PHS], RG 140, Korea Mission Secretaries Files, box 16, folders 13–21.

3. Japanese press reports excerpted in PHS, RG 140, box 16, folder 15.

4. U.S. Mission in Tokyo to secretary of state, 8 Mar. 1919, USNA, RG 59, 895.00/587; Morris to secretary of state, 15 Mar. 1919, RG 59, 895.00/572. Also see news report in NAUK, FO 262/1406, fol. 414.

5. Report cited in Lee, *Korean Nationalism*, 107; see also Timothy L. Savage, "The American Response to the Korean Independence Movement, 1910–1945," *Korean Studies* 20 (1996), 195. George Shannon McCune was then the general superintendent of schools in northern Korea, and he later became known as an expert in Eastern affairs (see *New York Times*, 6 Dec. 1941, 17). *PWW* shows no record that McCune ever met with Wilson. McCune was already known in Korea as an opponent of Japanese rule there; see PHS, box 16, folder 12.

6. Lee, "A Political Factor in the Rise of Protestantism in Korea," 135.

7. Morris to secretary of state, 21 Mar. 1919, USNA, RG 59, 895.00/586.

8. Report from British Consulate-General in Seoul, 13 May 1919, NAUK, FO 262/1406, fol. 158–160.

9. Reinsch to secretary of state, 12 Mar. 1919, USNA, RG 59, 895.00/570.

10. See Caldwell to secretary of state, 18 Mar. 1919, USNA, RG 59, 895.00/575. Also see Savage, "American Response," 196–197.

11. American Commission to secretary of state, 18 Mar. 1919; and Department of State to American Commission, 19 Mar. 1919, USNA, RG 59, 895.00/574.

12. Brown to Friends and Relatives of the Chosen Missionaries, 18 Apr. 1919, PHS, RG 140, 16:15; "A Statement on the Korean Situation by the Commission on Relations

with the Orient of the Federal Council of the Churches of Christ in America," May 1919, PHS, RG 140, 16:15.

13. A. E. Armstrong, "Notes on the Korean Uprising for Independence," 5 Apr. 1919, PHS, RG 140, 16:15; Blair to Brown, 12 July 1919, RG 140, 16:13.

14. Lee, "A Political Factor in the Rise of Protestantism in Korea," 137–138. See also Harry A. Rhodes, ed., *History of the Korea Mission, Presbyterian Church, U.S.A.*, vol. 1, *1884–1934* (Seoul: Presbyterian Church of Korea, Department of Education, 1934), 500–502.

15. For example, Koreans in the Vladivostok region in Russia paraded for Korean independence several times during March. Caldwell to secretary of state, 17 Mar. 1919, USNA, RG 59, 895.00/606; and 18 Mar. 1919, RG 59, 895.00/573.

16. The government brought together three groups, which all agreed on the need for Korean independence but differed on the preferred means to achieve this goal. The "militarists," based in Manchuria, worked to organize armed resistance against the Japanese. They were more conservative and usually loyal to the deposed dynasty. The "gradualists," led by An Ch'ang-ho, felt that Koreans were not yet capable of complete independence and needed a long-term program of cultural and economic development under Japanese tutelage before they could achieve it. At the height of the Wilsonian moment, however, the most influential group was the "propagandists," led by Rhee, Jaisohn, and Kim. They were largely Western-educated and wanted to focus on propaganda efforts directed at the foreign powers, especially the United States. Rhee and Kim saw guerrilla activities as dangerous, since they merely provided the Japanese with excuses for further oppression, and they felt that the only way to win independence was by "appealing to the conscience of the Western powers." Lee, *Korean Nationalism*, 140–141.

17. Lee, *Korean Nationalism*, 130–131.

18. Carl Crow, "President Wilson['s] Eyes & Ears," pp. 9–14, unpublished typescript, Crow Papers.

19. KNA to Wilson, 7 Apr. 1919, USNA, RG 59, 895.01/2; KNA to Polk, 14 Apr. 1919, RG 59, 895.00/596.

20. Rhee to Polk, 19 June 1919, USNA, RG 59, 895.01/4; Rhee to Wilson, 27 June 1919, RG 59, 895.01/8. Emphasis in original.

21. On the position of the State Department, see, for example, Grew to Hornbeck, 28 Mar. 1919, USNA, RG 256, 895.00/8

22. Oliver, *Syngman Rhee*, 110–113, 132. Oliver, who was Rhee's U.S. publicity agent in the 1940s and 1950s, may have embellished the account somewhat, but there is also other evidence to suggest that Rhee had at least some contact with Wilson in his Princeton days. See, e.g., Rhee to Wilson, 1 July 1910, LOC, WWP, series 2, reel 19.

23. Polk to Lansing, 1 Mar. 1919, Hornbeck Papers, box 329, folder "Paris Peace Conference: Korea at the Peace Conference"; Rhee to Chung, 5 Mar. 1919; Ahn to Rhee, 14 Mar. 1919; Rhee to Kim, 7 Apr. 1919, all in Institute for Modern Korean Studies, ed., *The Syngman Rhee Telegrams*, 4 vols. (Seoul: JoongAng Ilbo and IMKS, 2000), 1:20, 33. Also see *Young Korea* 1:3 (May 1919), p. 83.

24. "Koreans Petition Wilson," *New York Times*, 17 Mar. 1919, 2.

25. Savage, "American Response," 201–204.

26. Oliver, *Syngman Rhee*, 143.

27. Jaisohn had already established in Philadelphia the Bureau of Information for the Republic of Korea, of which he was the director. See Jaisohn to McMillan, 7 Jan. 1919, PHS, RG 140, 16:13.

28. Baldwin, "The March First Movement," 148–149. On the preparations, see also the invitations sent to various Korean activists in the United States in *Syngman Rhee Telegrams*, 1:84–86.

29. Cited in "Philadelphia Congress," *Young Korea* 1:3 (May 1919), p. 90. Also see Choy, *Koreans in America*, 154.

30. "First Korean Congress," Philadelphia, 14–16 Apr. 1919, pp. 29–30, minutes filed in USNA, RG 59, 895.00/647.

31. Ibid., 69.

32. Ibid., 33–34; *Young Korea* 1:3 (May 1919), pp. 90–91.

33. "First Korean Congress," 55.

34. Jaisohn, who wanted the campaign to resonate with the U.S. public, explained that this phrase was especially appropriate because it had neither Latin nor French origins but was a "true Anglo-Saxon" phrase. Ibid., 70–71.

35. *Korean Publication* 1:1 (Mar. 1919), back cover.

36. The first two issues (Mar. and Apr. 1919) were published under the title *Korean Publication*, and the third (May) was titled *Young Korea*; thereafter the title was changed to *Korea Review*.

37. See, e.g., Henry Chung, *The Oriental Policy of the United States* (New York: Revell, 1919); and Chung, *The Case of Korea* (New York: Revell, 1921).

38. "Egypt and Korea," *New York Times*, 20 Mar. 1919, 12; Henry Chung, "Korea's Appeal: Asks for an Opportunity to Show Fitness for Self-Government," *Young Korea* 1:3 (May 1919), 78.

39. Syngman Rhee, "Korea against Japan," *New York Times*, 18 May 1919, 38. Ladd's impressions of Korea were based on a brief visit there some yeas before. See George Trumbull Ladd, *In Korea with Marquis Ito* (New York: Scribner's, 1908); also Andre Schmid, *Korea between Empires, 1895–1919* (New York: Columbia University Press, 2002), 163–164.

40. See, e.g., "A Summary of Korea's Situation: 'Belgium in Asia,' " and Rev. P. K. Yoon, "The Belgium of the Orient," *Young Korea* 1:3 (May 1919), 68–70, 94–95.

41. Lee to Coolidge, 29 May 1919, Hornbeck Papers, box 270, folder "Korea: Peace Conference."

42. "First Korean Congress," 41–46, 61–68, 79–82, and photo after p. 56; *Young Korea* 1:3 (May 1919), 93–94. See also Rhee to Kim, 17 Apr. 1919, in *Syngman Rhee Telegrams*, 1:135; Lee, *Korean Nationalism*, 79–82. For the impact of the American Declaration of Independence on subsequent independence movements, see David Armitage, *The Declaration of Independence: A Global History* (Cambridge, Mass.: Harvard University Press, 2007).

43. Reported in Reinsch to the secretary of state, 16 Feb. 1919, USNA, RG 59, 895.00/581.

44. Bonsal, *Suitors and Suppliants*, 222–225.

45. Hornbeck to Grew, 25 Mar. 1919; and Grew to Hornbeck, 28 Mar. 1919, USNA, RG 256, 895.00/8.

46. *The Claim of the Korean People and Nation for Liberation from Japan and for the Reconstitution of Korea as an Independent State* (Paris: Korean Delegation to the Peace Conference, Apr. 1919), enclosed in Kim to Wilson, 12 May 1919, USNA, RG 256, 895.00/17. A copy of the pamphlet was sent to the American Commission adviser E. T. Williams, 13 May 1919, RG 256, 895.00/16.

47. Kim to Wilson, 12 May 1919, USNA, RG 256, 895.00/17.

48. Close to Kim, 16 May 1919, LOC, WWP, series 5b, reel 406; Baldwin, "The March First Movement," 147–148.

49. Kim to Lloyd George, 12 May 1919, USNA, RG 256, 895.00/17.

50. Kim to Wilson, 24 May 1919, LOC, WWP, series 5b, reel 408.

51. Kerr to Foreign Office, 30 May 1919, NAUK, FO 608/211, fol. 430–432; MAE, Papiers d'Agents 166 (PA-AP), André Tardieu, folder 403 (Asie), pp. 135–155. Another note, Rhee to British delegation, dated 16 June 1919, sought British good offices, as per the 1883 bilateral treaty, to help present the Korean case in Paris. It, too, met with no response. FO 608/211, fol. 443–444.

52. Young L. Park of United Asiatic Society of Detroit, Michigan, to Peace Conference, NAUK, FO 608/211, fol. 436–439; a copy of the petition was also sent to the Chinese delegation, WJB, RG 03–37, box 31, vol. 4.

53. Hyunsoon to Wilson, 5 Mar. 1919, Hornbeck Papers, box 270, folder "Korean Petitions." Also see there Kinshung to Wilson, 25 Jan. 1919; Korean National Independence Union to Lansing, 6 Mar. 1919, WWP, series 5b, reel 394.

54. Kim to Hornbeck, 14 June 1919, and Hornbeck to Kirk, 21 June 1919, in Hornbeck Papers, box 270, folder "Korea: Peace Conference"; Kim to Clemenceau, 11 June 1919, NAUK, FO 608/211, fol. 434–435; Kim to Chinese delegation, 16 June 1919, WJB, RG 03–37, box 31, vol. 1.

55. Bonsal, *Suitors and Suppliants*, 226. On Kim's frustrated efforts in Paris, see also Baldwin, "The March First Movement," 143–148.

56. *Korea Review* 1:7 (Sept. 1919), 14.

57. Frederick R. Dickinson, *War and National Reinvention: Japan in the Great War, 1914–1919* (Cambridge, Mass.: Harvard University Asia Center, 1999), 177–178; also see 202–203.

58. Dickinson, *War and National Reinvention*, 228, 235. On Yoshino, see Wells, "Background to the March First Movement," 9.

59. See Miwa Kimitada, "Japanese Opinions on Woodrow Wilson in War and Peace," *Monumenta Nipponica* 22:3–4 (1967), 388–389. Some scholars have emphasized the impact of the Russian Revolution on these postwar developments in Japan, but recent scholarship suggests that it was Wilson rather than Lenin who had the preponderant impact. Frederick Dickinson argues that in the immediate postwar period, the governing Japanese elites considered Wilson's calls for democracy and internationalism, rather than Bolshevism, as the most dangerous threat to the political structure of imperial Japan. Dickinson, *War and National Reinvention*, 179–180.

60. Dickinson, *War and National Reinvention*, 227–231, 237.

61. Baldwin, "The March First Movement," 168; see 163–168 for the reasons for this miscalculation.

62. Ku, *Korea under Colonialism*, 108–117.

63. Robinson, *Cultural Nationalism*, 44–45; Eckert et al., *Korea Old and New*, 281–285.

64. Kim to Lansing, 28 Aug. 1919, USNA, RG 59, 895.00/655; "Koreans Demand Real Independence," *Korea Review* 1:8 (Oct. 1919), 8–9. Also see Rhee's proclamations reported in the *New York Times*, 21 Aug. 1919, 19; 25 Aug. 1919, 2; 1 Sept. 1919, 2.

65. Curtis to Tumulty, 1 May 1919, USNA, RG 256, 895.99/21; the Federal Council of Protestant Evangelical Missions to Baron Saito, 29 Sept. 1919, RG 59, 895.00/667. Similar sentiments were expressed by a Presbyterian group in Pasadena, Calif., in Youngblood to Lansing, 22 Oct. 1919, RG 59, 895.00/664.

66. DOS to the Friends of Korea, 20 Apr. 1920, in USNA, RG 59, 895.00/675. The same policy remained in place in subsequent years; see, for example, correspondence regarding a petition sent to the White House by Soon Hyun, the "Representative of the President of the Provisional Government of Republic of Korea." Hughes to Christian, 16 May 1921, RG 59, 895.00/691.

67. *Korea Review* 1:6 (Aug. 1919), 7–8; *Korea Review* 1:8 (Oct. 1919), 13. See also Baldwin, "The March First Movement," 150–151. In 1950, the Republic of Korea awarded Dolph a posthumous Medal of Honor for his services. See "11 Who Aided Korea Will Get High Honor," *New York Times*, 28 Feb. 1950, 21.

68. Senate session, 13 Oct. 1919, *Congressional Record*, 58:6812–6826, cited in Baldwin, "The March First Movement," 153; *New York Times*, 14 Oct. 1919, 2.

69. See also petitions of 25 May 1920, USNA, RG 59, 895.00/679; 22 July 1920, RG 59, 895.00/686; 14 Sept. 1921, RG 59, 895.00/696. Also see Savage, "American Response," 204–206.

70. Frank Hoffmann, "The Muo Declaration: History in the Making," *Korean Studies* 13 (1989), 40 n. 41. The Second International, formed in 1889, was led by Social Democrats and opposed by the Russian Bolsheviks. It collapsed in 1920 and was replaced by the Bolshevist Third International, or Comintern.

71. Frank Prentiss Baldwin, Jr., "The March First Movement: Korean Challenge and Japanese Response" (Ph.D. diss., Columbia University, 1969), 219. Also see Dae-sook Suh, *The Korean Communist Movement, 1918–1948* (Princeton, N.J.: Princeton University Press, 1967), 55–56.

72. Schmid, *Korea between Empires*, 251–257.

73. *Constitution of the Republic of Korea* (Seoul: Office of Public Information, Republic of Korea, 1952), 1.

74. Lee, *Korean Nationalism*, 123–125.

CONCLUSION

1. Kim's address is printed in the *Korea Review* 1:7 (Sept. 1919), 10–11.

2. Sun Yat-sen, *San Min Chu I: The Three Principles of the People*, trans. Frank W. Price (Shanghai: Institute of Pacific Relations, 1929), 84.

3. Robert T. Pollard, *China's Foreign Relations, 1917–1931* (New York: MacMillan, 1933), chaps. 7–11. Pollard, writing in 1932, concludes by noting (p. 400) that "one who remembers the treatment meted out to China at Paris" could not avoid being struck by the change of China's international position since then. If before the World

War China had accepted her "humiliating status" in international affairs, now "she demands the rights of a sovereign nation, and during the past ten years the powers have gone far toward recognizing the justice of her demands." See also Akira Iriye, *After Imperialism: The Search for a New Order in the Far East, 1921–1931* (Cambridge, Mass.: Harvard University Press, 1965), esp. Part Three.

4. Incomplete and unpublished review of Bertrand Russell's *Roads to Freedom* (1918), written sometime after April 1919, NMML, Jawaharlal Nehru Papers, Writings & Speeches, serial no. 21. In the context of his own review, Nehru's citation of Russell implies that the "millennium" that had collapsed was the Wilsonian program, though Russell wrote this passage in March 1918 in reference to the failure of the Russian Revolution to spread elsewhere in Europe. The passage is found in Bertrand Russell, *Roads to Freedom* (1918; rpt., London: Unwin, 1977), 120.

5. S. Gopal, ed., *Selected Works of Jawaharlal Nehru*, 15 vols. (New Delhi: Orient Longman, 1972–1981), 4:185; Spear, *Oxford History*, 346–354.

6. "Tumas Wudru Wilsun," published 5 Feb. 1924 in the journal *Al-Siyasa* [Politics] and reproduced in Muhammad Husayn Haykal, *Fi Awqat al-Faragh: Majmu'at Rasa'il Adabiyya Ta'rikhiyya Akhlaqiyya Falsafiyya* [In Times of Leisure: A Collection of Writings on Culture, History, Morality, and Philosophy] (Cairo: al-Matba'a al-'Asriyya, 1925), 150–151.

7. Gamal 'Abd al-Nasir, *al-Majmu'a al-Kamila li-Khutab wa-Ahadith wa-Tasrihat Gamal 'Abd al-Nasir* [The Complete Collection of the Speeches, Interviews, and Declarations of Gamal Abdel Nasser], ed. Ahmad Yusuf Ahmad (Beirut: Markaz Dirasat al-Wahda al-'Arabiyya, 1995), 3:231–232. For the international context of Nasser's statement, see Peter L. Hahn, *The United States, Great Britain, and Egypt, 1945–1956: Strategy and Diplomacy in the Early Cold War* (Chapel Hill: University of North Carolina Press, 1991), 155–179.

8. George Creel, *The War, the World and Wilson* (New York: Harper, 1920), 161–162.

9. E.g., "Mei zhi duli jinian" [America's Independence Day], *Shenbao*, 4 July 1918, 11, where there is emphasis on the U.S. "democratic spirit" and its commitment to "uphold justice and humanity in the world."

10. An Address in the Indianapolis Coliseum, 4 Sept. 1919, *PWW*, 63:26–27.

11. This story is recounted in detail in Cooper, *Breaking the Heart*, esp. chap. 8.

12. Geoffrey Barraclough, *An Introduction to Contemporary History* (New York: Basic, 1964), title of chap. 6.

13. John A. Hall, *International Orders* (Cambridge, Mass.: Blackwell, 1996), 28.

BIBLIOGRAPHY

Primary Sources

Archival Collections

China

Waijiaobu (Chinese Foreign Ministry) Archives, Institute of Modern History, Academia Sinica, Taipei, Taiwan
Record Group 03–37, Bali hehui (Paris Peace Conference)
Record Group 03–12, zhu Mei shiguan baocun dangan (Archive of the Embassy to the United States)

France

Archives du Ministère des Affaires Etrangères, Quai d'Orsay, Paris
Papiers d'Agents, André Tardieu
Correspondance Politique et Commerciale, 1914–1940: A. Paix
Service Historique de l'Armée de Terre, Vincennes
Série 5 N, Cabinet du Ministre
Série 6 N, Fond Clemenceau

Great Britain

India Office Records, British Library, London
L/PJ/6, Annual Files of the Public and Judicial Department
L/PS/11, Political and Secret Annual Files, 1912–1930
V/26, Committee and Commission Reports
V/26/262, Records of the Hunter Commission, 1919–1920
L/R/5, Indian Press Summaries
L/R/5/89–96, United Provinces, 1914–1921
L/R/5/119–129, Madras, 1914–1921
L/R/5/169–179, Bombay, 1914–1921
L/R/5/195–202, Punjab, 1914–1921
National Archives of the United Kingdom, Kew, England
FO 262, Embassy and Consulates, Japan: General Correspondence
FO 371, Foreign Office Political Departments: General Correspondence from 1906
FO 410, Foreign Office Confidential Print Japan, 1859–1957
FO 608, British Delegation to Peace Conference, Correspondence and Papers 1918–1920

India

National Archives of India, New Delhi
Home Department Political Branch Files
Private Archives
G. S. Khaparde Papers
Lala Lajpat Rai Papers
Edwin Samuel Montagu Papers
V. S. Srinivasa Sastri Papers

Nehru Memorial Museum and Library, New Delhi
All-India Congress Committee Records
Poona District Congress Committee Records
Private Papers
Chelmsford Papers
Mohan Madan Malaviya Papers
Jawaharlal Nehru Papers
Motilal Nehru Papers
B. G. Tilak Papers

United States

Bancroft Library, University of California, Berkeley
Edward Thomas Williams Papers
Hoover Institution Archives, Stanford University
Stanley K. Hornbeck Papers
Library of Congress, Washington, D.C.
Ray Stannard Baker Papers
Stephen Bonsal Papers
Robert Lansing Papers
Breckinridge Long Papers
Woodrow Wilson Papers
Manuscripts and Archives, Yale University Library, New Haven, Connecticut
William C. Bullitt Papers
Edward M. House Diary and Papers
Frank Lyon Polk Papers
Chengting Thomas Wang Papers
William Wiseman Papers
Seeley G. Mudd Manuscript Library, Princeton University, Princeton, New Jersey
Ray Stannard Baker Papers
Woodrow Wilson Collection
Presbyterian Historical Society, Philadelphia, Pennsylvania
Record Group 140, Korea Mission Secretaries Files
Rare Book and Manuscript Library, Columbia University, New York
James Shotwell Papers (George Louis Beer Diary)
V. K. Wellington Koo Papers
Reminiscences of V. K. Wellington Koo: Oral History
State Historical Society of Wisconsin, Madison, Wisconsin
Paul S. Reinsch Papers
U.S. National Archives, College Park, Maryland
Record Group 59, General Records of the Department of State
Records of the Department of State Relating to the Internal Affairs of China, 1910–1929 (M-329)
Records of the Department of State Relating to the Internal Affairs of Egypt, 1910–1929 (M-571)

Records of the Department of State Relating to the Internal Affairs of India and Burma, 1910–1929 (M-335)

Records of the Department of State Relating to the Internal Affairs of Korea (Chosen), 1910–1929 (M-426)

Records of the Department of State Relating to the Internal Affairs of Persia, 1910–1929 (M-715)

Record Group 256, Records of the American Commission to Negotiate Peace

General Records of the American Commission to Negotiate Peace, 1918–1931 (M-820)

Western Historical Manuscript Collection, University of Missouri, Columbia

Carl Crow Papers

Newspapers and Periodicals

Al-Ahram (Cairo)

Amrita Bazar Patrika (Calcutta)

Chinese Social and Political Science Review (Beijing)

Dagongbao (Tianjin)

Far Eastern Political Science Review (Guangzhou)

Guomin Gongbao (Beijing)

Korean Publication (Philadelphia; continued as *Young Korea*)

Korea Review (Philadelphia)

Los Angeles Times

Mahratta (Poona)

Manchester Guardian

Millard's Review (Shanghai)

Modern Review (Calcutta)

Nation (New York City)

New India (Madras)

New York Times

North China Star (Tianjin)

Peking Leader (Beijing)

Shenbao (Shanghai)

Shibao (Shanghai)

Times (London)

Tribune (Lahore)

Xin Chao [New Tide] (Beijing)

Xin Qingnian [New Youth] (Beijing)

Young India (Ahmedabad)

Young India (New York City)

Young Korea (Philadelphia; continued as *Korea Review*)

Contemporary Pamphlets, Reports, and Special Publications

America's Position on the Shantung Question. Shanghai: Weekly Review of the Far East, 1922.

China's Claims at the Peace Table. New York: Chinese Patriotic Committee, 1919.

China vs. Japan. New York: Chinese Patriotic Committee, 1919.

Chinese Delegation to the Paris Peace Conference. *Canyu Ouzhou heping dahui fenlei baogao* [Report on Participation in the European Peace Conference]. Washington, D.C.: Chinese Legation, n.d.

——. *The Claim of China: Submitting for Abrogation by the Peace Conference the Treaties and Notes Made and Exchanged by and between China and Japan on May 25, 1915, as a Transaction Arising out of and Connected with the War between the Allied and Associated States and the Central Powers*. Paris: Impr. de Vaugirard, 1919.

The Claim of the Korean People and Nation for Liberation from Japan and for the Reconstitution of Korea as an Independent State. Paris: Korean Delegation to the Peace Conference, April 1919.

Egyptian Delegation to the Peace Conference. *Collection of Official Correspondence from November 11, 1918 to July 14, 1919*. Paris: Published by the Delegation, 1919.

Might or Right? The Fourteen Points and the Disposition of Kiao-Chau. New York: Chinese Patriotic Committee, 1919.

Report of the Committee Appointed by the Government of India to Investigate the Disturbances in the Punjab, etc. London: His Majesty's Stationery Office, 1920.

Self-Determination for India. London: India Home Rule League, 1918.

The Shantung Question: A Statement of China's Claim Together with Important Documents Submitted to the Peace Conference in Paris. San Francisco: Chinese National Welfare Society in America, 1 August 1919.

Telegrams Received by the Chinese Delegation in Support of Their Stand on the Shantung Question. Paris: [Chinese Delegation, 1919].

Who's Who in China, 2d ed. Shanghai: Millard's Review, 1920.

Document Collections, Memoirs, and Contemporary Accounts

'Abd al-Nāṣir, Gamāl. *al-Majmū'a al-Kāmila li-Khutāb wa-Aḥādīth wa-Taṣriḥāt Gamāl 'Abd al- Nāṣir* [The Complete Collection of the Speeches, Interviews, and Declarations of Gamal Abdel Nasser]. Aḥmad Yūsuf Aḥmad, ed. Beirut: Markaz Dirāsāt al-Waḥda al-'Arabīyya, 1995.

'Abd al-Nūr, Fakhrī. *Mudhakkirāt Fakhrī 'Abd al-Nūr: Thawrat 1919, Dawr Sa'd Zaghlūl wal-Wafd fi al-Ḥaraka al-Waṭaniyya* [The Memoirs of Fakhri 'Abd al-Nur: The 1919 Revolution, the Role of Sa'd Zaghlul and the Wafd in the National Movement]. Cairo: Dār al-Shurūq, 1992.

'Allūba, Muḥammad 'Alī. *Dhikriyyāt Ijtimā'iyya wa-Siyāsiyya* [Social and Political Memoirs]. Cairo: Al-Hay'a al-Miṣriyya al-'Āmma lil-Kitāb, 1988.

Baker, Ray Stannard. *What Wilson Did at Paris*. Garden City, N.Y.: Doubleday, Page, 1922.

——. *Woodrow Wilson and World Settlement*. 3 vols. Garden City, N.Y.: Doubleday, Page, 1922.

Bonsal, Stephen. *Unfinished Business*. Garden City, N.Y.: Doubleday, Doran, 1944.

——. *Suitors and Suppliants: The Little Nations at Versailles*. New York: Prentice-Hall, 1946.

British Documents on Foreign Affairs: Reports and Papers from the Confidential Print. Frederick, MD: University Publications of America, 1983–2000.

Part II, Series E: Asia, 1914–1939.
Part II, Series G: Africa, 1914–1939.
Part II, Series H: The First World War, 1914–1918.
Part II, Series I: The Paris Peace Conference, 1919.

Chen Duxiu. *Duxiu wencun* [The Surviving Writings of Chen Duxiu]. Hefei: Anhui renmin chubanshe, 1987.

Chirol, Valentine. *Indian Unrest.* London: Macmillan, 1910.

Chung, Henry. *The Oriental Policy of the United States.* New York: Revell, 1919.

——. *The Case of Korea.* New York: Revell, 1921.

Congressional Record. Washington, D.C.: U.S. Government Printing Office, 1873–.

Congress Presidential Addresses. A. M. Zaidi, ed. 6 vols. New Delhi: Indian Institute of Applied Political Research, 1986.

Constitution of the Republic of Korea. Seoul: Office of Public Information, Republic of Korea, 1952.

Creel, George. *Complete Report of the Chairman of the Committee on Public Information.* Washington, D.C.: U.S. Government Printing Office, 1920.

——. *How We Advertised America: The First Telling of the Amazing Story of the Committee on Public Information That Carried the Gospel of Americanism to Every Corner of the Globe.* New York: Harper, 1920.

——. *The War, the World and Wilson.* New York: Harper, 1920.

Crow, Carl. *I Speak for the Chinese.* New York: Harper, 1937.

——. *China Takes Her Place.* New York: Harper, 1944.

Fahmī, ʿAbd al-Raḥman. *Mudhakkirāt ʿAbd al-Raḥman Fahmī: Yawmiyyāt Miṣr al-Siyāsiyya* [The Memoirs of ʿAbd al-Rahman Fahmi: A Diary of Egyptian Politics]. 2 vols. Yūnān Labīb Rizq, ed. Cairo: Al-Hay'a al-Miṣriyya lil-Kitāb, 1988–1993.

Farīd, Muḥammad. *Awrāq Muḥammad Farīd* [The Papers of Muhammad Farid]. Musṭafā al-Naḥḥās Jabr, ed. 2 vols. Cairo: Al-Hay'a al-Miṣriyya al-ʿĀmma lil-Kitāb, 1978–1986.

Gandhi, M. K. *Hind Swaraj* [Indian Home Rule]. 1908, 5th ed. Madras: Ganesh, 1922.

——. *Gokhale: My Political Guru.* Ahmedabad: Navajivan, 1955.

——. *The Collected Works of Mahatma Gandhi.* 90 vols. Delhi: Publications Division, Ministry of Information and Broadcasting, Government of India, 1958–.

Gokhale, G. K. *Speeches and Writings of Gopal Krishna Gokhale.* D. G. Karve and D. V. Ambekar, eds. 3 vols. Bombay: Asia Publishing House, 1966.

Gracie, David M., ed. *Gandhi and Charlie: The Story of a Friendship, as Told through the Letters and Writings of Mohandas K. Gandhi and Rev'd Charles Freer Andrews.* Cambridge, Mass.: Cowley, 1989.

Hansen, Harry. *The Adventures of the Fourteen Points.* New York: Century, 1919.

Haykal, Muḥammad Ḥusayn. "Tūmās Wūdrū Wilsun," in *Fī Awqāt al-Farāgh: Majmūʿāt Rasā'il Adabiyya Ta'rīkhiyya Akhlāqiyya Falsafiyya* [In Times of Leisure: A Collection of Writings on Culture, History, Morality, and Philosophy]. Cairo: al-Maṭbaʿa al-ʿAṣriyya, 1925, pp. 149–156. Originally published 5 Feb. 1924 in the journal *Al-Siyāsa* [Politics].

——. *Mudhakkirāt fi al-Siyāsa al-Miṣriyya* [Memoirs of Egyptian Politics]. 2 vols. Cairo: Dār al-Maʿārif, 1977.

Ho Chi Minh. *Ho Chi Minh: Textes, 1914–1969*. Alain Ruscio, ed. Paris: L'Harmattan, 1990.

House, Edward Mandell, and Charles Seymour, eds. *What Really Happened at Paris: The Story of the Peace Conference, 1918–1919, by American Delegates*. New York: Scribner's, 1921.

Hu Shi. *Hu Shi liuxue riji* [Hu Shi's Diary while Studying Abroad]. Changsha: Yuelu shu she, 2000.

Hu Suh [Hu Shi]. "Intellectual China in 1919," *Chinese Social and Political Science Review* 4:4 (1919), 345–355.

Jayakar, M. R. *The Story of My Life*. Bombay: Asia Publishing House, 1958.

Kang, Hildi, comp. *Under the Black Umbrella: Voices from Colonial Korea, 1910–1945*. Ithaca, N.Y.: Cornell University Press, 2001.

Kang Youwei. *Ta t'ung shu: The One-World Philosophy of K'ang Yu-wei*. Laurence G. Thompson, trans. London: Allen & Unwin, 1958.

——. *Kang Youwei zhenglun ji* [The Political Writings of Kang Youwei]. Yang Zhijun, ed. 2 vols. Beijing: Zhonghua shuju, 1981.

Keynes, John Maynard. *The Economic Consequences of the Peace*. London: Macmillan, 1919.

Khamsīn 'Āmā 'alā Thawrat 1919 [The 1919 Revolution after Fifty Years]. Cairo: Mu'assasat al-Ahrām, Markaz al-Wathā'iq wal-Buḥūth al-Ta'rīkhiyya li-Miṣr al-Mu'āṣira, 1970.

King, Wunsz. *China at the Paris Peace Conference in 1919*. Jamaica, N.Y.: St. John's University Press, 1961.

Koo, V. K. Wellington. *The Wellington Koo Memoir*. 7 vols. New York: Columbia University, East Asian Institute, 1976. (Chinese Oral History Project microfilm publication)

Koo, V. K. Wellington, and Cheng-ting T. Wang. *China and the League of Nations*. London: Allen & Unwin, 1919.

Ladd, George Trumbull. *In Korea with Marquis Ito*. New York: Scribner's, 1908.

Lajpat Rai, Lala. *The United States of America: A Hindu's Impressions and a Study*. Calcutta: Chatterjee, 1916.

——. *Young India: An Interpretation and a History of the Nationalist Movement from Within*. New York: Huebsch, 1916.

——. *Autobiographical Writings*. Vijaya Chandra Joshi, ed. Delhi and Jullundur: University Publishers, 1965.

——. *Writings and Speeches*. 2 vols. Vijaya Chandra Joshi, ed. Delhi and Jullundur: University Publishers, 1966.

——. *The Story of My Life*. Joginder Singh Dhanki, ed. New Delhi: Gitanjali Prakashan, 1978.

——. *Selected Documents of Lala Lajpat Rai, 1906–1928*. Ravindra Kumar, ed. 5 vols. New Delhi: Anmol, 1992.

——. *Perspectives on Indian National Movement: Selected Correspondence of Lala Lajpat Rai*. Joginder Singh Dhanki, ed. New Delhi: National Book Organisation, 1998.

Lansing, Robert. *The Peace Negotiations: A Personal Narrative*. Boston: Houghton Mifflin, 1921.

Lenin, V. I. *The State and Revolution*. London: British Socialist Party, 1919.

——. *Imperialism: The Highest Stage of Capitalism*. Moscow: Foreign Languages Publishing House, 1920.

——. *Collected Works*, 45 vols. Moscow: Progress, 1960–1970.

Li Dazhao. *Li Dazhao wenji* [Writings of Li Dazhao]. 5 vols. Beijing: Renmin chubanshe, 1999.

Liang Qichao. *Liang Qichao quanji* [The Complete Works of Liang Qichao]. 10 vols. Beijing: Beijing chubanshe, 1999.

Link, Arthur S., ed. *The Papers of Woodrow Wilson*. 69 vols. Princeton, N.J.: Princeton University Press, 1966–1994.

Lloyd George, David. *British War Aims: Statement by the Prime Minister, the Right Honourable David Lloyd George, on January 5, 1918*. London: Hazell, Watson & Viney, 1918.

——. *Memoirs of the Peace Conference*. 2 vols. New Haven, Conn.: Yale University Press, 1939.

Lou Tseng-tsiang. *Souvenirs et pensées: Lettre à mes amis de Grande-Bretagne et d'Amérique*. 1948. Reprint, Paris: Dominique Martin Morin, 1993.

Mantoux, Paul. *The Deliberations of the Council of Four (March 24–June 28, 1919): Notes of the Official Interpreter*. 2 vols. Arthur S. Link with Manfred F. Boemeke, trans. and eds. Princeton, N.J.: Princeton University Press, 1992.

Mao Zedong. *Mao's Road to Power: Revolutionary Writings, 1912–1949*. Stuart R. Schram, ed. Armonk, N.Y.: Sharpe, 1992.

McCurdy, Charles A. *A Clean Peace: The War Aims of British Labour: Complete Text of the Official War Aims Memorandum of the Inter-Allied Labour and Socialist Conference, Held in London, February 23, 1918*. New York: Doran, 1918.

McKenzie, Frederick A. *The Tragedy of Korea*. London: Hodder and Stoughton, 1908.

The Messages and Papers of Woodrow Wilson. Albert Shaw, ed. 2 vols. New York: Review of Reviews Corporation, 1924.

Millard, Thomas F. *Democracy and the Eastern Question: The Problem of the Far East as Demonstrated by the Great War, and Its Relation to the United States of America*. New York: Century, 1919.

——. *The Shantung Case at the Conference*, 2d ed. Shanghai: Millard's Review of the Far East, 1921.

Miller, David Hunter. *My Diary at the Conference at Paris*. 2 vols. New York: Printed for the author by the Appeal Printing Company, 1924.

——. *The Drafting of the Covenant*. 2 vols. New York: Putnam's, 1928.

Montagu, Edwin Samuel. *An Indian Diary*. London: Heinemann, 1930.

Nehru, Jawaharlal. *Jawaharlal Nehru: An Autobiography*. London: Lane, 1936.

——. *Selected Works of Jawaharlal Nehru*. S. Gopal, gen. ed. 15 vols. New Delhi: Orient Longman, 1972–1981.

Nicolson, Harold. *Peacemaking 1919*. New York: Harcourt, Brace, 1939.

Papers Relating to the Foreign Relations of the United States: The Lansing Papers, 1914–1920. 2 vols. Washington, D.C.: U.S. Government Printing Office, 1939–1940.

Papers Relating to the Foreign Relations of the United States: The Paris Peace Conference, 1919. 13 vols. Washington, D.C.: U.S. Government Printing Office, 1942–1947.

Poole, Ernest. *The Bridge: My Own Story*. New York: Macmillan, 1940.

Powell, John B. *My Twenty-Five Years in China*. New York: Macmillan, 1945.

Reinsch, Paul. *An American Diplomat in China*. Garden City, N.Y.: Doubleday, 1922.

Rhee, Syngman. *The Syngman Rhee Telegrams*. Institute for Modern Korean Studies, ed. 4 vols. Seoul: JoongAng Ilbo and IMKS, 2000.

Roy, M. N. *M. N. Roy's Memoirs*. Bombay: Allied, 1964.

——. *Selected Works of M. N. Roy*. Sibnarayan Ray, ed. 4 vols. New Delhi: Oxford University Press, 1987.

Russell, Bertrand. *Roads to Freedom*. 1918. Reprint, London: Unwin, 1977.

Salīm, Muḥammad Kāmil. *Thawrat 1919 kamā 'Ishtuha wa-'Araftuha* [The 1919 Revolution as I Lived and Knew It]. Cairo: Mu'assasat Akhbār al-Yawm, 1975.

Al-Sayyid, Ahmad Lutfī. *Qiṣṣat Hayātī* [The Story of My Life]. Cairo: Dār al-Hilāl, 1962.

Selected Documents on the Constitutional History of the British Empire and Commonwealth. Vol. 6: *The Dominions and India since 1900*. Frederick Madden and John Darwin, eds. Westport, Conn.: Greenwood, 1993.

Sha'rawi, Huda. *Harem Years: The Memoirs of an Egyptian Feminist, 1879–1924*. Margot Badran, ed. New York: Feminist Press, 1987.

Shotwell, James T. *At the Paris Peace Conference*. New York: Macmillan, 1937.

Ṣidqī, Ismā'īl. *Mudhakkirāti* [My Memoirs]. Sāmī Abu al-Nūr, ed. Cairo: Madbūlī, 1991.

Suh, Dae-sook, ed. *Documents of Korean Communism, 1918–1948*. Princeton, N.J.: Princeton University Press, 1970.

Sun Yat Sen. *Prescriptions for Saving China: Selected Writings of Sun Yat-sen*. Julie Lee Wei, Ramon H. Myers, and Donald G. Gillin, eds. Stanford, Calif.: Hoover Institution Press, 1994.

——. *San Min Chu I: The Three Principles of the People*, trans. Frank W. Price. Shanghai: Institute of Pacific Relations, 1929.

Thompson, Charles T. *The Peace Conference Day by Day: A Presidential Pilgrimage Leading to the Discovery of Europe*. New York: Brentano's, 1920.

Tilak, Bal Gangadhar. *Letters of Lokamanya Tilak*. M. D. Vidwans, ed. Poona: Kesari Prakashan, 1966.

——. *Selected Documents of Lokamanya Bal Gangadhar Tilak, 1880–1920*. Ravindra Kumar, ed. 4 vols. New Delhi: Anmol, 1992.

Treaty of Peace with Germany: Hearings before the Committee on Foreign Relations, United States Senate. Washington: U.S. Government Printing Office, 1919.

Tyau, Min-ch'ien T. Z. *China Awakened*. New York: Macmillan, 1922.

Wang, Chengting Thomas. "Looking Back and Looking Forward." Unpublished autobiography. Archives and Manuscripts, Yale University, New Haven, Conn.

Wells, H. G. *The War That Will End War*. London: Palmer, 1914.

——. *The Shape of Things to Come*. New York: Macmillan, 1933.

Williams, E. T. "Recollections." Unpublished typescript. E. T. Williams Papers, Bancroft Library, University of California, Berkeley.

Wilson, Woodrow. *Woodrow Wilson's Message for Eastern Nations, Selected by Himself from His Public Addresses*. Calcutta: Association Press, 1925.

Yim, Louise. *My Forty Year Fight for Korea*. New York: Wyn, 1951.

Zaghlūl, Sa'd. *Mudhakkirāt Sa'd Zaghlūl* [The Diaries of Sa'd Zaghlul]. 'Abd al-'Aẓīm Ramaḍān, ed. 9 vols. Cairo: Al-Hay'a al-Miṣriyya al-'Āmma lil-Kitāb, 1987–1998.

Zou Rong. *The Revolutionary Army*. John Lust, trans. The Hague: Mouton, 1968.

SECONDARY SOURCES: ARTICLES, BOOKS, DISSERTATIONS

Adas, Michael. "Contested Hegemony: The Great War and the Afro-Asian Assault on the Civilizing Mission Ideology," *Journal of World History* 15:1 (2004), 31–63.

"*AHR* Conversation: On Transnational History," *American Historical Review* 111:5 (2006).

Albertini, Rudolf Von. "The Impact of Two World Wars on the Decline of Colonialism," *Journal of Contemporary History* 4:1 (1969), 17–35.

——. *Decolonization: The Administration and Future of the Colonies, 1919–1960*. Francisca Garvie, trans. Garden City, N.Y.: Doubleday, 1971.

Ambrosius, Lloyd E. "The Orthodoxy of Revisionism: Woodrow Wilson and the New Left," *Diplomatic History* 3 (1977), 199–214.

——. *Woodrow Wilson and the American Diplomatic Tradition: The Treaty Fight in Perspective*. Cambridge: Cambridge University Press, 1987.

——. *Wilsonian Statecraft: Theory and Practice of Liberal Internationalism during World War I*. Wilmington, Del.: Scholarly Resources, 1991.

——. *Wilsonianism: Woodrow Wilson and His Legacy in American Foreign Relations*. New York: Palgrave Macmillan, 2002.

Anderson, Benedict. *Imagined Communities: Reflections on the Origin and Spread of Nationalism*. Rev. ed. London: Verso, 1991.

Anderson, Carol. *Eyes off the Prize: The United Nations and the African American Struggle for Human Rights, 1944–1955*. Cambridge: Cambridge University Press, 2003.

'Aqqād, 'Abbās Mahmūd. *Sa'd Zaghlūl: Sīrah wa-Taḥiyya* [Sa'd Zaghlul: A Biography and Salute]. Cairo: Dār al-Shurūq, 1975.

Armitage, David. *The Declaration of Independence: A Global History*. Cambridge, Mass.: Harvard University Press, 2007.

Auslin, Michael R. *Negotiating with Imperialism: The Unequal Treaties and the Culture of Japanese Diplomacy*. Cambridge, Mass.: Harvard University Press, 2004.

Ayalon, Ami. *The Press in the Arab Middle East: A History*. New York: Oxford University Press, 1995.

Aydin, Cemil. "A Global Anti-Western Moment? The Russo-Japanese War, Decolonization, and Asian Modernity," in Sebastian Conrad and Dominic Sachsenmaier, eds., *Conceptions of World Order: Global Historical Approaches*. New York: Palgrave Macmillan, 2007, pp. 213–236.

Badran, Margot. *Feminists, Islam and Nation: Gender and the Making of Modern Egypt*. Princeton, N.J.: Princeton University Press, 1995.

Bakshi, S. R. *Home Rule Movement*. New Delhi: Capital, 1984.

Baldwin, Frank Prentiss, Jr. "The March First Movement: Korean Challenge and Japanese Response." Ph.D. diss., Columbia University, 1969.

Baritz, Loren. *Backfire: A History of How American Culture Led Us into Vietnam and Made Us Fight the Way We Did*. New York: Morrow, 1985.

Barraclough, Geoffrey. *An Introduction to Contemporary History*. New York: Basic, 1964.

Barrier, N. Gerald. *Banned: Controversial Literature and Political Control in British India, 1907–1947*. Columbia, Mo.: University of Missouri Press, 1974.

Beckert, Sven. "Emancipation and Empire: Reconstructing the Worldwide Web of Cotton Production in the Age of the American Civil War," *American Historical Review* 109:5 (2004), 1405–1438.

Beisner, Robert L. *Twelve against Empire: The Anti-Imperialists, 1898–1900*. New York: McGraw-Hill, 1968.

Beloff, Max. *Imperial Sunset*, vol. 1: *Britain's Liberal Empire, 1897–1921*. New York: Knopf, 1970.

Bender, Thomas, ed. *Rethinking American History in a Global Age*. Berkeley: University of California Press, 2001.

Bishku, Michael B. "The British Press and the Future of Egypt, 1919–1922," *International History Review* 8:4 (1986), 604–609.

——. "Intrigue, Propaganda and the Press: British Perceptions of and Reactions to the 1919 Egyptian Uprising," *Journal of Newspaper and Periodical History* 4:1 (1987–1988), 29–35.

Blumenthal, Henry. "Woodrow Wilson and the Race Question," *Journal of Negro History* 48:1 (1963), 1–21.

Boemeke, Manfred F., Gerald D. Feldman, and Elisabeth Glaser, eds. *The Treaty of Versailles: A Reassessment after 75 Years*. Cambridge: Cambridge University Press, 1998.

Boersner, Demetrio. *The Bolsheviks and the National and Colonial Question (1917–1928)*. Geneva: Droz, 1957.

Bondurant, Joan V. *Conquest of Violence: The Gandhian Philosophy of Conflict*. New rev. ed. Princeton, N.J.: Princeton University Press, 1988.

Borgwardt, Elizabeth. *A New Deal for the World: America's Vision for Human Rights*. Cambridge, Mass.: Harvard University Press, 2005.

Borstelmann, Thomas. *The Cold War and the Color Line: American Race Relations in the Global Arena*. Cambridge, Mass.: Harvard University Press, 2001.

Bose, A. C. "Indian Revolutionaries during the First World War: A Study of Their Aims and Weaknesses," in DeWitt C. Ellinwood and S. D. Pradhan, eds., *India and World War I*. New Delhi: South Asia Books, 1978, pp. 109–126.

Bose, Sugata, and Ayesha Jalal. *Modern South Asia: History, Culture, Political Economy*. London: Routledge, 1998.

Bradley, Mark Philip. *Imagining Vietnam & America: The Making of Postcolonial Vietnam, 1919–1950*. Chapel Hill: University of North Carolina Press, 2000.

Brands, H. W. *India and the United States: The Cold Peace*. Boston: Twayne, 1990.

Brindley, Ronan. "Woodrow Wilson, Self-Determination and Ireland, 1918–1919: A View from the Irish Newspapers," *Éire-Ireland* 23:4 (1988), 62–80.

Brown, Giles T. "The Hindu Conspiracy, 1914–1917," *Pacific Historical Review* 17:3 (1948), 299–310.

Brown, Judith M. *Gandhi's Rise to Power: Indian Politics, 1915–1922*. Cambridge: Cambridge University Press, 1972.

——. "War and the Colonial Relationship: Britain, India, and the War of 1914–18," in DeWitt C. Ellinwood and S. D. Pradhan, eds., *India and World War I*. New Delhi: South Asia Books, 1978, pp. 19–48.

——. *Modern India: The Origins of an Asian Democracy*. 2d ed. Oxford: Oxford University Press, 1994.

Buitenhuis, Peter. "Selling the Great War," *Canadian Review of American Studies* 7:2 (Fall 1976), 139–150.

Bull, Hedley, and Adam Watson, eds. *The Expansion of International Society*. New York: Oxford University Press, 1984.

Calhoun, Frederick S. *Uses of Force and Wilsonian Foreign Policy*. Kent, Ohio: Kent State University Press, 1993.

Callahan, Michael D. *Mandates and Empire: The League of Nations and Africa, 1914–1931*. Brighton, England: Sussex Academic Press, 1999.

——. *A Sacred Trust: The League of Nations and Africa, 1929–1946*. Brighton, England: Sussex Academic Press, 2004.

Carrère d'Encausse, Hélène, and Stuart R. Schram. *Marxism and Asia: An Introduction with Readings*. London: Allen Lane/Penguin, 1969.

Cashman, Richard I. *The Myth of the Lokamanya: Tilak and Mass Politics in Maharashtra*. Berkeley: University of California Press, 1975.

Cassese, Antonio. *Self-Determination of Peoples: A Legal Reappraisal*. Cambridge: Cambridge University Press, 1995.

Chadha, Yogesh. *Gandhi: A Life*. New York: Wiley, 1997.

Chakrabarty, Dipesh. *Provincializing Europe: Postcolonial Thought and Historical Difference*. Princeton, N.J.: Princeton University Press, 2000.

Chamberlain, M. E. *Decolonization: The Fall of the European Empires*. Oxford: Oxford University Press, 1985.

Chan, F. Gilbert. "The American Revolution and the Rise of Afro-Asian Nationalism, with Special Reference to Sun Yat-Sen and the Chinese Experience," *Asian Profile* 10:3 (1982), 209–219.

Chandra, Bipan, et al. *India's Struggle for Independence, 1857–1947*. New Delhi: Viking, 1988.

——. *Nationalism and Colonialism in Modern India*. New Delhi: Orient Longman, 1996.

Chandra, Vipan. *Imperialism, Resistance, and Reform in Late Nineteenth-Century Korea: Enlightenment and the Independence Club*. Berkeley: Center for Korean Studies, Institute of East Asian Studies, University of California, 1988.

Chang, Gordon H. "Whose 'Barbarism'? Whose 'Treachery'? Race and Civilization in the Unknown United States–Korea War of 1871," *Journal of American History* 89:4 (2003), 1331–1365.

Chang, Hao. *Chinese Intellectuals in Crisis: Search for Order and Meaning, 1890–1911*. Berkeley: University of California Press, 1987.

Charmley, John. *Lord Lloyd and the Decline of the British Empire*. New York: St. Martin's, 1987.

Chatterjee, Partha. *Nationalist Thought and the Colonial World: A Derivative Discourse?* Minneapolis: University of Minnesota Press, 1986.

——. *The Nation and Its Fragments: Colonial and Postcolonial Histories.* Princeton, N.J.: Princeton University Press, 1993.

Chay, John. "The American Image of Korea to 1945," in Youngnok Koo and Dae-sook Suh, eds., *Korea and the United States: A Century of Cooperation.* Honolulu: University of Hawaii Press, 1984, pp. 53–76.

Chen, Joseph T. "The May Fourth Movement Redefined," *Modern Asian Studies* 4:1 (1970), 63–81.

Chi, Madeleine. "China and Unequal Treaties at the Paris Peace Conference of 1919," *Asian Profile* 1:1 (1973), 49–61.

Chow Tse-tsung. *The May Fourth Movement: Intellectual Revolution in Modern China.* Cambridge, Mass.: Harvard University Press, 1960.

——. *Research Guide to the May Fourth Movement.* Cambridge, Mass.: Harvard University Press, 1963.

Choy, Bong-youn. *Koreans in America.* Chicago: Nelson-Hall, 1979.

Chu, Pao-chin. *V. K. Wellington Koo: A Case Study of China's Diplomat and Diplomacy of Nationalism, 1912–1966.* Hong Kong: Chinese University Press, 1981.

Clark, Donald N. " 'Surely God Will Work Out Their Salvation': Protestant Missionaries in the March First Movement," *Korean Studies* 13 (1989), 42–75.

Clements, Kendrick A. *Woodrow Wilson: World Statesman.* 1987. Reprint, Chicago: Dee, 1999.

——. *The Presidency of Woodrow Wilson.* Lawrence: University Press of Kansas, 1992.

Cobban, Alfred. *National Self-Determination.* Oxford: Oxford University Press, 1944.

Cohen, Warren I. "America and the May Fourth Movement: The Response to Chinese Nationalism, 1917–1921," *Pacific Historical Review* 35:1 (1966), 83–100.

——. *America's Response to China: An Interpretive History of Sino-American Relations.* New York: Wiley, 1971.

Cole, Juan R. I. *Colonialism and Revolution in the Middle East: Social and Cultural Origins of Egypt's 'Urabi Movement.* Princeton, N.J.: Princeton University Press, 1993.

Connelly, Matthew. "Taking Off the Cold War Lens: Visions of North-South Conflict during the Algerian War for Independence," *The American Historical Review* 105:3 (2000), 739–769.

——. *A Diplomatic Revolution: Algeria's Fight for Independence and the Origin of the Post–Cold War Era.* New York: Oxford University Press, 2002.

Contee, Clarence G. "Dubois, the NAACP, and the Pan-African Congress of 1919," *Journal of Negro History* 57:1 (1972), 13–28.

Conyne, G. R. *Woodrow Wilson: British Perspectives, 1912–1921.* London: Macmillan, 1992.

Cooper, John Milton, Jr. *The Vanity of Power: American Isolationism and the First World War, 1914–1917.* Westport, Conn.: Greenwood, 1969.

——." 'An Irony of Fate': Woodrow Wilson's Pre–World War I Diplomacy," *Diplomatic History* 3:4 (1979), 425–437.

——. *The Warrior and the Priest: Woodrow Wilson and Theodore Roosevelt.* Cambridge, Mass.: Harvard University Press, 1983.

——. "Fool's Errand or Finest Hour: Woodrow Wilson's Speaking Tour in September 1919," in John Milton Cooper, Jr., and Charles E. Neu, eds., *The Wilson Era.* Arlington Heights, Ill.: Harlan Davidson, 1991, pp. 198–220.

——. *Breaking the Heart of the World: Woodrow Wilson and the Fight for the League of Nations.* Cambridge: Cambridge University Press, 2001.

Cooper, John Milton, Jr., and Charles E. Neu, eds. *The Wilson Era.* Arlington Heights, Ill.: Harlan Davidson, 1991.

Coventry, Donald C. "The Public Career of Sir Francis Reginald Wingate, High Commissioner for Egypt: 1917–1919." Ph.D. diss., American University, 1989.

Craft, Stephen G. "Angling for an Invitation to Paris: China's Entry into the First World War," *International History Review* 16:1 (1994), 1–24.

——. "John Bassett Moore, Robert Lansing, and the Shandong Question," *Pacific Historical Review* 66:2 (1997), 231–249.

——. *V. K. Wellington Koo and the Emergence of Modern China.* Lexington, Ky.: University Press of Kentucky, 2004.

Crane, Daniel M., and Thomas A. Breslin. *An Ordinary Relationship: American Opposition to Republican Revolution in China.* Miami: Florida International University Press, 1986.

Crosby, Earl W. "Progressive Segregation in the Wilson Administration," *Potomac Review* 6:2 (1973), 41–57.

Curry, George. "Woodrow Wilson, Jan Smuts and the Versailles Settlement," *American Historical Review* 66 (1961), 968–986.

Curry, Roy Watson. *Woodrow Wilson and Far Eastern Policy, 1913–1921.* New York: Bookman, 1957.

Daly, M. W. *The Sirdar: Sir Reginald Wingate and the British Empire in the Middle East.* Philadelphia: American Philosophical Society, 1997.

——. "The British Occupation," in M. W. Daly, ed., *The Cambridge History of Egypt,* vol. 2. Cambridge: Cambridge University Press, 1998, pp. 239–251.

Daly, M. W., ed. *The Cambridge History of Egypt.* Vol. 2. Cambridge: Cambridge University Press, 1998.

Darwin, John. *Britain, Egypt and the Middle East: Imperial Policy in the Aftermath of War, 1918–1922.* London: Macmillan, 1981.

Dawley, Alan. *Changing the World: American Progressives in War and Revolution.* Princeton, N.J.: Princeton University Press, 2003.

Deeb, Marius. "The 1919 Popular Uprising: A Genesis of Egyptian Nationalism," *Canadian Review of Studies in Nationalism* 1:1 (1973), 106–119.

——. *Party Politics in Egypt: The Wafd and Its Rivals, 1919–1939.* London: Ithaca, 1979.

Dhanki, J. S. *Lala Lajpat Rai and Indian Nationalism.* Jalandhar, India: ABS, 1990.

Dharmavira. *Lala Har Dayal and Revolutionary Movements of His Times.* New Delhi: India Book, 1970.

Dickinson, Frederick R. *War and National Reinvention: Japan in the Great War, 1914–1919.* Cambridge, Mass.: Harvard University Asia Center, 1999.

Dignan, Don. "The Hindu Conspiracy in Anglo-American Relations during World War I," *Pacific Historical Review* 40:1 (1971), 57–76.

Dikholkar, Manisha. *The History of India's Freedom Struggle in Britain: British Reaction and Responses (1885–1920)*. Bombay: Himalaya, 1996.

Dirlik, Arif. *The Origins of Chinese Communism*. New York: Oxford University Press, 1989.

Duara, Prasenjit. *Rescuing History from the Nation: Questioning Narratives of Modern China*. Chicago: University of Chicago Press, 1995.

——. "Transnationalism and the Predicament of Sovereignty: China, 1900–1945," *American Historical Review* 102:4 (1997), 1030–1051.

——. *Sovereignty and Authenticity: Manchukuo and the East Asian Modern*. Lanham, Md.: Rowman & Littlefield, 2003.

Duara, Prasenjit, ed. *Decolonization: Perspective from Now and Then*. London: Routledge, 2004.

Duiker, William J. *Ts'ai Yuan-pei: Educator of Modern China*. University Park: Pennsylvania State University Press, 1977.

Eckert, Carter J., Ki-Baik Lee, Young Ick Lew, Michael Robinson, and Edward W. Wagner. *Korea Old and New: A History*. Cambridge, Mass.: Harvard University Press, 1990.

Egerton, George W. "The Lloyd George Government and the Creation of the League of Nations," *American Historical Review* 79 (1974), 419–444.

——. "Britain and 'the Great Betrayal': Anglo-American Relations and the Struggle for United States Ratification of the Treaty of Versailles, 1919–1920," *Historical Journal* 21 (1978), 885–911.

——. *Great Britain and the Creation of the League of Nations: Strategy, Politics and International Organization, 1914–1919*. Chapel Hill: University of North Carolina Press, 1978.

Elleman, Bruce A. "Did Woodrow Wilson Really Betray the Republic of China at Versailles?" *American Asian Review* 13:1 (1995), 1–28.

Ellinwood, DeWitt C., and S. D. Pradhan, eds. *India and World War I*. New Delhi: South Asia Books, 1978.

Embree, Ainslie T. "The Function of Gandhi in Indian Nationalism," in Paul F. Power, ed., *The Meanings of Gandhi*. Manoa: University of Hawaii Press, 1971, pp. 59–76.

Esposito, David M. "Woodrow Wilson and the Origins of the AEF," *Presidential Studies Quarterly* 19 (1989), 127–140.

——. *The Legacy of Woodrow Wilson: American War Aims in World War I*. Westport, Conn.: Praeger, 1996.

Fairbank, John K., ed. *The Chinese World Order: Traditional China's Foreign Relations*. Cambridge, Mass.: Harvard University Press, 1968.

——. *The Cambridge History of China*. Vol. 12: *Republican China 1912–1949, Part I*. Cambridge: Cambridge University Press, 1983.

Ferguson, Niall. *The Pity of War*. London: Allen Lane/Penguin, 1998.

Ferrell, Robert H. *Woodrow Wilson and World War I, 1917–1921*. New York: Harper & Row, 1985.

Fic, Victor M. *The Collapse of American Policy in Russia and Siberia, 1918: Wilson's Decision Not to Intervene*. Boulder: University of Colorado Press, 1995.

Fifield, Russell H. *Woodrow Wilson and the Far East: The Diplomacy of the Shantung Question*. Hamden, Conn.: Archon, 1965.

Finnemore, Martha, and Kathryn Sikkink. "International Norm Dynamics and Political Change," *International Organization* 52:4 (1998), 887–917.

Fleming, Denna Frank. *The United States and the League of Nations, 1918–1920*. New York: Putnam's, 1932.

Floto, Inga. *Colonel House in Paris: A Study of American Policy at the Paris Peace Conference, 1919*. Princeton, N.J.: Princeton University Press, 1973.

Foglesong, David S. *America's Secret War against Bolshevism: U.S. Intervention in the Russian Civil War, 1917–1920*. Chapel Hill: University of North Carolina Press, 1995.

——. "The United States, Self-Determination, and the Struggle against Bolshevism in the Eastern Baltic Region, 1918–1920," *Journal of Baltic Studies* 26 (1995), 107–144.

Fowler, William B. *British-American Relations 1917–1918: The Role of Sir William Wiseman*. Princeton, N.J.: Princeton University Press, 1969.

Franklin, John Hope. " 'Birth of a Nation': Propaganda as History," *Massachusetts Review* 20:3 (1979), 417–434.

Freud, Sigmund, and William C. Bullitt. *Thomas Woodrow Wilson, Twenty Eighth President of the United States: A Psychological Study.* Boston: Houghton Mifflin, 1967.

Fromkin, David. *A Peace to End All Peace: Creating the Modern Middle East, 1914–1922*. New York: Holt, 1989.

Fung, Allen Yuk-Lun. "The Struggle over the Constitution: Chinese Politics, 1917–1919." Ph.D. diss., Harvard University, 1996.

Furth, Charlotte. "Intellectual Change: From the Reform Movement to the May Fourth Movement, 1895–1920," in John K. Fairbank, ed., *The Cambridge History of China*. Vol. 12: *Republican China 1912–1949, Part I*. Cambridge: Cambridge University Press, 1983, pp. 354–364.

Gaddis, John Lewis. *We Now Know: Rethinking Cold War History.* New York: Oxford University Press, 1997.

Gallagher, John. "Nationalisms and the Crisis of Empire, 1919–1922," *Modern Asian Studies* 15:3 (1981), 355–368.

Gallicchio, Marc. *The African American Encounter with Japan & China: Black Internationalism in Asia, 1895–1945*. Chapel Hill: University of North Carolina Press, 2000.

Gardner, Arthur Leslie. "The Korean Nationalist Movement and An Ch'ang-Ho, Advocate of Gradualism." Ph.D. diss., University of Hawaii, 1979.

Gardner, Lloyd C. "Woodrow Wilson and the Mexican Revolution," in Arthur S. Link, ed., *Woodrow Wilson and a Revolutionary World, 1913–1921*. Chapel Hill: University of North Carolina Press, 1982, pp. 3–48.

——. *A Covenant with Power: America and World Order from Wilson to Reagan*. London: Macmillan, 1984.

——. *Safe for Democracy: The Anglo-American Response to Revolution, 1913–1923*. New York: Oxford University Press, 1984.

Gelfand, Lawrence E. *The Inquiry: American Preparations for Peace, 1917–1919*. New Haven, Conn.: Yale University Press, 1963.

Gellner, Ernest. *Nations and Nationalism*. Ithaca, N.Y.: Cornell University Press, 1983.

George, Alexander L., and Juliette L. George. *Woodrow Wilson and Colonel House: A Personality Study*. New York: Dover, 1964.

Gershoni, Israel. "Between Ottomanism and Egyptianism: The Evolution of 'National Sentiment' in the Cairene Middle Class as Reflected in Najib Mahfuz's *Bayn Al-Qasrayn*," *Asian and African Studies* 17:1–3 (1983), 227–263.

——. "The Egyptian Nationalist Movement: A Self-Portrait, 1904–1919," *Asian and African Studies* 27:3 (1993), 313–341.

Gershoni, Israel, and James Jankowski. *Egypt, Islam and the Arabs: The Search for Egyptian Nationhood, 1900–1930*. New York: Oxford University Press, 1986.

Ghose, Sankar. *Socialism and Communism in India*. Bombay: Allied, 1971.

Gilderhus, Mark. *Pan American Visions: Woodrow Wilson in the Western Hemisphere, 1913–1921*. Tucson: University of Arizona Press, 1986.

Godshall, Wilson Leon. "The International Aspects of the Shantung Question." Ph.D. diss., University of Pennsylvania, 1923.

Goldberg, Ellis. "Peasants in Revolt, Egypt 1919," *International Journal of Middle East Studies* 24:2 (1992), 261–280.

Goldschmidt, Arthur, Jr. *Modern Egypt: The Formation of a Nation-State*. Boulder, Colo.: Westview, 1988.

——. *Biographical Dictionary of Modern Egypt*. Cairo: American University in Cairo Press, 2000.

Goldstein, Erik. *Winning the Peace: British Diplomatic Strategy, Peace Planning, and the Paris Peace Conference, 1916–1920*. New York: Oxford University Press, 1991.

Goldstein, Judith, and Robert O. Keohane, eds. *Ideas and Foreign Policy: Beliefs, Institutions and Political Change*. Ithaca, N.Y.: Cornell University Press, 1993.

Gong, Gerrit W. *The Standard of 'Civilization' in International Society*. Oxford: Clarendon, 1984.

Gordon, Andrew. *A Modern History of Japan: From Tokugawa Times to the Present*. New York: Oxford University Press, 2003.

Gordon, Leonard A. *Bengal: The Nationalist Movement, 1876–1940*. New York: Columbia University Press, 1974.

Graebner, Norman A., ed. *Ideas and Diplomacy: Readings in the Intellectual Traditions of American Foreign Policy*. New York: Oxford University Press, 1964.

Graham, Sally Hunter. "Woodrow Wilson, Alice Paul, and the Woman Suffrage Movement," *Political Science Quarterly* 98 (1983–1984), 665–679.

Green, Martin. *Gandhi: Voice of a New Age Revolution*. New York: Continuum, 1993.

Greenfeld, Liah. *Nationalism: Five Roads to Modernity*. Cambridge, Mass.: Harvard University Press, 1992.

——. "Transcending the Nation's Worth," *Daedalus* 122:3 (1993), 47–62.

Grieder, Jerome B. *Hu Shih and the Chinese Renaissance: Liberalism in the Chinese Revolution, 1917–37*. Cambridge, Mass.: Harvard University Press, 1970.

Grimal, Henri. *Decolonization: The British, French, Dutch and Belgian Empires, 1919–1963*. Stephan De Vos, trans. 1965. Reprint, Boulder, Colo.: Westview, 1978.

Gundappa, D. V. "Liberalism in India," *Confluence* 5:3 (1956), 216–228.

Hahm, Pyong-choon. "The Korean Perception of the United States," in Youngnok Koo and Dae-sook Suh, eds., *Korea and the United States: A Century of Cooperation*. Honolulu: University of Hawaii Press, 1984, pp. 23–52.

Hahn, Peter. *The United States, Great Britain, and Egypt, 1945–1956: Strategy and Diplomacy in the Early Cold War.* Chapel Hill: University of North Carolina Press, 1991.

Haithcox, John P. "The Roy-Lenin Debate on Colonial Policy: A New Interpretation," *Journal of Asian Studies* 23:1 (1963), 93–101.

——. *Communism and Nationalism in India: M. N. Roy and Comintern Policy, 1920–1939*. Princeton, N.J.: Princeton University Press, 1971.

Hall, John A. "Nationalisms: Classified and Explained," *Daedalus* 122:3 (1993), 1–28.

——. *International Orders*. Cambridge, Mass.: Blackwell, 1996.

Hamel, William Christopher. "Race and Responsible Government: Woodrow Wilson and the Philippines." Ph.D. diss., Michigan State University, 2002.

Han, Woo-keun. *The History of Korea*. Lee Kyung-shik, trans. Seoul: Eul-yoo, 1970.

Hancock, W. K. *Smuts: The Sanguine Years, 1870–1919*. Cambridge: Cambridge University Press, 1962.

Hapgood, David. *Charles R. Crane: The Man Who Bet on People*. [Hanover, N.H.:] Institute of Current World Affairs, 2000.

Harrington, Fred Harvey. *God, Mammon, and the Japanese: Dr. Horace N. Allen and Korean-American Relations, 1884–1905*. Madison: University of Wisconsin Press, 1944.

Harris, Sally. *Out of Control: British Foreign Policy and the Union of Democratic Control, 1914–1918*. Hull, England: University of Hull Press, 1996.

Harrison, Henrietta. "Newspapers and Nationalism in Rural China 1890–1929," *Past & Present* 166 (2000), 181–204.

Hatada, Takashi. *A History of Korea*. Warren W. Smith, Jr., and Benjamin H. Hazard, trans. Santa Barbara, Calif.: ABC-Clio, 1969.

Hay, Stephen N. "Rabindranath Tagore in America," *American Quarterly* 14:3 (1962), 439–463.

Headrick, Daniel R. *The Tentacles of Progress: Technology Transfer in the Age of Imperialism, 1850–1940*. New York: Oxford University Press, 1988.

——. *The Invisible Weapon: Telecommunications and International Politics, 1851–1945*. New York: Oxford University Press, 1991.

Heater, Derek Benjamin. *National Self-Determination: Woodrow Wilson and His Legacy*. New York: St. Martin's, 1994.

Heckscher, August. *Woodrow Wilson*. New York: Scribner's, 1991.

Heehs, Peter. *India's Freedom Struggle, 1857–1947: A Short History*. New Delhi: Oxford University Press, 1988.

Henderson, Paul V. N. "Woodrow Wilson, Victoriano Huerta, and the Recognition Issue in Mexico," *Americas: A Quarterly Review of Inter-American Cultural History* 41:2 (1984), 151–176.

Hilderbrand, Robert C. *Power and the People: Executive Management of Public Opinion in Foreign Affairs, 1897–1921*. Chapel Hill: University of North Carolina Press, 1981.

Hobsbawm, Eric. *Nations and Nationalism since 1780: Programme, Myth, Reality.* Cambridge: Cambridge University Press, 1990.

——. *The Age of Extremes: A History of the World, 1914–1991*. New York: Pantheon, 1994.

Hoffmann, Frank. "The Muo Declaration: History in the Making," *Korean Studies* 13 (1989), 22–41.

Hoganson, Kristin. "Stuff It: Domestic Consumption and the Americanization of the World Paradigm," *Diplomatic History* 30:4 (2006), 571–594.

Holland, R. F. *European Decolonization, 1918–1981: An Introductory Survey*. New York: St. Martin's, 1985.

Hoover, Karl. "The Hindu Conspiracy in California, 1913–1918," *German Studies Review* 8:2 (1985), 245–261.

Hope, A. Guy. *America and Swaraj*. Washington, D.C.: Public Affairs Press, 1968.

Hourani, Albert. *Arabic Thought in the Liberal Age, 1798–1939*. Cambridge: Cambridge University Press, 1962.

Hsiao Kung-chuan. *A Modern China and a New World: Kang Yu-wei, Reformer and Utopian, 1858–1927*. Seattle: University of Washington Press, 1975.

Hsü, Immanuel C. Y. *The Rise of Modern China*. 6th ed. New York: Oxford University Press, 2000.

Hu Shizhang. *Stanley K. Hornbeck and the Open Door Policy, 1919–1937*. Westport, Conn.: Greenwood, 1995.

Huang, Philip. *Liang Ch'i-ch'ao and Modern Chinese Liberalism*. Seattle: University of Washington Press, 1972.

Hunt, Michael H. *The Making of a Special Relationship: The United States and China to 1914*. New York: Columbia University Press, 1983.

——. *Ideology and U.S. Foreign Policy*. New Haven, Conn.: Yale University Press, 1987.

——. "Internationalizing U.S. Diplomatic History: A Practical Agenda," *Diplomatic History* 15:1 (1991), 1–11.

——. *The Genesis of Chinese Communist Foreign Policy*. New York: Columbia University Press, 1996.

Huthmacher, J. J., and W. I. Susman, eds. *Wilson's Diplomacy: An International Symposium*. Cambridge, Mass.: Schenkman, 1973.

Iriye, Akira. *After Imperialism: The Search for a New Order in the Far East, 1921–1931*. Cambridge, Mass.: Harvard University Press, 1965.

——. "Culture and Power: International Relations as Intercultural Relations," *Diplomatic History* 3:2 (1979), 115–128.

——. "The Internationalization of History," *American Historical Review* 94:1 (1989), 1–10.

——. *The Globalizing of America, 1913–1945*. Vol. 3 of *The Cambridge History of American Foreign Relations*, Warren I. Cohen, series ed. New York: Cambridge University Press, 1993.

——. *Cultural Internationalism and World Order.* Baltimore, Md.: Johns Hopkins University Press, 1997.

——. "Transnational History," *Contemporary European History* 13:2 (2004), 211–222.

Isaacs, Harold R. *Scratches on Our Minds: American Images of China and India.* New York: John Day, 1958.

Israel, Jerry. *Progressivism and the Open Door: America and China, 1905–1921.* Pittsburgh, Pa.: University of Pittsburgh Press, 1971.

——. "Carl Crow, Edgar Snow, and Shifting American Journalistic Perceptions of China," in Jonathan Goldstein, Jerry Israel, and Hilary Conroy, eds., *America Views China: American Images of China Then and Now.* Bethlehem, Pa.: Lehigh University Press, 1991, pp. 148–168.

Jacobson, Matthew Frye. *Barbarian Virtues: The United States Encounters Foreign Peoples at Home and Abroad, 1876–1917.* New York: Hill and Wang, 2000.

Jauhri, R. C. *American Diplomacy and Independence for India.* Bombay: Vora, 1970.

Jeffery, Keith. *The British Army and the Crisis of Empire, 1918–22.* Manchester, England: Manchester University Press, 1984.

Jensen, Joan M. "The 'Hindu Conspiracy': A Reassessment," *Pacific Historical Review* 48:1 (1979), 65–83.

Johnson, David, Andrew J. Nathan, and Evelyn S. Rawski, eds. *Popular Culture in Late Imperial China.* Berkeley: University of California Press, 1985.

Johnson, Robert David. "Article XI in the Debate on the United States' Rejection of the League of Nations," *International History Review* 15 (1993), 502–524.

——. *The Peace Progressives and American Foreign Relations.* Cambridge, Mass.: Harvard University Press, 1995.

Judge, Joan. *Print and Politics: "Shibao" and the Culture of Reform in Late Qing China.* Stanford, Calif.: Stanford University Press, 1996.

Karl, Rebecca E. "Creating Asia: China in the World in the Beginning of the Twentieth Century," *American Historical Review* 103:4 (1998), 1096–1118.

——. *Staging the World: Chinese Nationalism at the Turn of the Twentieth Century.* Durham, N.C.: Duke University Press, 2002.

Karsh, Efraim, and Inari Karsh. *Empires of the Sand: The Struggle for Mastery in the Middle East, 1789–1923.* Cambridge, Mass.: Harvard University Press, 1999.

Kaushik, Karuna. *Russian Revolution & Indian Nationalism: Studies of Lajpat Rai, Subhas Chandra Bose & Rammanohar Lohia.* Delhi: Chanakya, 1984.

Kawamura, Noriko. "Wilsonian Idealism and Japanese Claims at the Paris Peace Conference," *Pacific Historical Review* 66:4 (1997), 503–526.

Kedourie, Elie. "Sa'd Zaghlul and the British," in his *The Chatham House Version and Other Middle-Eastern Studies.* New York: Praeger, 1970, pp. 82–159.

——. *Nationalism.* 4th ed. Oxford: Blackwell, 1993.

Kedourie, Elie, ed. *Nationalism in Asia and Africa.* New York: World, 1970.

Keegan, Nicholas M. "From Chancery to Cloister: The Chinese Diplomat Who Became a Benedictine Monk," *Diplomacy & Statecraft* 10:1 (1999), 172–185.

Keer, Dhananjay. *Lokamanya Tilak: Father of the Indian Freedom Struggle.* 2d ed. Bombay: Popular Prakashan, 1969.

Kennan, George. *American Diplomacy, 1900–1950*. Chicago: University of Chicago Press, 1951.

——. *Soviet-American Relations, 1917–1920*. 2 vols. Princeton, N.J.: Princeton University Press, 1956–1958.

Kennedy, David M. *Over Here: The First World War and American Society*. New York: Oxford University Press, 1980.

Kennedy, Paul M. "The Theory and Practice of Imperialism," *Historical Journal* 20:3 (1977), 761–769.

——. *The Realities behind Diplomacy: Background Influences on British External Policy, 1865–1980*. London: Allen & Unwin, 1981.

——. "The First World War and the International Power System," *International Security* 9:1 (1984), 7–40.

Kennedy, Ross A. "Woodrow Wilson, World War I, and an American Conception of National Security," *Diplomatic History* 25:1 (2001), 1–31.

Kernek, Sterling J. *Distractions of Peace during War: The Lloyd George Government's Reactions to Woodrow Wilson, December 1916–November 1918*. Philadelphia: American Philosophical Society, 1975.

Kerney, James. *The Political Education of Woodrow Wilson*. New York: Century, 1926.

Keylor, William R. "Versailles and International Diplomacy," in Manfred F. Boemeke, Gerald D. Feldman, and Elisabeth Glaser., eds., *The Treaty of Versailles: A Reassessment after 75 Years*. Cambridge: Cambridge University Press, 1998, pp. 469–506.

Khalidi, Rashid, ed. *The Origins of Arab Nationalism*. New York: Columbia University Press, 1991.

Kiang, Wen-han. *The Chinese Student Movement*. New York: King's Crown, 1948.

Kim, Han-Kyo. "The Declaration of Independence, March 1, 1919: A New Translation," *Korean Studies* 13 (1989), 1–4.

Kim, Hyung-chan. *Tosan Ahn Ch'ang-ho: A Profile of a Prophetic Patriot*. Seoul: Tosan Memorial Foundation, 1996.

Kim, Hyung-chan, and Wayne Patterson, eds. *The Koreans in America, 1882–1974*. New York: Oceana, 1974.

Kim, Warren Y. *Koreans in America*. Seoul: Po Chin Chai, 1971.

Kimball, Warren F. *The Juggler: Franklin Roosevelt as Wartime Statesman*. Princeton, N.J.: Princeton University Press, 1991.

Kimitada, Miwa. "Japanese Opinions on Woodrow Wilson in War and Peace," *Monumenta Nipponica* 22:3–4 (1967), 368–389.

Kissinger, Henry. *Diplomacy*. New York: Simon & Schuster, 1994.

Knock, Thomas J. "Kennan versus Wilson," in John Milton Cooper, Jr., and Charles E. Neu, eds., *The Wilson Era*. Arlington Heights, Ill.: Harlan Davidson, 1991, pp. 302–326.

——. *To End All Wars: Woodrow Wilson and the Quest for a New World Order*. 1992. Reprint, Princeton, N.J.: Princeton University Press, 1995.

Koo, Youngnok, and Dae-sook Suh, eds. *Korea and the United States: A Century of Cooperation*. Honolulu: University of Hawaii Press, 1984.

Krüger, Horst. "Indian National Revolutionaries in Paris before World War I," *Archív Orientální* 45 (1977), 329–339.

Ku, Dae-yeol. *Korea under Colonialism: The March First Movement and Anglo-Japanese Relations*. Seoul: Seoul Computer Press, 1985.

Kuhn, Philip A. *Origins of the Modern Chinese State*. Stanford, Calif.: Stanford University Press, 2002.

Kumar, R., ed. *Essays on Gandhian Politics: The Rowlatt Satyagraha of 1919*. Oxford: Clarendon, 1971.

Kumar, Ravinder. "From Swaraj to Purna Swaraj: Nationalist Politics in the City of Bombay, 1920–32," in D. A. Low, ed., *Congress and the Raj: Facets of the Indian Struggle, 1917–1947*. London: Heinemann, 1977, pp. 77–106.

Laqueur, Walter Z. *Communism and Nationalism in the Middle East*. 3d ed. London: Routledge & Kegan Paul, 1961.

Lāshīn, 'Abd al-Khāliq. *Sa'd Zaghlūl wa-Dawruhu fi al-Siyāsa al-Miṣriyya* [Sa'd Zaghlul and His Role in the Politics of Egypt]. Cairo: Maktabat Madbūlī, 1975.

Latham, Earl, ed. *The Philosophies and Policies of Woodrow Wilson*. Chicago: University of Chicago Press, 1958.

Lauren, Paul Gordon. "Human Rights in History: Diplomacy and Racial Equality at the Paris Peace Conference," *Diplomatic History* 3 (1978), 257–278.

——. *Power and Prejudice: The Politics and Diplomacy of Racial Discrimination*. 2d ed. Boulder, Colo.: Westview, 1996.

Lawrence, Mark Atwood. *Assuming the Burden: Europe and the American Commitment to War in Vietnam*. Berkeley: University of California Press, 2005.

Lazo, Dimitri D. "A Question of Loyalty: Robert Lansing and the Treaty of Versailles," *Diplomatic History* 9:1 (1985), 35–53.

Lee, Chong-sik. *The Politics of Korean Nationalism*. Berkeley: University of California Press, 1963.

——. *The Korean Workers' Party: A Short History*. Stanford, Calif.: Hoover Institution Press, 1978.

Lee Feigon. *Chen Duxiu, Founder of the Chinese Communist Party*. Princeton, N.J.: Princeton University Press, 1983.

Lee, Ki-baik. *A New History of Korea*. Edward W. Wagner with Edward J. Shultz, trans. Cambridge, Mass.: Harvard University Press, 1984.

Lee, Leo and Andrew J. Nathan, "The Beginnings of Mass Culture," in David Johnson, Andrew J. Nathan, and Evelyn S. Rawski, eds., *Popular Culture in Late Imperial China*. Berkeley: University of California Press, 1985, pp. 368–378.

Lee, Timothy S. "A Political Factor in the Rise of Protestantism in Korea: Protestantism and the 1919 March First Movement," *Church History* 69:1 (2000), 116–142.

Levenson, Joseph. *Liang Chi-chao and the Mind of Modern China*. Cambridge, Mass.: Harvard University Press, 1953.

——. *Confucian China and Its Modern Fate: A Trilogy*. Berkeley: University of California Press, 1968.

Levin, N. Gordon. *Woodrow Wilson and World Politics: America's Response to War and Revolution*. New York: Oxford University Press, 1968.

Li Danyang. "Makesi xueshuo yanjiuhui yu Zhongguo gongchanzhuyi zuzhi de qiyuan" [The Society for the Study of Marxism and the Origins of Communist

Organization in China], *Shixue yuekan* [Journal of Historical Science] 6 (2004), 51–59.

Li, Tien-yi. *Woodrow Wilson's China Policy, 1913–1917*. New York: Twayne, 1952.

Link, Arthur S. *Wilson the Diplomatist: A Look at His Major Foreign Policies*. Baltimore, Md.: Johns Hopkins University Press, 1957.

——. *The Higher Realism of Woodrow Wilson and Other Essays*. Nashville, Tenn.: Vanderbilt University Press, 1971.

Link, Arthur S., ed. *Woodrow Wilson and a Revolutionary World, 1913–1921*. Chapel Hill: University of North Carolina Press, 1982.

Lloyd, George Ambrose. *Egypt since Cromer*. 2 vols. London: Macmillan, 1933.

Lo, Jung-pang, ed. *K'ang Yu-wei: A Biography and a Symposium*. Tucson: University of Arizona Press, 1967.

Logevall, Fredrik. *Choosing War: The Lost Chance for Peace and the Escalation of War in Vietnam*. Berkeley: University of California Press, 1999.

Lone, Stewart, and Gavan McCormack. *Korea since 1850*. New York: St. Martin's, 1993.

Low, D. A. *Government Archives in South Asia: A Guide to the National and State Archives in Ceylon, India and Pakistan*. Cambridge: Cambridge University Press, 1969.

Low, D. A., ed. *Congress and the Raj: Facets of the Indian Struggle, 1917–1947*. London: Heinemann, 1977.

Lunardini, Christine A. "Standing Firm: William Monroe Trotter's Meetings with Woodrow Wilson, 1913–1914," *Journal of Negro History* 64:3 (1979), 244–264.

Lunardini, Christine A., and Thomas J. Knock. "Woodrow Wilson and Woman Suffrage: A New Look," *Political Science Quarterly* 95 (1980–1981), 655–671.

Lynch, Allen. "Woodrow Wilson and the Principle of 'National Self-Determination': A Reconsideration," *Review of International Studies* 28 (2002), 419–436.

MacKinnon, Stephen R. "Toward a History of the Chinese Press in the Republican Period," *Modern China* 23:1 (1997), 3–32.

MacMillan, Margaret. *Paris 1919: Six Months That Changed the World*. New York: Random House, 2002.

Maddox, Robert James. *The Unknown War with Russia: Wilson's Siberian Intervention*. San Rafael, Calif.: Presidio, 1977.

Maier, Charles S. *Recasting Bourgeois Europe: Stabilization in France, Germany, and Italy in the Decade after World War I*. Princeton, N.J.: Princeton University Press, 1975.

Makdisi, Ussama. " 'Anti-Americanism' in the Arab World: An Interpretation of a Brief History," *Journal of American History* 89:2 (2002), 538–557.

Mamatey, Victor S. *The United States and East Central Europe, 1914–1918: A Study in Wilsonian Diplomacy and Propaganda*. Princeton, N.J.: Princeton University Press, 1957.

Manela, Erez. "Good Will and Bad: Rethinking US-Egyptian Contacts in the Interwar Years," *Middle Eastern Studies* 38:1 (2002), 71–89.

——. "A Man Ahead of His Time? Wilsonian Globalism and the Doctrine of Preemption," *International Journal* 60:4 (2005), 1115–1124.

——. "Imagining Woodrow Wilson in Asia: Dreams of East-West Harmony and the Revolt against Empire in 1919," *American Historical Review* 111:5 (2006), 1327–1351.

Margulies, Herbert F. *The Mild Reservationists and the League of Nations Controversy in the Senate*. Columbia: University of Missouri Press, 1989.

Marks, Sally. *The Ebbing of European Ascendancy: An International History of the World 1914–1945*. London: Arnold, 2002.

Marston, F. S. *The Peace Conference of 1919: Organization and Procedure*. Oxford: Oxford University Press, 1944.

Martel, Gordon. "The Meaning of Power: Rethinking the Decline and Fall of Great Britain," *International History Review* 13:4 (1991), 662–694.

Martin, Laurence W. *Peace without Victory: Woodrow Wilson and the British Liberals*. New Haven, Conn.: Yale University Press, 1958.

Mathur, L. P. *Indian Revolutionary Movement in the United States of America*. Delhi: Chand, 1970.

Matsuo, Kazuyuki. "American Propaganda in China: The U.S. Committee on Public Information, 1918–1919," *Journal of American and Canadian Studies* [Japan] 14 (1996), 19–42.

May, Ernest R. *The World War and American Isolation, 1914–1917*. Cambridge, Mass.: Harvard University Press, 1959.

——. *Imperial Democracy: The Emergence of America as a Great Power*. New York: Harcourt, Brace & World, 1961.

——. *American Imperialism: A Speculative Essay*. New York: Atheneum, 1968.

Mayall, James. *Nationalism and International Society*. Cambridge: Cambridge University Press, 1990.

Mayer, Arno J. *Wilson vs. Lenin: Political Origins of the New Diplomacy, 1917–1918*. Cleveland, Ohio: World, 1964.

——. *Politics and Diplomacy of Peacemaking: Containment and Counterrevolution at Versailles, 1918–1919*. New York: Knopf, 1967.

McDermott, Kevin, and Jeremy Agnew, eds. *The Comintern: A History of International Communism from Lenin to Stalin*. London: Macmillan, 1996.

McIntyre, John D., Jr. *The Boycott of the Milner Mission: A Study in Egyptian Nationalism*. New York: Lang, 1985.

McKillen, Elizabeth. "Ethnicity, Class, and Wilsonian Internationalism Reconsidered: The Mexican-American and Irish-American Immigrant Left and U.S. Foreign Relations, 1914–1922," *Diplomatic History* 25:4 (Fall 2001), 553–587.

McPherson, Alan. *Yankee No!: Anti-Americanism in U.S.-Latin American Relations*. Cambridge, Mass.: Harvard University Press, 2003.

Meaney, Neville K. "Arthur S. Link and Thomas Woodrow Wilson," *Journal of American Studies* 1:1 (1967), 119–126.

Meisner, Maurice. *Li Ta-chao and the Origins of Chinese Marxism*. Cambridge, Mass.: Harvard University Press, 1967.

Mervin, David. "Henry Cabot Lodge and the League of Nations," *Journal of American Studies* 4:2 (1971), 201–214.

Meyer, John W., John Boli, George M. Thomas, and Francisco O. Ramirez. "World Society and the Nation-State," *American Journal of Sociology* 103:1 (1997), 144–181.

Minault, Gail. *The Khilafat Movement: Religious Symbolism and Political Mobilization in India*. New York: Columbia University Press, 1982.

Mitter, Rana. *A Bitter Revolution: China's Struggle with the Modern World*. New York: Oxford University Press, 2004.

Mock, James R., and Cedric Larson. *Words That Won the War: The Story of the Committee on Public Information, 1917–1919*. Princeton, N.J.: Princeton University Press, 1939.

Mommsen, Wolfgang J. *Theories of Imperialism*. New York: Random House, 1980.

Monroe, Elizabeth. *Britain's Moment in the Middle East, 1914–1971*. New rev. ed. Baltimore, Md.: Johns Hopkins University Press, 1981.

Moore, James R. "Woodrow Wilson and Post-Armistice Diplomacy: Some French Views," *Reviews in American History* 2:2 (1974), 207–213.

Moynihan, Daniel Patrick. *On the Law of Nations*. Cambridge, Mass.: Harvard University Press, 1990.

Mulder, John M., Ernest M. White, and Ethel S. White, comps. *Woodrow Wilson: A Bibliography*. Westport, Conn.: Greenwood, 1997.

Mu'nis, Husayn. *Dirasāt fi Thawrat 1919*. Cairo: Dār al-Ma'ārif, 1976.

Murthy, Nadig Krishna. *Indian Journalism: Origin, Growth and Development of Indian Journalism, from Asoka to Nehru*. Mysore, India: University of Mysore, 1966.

Muzumdar, Haridas T. *America's Contributions to India's Freedom*. Allahabad, India: Central Book Depot, 1962.

Naidis, Mark. "Propaganda of the *Gadar* Party," *Pacific Historical Review* 20:3 (1951), 251–260.

Nairn, Tom. "Internationalism and the Second Coming," *Daedalus* 122:3 (1993), 155–170.

Najjār, Husayn Fawzī. *Sa'd Zaghlūl: Al-Za'īm wal-Za'āma* [Sa'd Zaghlul: The Leader and the Leadership]. Cairo: Maktabat Madbūlī, 1986.

Natarajan, S. *A History of the Press in India*. Bombay: Asia Publishing House, 1962.

Nathan, Andrew J. *Peking Politics, 1918–1923*. Berkeley: University of California Press, 1976.

——. *Chinese Democracy*. New York: Knopf, 1985.

Nickles, David Paull. *Under the Wire: How the Telegraph Changed Diplomacy*. Cambridge, Mass.: Harvard University Press, 2003.

Ninkovich, Frank. *Modernity and Power: A History of the Domino Theory in the Twentieth Century*. Chicago: University of Chicago Press, 1994.

——. *The Wilsonian Century: US Foreign Policy since 1900*. Chicago: University of Chicago Press, 1999.

——. "The United States and Imperialism," in Robert D. Schulzinger, ed., *A Companion to American Foreign Relations*. Malden, Mass.: Blackwell, 2003, pp. 79–102.

Noble, George Bernard. *Policies and Opinions at Paris, 1919: Wilsonian Diplomacy, the Versailles Peace, and French Public Opinion*. New York: Macmillan, 1935.

O, Se-ŭng. *Dr. Philip Jaisohn's Reform Movement, 1896–1898: A Critical Appraisal of the Independence Club*. Lanham, Md.: University Press of America, 1995.

Oliver, Robert T. *Syngman Rhee: The Man behind the Myth*. New York: Dodd Mead, 1954.

Osgood, Robert E. *Ideals and Self-Interest in America's Foreign Relations: The Great Transformation of the Twentieth Century.* Chicago: University of Chicago Press, 1953.

Owen, Roger, and Bob Sutcliffe, eds. *Studies in the Theory of Imperialism.* London: Longman, 1972.

Parsons, Edward B. "Some International Implications of the 1918 Roosevelt-Lodge Campaign against Wilson and a Democratic Congress," *Presidential Studies Quarterly* 19 (1989), 141–157.

Parvate, T. V. *Bal Gangadhar Tilak: A Narrative and Interpretive Review of His Life, Career and Contemporary Events.* Ahmedabad, India: Navajivan, 1958.

Pedersen, Susan. "Settler Colonialism at the Bar of the League of Nations," in Caroline Elkins and Susan Pedersen, eds., *Settler Colonialism in the Twentieth Century: Projects, Practices, Legacies.* New York: Routledge, 2005, pp. 113–134.

——. "The Meaning of the Mandate System: An Argument," *Geschichte und Gesellschaft* 32 (2006), 1–23.

Philpott, Daniel. *Revolutions in Sovereignty: How Ideas Shaped Modern International Relations.* Princeton, N.J.: Princeton University Press, 2001.

Piott, Steven L. *Holy Joe: Joseph W. Folk and the Missouri Idea.* Columbia: University of Missouri Press, 1998.

Plummer, Brenda Gayle. "The Changing Face of Diplomatic History: A Literature Review," *The History Teacher* 38:3 (2005), 385–400.

Pollard, Robert T. *China's Foreign Relations, 1917–1931.* New York: Macmillan, 1933.

Pomerance, Michla. "The United States and Self-Determination: Perspectives on the Wilsonian Conception," *American Journal of International Law* 70 (1976), 1–27.

——. *Self-Determination in Law and Practice: The New Doctrine in the United Nations.* Boston: Hingham, 1982.

Power, Paul F., ed. *The Meanings of Gandhi.* Manoa: University of Hawaii Press, 1971.

Pradhan, G. P., and A. K. Bhagwat. *Lokamanya Tilak: A Biography.* Bombay: Jaico, 1959.

Price, Don C. *Russia and the Roots of the Chinese Revolution, 1896–1911.* Cambridge, Mass.: Harvard University Press, 1974.

Price, Ruth. *The Lives of Agnes Smedley.* New York: Oxford University Press, 2005.

Pugach, Noel H. "Making the Open Door Work: Paul S. Reinsch in China, 1913–1919," *Pacific Historical Review* 38:2 (1969), 157–175.

——. "American Friendship for China and the Shantung Question at the Washington Conference," *Journal of American History* 64:1 (June 1977), 67–86.

——. *Paul S. Reinsch: Open Door Diplomat in Action.* Millwood, N.Y.: KTO, 1979.

Qureshi, M. Naeem. *Pan-Islam in British Indian Politics: A Study of the Khilafat Movement, 1918–1924.* Leiden, Netherlands: Brill, 1999.

Rāfiʿī, ʿAbd al-Raḥman. *Thawrat Sanat 1919: Tarīkh Miṣr al-Qawmī min Sanat 1914 ilā Sanat 1921* [The 1919 Revolution: The National History of Egypt, 1914–1921]. Cairo: Maktabat al-Nahḍa al-Miṣriyya, 1955.

Ramaḍan, ʿAbd al-ʿAẓim. *Thawrat 1919 fi Ḍaw' Mudhakkirāt Saʿd Zaghlūl* [The 1919 Revolution in Light of Saʿd Zaghlul's Memoirs]. Cairo: Al-Hay'ah al-Miṣriyya al-ʿĀmma lil-Kitāb, 2002.

Rao, Vasant D. "Tilak's Attitude towards the Montagu-Chelmsford Reforms," *Journal of Indian History* 56 (1978), 169–181.

Rathore, Naeem Gul. "Indian Nationalist Agitation in the United States: A Study of Lala Lajpat Rai and the India Home Rule League of America, 1914–1920." Ph.D. diss., Columbia University, 1965.

Raucher, Alan. "American Anti-Imperialists and the Pro-India Movement, 1900–1932," *Pacific Historical Review* 43 (1974), 83–110.

Read, Donald. *The Power of News: The History of Reuters*. 2d ed. New York: Oxford University Press, 1999.

Reed, James. *The Missionary Mind and American East Asia Policy, 1911–1915*. Cambridge, Mass.: Council on East Asian Studies, Harvard University, 1983.

Rees, Tim, and Andrew Thorpe, eds. *International Communism and the Communist International, 1919–43*. New York: St. Martin's, 1998.

Reid, Donald Malcolm. "The 'Urabi Revolution and the British Conquest, 1879–1882," in M. W. Daly, ed., *The Cambridge History of Egypt*, vol. 2. Cambridge: Cambridge University Press, 1998, pp. 217–238.

Rhodes, Harry A., ed. *History of the Korea Mission, Presbyterian Church, U.S.A.* Vol. 1: *1884–1934*. Seoul: Presbyterian Church of Korea, Department of Education, 1934.

Robinson, Michael Edson. *Cultural Nationalism in Colonial Korea, 1920–1925*. Seattle: University of Washington Press, 1988.

Robinson, Ronald. "Non-European Foundations of European Imperialism: Sketch for a Theory of Collaboration," in Roger Owen and Bob Sutcliffe, eds., *Studies in the Theory of Imperialism*. London: Longman, 1972, pp. 117–142.

Rochester, Stuart I. *American Liberal Disillusionment in the Wake of World War I*. University Park: Pennsylvania State University Press, 1977.

Rodgers, Daniel T. *Atlantic Crossings: Social Politics in a Progressive Age*. Cambridge, Mass.: Belknap, 1998.

Rosenberg, Emily S. *Spreading the American Dream: American Economic and Cultural Expansion, 1890–1945*. New York: Hill and Wang, 1982.

——. *Financial Missionaries to the World: The Politics and Culture of Dollar Diplomacy, 1900–1930*. Cambridge, Mass.: Harvard University Press, 1999.

Rosenberg, Jonathan. "For Democracy, Not Hypocrisy: World War and Race Relations in the United States, 1914–1919," *International History Review* 21:3 (1999), 592–625.

——. *How Far the Promised Land: World Affairs and the American Civil Rights Movement from the First World War to Vietnam*. Princeton, N.J.: Princeton University Press, 2005.

Ryland, Shane. "Edwin Montagu in India, 1917–1918: Politics of the Montagu-Chelmsford Report," *South Asia* 3 (1973), 79–92.

Saini, Krishnan G. "The Economic Aspects of India's Participation in the First World War," in DeWitt C. Ellinwood and S. D. Pradhan, eds., *India and World War I*. New Delhi: South Asia Books, 1978, pp. 141–176.

Sareen, Tilak Raj. *Russian Revolution and India, 1917–1921*. New Delhi: Sterling, 1977.

——. *Russian Revolution and India: A Study of Soviet Policy towards the Indian National Movement, 1922–29*. New Delhi: Sterling, 1978.

Sarkar, Sumit. *The Swadeshi Movement in Bengal, 1903–1908*. New Delhi: People's, 1973.

——. *Modern India, 1885–1947*. 2d ed. London: Macmillan, 1989.

Savage, Timothy L. "The American Response to the Korean Independence Movement, 1910–1945," *Korean Studies* 20 (1996), 189–231.

Schiffrin, Harold Z. *Sun Yat-sen: Reluctant Revolutionary*. Boston: Little, Brown, 1980.

Schild, Georg. *Between Ideology and Realpolitik: Woodrow Wilson and the Russian Revolution, 1917–1921*. Westport, Conn.: Greenwood, 1995.

Schmid, Andre. *Korea between Empires, 1895–1919*. New York: Columbia University Press, 2002.

Schmidt, Hans. "Democracy for China: American Propaganda and the May Fourth Movement," *Diplomatic History* 22:1 (1998), 1–28.

Schrecker, John E. *Imperialism and Chinese Nationalism: Germany in Shantung*. Cambridge, Mass.: Harvard University Press, 1971.

Schroeder, Paul W. *The Transformation of European Politics, 1763–1848*. New York: Oxford University Press, 1994.

Schulte Nordholt, Jan Willem. *Woodrow Wilson: A Life for World Peace*. Herbert H. Rowen, trans. Berkeley: University of California Press, 1991.

Schulzinger, Robert D. *A Time for War: The United States and Vietnam, 1941–1975*. New York: Oxford University Press, 1997.

Schwabe, Klaus. *Woodrow Wilson, Revolutionary Germany, and Peacemaking, 1918–1919: Missionary Diplomacy and the Realities of Power*. Rita Kimber and Robert Kimber, trans. Chapel Hill: University of North Carolina Press, 1985.

Schwarcz, Vera. *The Chinese Enlightenment: Intellectual Trends and the Legacy of the May Fourth Movement of 1919*. Berkeley: University of California Press, 1986.

Schwartz, Benjamin I., ed. *Reflections on the May Fourth Movement: A Symposium*. Cambridge, Mass.: East Asian Research Center, Harvard University, 1972.

Scully, Eileen P. *Bargaining with the State from Afar: American Citizenship in Treaty Port China, 1844–1942*. New York: Columbia University Press, 2001.

Searle, Geoffrey. *The Quest for National Efficiency: A Study in British Politics and Political Thought, 1899–1914*. Oxford: Blackwell, 1971.

Sen, S. P., ed. *Dictionary of National Biography*. 4 vols. Calcutta: Institute of Historical Studies, 1974.

Seshachari, Candadai. *Gandhi and the American Scene: An Intellectual History and Inquiry*. Bombay: Nachiketa, 1969.

Seth, Sanjay. "Rewriting Histories of Nationalism: The Politics of 'Moderate Nationalism' in India, 1870–1905," *American Historical Review* 104:1 (1999), 95–116.

Seymour, Charles. *American Diplomacy during the World War*. Baltimore, Md.: Johns Hopkins University Press, 1934.

——. *American Neutrality, 1914–1917: Essays on the Causes of American Intervention in the World War*. New Haven, Conn.: Yale University Press, 1935.

Sheridan, James E. *Chinese Warlord: The Career of Feng Yü-hsiang*. Stanford, Calif.: Stanford University Press, 1966.

Shimazu, Naoko. *Japan, Race and Equality: The Racial Equality Proposal of 1919*. London: Routledge, 1998.

Singh, Diwakar Prasad. *American Attitude towards the Indian Nationalist Movement*. New Delhi: Munshiram Manoharlal, 1974.

Singh, Harnam. *The Indian National Movement and American Opinion*. New Delhi: Rama Krishna, 1962.

Sisson, Richard, and Stanley Wolpert, eds. *Congress and Indian Nationalism: The Pre-Independence Phase*. Berkeley: University of California Press, 1988.

Skidelsky, Robert. *John Maynard Keynes: A Biography*. London: Macmillan, 1983.

Smith, Charles D. *Islam and the Search for Social Order in Modern Egypt: A Biography of Muhammad Husayn Haykal*. Albany: State University of New York Press, 1983.

Smith, Daniel M. *The Great Departure: The United States and World War I, 1914–1920*. New York: Wiley, 1965.

Smith, Gaddis. *Woodrow Wilson's Fourteen Points after 75 Years*. New York: Carnegie Council on Ethics and International Affairs, 1993.

Smith, Jeremy. *The Bolsheviks and the National Question, 1917–1923*. London: Macmillan, 1999.

Smith, Ray T. "V. S. Srinivasa Sastri and the Moderate Style in Indian Politics," *South Asia* 2 (1972), 81–100.

Smith, Tony. *America's Mission: The United States and the Worldwide Struggle for Democracy in the Twentieth Century*. Princeton, N.J.: Princeton University Press, 1994.

Spear, Percival. *The Oxford History of Modern India, 1740–1975*. 2d ed. Oxford: Oxford University Press, 1978.

Spence, Jonathan D. *The Gate of Heavenly Peace: The Chinese and Their Revolution, 1895–1980*. New York: Viking, 1981.

——. *Chinese Roundabout: Essays in History and Culture*. New York: Norton, 1992.

——. *The Search for Modern China*. 2d ed. New York: Norton, 1999.

Startt, James D. "American Propaganda in Britain during World War I," *Prologue* 28:1 (1996), 17–33.

Steigerwald, David. *Wilsonian Idealism in America*. Ithaca, N.Y.: Cornell University Press, 1994.

——. "The Reclamation of Woodrow Wilson?" *Diplomatic History* 23:1 (Winter 1999), 79–99.

Stein, Burton. *A History of India*. Oxford: Oxford University Press, 1998.

Stevenson, David. "French War Aims and the American Challenge, 1914–1918," *Historical Journal* 22:4 (1979), 877–894.

——. *The First World War and International Politics*. Oxford: Oxford University Press, 1988.

Stoessinger, John G. *Crusaders and Pragmatists: Movers of Modern American Foreign Policy*. 2d ed. New York: Norton, 1985.

Suh, Dae-sook. *The Korean Communist Movement, 1918–48*. Princeton, N.J.: Princeton University Press, 1967.

Sunoo, Sonia Shinn. *Korea Kaleidoscope: Oral Histories*. Davis, Calif.: Korean Oral History Project, 1982.

Suri, Jeremi. *Power and Protest: Global Revolution and the Rise of Détente*. Cambridge, Mass.: Harvard University Press, 2003.

Tai, Hue-Tam Ho. *Radicalism and the Origins of the Vietnamese Revolution*. Cambridge, Mass.: Harvard University Press, 1992.

Tang Xiaobing. *Global Space and the Nationalist Discourse of Modernity: The Historical Thinking of Liang Qichao*. Stanford, Calif.: Stanford University Press, 1996.

Tang Zhenchang. *Cai Yuanpei Zhuan* [The Biography of Cai Yuanpei]. Shanghai: Shanghai renmin chubanshe, 1985.

Tao Wenzhao. *Zhong Mei guanxi shi, 1911–1950* [Sino-American Relations, 1911–1950]. Chongqing: Chongqing Press, 1993.

Temperley, H. W., ed. *A History of the Peace Conference of Paris*. 6 vols. London: Frowde and Hodder & Stoughton, 1920–1924.

Terry, Janice J. "Official British Reaction to Egyptian Nationalism after World War I," *Al-Abhath* 21:2–4 (1968), 15–29.

——. *The Wafd, 1919–1952*. London: Third World Centre for Research and Publishing, 1982.

Thompson, John A. "Woodrow Wilson and World War I: A Reappraisal," *Journal of American Studies* 19 (1985), 325–348.

——. *Reformers and War: American Progressive Publicists and the First World War.* Cambridge: Cambridge University Press, 1987.

——. "More Tactics than Strategy: Woodrow Wilson and World War I, 1914–1919," in William N. Tilchin and Charles E. Neu, eds., *Artists of Power: Theodore Roosevelt, Woodrow Wilson, and Their Enduring Impact on U.S. Foreign Policy.* Westport, Conn.: Praeger Security International, 2006, pp. 95–115.

Thompson, John M. *Russia, Bolshevism, and the Versailles Peace*. Princeton, N.J.: Princeton University Press, 1966.

Thornton, A. P. *Imperialism in the Twentieth Century.* Minneapolis: University of Minnesota Press, 1977.

——. *The Imperial Idea and Its Enemies*. 2d ed. London: Macmillan, 1985.

Thorsen, Niels Aage. *The Political Thought of Woodrow Wilson, 1875–1910*. Princeton, N.J.: Princeton University Press, 1988.

Throntveit, Trygve. "The Fable of the Fourteen Points." Paper delivered at the Princeton Institute for International and Regional Studies, Princeton University, April 8, 2006.

Tilchin, William N., and Charles E. Neu, eds. *Artists of Power: Theodore Roosevelt, Woodrow Wilson, and Their Enduring Impact on U.S. Foreign Policy.* Westport, Conn.: Praeger Security International, 2006.

Tillman, Seth P. *Anglo-American Relations at the Paris Peace Conference of 1919.* Princeton, N.J.: Princeton University Press, 1961.

Tilly, Charles. "National Self-Determination as a Problem for All of Us," *Daedalus* 122:3 (1993), 29–36.

Tinker, Hugh. "India in the First World War and After," *Journal of Contemporary History* 3:4 (1968), 89–107.

——. *The Ordeal of Love: C. F. Andrews and India*. New Delhi: Oxford University Press, 1979.

Townsend, James. "Chinese Nationalism," *Australian Journal of Chinese Affairs* 27 (1992), 97–130.

Trachtenberg, Marc. "Versailles after Sixty Years," *Journal of Contemporary History* 17 (1982), 487–506.

Trani, Eugene P. "Woodrow Wilson, China, and the Missionaries, 1913–1921," *Journal of Presbyterian History* 49:4 (1971), 328–351.

Trow, Clifford W. "Woodrow Wilson and the Mexican Interventionist Movement of 1919," *Journal of American History* 58:1 (1971), 46–72.

Tung, William L. *V. K. Wellington Koo and China's Wartime Diplomacy.* New York: Center of Asian Studies of St. John's University, 1977.

Tuteja, K. L. "Jallianwala Bagh: A Critical Juncture in the Indian National Movement," *Social Scientist* 25 (1997), 25–61.

Unterberger, Betty Miller. "Woodrow Wilson and the Russian Revolution," in Arthur S. Link, ed., *Woodrow Wilson and a Revolutionary World, 1913–1921.* Chapel Hill: University of North Carolina Press, 1982, pp. 49–104.

——. *The United States, Revolutionary Russia, and the Rise of Czechoslovakia.* Chapel Hill: University of North Carolina Press, 1989.

——. "The United States and National Self-Determination: A Wilsonian Perspective," *Presidential Studies Quarterly* 26 (1996), 926–941.

Vatikiotis, P. J. *The History of Modern Egypt.* 4th ed. Baltimore, Md.: Johns Hopkins University Press, 1991.

Vaughn, Stephen. *Holding Fast the Inner Lines: Democracy, Nationalism, and the Committee on Public Information.* Chapel Hill: University of North Carolina Press, 1980.

Venkataramani, M. S., and B. K. Shrivstava. *Quit India: The American Response to the 1942 Struggle.* New Delhi: Vikas, 1979.

Verma, Dina Nath. "Some International Aspects of India's Constitutional Development," *Quarterly Review of Historical Studies* [Calcutta] 8:3 (1968–1969), 165–170.

Walker, Dennis. "Pan-Islamism as a Modern Ideology in the Egyptian Independence Movement of Mustafa Kamil," *Hamdard Islamicus* 17:1 (1994), 57–109.

Walworth, Arthur. *Woodrow Wilson.* 3d ed. New York: Norton, 1978.

——. *Wilson and His Peacemakers: American Diplomacy at the Paris Peace Conference, 1919.* New York: Norton, 1986.

Wang, Tsi C. *The Youth Movement in China.* New York: New Republic, 1927.

Wang Xiaode. "Yimian lishi de jingzi: Ping Wudeluo Weierxun de 'shimingguan' " [A Mirror of History: Woodrow Wilson's View on America's "Mission"], *Shijie Lishi* [World History] 1993:2, 74–82.

——. *Mengxiang yu xianshi: Wei-er-xun "lixiang zhuyi" waijiao yanjiu* [Dream and Reality: A Study of Wilson's "Idealistic" Foreign Policy]. Beijing: Chinese Social Studies Press, 1995.

Watt, Donald Cameron. *Succeeding John Bull: America in Britain's Place, 1900–1975.* Cambridge: Cambridge University Press, 1984.

Wells, Kenneth M. "Background to the March First Movement: Koreans in Japan, 1905–1919," *Korean Studies* 13 (1989), 5–21.

West, Rachel. *The Department of State on the Eve of the First World War.* Athens: University of Georgia Press, 1978.

White, William Allen. *Woodrow Wilson: The Man, His Time and His Task.* Boston: Houghton Mifflin, 1925.

Wilbur, C. Martin. *Sun Yat-sen: Frustrated Patriot.* New York: Columbia University Press, 1976.

Williams, Joyce G. *Colonel House and Sir Edward Grey: A Study in Anglo-American Diplomacy*. Lanham, Md.: University Press of America, 1984.

Williams, William A. *The Tragedy of American Diplomacy*. 2d ed. New York: Dell, 1972.

Wilz, John Edward. "Did the United States Betray Korea in 1905?" *Pacific Historical Review* 16 (1985), 243–270.

Wimer, Kurt. "Woodrow Wilson Tries Conciliation: An Effort That Failed," *Historian* 25 (1963), 419–438.

Wingate, Ronald. *Wingate of the Sudan: The Life and Times of General Sir Reginald Wingate*. London: Murray, 1955.

Wolgemuth, Kathleen L. "Woodrow Wilson and Federal Segregation," *Journal of Negro History* 44:2 (1959), 158–173.

Wolper, Gregg. "The Origins of Public Diplomacy: Woodrow Wilson, George Creel, and the Committee on Public Information." Ph.D. diss., University of Chicago, 1991.

——. "Wilsonian Public Diplomacy: The Committee on Public Information in Spain," *Diplomatic History* 17:1 (1993), 17–34.

Wolpert, Stanley A. *Tilak and Gokhale: Revolution and Reform in the Making of Modern India*. Berkeley: University of California Press, 1962.

——. "Congress Leadership in Transition: Jinnah to Gandhi, 1914–1920," in DeWitt C. Ellinwood and S. D. Pradhan, eds., *India and World War I*. New Delhi: South Asia Books, 1978, pp. 127–140.

——. *A New History of India*. 6th ed. New York: Oxford University Press, 2000.

Wood, Ge-Zay. *The Shantung Question: A Study in Diplomacy and World Politics*. New York: Revell, 1922.

Woodward, David R. "The Origins and Intent of David Lloyd George's January 5 War Aims Speech," *Historian* 34 (1971), 22–39.

Xiang Liling. *Zhong-Mei guanxi shang de yi ci quzhe: Cong Bali hehui dao Huasheng-dun huiyi* [A Tortuousity [*sic*] in Sino-U.S. Relations: From the Paris Peace Conference to the Washington Conference]. Shanghai: Fudan University Press, 1993.

Xu Guoqi. *China and the Great War: China's Pursuit of a New National Identity and Internationalization*. Cambridge: Cambridge University Press, 2005.

Zang, Shijun. *Kang Youwei datong sixiang yanjiu* [A Study of Kang Youwei's "Datong" Thought]. Guangzhou, China: Guangdong gaodeng jiaoyu chubanshe, 1997.

Zayyid, Maḥmūd. "Nash'at ḥizb al-Wafd, 1918–1924" [The Establishment of the Wafd Party, 1918–1924], *Al-Abhath* 15:2 (1962), 242–280.

Zhang Chunlan. "Gu Weijun di hehui waijiao: Yi shouhui shandong zhuquan wenti wei zhongxin" [Wellington Koo's Diplomacy at the Paris Peace Conference: A Study of His Role in the Shandong Question], *Bulletin of the Institute of Modern History, Academia Sinica* 23:2 (1994), 29–54.

Zhang Wei. "Origin and Political History of the Modern Chinese Press." Working Paper No. 59. Perth, Australia: Asia Research Centre, Murdoch University, 1996.

Zhang Yongjin. *China in the International System, 1918–1920: The Middle Kingdom at the Periphery*. Oxford: St. Anthony's/Macmillan, 1991.

Zhao, Suisheng. *A Nation-State by Construction: Dynamics of Modern Chinese Nationalism*. Stanford, Calif.: Stanford University Press, 2004.

INDEX